The SENSE OF MUSIC

The SENSE OF MUSIC

Stephen Brown

Southern Illinois University, Edwardsville

HARCOURT BRACE JOVANOVICH, PUBLISHERS

San Diego   New York   Chicago   Austin   Washington, D.C.

London   Sydney   Tokyo   Toronto

Preface

Making music is a matter of choices. "Why these things and not others?" as Beaumarchais's Figaro remarks. An infinite combination of factors influences the choices that finally result in music. A given sound may result from a composer's whim or a composer's genius, from a need to make art or a need to make money, from an audience's demand or an inner necessity, from the requirements of a musical form or style, from the potentials or the limitations of a particular instrument or a particular player, or from the particular player's needs, emotions, or inventiveness. In short, the fundamental questions about choices—why these things and not others—are finally unanswerable in any truly permanent or objective way. This does not mean, however, that the questions should not be asked. Basic to this book is the assumption that asking such questions and arriving at answers—however provisional or arguable they may be—is the key to a wider and deeper understanding of music.

The Sense of Music is divided into three sections. The first section, "Fundamentals," reviews the essential vocabulary for talking about music, including the basics of music notation. This section is as concise and efficient as possible; all of the concepts that are sketched in here appear in more fleshed-out form in the discussions of particular musical examples that occur in later sections. In this first section I introduce the various categories for discussing music (melody, harmony, rhythm, form, texture, timbre, and function) which provide the basis for the detailed summaries following each musical example in the book.

The second section of the book illustrates a sampling of musical forms. Although it does not attempt to be comprehensive, this section does treat a variety of forms from the small to the large (a single phrase, a song, a piano piece, a concerto, a symphony, an opera), including a variety of periods and styles. In each case, I discuss a whole work rather than an excerpt, and I use the discussion to focus on certain issues and approaches that do not fit easily into the later, chronological discussion (for example, the relationship between performer and music, the general question of operatic conventions, and the different levels on which words and music can relate).

In the final and largest section of the book, I discuss a number of historical styles. My purpose is to use important and characteristic musical examples to convey a sense of each period's style in order to give the student a framework for understanding.

Within each period, I focus on composers rather than on genres. Therefore the discussion of Beethoven's life and works is found all together, not divided among discussions of the Classical piano sonata, symphony, and string quartet. Information about composers' professional lives and their careers is stressed since this information helps locate the composer in relationship to society. I provide materials for comparison (Mozart's *Don Giovanni* and Strauss's *Don Juan,* for example), and I present a sufficient quantity of examples for the instructor to be able to choose among them, if desired. In treating vocal music, I pay particularly close attention to the words, since these texts can serve as bridges between the music and the larger cultural concerns of the time. While my principal emphasis is on the high-art tradition, I also give weight to folk and popular styles and to the major influence of African music in the twentieth century.

My approach through all of this is example-oriented. Within the discussion of particular examples, the focus is on small-scale events; that is, the musical nuances that seem central to the work's identity. In asking "Why these things and not others?," I want the student to know about particular choices the composer makes: Why this note, this rhythm, this instrument is the right, the necessary one.

Above all, I have kept in mind a principle that can be summarized in a sentence from a novel by Malcolm Bradbury: "Information without context or framework is noise." I hope that I succeed in avoiding such noise and that I instead provide the means to a deeper sense of music.

I want to acknowledge a number of people who helped me write this book. Thanks first to my colleague Paul Gaston, without whose help this project would never have gotten off the ground. Thanks also to two of my teachers: James Ackerman, of Harvard University, who told me always to argue from evidence, and Harold Zabrack, my longtime piano teacher, now at Westminster Choir College, who taught me where to look for musical nuance.

Thanks to many others who assisted me at various stages, including my wife, Lisbeth Brown, and my father, Dr. Julius Brown, who read a great deal and listened to a great deal more. Thanks to the staff of Lovejoy Library, especially Barbara Zimmermann—I hope her superiors never find out how much time she wasted looking things up for me; to my colleagues at Southern Illinois University at Edwardsville, who were unfailingly helpful whenever called upon; to Ken Herman; Ted Lynn, Los Angeles Valley College; and Elyse Mach, Northeastern Illinois University, who carefully and thoughtfully reviewed the manuscript; to Jane Carey, designer; Lynne Bush, production manager; Rebecca Lytle, art editor; Margie Rogers, manuscript editor; and Pat Zelinka, production editor, at Harcourt Brace Jovanovich, who labored so hard turning manuscript into book; and especially to Albert Richards, acquisitions editor, whose initial and continuing enthusiasm provided much-needed encouragement all along the way. Thanks, finally, to my students for their questions.

Stephen Brown

Contents

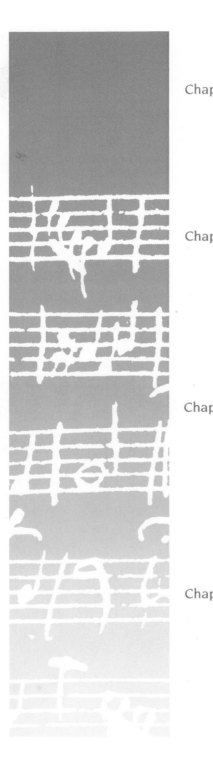

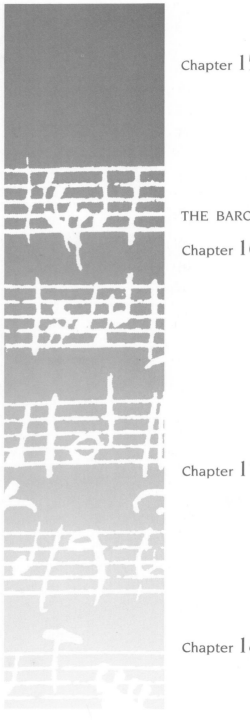

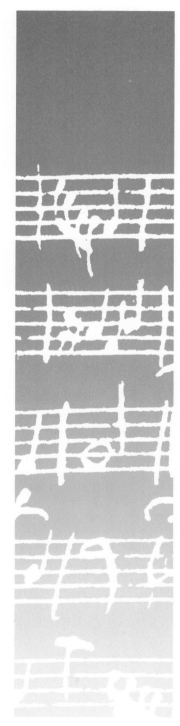

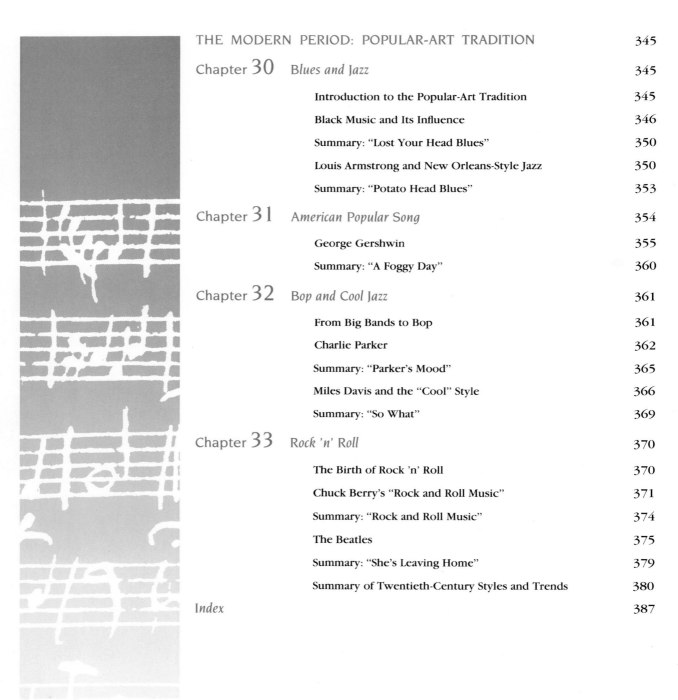

The SENSE OF MUSIC

Fundamentals

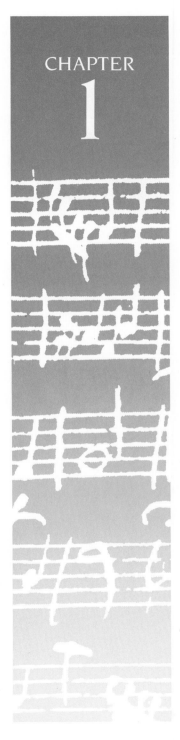

The Basics of Music Notation

Building a Music Vocabulary

Location and Duration

Music is made of sounds. To paraphrase the late jazz saxophonist Eric Dolphy, it's in the air and then it's gone. When we try to talk about music, we're really talking about memories of sounds we have heard. This is one of the things that makes the study of music difficult. It is also one of the reasons for learning the basics of music notation—to be able to picture certain aspects of music and to acquire words to describe the pictures.

There are two levels of music-reading. The first level is the performer's, who must be able to translate the musical symbol instantly into a sound on an instrument. This sort of skill takes years to develop, but, luckily, it is not a skill you need in order to study music as a listener. All you need is a grasp of the basic way in which notation describes two aspects of music: the location and the duration of musical sounds. This is important because the crucial decisions which a composer makes are so often seemingly small ones. A sixteenth note is used instead of an eighth note; a D flat instead of a D natural; a minor chord in-

Composer writing music.

stead of a major one; a note is played on the first beat of the measure instead of the third beat. The basic vocabulary of music notation makes it possible to picture musical events like these and to talk about them.

Melodic Lines

The simplest skill for a listener is also one of the most useful ones—to be able to follow the outline of a melody. The basic rule is that higher notes are written higher, and lower notes are written lower, and this is really the only information absolutely necessary in order to follow a musical line. In detail, the system works like this: five lines are drawn. This is called the **staff.** A note can be located either on a line or on a space; extra lines and spaces can be added above or below the staff. Draw a staff, place notes on it, and you have created a melody.

A melody

Intervals

A melody is defined by the relationships between its notes. These relationships can be named. Look at two notes on a staff. Count the line or space on which the first note rests as "one," and count every line and space until you reach the second note, and you will have the name for the interval between the two notes. When two notes are identical, it is called a **unison;** an interval of eight notes is called an **octave.**

Second   Unison   Third   Octave   Fifth   Seventh   Fourth

Names of Notes

Having a sense of the relationships between the notes is more important than knowing the names of the notes, but knowing the names of the notes is valuable too. The names are defined by **clef** signs. The **treble clef** sign is a large G; it circles the second line of the staff, defining that line as the one on which the note G will be located. Most of the examples in this book will use the G or treble clef. The other common clef is the **bass clef;** its sign is a script F with two dots around the line on which the note F will be found.

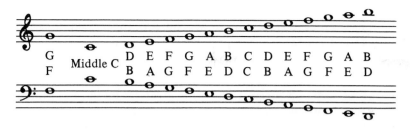

Treble and bass clefs and names of notes

Scale

What complicates this system is the problem of dealing with half steps. Even in the standard, eight-note scale, familiar as the "do-re-mi" (or diatonic) scale, the steps are not all equal. There are half steps between the third and fourth notes, and again between the seventh and eighth notes.

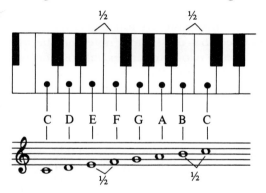

C-major scale, showing half steps on the piano keyboard and in notation

As long as this scale starts on C there is no great difficulty. But to start it on, for example, A and still have all the whole-step and half-step relationships come out right requires the use of symbols to raise certain notes by half a step.

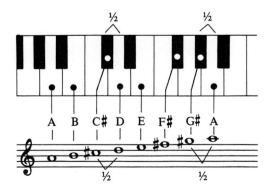

A-major scale on the piano keyboard and in notation

The sharp sign (♯) raises a note a half step; the flat sign (♭) lowers it a half step; the natural sign (♮) takes a note which has been sharped or flatted and returns it to its normal state.

Key and Accidental

To write a piece in the **key** of A means to base the piece on the notes of the A scale. If the composer wants the same notes sharped all through the piece, he or she will write a **key signature** at the beginning which will establish that the notes F, C, and G will be sharped throughout.

Key signature of A

Sharps, flats, or naturals which are not established by the key signature, but which are instead inserted individually into the music, are called **accidentals.**

In reading this, you may have noticed that the bottom note and the top note of the scale share the same name. These two notes are exactly one octave apart; they are so similar in sound that if played together they merge almost indistinguishably. The most common scales are made of a series of eight notes running from the bottom note to the top note of an octave, although other assortments of notes are possible. In writing melodies, composers usually limit their choices by using the notes from a single scale or **mode.** The melody shown on page 4 uses an assortment of notes called the Aeolian mode; it can also be called a "natural minor" scale based on A. The important point is that this scale or mode provides an assortment of notes—A, B, C, D, E, F, G, A—to choose from, and as long as this scale is used, the music will keep a certain consistency.

A B C D E F G A

Aeolian mode, or natural minor scale based on A

A B B C D E C A G A A B B C A

A melody based on the Aeolian mode.

Here are some other scales and modes used in music seen later in this book:

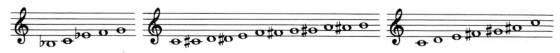

Pentatonic (five-note) scale   Chromatic (half-step) scale   Whole-tone scale (no half steps)

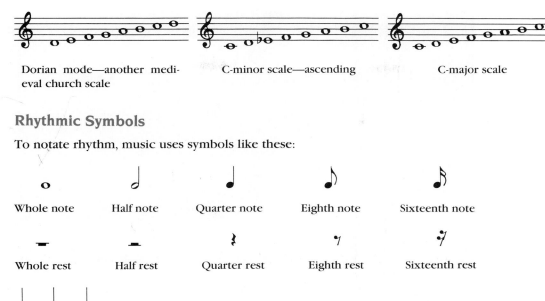

Dorian mode—another medieval church scale

C-minor scale—ascending

C-major scale

Rhythmic Symbols

To notate rhythm, music uses symbols like these:

Whole note   Half note   Quarter note   Eighth note   Sixteenth note

Whole rest   Half rest   Quarter rest   Eighth rest   Sixteenth rest

Half tied to quarter—same as dotted half note (in other words, the dot behind the note means that it is to be held half again as long)

Quarter tied to eighth—same as dotted quarter

Eighth tied to sixteenth—same as dotted eighth

Triplet—three eighth notes in the duration of one quarter note

Notes "beamed" together

Again, what the notation describes is relationships. The half note lasts half as long as the whole note and twice as long as the quarter note. These are commonly called **durations,** but that term is not exactly accurate, since nothing in this system specifies exactly how long a note is to be held, only how long it will

"Gee . . . Look at all the little black dots."

Drummer beating rhythm.

be held in relationship to another note. Sometimes a composer will give a benchmark indication, a metronome* marking like M.M. = 120. This shows that there will be 120 quarter notes per minute; in other words, a quarter note will last one-half second.

Tempo

In practice, composers give performers considerable freedom to interpret the speed, or **tempo,** of a composition. Any five performances of a given piece are likely to have five different tempos. Usually, the composer is content to give a general instruction, often in Italian, like *Allegro* or *Adagio,* and then allow the performer the freedom to interpret within that general indication. Some common tempo indications are:

> *Adagio* very slow
>
> *Andante* rather slow
>
> *Moderato* moderate
>
> *Allegretto* a little fast
>
> *Allegro* fast
>
> *Presto* very fast
>
> *Ritardando* gradually slower (abbreviated "rit.")
>
> *Accelerando* gradually faster
>
> *Rubato* variable tempo
>
> *A tempo* back to original tempo

*A metronome is a mechanical device which gives audible clicks at given rates. For example, it can be set to give 120 clicks per minute.

Beat

What most familiar music has, and what helps makes sense of this system, is the **beat**—a regular, recurring pulse to the music. At the beginning of a piece, the composer will define the beat, indicating, for example, that a quarter note will equal one beat, or that an eighth note will equal one beat. These beats rarely arrive with equal strength. Usually, they break down into patterns of strong and weak. ONE-two-three, ONE-two-three, or ONE-two-*three*-four, ONE-two-*three*-four. Again, the composer can define this grouping at the beginning, by saying how many beats there will be in each group, or **measure.** This is the **time signature.** A time signature of ⅜ shows that there will be three beats in each measure, and that an eighth note will receive one beat. A time signature of ¼ (the most common time signature) indicates that there will be four beats in each measure, and that a quarter note will receive one beat.

In writing music, each measure or group of beats is identified by a **bar line.** The beats are regular; a single beat can be supplied by different combinations of notes. A four-beat measure could include four quarter notes, or two quarter notes and a half note, or a half rest and four eighth notes, and so on.

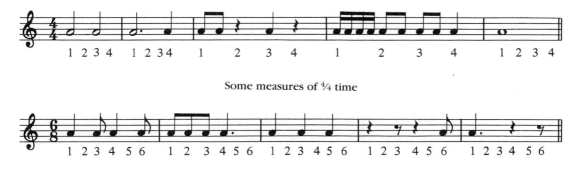

Some measures of ¼ time

Some measures of ⅝ time

These are just the basics of location and duration. But they should be enough for you to be able to make some connection between the sounds in the air and the notes on the page.

Melody, Harmony, and Rhythm

Melody, harmony, and rhythm are the three most basic elements of music. I will not attempt an all-inclusive discussion of them here, since we will be talking about melody, harmony, and rhythm throughout this book. My purpose now is to introduce some basic vocabulary which will make those later discussions easier.

Melody

A **melody** is simply a series of notes heard one after the other. There is nothing easier to write. Give each note of a scale a number:

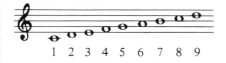

1 2 3 4 5 6 7 8 9

Numbers assigned to the notes of a scale

A melody can then be made from any sequence of numbers: telephone, Social Security, even a lottery number. For example, here is a ten-million-dollar lottery number—9, 15, 17, 23, 26, 27—which does not make a ten-million-dollar melody:

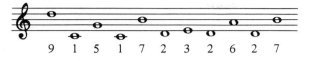

9   1   5   1   7   2   3   2   6   2   7

Lottery number translated into melody

But what we remember about a melody is something more than just the succession of tones. The pattern created by the durations of the tones is essential to the melody's character. For example, this:

Sounds very unlike this:

Opening theme from Beethoven's Fifth Symphony

A better working definition for melody might be "A succession of tones and durations which creates an identifiable pattern." When this pattern is not just memorable but also easily singable, then it is often called a **tune;** when (as is the case with the Beethoven melody shown above) it is used as the basis for an extended work, it is called a **theme.** When a fragment of that theme is broken off but still stays identifiable, it is called a **motive.**

Sometimes, though, music has melodies which approach the pure definition of "a succession of tones." For example, a jazz bass player might play a pattern like this:

Jazz bass line

This is not particularly identifiable or memorable, but it is a kind of melody, and can be referred to as such, although a more exact term might be "melodic line." In any music where several different instruments or voices are heard, there are likely to be subsidiary melodies of this sort.

The basic words for describing melody simply describe the melody's direction (ascending, descending, static) and the character of its intervals—that is, whether it moves primarily by steps, in which case its motion is called stepwise or conjunct, or if it moves primarily by skips, in which case it is called disjunct. The lottery melody uses disjunct motion; the jazz bass line is primarily conjunct.

Harmony

If a melody is tones heard one after another, then a **harmony** is tones heard together. Again, there is no great trick to writing one. We could make one harmony out of the first five notes of the lottery melody and another from the last six notes. These are not unknown combinations, although they are both a little dissonant, which means that they have a harsh or jangling effect. The dissonance can be relaxed or resolved into a more pleasing, "harmonious" harmony:

Jazz bass player
Charlie Mingus.

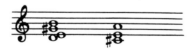

Relatively   Relatively   Relatively   Relatively
dissonant   consonant   dissonant   consonant

I stress the word "relatively" because there is nothing absolute about **consonance** and **dissonance.** The same harmony which is dissonant in one situation can be consonant in another. For example, the last "relatively consonant" harmony above becomes the dissonant member of this pair:

Relatively   Relatively
dissonant   consonant

Harmonies like these, where the notes are heard in one block of sound, are called **chords.** The standard way to create chords is to build them out of scales. Again, there is nothing difficult about the basic elements of the process. Choose a scale; pick a tone from the scale, calling it the **root** of your chord; starting on that tone use every other tone until you have three tones together, and you will have a chord. Three-note chords of this sort are called **triads.**

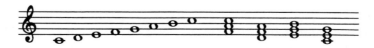

C scale and some triadic chords made from it

When triadic chords are broken up and played as melodies, they are called **arpeggios.**

Arpeggio based on A triads

An important expressive quality in chords has to do with whether they are **major** or **minor.** The difference is just a difference of a half step. Lowering the middle note of the triad, the third, by a half step, changes the chord's quality profoundly. This lowered third is called a minor third, and the chord it creates, a minor chord.

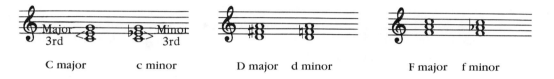

C major   c minor   D major   d minor   F major   f minor

Although triads are basic to most chord construction, other tones are often added. The most common of these is the seventh. The sound of the chord can be altered further by changing the position of the tones within it, or by playing some of its tones more than once.

C-major   C-major   Seventh added   Same chord with third
triad   seventh   below the root   doubled and seventh tripled

On paper, harmonies are written vertically, while melodies are written horizontally. In practice, harmonies also have horizontal movement. Dissonance creates tension, which consonance releases. From this basic principle it is possible to create long series of chords which flow from one to the next and which are called chord **progressions.** The methods for doing this are a great invention of Western music, and we will see them develop in Part Three of this book. Briefly, the methods revolve around the idea of a tonal center—one tone which is established as the "home" tone. In the key of A, that tone is A, and the chords tend to progress away from and ultimately back to a chord based on A. Along the way, other tonal centers may be used, sometimes for only a moment, sometimes for extended periods. Whenever a progression of chords seems to arrive at a conclusion, whether final at the end of a piece, or temporary at the end of phrase or section, it is called a **cadence.**

A cadence leading to a D-major chord

Rhythm

Rhythm is the way musical sounds are organized in time. Many art forms have no need for this sort of time organization. Painting, architecture, poetry, and novels all give the viewer the chance to organize the experience on his or her own, unlike music, which must impose its own time-organization on the listener. The organization can be loose. A singer, for example, can be left free to sing words in a conversational rhythm. Religious chant is often left ungoverned by any rhythmic pulse. But, as we discussed in looking at rhythmic notation, most familiar music is organized by the regular pulse of a beat, and the beats are grouped into measures. This is the basic, underlying rhythmic pattern of the music. Above it, the harmonies and melodies often have their own rhythms. Most compositions that use chord progressions establish a certain pace of

Trumpet player creating melody and rhythm for a young listener.

rhythmic change. A new chord might arrive on the first beat of every measure—not invariably, but just as a general pace to the chord changes. This is called the **harmonic rhythm.**

Above the harmonic rhythm, the melody will have its own rhythmic patterns, usually involving contrasts between notes of shorter and longer durations. The theme of Beethoven's Fifth Symphony is fairly easily recognized by just its rhythmic pattern: short-short-short long, short-short-short long. The song "Yesterday" becomes: short-short long, short-short-short-short-short-short-long-short-long.

The commas in these odd-looking statements are at the points which seem natural for a breath or pause. In musical terms, these are **phrases.** Sometimes the composer indicates these in the written music by means of a curved line over the notes; sometimes they are just implicit in the music. The phrase has been called a musical sentence, but that is a little misleading. Think of "The Star-Spangled Banner." The first sentence of that song breaks down into four phrases: "O say can you see / by the dawn's early light / what so proudly we hailed / at the twilight's last gleaming." These phrases establish a kind of rhythmic pattern of their own—through most of the song each phrase lasts for six beats. One of the nice effects in the "Star-Spangled Banner" occurs near the end, when for the line "O say does that Star-Spangled Banner yet wave" there is a phrase which suddenly lengthens out to a full twelve beats. As is the case with all of the patterns we have been talking about, melodic, harmonic, or rhythmic, half the reason for making them is the effect to be gained from breaking them.

Music's Traditional Functions

Six Traditional Functions

Form follows function. Music changes its forms as it is designed to fulfill a variety of different functions. These can be various indeed. One composer may write a war requiem to mourn those killed in battle; another might design music for dancing. Whether the function is sacred or commercial, the music will take particular shapes in response to particular needs.

Some of the considerations which govern musical form are mundane, everyday, obvious things. You cannot bring a thousand people together at a church service and give them seven minutes of harmonica solo. Nor would an audience gathered together to dance away a few hours on a Saturday night be much entertained by music organized in slow, processional, funereal rhythms. So before looking more closely at some specific musical forms in Part Two, it seems worthwhile to consider some of the traditional musical functions. As a guide, J. H. Kwabena Nketia's *African Music in Ghana* will be used. It describes a number of the functions that music fulfills in traditional African society. While

Music is an integral part of African tribal customs.

contemporary Western culture is far removed from the culture Nketia discusses, many of music's roles remain the same.

Worship

Music in many cultures plays a role in religious ceremony. As religions are various, so is the music that serves them. Catholic mass, Protestant hymn, and Jewish chant all have forms intimately connected to the rituals they support, and of course this is true of other world religions as well. There are a number of reasons for the connection between music and religious ceremony. Perhaps the most important is simply that the normal human conversational voice seems inadequate for addressing a god or gods. Music can raise such utterances to a different level. In public worship, music can serve a communal function. Whether the worshipping group is performing the music itself or only listening to the performance of others, the music can help each member of the group to sense that he or she is sharing the experience with the other participants. A more practical reason for music's presence in worship is to function as a mnemonic, an aid to memory; the easily-learned musical patterns help the worshippers to remember the words and actions of the ceremonies. Finally, there is a function which can be called "beauty as argument." Many religions have felt that the beauty of music, like the beauty of art, can in itself provide convincing arguments that their faith's tenets are true ones.

Life-Cycle Events

The major events in an individual's life—birth, coming-of-age, marriage, and death—are frequently marked by celebration, and the celebration frequently requires music. Here, music's ability to make an individual experience into a communal one is paramount. In a funeral ceremony, for example, music might, ideally, take private sorrows and turn them into something shared and therefore more easily borne.

Work

The traditional idea of work songs or work music has largely disappeared from our culture, perhaps because of the changes in the nature of the tasks which people perform in modern industrialized society. In cultures which do not share our sort of high technology, much of the work must be done by groups of people repeating actions together. Grinding grain, for example, breaking stone, planting rice, or moving logs, require concerted actions. It is not just music's role to make the different individuals' actions chime together, but also to match the individual's rhythms with the rhythms of the tasks. Thus many traditional cultures have specific songs for specific jobs. Perhaps in a very watered-down way the music piped into supermarkets, or played on the radio in gas-stations, or even the music listened to while driving a car or washing the dishes fulfills some of this traditional function.

Rule

Rulers, whether village chieftains or English kings, have long sensed the value of music to increase their importance and the awe in which they are held. This is not a concept of music which fits too well with democratic ideals, and in the United States, all the President gets is a band playing "Hail to the Chief." But in other cultures and times, the desire of rulers to have music associated with them has been an enormously powerful factor in causing music to be written, played, and remembered. A good deal of the music listened to today was originally written for the greater glory of rulers, and was as much a part of the trappings of office as the throne or the crown.

The parade music of marching bands has its roots in war music.

War

It would be hard to imagine anything more peaceful-seeming than a summer parade down a small-town main street. Nevertheless, the music in that parade is, at its root, war music. This is why marching bands march, wear uniforms, and are often accompanied by drill teams complete with flags and rifles. In this instance the musical sword has been beaten into a trombone. But it should remind us that music, along with its ability to organize a group of people into a shared task like marching, also has the ability to incite. Patriotic songs and marching music can be weapons, in the sense of being instruments of war.

Recreation

This is the primary function of music in the Western world today, and it includes a great diversity of musical types, many of which will be discussed later in this book. Among them are examples which originally had some other function, but have now been taken over for recreational use. The march music mentioned earlier is an example of this; it is not unusual to hear church music in concert halls; and so on. But it should be remembered that music originally designed for some nonrecreational function will have a form that was to some degree determined by the nature of the original function. Work songs, for example, will bear the rhythm of the task they were designed to aid, even when sung by a modern-day folksinger who may never have lifted a sledgehammer.

A Walkman provides private recreational music.

Within the general category of recreational music are some subcategories. One is that of *incidental* music, where music serves as the accompaniment for some other recreational activity: films, for example, television dramas, even circuses or baseball games. Another category is *dance* music. For many cultures this has been a primary source of demand for music, as it is in popular culture today. A third category can be called *private,* referring here to music which has no public function, but exists only for individual expression or communication. Our culture has developed the most extreme version of this—the Sony Walkman—and this kind of technology dominates our musical scene today. People listen to radios in their cars, to their record players at home, to cassettes on their headsets—and music which may have been designed for a public or communal function turns into something which tends to isolate the individual and to separate him or her from the crowd. But in a sense, even this is nothing new. Long before the invention of the Walkman, people hummed or whistled or just listened to the music playing inside their heads—as of course they still do.

The subcategory I have left for last is perhaps the most important one for this book. It is *concert* music—music which is designed for an audience's aesthetic enjoyment, and which is listened to because it is beautiful and pleasing. As indicated above, music used for this purpose may originally have been designed for some other function. Or, as is often the case, it may derive its form from music which serves other functions. Chopin, for example, wrote a number of piano pieces he called "Mazurkas." They were intended for a pianist to play, while an audience sat and listened. But the origin of the mazurka is a dance, and the rhythms Chopin used in these piano pieces were the rhythms which went with the physical movements of the dance. This is not a rare or unusual example. The literature of concert music is filled with formal elements taken from music originally designed to fit dance, march, hymn, mass, drama, festival, and ceremony.

From this it should be clear that the function of concert music tolerates a tremendous variety of individual forms; indeed, the function of providing aesthetic pleasure is one which *demands* a great variety of forms. Before examining these forms in more detail, we will look at the materials with which they are made.

CHAPTER

4

Timbres: The Ways of Making Musical Sound

Sound

When a stone is dropped into a still pool of water, its impact makes two kinds of waves. We see as ripples the waves which the impact makes in the water. We hear as a "plop" the waves which the impact makes in the air. These waves of sound (more accurately described as areas of slightly more compressed air alternating with areas of slightly thinner air, or *compression* and *rarefaction*) must strike our ears with a certain *frequency* for us to detect the effect as sound. Sound waves which strike our ears with a frequency of less than 16 cycles per second (called *hertz,* abbreviated *Hz*) are generally inaudible, as are those which reach our ears at frequencies above approximately 20,000 Hz. The sound waves produced by striking the lowest note on the piano reach our ears at a frequency of about 30 Hz, those of the piano's highest note at about 4,000 Hz. It is the frequency, and only the frequency, which determines the highness or lowness of the sound; that is, its **pitch.** The loudness or softness of the sound is determined not by the frequency but by the size of the waves, or their *amplitude.*

Most sounds are not this simple; they have more to them than just one frequency. Sounds which we think of as "musical" are generally simpler than sounds we think of as "noise," in that the musical sound usually has one principal pitch which we hear more than any other. But other, subsidiary pitches exist within even a musical sound. These are called **harmonics.** When a violin makes a sound at a given pitch, and then a flute makes a sound at the same pitch, they sound different because their harmonics are different. Similarly, when two people sing the same note, the different harmonics in the sounds they produce are what make their voices different and distinct.

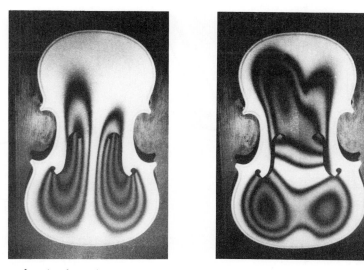

Holograms showing how the violin resonates at different frequencies.

To make music, then, requires instruments and/or voices which will produce sounds at a variety of frequencies, giving different pitches; at a variety of amplitudes, giving different degrees of loudness; and with a variety of different assortments of harmonics, giving different tone colors, or **timbres.**

Musical Instruments

The strings

Stretch a string and pluck it, and it will vibrate. The shorter, thinner, and more tightly stretched the string, the faster the vibrations and the higher the pitch. Thus, on a guitar, the strings which produce the higher pitches are thinner and stretched tighter than those which produce the lower pitches. But if the guitarist wishes to make a given string produce a higher tone, he or she shortens its vibrating length by pressing it to the fingerboard, so that it can only vibrate

STRINGS

violin

viola

'cello

bass viol

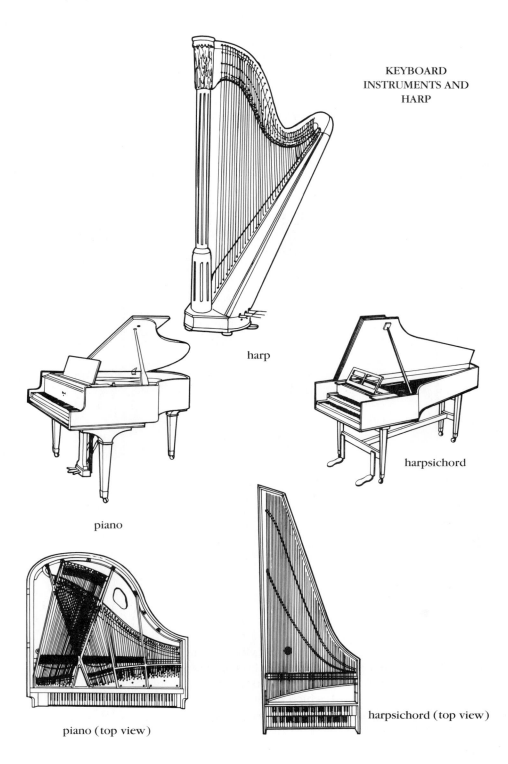

KEYBOARD
INSTRUMENTS AND
HARP

harp

harpsichord

piano

piano (top view)

harpsichord (top view)

between the point of pressure and the point where it is fixed. In the orchestra, the various members of the violin family are constructed on the same principle. The violin itself is the smallest of this family; it has the shortest strings, and it is therefore the highest pitched. The other members of the violin family, in order of increasing size and lower pitch range, are the viola, the violoncello (usually called simply the 'cello) and the double-bass, or bass viol. While the strings of the violin family may be set in motion by plucking them like a guitar's (the technical term for this is *pizzicato*), usually they are bowed. The bow running across the string produces a more constant level of volume than does plucking.

Violins and guitars are both designed with a resonating chamber—a box which receives the initial vibrations of the strings and sends them out again, mixed and magnified. This may not sound like an important function, but it is in fact a crucial one. The difference between one resonating chamber and another is the difference between a student violin and a Stradivarius,* a difference audible enough in the concert hall to be worth many thousands of dollars (in fact, about half a million) in the auction room.

The other principal instruments whose sound is made by strings are the harp, the piano, and the harpsichord. Unlike the members of the guitar and violin families, where only a few strings are used and the player gets different pitches by shortening the effective length of the string with the fingers, these instruments present the player with a string for each note. (The harp does have pedals which can tighten each string enough to raise it two half steps.) The strings of the harp are plucked with the fingers; those of the piano are hit by hammers set in motion by striking keys; and those of the harpsichord are plucked by a plectrum made of quill or leather (or, today, plastic), also set in motion through a keyboard.

Winds

The Woodwinds.

The woodwinds are called woodwinds because they depend upon player-supplied wind, and because they or their ancestors were made of wood. It is the player's wind vibrating inside the instrument which makes the sound. The longer the column of air inside the instrument, the lower will be the sound. Woodwind instruments therefore have a series of holes, sometimes covered with the fingers directly, sometimes covered by keys. When all the holes are covered, the length of the column of air is equal to the length of the entire instrument. As the keys are opened, the column of air becomes shorter and the pitch higher. But more pitches are available than the number of holes indicates. The player, by over-blowing, can force the air column to vibrate in halves or thirds, thus enabling higher ranges of pitches to be produced.

The initial setting-in-motion of the air column can be accomplished in several ways. In the flutes, it is simply the player's breath moving across an opening—the same way a note is produced by blowing across a bottle. In the

WOODWINDS

flute

clarinet

saxophone

oboe

*A violin made by Antonio Stradivari, who worked in Cremona, Italy, between about 1660 and 1737. Some 400 of his violins still exist today.

(*Woodwinds continued on next page*)

WOODWINDS
(continued)

single-reed instruments, like the clarinets and saxophones, it is a reed vibrating against a mouthpiece which sets the column of air in motion. In the double-reed instruments, like the oboe and the bassoon, two halves of a reed vibrate against each other.

Brass.   The sounds coming from the brass instruments—trumpets, trombones, French horns, tubas—are, like those of the woodwinds, caused by vibrating columns of air inside the instruments. (Brass and woodwinds are together classed as wind instruments). What starts the column vibrating here, though, are the player's lips pressed into a cup-shaped mouthpiece. Earlier, I spoke of the way a woodwind player can overblow and cause the column of air to vibrate in halves or thirds. This process is even more important for the brass player. "Overblow" may be a misleading word, since it implies mere huffing and

bassoon

BRASS

trumpet

bugle

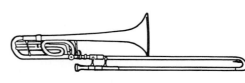

trombone

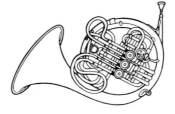

French horn

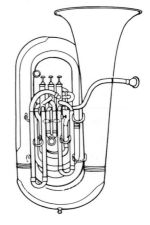

tuba

contrabassoon

puffing. The process is considerably more complicated than that. It may involve such things as the shape the lips take and their degree of tension, in addition to the intensity of the stream of air, its shape, direction, and focus. The tone the player produces may be the fundamental tone caused by the vibration of the entire column of air, or any one of a considerable series of harmonics as the air column vibrates in halves, thirds, quarters, etc. In practice, the lowest notes commonly used on the brass instruments are not the fundamentals but those based on the first harmonic, where the air column vibrates in halves.

On an instrument like the bugle, the player has only the air column in the instrument to work with. This severely limits the number of tones that are practical. "Taps" is a familiar bugle tune; it uses the third, fourth, fifth, and sixth harmonics. In order to play music more flexible than this, it is helpful to have different-sized air columns to choose from. In the brass instruments, this is usually effected by means of valves which bring different lengths of tubing into play. An exception is the slide trombone, where the player's movement of the slide directly lengthens or shortens the length of the air column.

Percussion

With the percussion instruments, sound is made as it is in the example we began with—the plop of a stone into water. That is, the principal sound is caused

High-speed photographic study of lips vibrating in a trombone mouthpiece.

PERCUSSION

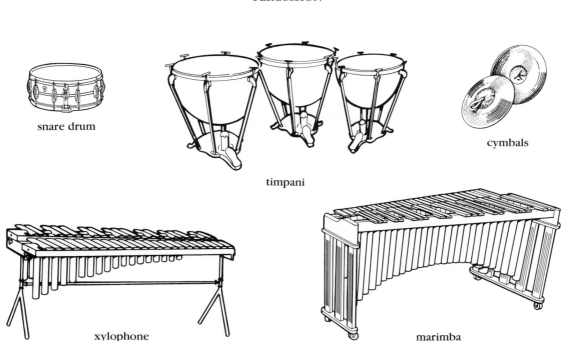

snare drum

timpani

cymbals

xylophone

marimba

by the actual impact of one surface against another. With some percussion instruments we are mostly conscious of just the sound of the impact; with others, there is a consistent enough after-ring to give a sense of definite pitch. In the first group are classed such instruments as the snare drum and cymbals; in the second are such instruments as the timpani (kettle drums) and the xylophone. The drums, like the stringed instruments, consist mainly of two elements: something to vibrate (in this case a membrane stretched over the head of the drum) and somewhere for the vibration to resonate (in this case the body of the drum). The tighter and smaller the membrane, the higher the pitch of its sound. Instruments like the xylophone and its relatives are similar in design to a piano (which is itself often classified and used as a percussion instrument) in that there is a separate element for each pitch. In the xylophone and marimba, these elements are blocks of wood (in the glockenspiel, they are strips of metal) which the player strikes with mallets.

Human Voice

Humans do not need instruments to make music. Such actions as clapping and whistling produce sounds in ways similar to those used by instruments like the drum and the flute. The principal human instrument, though, is the voice. The voice is like a stringed instrument in its use of vibrating cords and resonating chambers; it is like a woodwind in that the cords are set vibrating by air. Briefly, what happens is that air is forced out of the lungs; it passes through the larynx, in which are located the vocal cords, which the air causes to vibrate. If the air is forced through with great pressure, the amplitude of the cords' vibration will be correspondingly great and the sound level loud; if the air pressure is less, the sound will be softer. Muscles surround and control the vocal cords; if the muscles tighten, the pitch of the sound will be higher; if they are relaxed, lower. Then, on the way out of the body, these vibrations pass by and through several cavities which themselves contain air. According to the shape of the cavities, the air will resonate to the original vibration and to various of its harmonics and thus influence the sound which is finally produced.

Certain elements of the means of vocal production are given to a person in much the same way as he or she might be handed a violin of given shape and quality. The longer and thicker the vocal cords, the lower the voice will be. The particular quality of the cords themselves, and of the shape of the resonating chambers, also must vary from person to person. At the same time, there are hundreds of muscles controlling the diaphragm, ribs, larynx, throat, tongue and mouth, altering tension and shape, and allowing training to change the nature of the vocal sound.

Like the string family, the human voice can be placed in certain categories describing the range of pitches it is capable of producing. The terms for high, medium, and low female voices are *soprano, mezzo-soprano,* and *alto* (or *con-*

tralto); the names for high, medium, and low male voices are *tenor, baritone,* and *bass.*

Electronic Amplification and Synthesis

Thus far, the means of making music we have discussed are similar to those which have been in use for countless centuries in countless different cultures. The twentieth century has created something new—music made or amplified electronically. In this case, what sets the air in motion is the vibrating cone of a speaker. What makes the speaker cone vibrate is an electromagnet. Changing electrical signals arriving at the electromagnet cause its force to vary, and as its force varies it moves closer to or farther away from a permanent magnet, moving the speaker cone with it. The changing electrical signals proceed from an amplifier, whose job, as its name implies, is to amplify other, original electrical signals. These signals may originate in different ways. One way is from a microphone, which is very like a speaker in reverse: sound in the air, made by, for example, a voice, causes a membrane inside the microphone to vibrate in response. As it vibrates, it varies an electrical signal, which then heads for the

Student composing at a synthesizer in a computer-music laboratory.

amplifier and speaker. But it is not necessary to start the original signal with a microphone. It is possible simply to introduce an electrical signal to the amplifier, which will then amplify it and send it on to the speaker. Different patterns of electrical signals will produce different kinds of sounds. Thus, sounds can be *electronically synthesized.* A synthesizer is a fancy device, but the essentials of its operation are no different from those which occur when a loose wire on a turntable sends a hum through the amplifier and out the speaker of a home stereo.

Musical Texture and Form

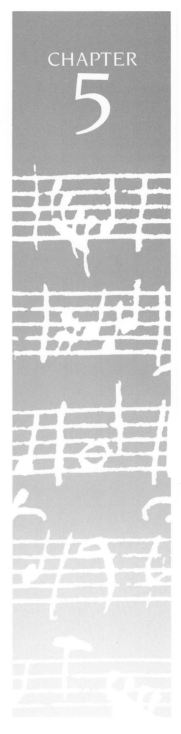

The different ways of making musical sounds add up to a tremendous array of possibilities for the composer. Anyone writing a work for a modern symphony orchestra will have approximately one hundred players available: about 65 strings, 15 woodwinds, 15 brass, and 5 percussion. This range and variety of instruments and voices imposes practically no limit on the degree of complexity with which a piece of music can be organized. A composer could design performances in which literally dozens of different musical ideas were being played simultaneously. The result would, of course, be merely chaotic to the listener. And this brings up the real limit the composer faces: the sensibilities of the listeners. In practical terms, a listener is able to make comfortable sense out of no more than three or four different—but related—musical ideas occurring simultaneously, and this is true whether the composer is designing the work for a 100-piece orchestra or a four-piece rock group. It is the way the different strands of music combine that defines the composition's *texture*.

Texture

Homophony

Pages 30 and 31 from the score of the first movement of Peter Ilyich Tchaikovsky's *Symphony No. 6*, the "Pathétique," (*see* page 31) show a large symphony orchestra at work: flutes, oboes, clarinets, bassoons, French horns, trumpets, trombones, tuba, timpani, violins, violas, 'cellos, and bass viols. At first glance, the score might look impossibly complex. But if we examine the opening measures carefully, we can see that all the instruments except for the violins and violas are playing a similar pattern of repeated eighth notes, without much melodic change.

Two measures of the second flute part

If listened to by itself, this would not offer much to keep the ear interested. It is a background pattern, an accompaniment to the main melody, which appears in the higher strings (violins and violas).

Two measures from the second violin part

So although Tchaikovsky is using a full orchestra here, and achieving a kind of lush and rich sound obtainable in no other way, the relationship of the upper strings to the rest of the orchestra is virtually the same as that between a singer and a strumming guitar. The orchestral "strums" establish a rhythmic and harmonic backdrop for the melody.

In the fifth measure there is a change. Through the first four measures of our example, the first flute has been silent. Now, at a climactic moment, this flute joins in with the violins and violas. Underneath, in the brass, a little bit of counter-melody is added, played by the trumpets, trombones, and tuba, with timpani rolls supporting them. During these measures, then, we hear a melody, a related counter-melody, and rhythmic-chordal accompaniment. It is a grand moment, and virtually the entire orchestra is playing, but there are just three basic musical ideas being used, and they exist in close relationship to one another. This sort of musical texture, where one melody clearly dominates

Figure 5–1
Pages 30 and 31 of Tchaikovsky's *Symphony No. 6*

(Continued on next page.)

The Chicago Symphony Orchestra.

while the other elements support it, primarily with chordal harmonies, is called **homophony.**

Polyphony

Another kind of texture can be seen in a brief example by Johann Sebastian Bach—the opening six measures of the first fugue from his book of préludes and fugues, *The Well-Tempered Clavier,* from 1722. Where the Tchaikovsky example was homophonic, this work is **polyphonic** (many-voiced). That is, instead of one dominant musical idea, with the other ideas supporting it, each voice in this composition is of roughly equal importance. **Voice** here means an individual musical line. The work has four such voices. So although it is written for a solo keyboard instrument, it is more complex, musically, than the Tchaikovsky excerpt designed for full orchestra. In the Bach excerpt, the composer's problem is to create a musical texture of four independent and equal musical lines, without letting the music become confused or incomprehensible. Again, the limiting element is the listener's ear. How can four separate voices be so balanced as to maintain a clear and understandable relationship one to the other, while still retaining independent identities?

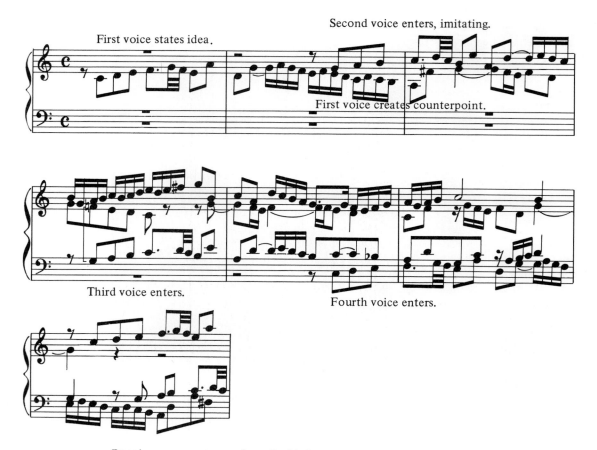

Opening seven measures from Bach's fugue

Bach starts off with a single line and a single idea. Midway through the second measure, the second voice enters—above the first—but imitating the first voice's initial statement. This is called, simply enough, **imitation.** While the second voice is imitating the first voice's statements, the first voice develops a melodic line which runs counter to the original statement. That is, it tends to run in directions opposite to the original statement's and with a different pattern of durations; where the original statement (now in the second voice) gives us eighth notes, this line uses sixteenth notes, and so on. This is **counterpoint:** a musical line, which, by its contrast with another musical line, asserts its own independence and identity. But the act of replying to the original idea ties the counterpoint closely to it, just as in a verbal dialogue opposing points of view are more closely related than separate, independent statements would be.

Another factor which helps to knit the voices together is the sense of harmonic progression. There is an implied sequence of chords underneath the various ideas, beginning with the C note which starts the piece. The work is in the key of C, which means that C is its tonal center. As the different voices enter and combine, they create chords. These chords progress through a sequence which takes them back to a cadence on C at measure seven. The individual voices, in all their movement, must still conform to the rules of this broader harmonic movement.

As the piece develops through these measures, the third and then the fourth voices enter. Each voice imitates the original statement, while an increasingly complex contrapuntal texture builds up in the other voices. But the reiteration of the familiar original idea, the close though contrasting relationship of melody to contrapuntal melody, and the general conformity to the rules of harmonic progression all serve to organize the work clearly and strongly enough to give the listener a sense of order. Imagine the equivalent in conversation: four people saying different things at the same time. The result would surely be chaos. If four people all sing different things at the same time according to rules like those Bach follows in his four-part fugue, a measure of clarity will result.

Although homophony and polyphony are the two principal ways in which musical textures are organized and made coherent, a piece of music does not have to use one or the other exclusively. Generally, it is possible to say that a piece is predominantly polyphonic or predominantly homophonic in texture, but many works combine elements of both. For instance, the counter-melody in the brass at the climax of the Tchaikovsky example is an example of counterpoint within a predominantly homophonic texture.

Form

Repetition, Contrast, Variation

We have seen how elements of melody, harmony and rhythm can be used to construct musical ideas, and we have seen how musical ideas can be supported and combined into musical textures. What remains is to see how these ideas can be shaped over time—the question of musical form. In music, time *is* organized. Perhaps this is necessary because music has such few external reference points. That is, it rarely accomplishes much in the way of imitating the material world, as paintings and poems and plays do. They can allow their organization to be imposed by the reality they imitate. Music's imitations must be of itself and, in fact, **repetition** is the essential element to musical form.

It follows from this that the simple rule for describing musical form is to list the repetitions, contrasts, and variations. For example, if you sing through the "Star-Spangled Banner," you will find that it breaks down into four parts. The first two are the same, the last two are different. The form can be described as AABC. Or try the Christmas carol "Deck the Halls." An idea is stated; it is repeated; and finally the original idea comes back. This pattern is described as AABA. One version of the tune gives a little variation at the end; this version can be described as AABA':

["A"—statement of idea]

["A"—statement repeated]

["B"—contrasting statement]

["A"—return to first statement]

[*or*—"A'"—variation on first statement]

"Deck the Halls"

Just because there are simple and basic ways of organizing music in time, do not think that they are used only in simple and basic music. In the small excerpt of Tchaikovsky's *Symphony No. 6* we looked at earlier (*see* page 30), the composer uses the same AABA formula found in "Deck the Halls." The melody in the second violin part begins:

It continues with the same melody, slightly varied:

Then a contrasting idea comes in:

Followed by a return to the first melody:

These examples are all relatively short. But the same kind of AABA pattern can be used over a much larger time span. Most first movements of symphonies,

First edition (1814) of "The Star-Spangled Banner"

sonatas, and concertos in the Classical period (approximately 1750–1825) are written in *sonata form,* to be discussed in greater detail later. Here I will mention just its broad outlines. First there is an exposition of the principal musical ideas (A). The exposition is, frequently, repeated (A). Then the ideas are varied and new ideas are added in a section called the development (B). There follows a return to the ideas of the exposition, called the recapitulation. Since the original ideas here occur in modified form, this section can be called (A′).

AABA is far from the only pattern available. A great deal of music depends on simple repetition—folk-song ballads, for example. Their form is often AAAAAAAA, etc. In **variation** form, the initial idea is changed each time it is restated: A A′ A″ A‴ A‴′ and so on. Two-part forms are called **binary;** they sometimes occur in AB or, more frequently, AAB patterns. The three-part form ABA is called **ternary,** or **song form.** Second movements of sonatas, concertos, and symphonies often follow this pattern. Last movements are often constructed on the **rondo form** pattern, whose basic form is ABACABA.

In contrapuntal works like the Bach fugue we looked at earlier, the interweaving of the voices does not allow for easy categorization of the music into A, B, and C sections. But the same principles of repetition, contrast, and variation apply there as well. The imitation of a musical idea in a different voice is a kind of repetition; the counterpoint is a kind of contrast. Indeed, what is most striking about the tremendous assortment of musical forms is the way they all tend to boil down to combinations of the elements of repetition, contrast, and variation. As was the case with musical texture, the limiting factor here is not the composer's imagination but the listener's. If the composer supplies all contrast and no repetition, the work will seem formless and chaotic. Too much repetition, and the work will seem boring, although of course a good idea can tolerate more repetition than a weak one. A mixture of these qualities is necessary for a work to have interest and excitement while still having coherence.

Compound Forms

Finally, these remarks about the ways in which music can be shaped over time apply in general to pieces of music heard continuously, without break—for example, a song, a movement from a symphony, or a single piano piece. When composers group pieces together to make larger works (called **compound forms**) like the song cycle, the symphony in four movements, or a series of twelve piano préludes, they usually introduce new material with each new piece or movement. Repetition of ideas from one section to the next is the exception rather than the rule. A common way to describe compound forms is to list the tempos—for example, the most typical form for sonatas and concertos is fast-slow-fast.

Talking about music is a little like talking about food. It's hard to discuss it while you're experiencing it, and afterwards you are left with memories which are hard to describe. The purpose of this discussion of music's fundamentals has been to supply some structure for ordering the memories of musical experience, by breaking that experience down into its elements of melody, harmony, rhythm, function, timbre, texture, and form; and to supply a vocabulary of names for the different components of musical experience.

Forms

A Single Phrase: Stevie Wonder's "You Are the Sunshine of My Life"

Combining Words and Music

Art is different from everyday existence. Ordinarily, we express our feelings to other people by the tones of voice we use, by our expressions, by our actions—but it is rare that we sing poetry to them. There is something artificial about a song, and in understanding what that something is we can gain a closer understanding of exactly what the songwriter has done. At the same time, there is much about art and song which is *not* artificial, much which is directly related to everyday existence. Finding these relationships makes it possible to understand how music can communicate.

As an example, we can look at the first phrase of Stevie Wonder's song, "You Are the Sunshine of My Life." The words to this phrase are, appropriately enough, "You are the sunshine of my life." We are immediately aware that something different from ordinary conversation is going on.

You are the sun - shine of___ my life,___

Several literary terms can be used to describe or characterize what is happening in this phrase. It is first of all a kind of metaphor: the "you" in the phrase is made equivalent to "sunshine," a poetic way of saying that "you are as essential to me and as warming and generally wonderful as sunshine is." The phrase can also be regarded as hyperbole—an exaggeration. And it is further a *cliché*—a phrase that has become familiar from frequent, often careless use. But saying that the phrase is a cliché need not be the same as saying that it is ineffective. What might be weak in a poem can be strong in a song lyric, and tired clichés can be revived by music.

Alternative Approaches and Solutions

So Stevie Wonder as lyricist has given Stevie Wonder as composer a particular problem: Take a phrase which because it is metaphoric and hyperbolic is not like ordinary conversation, and which at the same time is a cliché, and give it music which will communicate freshly and naturally the essence of the feeling the words contain. As an approach to Wonder's solution, I will try to show some other possible solutions, ones which do not work as well as his.

One approach is to start with the "music" of speech. As we talk we use a variety of different tonal levels, moving up and down constantly. (The stock method of imitating unhuman speech—"robot" speech, for example—is to talk on only one tonal level, in a monotone.) The principal difference between speech tones and song tones is that in a song a given tone is held long enough for our ears to become aware of a specific tonal level, a pitch. In speech, we slide over pitches so quickly that individual ones are not recognizable.

Another similarity between speech and music is that both are rhythmic. We pause after certain words, draw some syllables out, hurry others. For example, one way of saying the phrase from Wonder's song would be to draw out the word "You," then pause, then say the words "are the sunshine" fairly quickly, but with more emphasis on "sunshine," then pause again, and then say "of my life" fairly quickly, but holding longer the word "life." If I describe this way of saying the phrase in rhythmic notation, I come up with something like this:

Of course musical rhythm is different from speech rhythm, and what I have set down above is far more regular than the rhythms of actual speech, just as marching is more regular than walking.

In listening to the "melody" of speech we might hear a falling in tone level, or pitch, during the first three words of the phrase, then a rise to "sun," a fall to "shine," a slight rise during "of my" and a slight fall signifying the end of the phrase on the word "life." This pattern can be regularized into specific pitches for each of the words, and then set down in musical notation:

What this process has produced is a dull and essentially worthless piece of music, which should illustrate one basic point—that writing bad music is easy.

Stevie Wonder

You could take your own way of saying the phrase and go through a process similar to the one gone through above, and end up with your own piece of bad music. Of course the example could be livened up. By adding chord symbols which a pianist or guitar player could follow, and then making the rhythm more vital by delaying some notes so they come just after the main pulses of the beat, and forcing other notes to anticipate the pulses of the beat (a process familiar as **syncopation**), I can create a more passable rock version of the tune:

This is only a surface vitality, though; the music is still dull and empty. How to put something in it? Another approach would be to inject more meaning into the words by moving further away from the patterns of ordinary speech. For example, the first word, "You," could convey an intimate, enclosing kind of feeling. I might give it three descending notes all to itself. And since the sun is something high and constant, which fills every space with its light, then to symbolize it I could use high notes and a pattern which repeats and continues for a while. This is a songwriting technique called **"word-painting"** or "scene-painting." The result might look something like the following—more impressive, but still dull and lifeless:

Analysis of a Successful Solution

What then is the key to Stevie Wonder's solution? Why has his setting of these words proved convincing, fresh, and original? I will offer an explanation, which I stress is only a suggested explanation. Music is not a science. In the final analysis, there *is* no final analysis. Analyzing a piece of music is not like analyzing a chemical compound. There, an objective truth can be proved. Here, an explanation can be offered. It is best offered with evidence to support it, and perhaps, as in a court of law, the evidence will occasionally be so convincing as to remove all reasonable doubt. I hope that my explanations are correct and convincing—but I also hope that they are treated with reasonable doubt, not taken on faith.

My explanation of the workings of this particular musical phrase is that the key to its success lies in the way it opens up on the word "sunshine," especially on the second half of that word. I will try to show how this is accomplished.

To make something seem to "open up," you first have to establish it in a "closed down" form. Wonder does this by giving us no changes at all in the first part of the phrase. The melody and the harmonies stay the same for "You are the . . ." Then the changes start. The melody line moves up a note. In between the two syllables of the word "sunshine" the bass line drops a fifth, as the chords change. With the melody rising, the bass falling, and the harmonies shifting, we get a sense of expansion. And something unusual is happening in the rhythm. The syllable "shine" doesn't come where we would expect it to come. When we speak the word "sunshine," the accent comes on the first syllable, and the second syllable falls away in volume and emphasis. But here the second syllable is held just as long as the first syllable, and it arrives in between the first and second beats of the measure. This is a syncopated effect, where the note doesn't land on an expected beat and therefore calls attention to itself. And the melody reflects this: there is no melodic descent on the syllable "shine"; instead, the tune stays where it is for that syllable, and only falls downward after that point. So, in brief, everything in the music starts to expand at the syllable "sun," and instead of contracting again at the syllable "shine," it *stays* expanded. This slight gesture, this holding-out of the expansion, is something different from the average way we would speak or think the phrase, so it is not expected by us, and we feel the music opening up—flowering, if you will, in the sunshine.

Limits to Analysis

This is the point at which my explanation stops—the point where the discussion moves past the musical events, and past the question of just how these musical events communicate certain ideas or emotions, to the question of how the musical events can actually *cause* certain feelings in the listener. Most listeners will agree that Wonder has communicated the ideas and emotions in his phrase. Many, but not all, will agree that he has not just communicated them, he has evoked them in the listener's own mind. All I know with certainty is what everyone knows—that musical events do cause feelings in listeners. A song is not the reality it talks about. It is only words, metaphors, rhythms, and tones, combining, making and changing patterns. We can describe the ways in which these patterns are expressive, but certain fundamental questions remain. For example: how is it that a song can produce in us a reaction different from, yet just as real, and often even stronger, than the reaction which might be produced if we saw the reality the song describes?

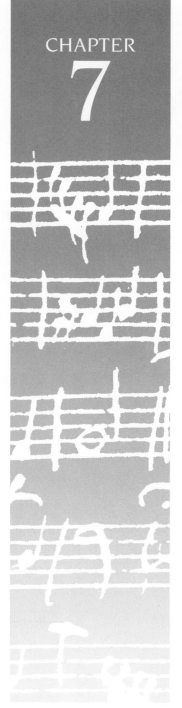

A Song: John Dowland's "Lady, If You So Spite Me"

Song

Most of what most people listen to when they listen to music today is song. Song pervades our popular culture—so much so that we hear people refer to *any* piece of music, even a Beethoven symphony, as a "song." Of course to be properly classified as a song, a work must have words; it will usually be sung by a solo singer; and it should be relatively short. These factors—shortness, small number of people needed for performance, contribution of words and music—have helped make song a universally popular medium of expression. But they have also made song seem so common, almost weed-like, that the form has not seemed so fit a subject for study as more monumental genres like the symphony.

And yet these same factors can be particularly valuable when it comes to studying the music of a given style or period. Principally important is the relationship between the words and the music. A song is not "pure" music in the way a symphony is, but its words do help us answer the question: What is the work *about?* We can speculate about the meaning of a Beethoven symphony, but about a Beethoven song we can be sure. A Beethoven symphony may be about "fate" or it may not. But if a Beethoven song talks about love, we can be fairly certain that love is indeed its subject.

In fact, even if the song is sung in German and you don't understand a word of that language, your safest bet is that it is about love. This might be a criticism of song as a form: its subject matter is so limited. For every song about fate, there must be a hundred about love. Even the songs which *are* about fate are likely to be about ill-fated love. Luckily—or unluckily—the ways of human love and relationships are so infinitely various and problematical that there is forever fresh material for poets and composers to write about.

John Dowland

John Dowland (1562–1626) was an English composer and performer on the lute at the time of Queen Elizabeth I; he and his contemporaries are therefore called "Elizabethans." The name is a little ironic in his case, since although recognized by many as the foremost composer and lutenist of the day, he never achieved employment in Queen Elizabeth's court. This was the great disappointment of his life. He did eventually acquire a court position under Elizabeth's successor, James, but most of his career was spent at courts in France and Denmark. As a songwriter-performer his situation parallels that of many popular musicians today. But where they sing to thousands in concerts or

Words and music for John Dowland's lute song, "Shall I Sue." The unusual placing of the parts is for the convenience of singers seated around a table.

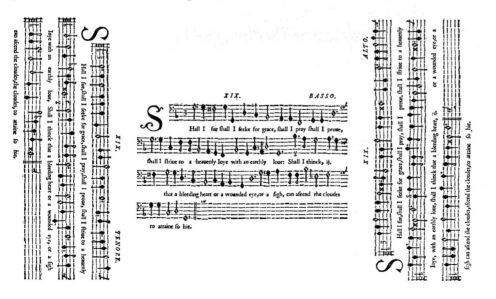

to millions on the radio, he performed to small numbers of upper-class ladies and gentlemen, and, logically enough, the love-lives of upper-class ladies and gentlemen frequently provide the subject matter of his songs.

The Song's Fictional Situation

In "Lady, If You So Spite Me," the "me" is one such gentleman, the "lady" a similarly aristocratic woman. This is the dramatized or fictionalized situation of the song. It doesn't matter if the singer is Dowland himself, or an actual upper-class gentleman of the time, or just a middle-class person who bought the published sheet music to learn at home; it doesn't even matter if the singer is a contemporary college student preparing a recital—whoever sings the song *becomes* for the moment the well-born gentleman singing to his lady.

La - dy, if you so   spite   me, so   spite_____ me,   where - fore do

you   so oft,   so   oft,   kiss,   kiss   and_ de - light   me?

Opening eight measures

Roberti (1430–96): *A Concert.* Instruments shown in this painting include the Renaissance lute (held by musician) and a pochette, a dancing-master's pocket violin (foreground). *(National Gallery, London)*

How Music Controls the Song's Text

Magnifying Text Meanings.   He begins with an opposition: she "spites" him—actively dislikes him—and yet she kisses and delights him. This is an opposition which the music catches and magnifies. Dowland repeats the words "so spite me," the added notes on the second "spite" communicating the emotional energy the word arouses in the singer. But his anger disappears as the melody turns soft and graceful when he thinks of how she kisses and delights him.

Illustrating Text Meanings.   His question, naturally enough, is "why?" If her emotional response to him is one of hate, why are her physical responses those of love? He suggests one possible reason:

Sure that my heart, oppressed and overcloyed,
May break thus overjoyed?

In other words, she may believe that by overwhelming him with love she can more easily break his heart. The phrase "may break" is another one which Dowland chooses to repeat and to illustrate with music. In this case he uses the repetition of the phrase to "break" the rhythmic pattern, an instance of word-painting:

Without the "break" the phrase would look something like this:

Not Dowland's setting

If this is in fact your plan, the singer continues, it's all right with me:

If you seek to spill me,
Come kiss me sweet, and kill me!
So shall your heart be eased,
And I shall rest content and die
    well-pleased.

Selecting Specific Meanings. This may at first seem like a noble sacrifice on the singer's part. But something unexpected occurs in the music. Again, we look at a repeated phrase: "and die." We would expect a slow, falling melodic line, gradually coming to rest. But Dowland gives us instead a rise to the highest and longest note of the song—in fact, the song's climactic moment:

Final four measures

What kind of death is this, we might ask, that you rise up towards, instead of sinking down into? For Dowland's Elizabethan audience, it was easy to answer. For them, the verb "to die" had a second meaning. It referred to the moment of sexual climax. Something of this meaning still survives in French, where the phrase "the little death"—"le petit mort"—refers to sexual release. Another French phrase is used to describe what is going on in the song at this point: *double entendre* (capable of being understood in two ways.)

In a sense, then, the whole song pivots on this phrase. Up until now, we have heard the man's complaints, coupled with his seeming acceptance of the woman's behavior. But Dowland makes his setting of the word "die" the musical climax of the song; this makes us hear the work in its meaning of sexual climax; and now it appears that the man, far from being victimized by the woman, is taking his pleasure from her. The song at first seemed to be about a woman teasing a man; now it turns out that the song itself is the man's way of teasing the woman.

We have seen the control the music can have on the words. It can magnify the meaning of words (by communicating the singer's extra emotional intensity); illustrate their meaning (through word-painting); and select specific meanings, as in the case of "to die," where one meaning is emphasized over another. These are specific instances of the music's control.

Creation of Context.   There is a more general sense in which the song keeps teasing us about the man's attitude, making us wonder if he is really depressed about the way the woman treats him, or is instead enjoying the way he's treating her. It is typical of the Elizabethan lute song style to switch in and out of the minor key. Even in songs which are thoroughly sad, the composer will introduce cadences on the major chord from time to time. But in this example the switches from minor to major seem well-calculated. Minor cadences occur around the phrases "spite me," "over-cloyed," "spill me," and "kill me." Dowland switches to major for "delight me," "overjoyed," and, finally, "die well pleased." This play between major and minor, along with shifts from short quick notes to long drawn-out ones, helps to define the singer's attitude for us, as he switches from anger to acceptance, from bitterness to contentment, from mock depression to smug pleasure.

By magnifying, illustrating, and selecting specific meanings, the music controls the song's text. By creating the mood or atmosphere behind the words, the music supplies the song's context. One of the major differences between Elizabethan song and contemporary popular song is that today's songwriters are much more concerned with context than with text. In other words, they are more concerned with creating mood and attitude than with magnifying, illustrating, or selecting meanings for particular words. Nevertheless, songwriters today, like those of Dowland's time some 400 years earlier, attempt through the combination of words and music to capture the particular inflections and shades of meaning of their contemporary culture. The successful song becomes like a time capsule. Its subject may be a common one like love, but if we can open it up to find the particularity of its attitude towards its common subject, we will be as close as we can get to the minds of its distant creators and listeners.

SUMMARY: *John Dowland's "Lady, If You So Spite Me"*

melody   A flexible melodic line which changes to fit particular inflections of meaning. The melody does have certain patterns which recur on an irregular basis. Most noticeable is a movement downwards by a half step, with a stress on the lower note (example: the opening phrase, where it occurs twice).

harmony   Alternates between major and minor cadences. Dissonance used frequently, but always resolved at the end of the phrase.

rhythm   The grouping of beats is irregular—there are no measures with set numbers of beats to each one. Dowland uses rhythm for expressive purposes, allowing a pattern to establish itself momentarily, then breaking it.

form   **Through-composed;** that is, no refrain or chorus, and no repeat of same music for different verses.

texture   The voice has the melody, of course, but the lute does not merely strum chords; rather, it intersperses the occasional chord among intricate counter-melodies. Thus the texture is both homophonic and polyphonic.

timbre   The most common instrumentation is voice and lute, but Elizabethan performance practices allow various combinations of strings as well. The traditional vocal timbre is the very high man's voice, counter-tenor.

function   Originally designed for intimately-scaled entertainments for aristocratic audiences. Also made available to a leisured middle- and upper-class public through commercial publishing.

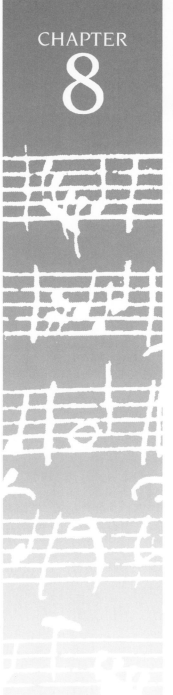

A Piano Piece: Chopin's Prélude in B Minor

Préludes

There is something odd about the title which Frédéric Chopin (1810–1849)* gave to his piece. A **prélude** is, traditionally, a short piece which introduces another work. Chopin wrote a collection of 24 préludes. They are all short, but they introduce nothing but themselves. Why then call them préludes? Chopin in his title is referring not so much to the traditional definition of a prélude as to a particular example of the form: Johann Sebastian Bach's collection of préludes and fugues called *The Well-Tempered Clavier*. More than one hundred years before Chopin, Bach (1685–1750)* wrote these to demonstrate the flexibility of a new system of tuning keyboard instruments, a "tempered," or "compromise" tuning, which allowed the composer to use every major and minor key. He succeeded in demonstrating the virtues of tempered tuning, but, more significantly, he illustrated such a wonderful variety of

*For additional biographical information on Chopin and Bach, *see* Chapters 23 and 18, respectively.

compositional and keyboard techniques that the *The Well-Tempered Clavier* became one of the central works in every pianist's education.

In calling his works préludes, and in writing one in each of the major and minor keys, the 28-year-old Chopin was in effect claiming that his works would illustrate the variety of his compositional and keyboard techniques just as Bach's had. It was in a sense an audacious, even a presumptuous claim, but it was a successful one. His préludes have, like Bach's, achieved a central place in the pianist's standard repertory.

The Problem of "Expression" in Music

Because the B Minor Prélude is such a standard work, and because its notes are relatively easy to learn, generations of pianists have studied it. Sometime in the learning process, most of them have probably heard their teachers say something like "Play with more expression." This is a standard sort of teacher's phrase, and one which students never seem to question. But what does it mean to play "expressively," and exactly what is the poor student supposed to express? The whole concept of "expression" in music is exceedingly vague and ill-defined. And yet most people listening to a good performance of the piece would agree that it is "expressive," that it is filled with emotion, although they would be hard pressed to define the emotion exactly.

A young girl's first piano recital.

Chopin's Prélude in B Minor

The piece begins with a melody in the left hand, a two-measure phrase which rises and falls in as thoroughly "minor" a manner as can be imagined (*See* Figure 8–1, example one. Note that two staffs are paired together. The left hand plays the lower staff and the right hand plays the upper one.) The melody follows the pattern of a climbing B-minor arpeggio, but at the second minor third it loses its energy, to fall slowly back to its starting point. The second two-measure phrase climbs higher, only to fall back once again. The third phrase is twice as long. It begins from a lower point and rises to a higher point than either of the first two phrases. As it starts to descend, it creates dissonance against the persistent throbbing pattern which has been playing above it in the right hand. The energy created by this dissonance seems to carry the melody up into the right hand; only at the very end of the phrase does it fall back towards the B-minor starting point once more.

The opening two-measure phrase now returns, exactly as it appeared at the start of the piece. The second phrase disrupts the pattern, moving quickly to a cadence in C major, stressed with repetitions of the C chord (Example two), as though the piece were suddenly coming to a happy ending. However, the throbbing motive in the right hand does not stop with the cadence. It continues, falling away from the C-major chord, towards a tense, dissonant chord (the technical name for which is a *diminished-seventh chord*—Example three) which marks the start of the long closing section. Here the melody, still in the left hand, falls—over a space of three measures—towards what sounds like the final cadence. But Chopin gives us what is called a **deceptive cadence.** Instead of ending on a B-minor chord, he substitutes a G-major chord at the last instant (Example four). The falling, closing melody then begins again, and this time does cadence on B minor. But the piece is not over yet. The right hand throbbing goes on, bringing back the opening phrase for the third and last time (Example five.) After its statement concludes, the throbbing pauses, returns for a second, and then ceases.

Specific Versus Abstract Interpretations

The previous section offered a description—at least a partial one—of the main events in the prélude. But the question remains: do these events possess meaning—that is, do they *express* something?

The novelist Amandine-Aurore Dupin, better known by her pseudonym George Sand, was Chopin's lover during the time the préludes were written. For her, the elements of the piece had specific meanings. Horribly specific, to our modern ears—she interpreted the "throbbing" motive in the right hand as cold drops of water dripping on the breast of a drowned man. If Chopin had really wanted us to have such a specific interpretation in mind he could have titled the piece something like *Death by Water* instead of *Prélude in B Minor.*

The opposite extreme is to think of the piece as totally abstract, as though it made no reference to human experience, but was only a pleasing arrange-

George Sand: *Frédéric Chopin* (1841).

Figure 8–1
Chopin's *Prélude in B Minor*
Example one: first phrase of the melody; Example two: C-major chords (arpeggios); Example three: diminished-seventh chord, start of closing section; Example four: deceptive cadence; Example five: return of opening phrase.

Caricature (1844) by Maurice Sand (George's son) of Chopin giving opera singer Pauline Viardot a piano lesson.

ment of sounds. This, as I suggested earlier, flies in the face of most listeners' intuitive sense that the work is charged with emotional content. To define that content, I suggest a middle course between the two extremes of the very specific and the very abstract.

The work Chopin created is like a vessel. Into it we can pour our own emotions, ideas, or stories. But the vessel is not infinitely elastic: it has a particular shape. A range of emotions, ideas, or stories will fit comfortably within it, but not every one. A listener's anger would not fit comfortably within this piece, nor would sheer bubbly happiness—but George Sand's story of a drowning man would fit, and so would an idea about the futility of human hope, and so would a number of emotional states. These need not be strictly defined. In listening to the piece, we need not have any intellectual awareness of how our consciousness is filling Chopin's design. We only know that the vessel is filled, the connection is made, and the experience is a satisfying one. It is for this sense of connection and communication—even validation—of the listener's emotional state that people are willing to sit quietly in rooms listening to sounds from piano or record-player.

The Performer as Interpreter

Which brings us back to the student struggling to perform the piece. For it is obvious that, while the notes on the page may be useful for analysis and discussion, looking at them will never create the kind of emotion-holding vessel we have been talking about—only sounds in the air can do that, and therefore the performer is necessary. But if the performer merely translates the notes directly into sounds, with the kind of exactness or precision we could expect from a computer, the result will be useless. The vessel will not take shape on its own. The performer must sense its contours, make them clear, and project them to the listener. In short, the performer has to "interpret" the piece, invest some of his or her own personality into the plain notes. The end result is something which differs from the precise or "computerized" version. We hear the performer's interpretation in the slight emphasis on one note rather than another, in subtle shifts of rhythm where one eighth note is held slightly longer than another eighth note next to it, in the use of the pedal, where some sounds are allowed to linger and others are cut short.

This interpretation requires more than an intellectual understanding of the piece and the technical skill to play it; the performer must, like the listener who enjoys the piece, establish, at some level, an intuitive connection with it. But what good is this as advice? Telling the struggling student "Establish an intuitive connection with the music" is even worse than saying "Play with more expression." This is not to say that it is impossible for teachers to give students good advice about playing, only to admit that such advice will not come in the form of simple generalizations.

Let me try to give some advice about a particular problem of interpretation—the two big C-major arpeggios (Example two). Played by themselves they seem like part of some happy ending. As such, they might be performed forcefully, the second arpeggio louder, more strongly marked and slower than the first. But in context the arpeggios are not a happy ending. C major isn't a chord which normally occurs in the key of B minor, and Chopin moves to it so quickly that it doesn't seem a stable or permanent resting place. In addition, as we noted before, the right-hand pulse does not stop but continues, quickly taking us out of C major and back towards B minor.

As a performer, your problem would be like that of a storyteller who, about mid-way through the tale, must give a hint that things will work out fine, although the listeners know that it is too soon for the plot to be resolved. You must then withdraw the hint and allow the story to continue towards its natural conclusion. One effective approach—not necessarily the only one—would be to arrive at the first C-major arpeggio with enough force to give the hint of resolution—but by the second arpeggio already to be drawing away from it. You can accomplish this by a variety of means—playing the second arpeggio more softly, for instance, or more delicately, or slower, or with a more flowing, connected (**legato**) touch. What finally matters is that you vary the two arpeggios so that a hint of resolution is given and then taken away. If you succeed in doing this, you will be playing "with expression," and fulfilling Chopin's ultimate aim in writing such a short but emotion-packed piece of music.

SUMMARY: *Chopin's* **Prélude No. 6, in B Minor**

melody	The characteristic shape of the typical melodic phrase can be described as a short steep climb, followed by a long gentle fall.
harmony	Minor mode. Use of dissonance, diminished-seventh chords.
rhythm	The right hand keeps a steady eighth-note pulse until almost the very end—but the performer is expected to treat the pulse of the music with flexibility (**rubato).**
form	Two short phrases and a long phrase comprise the initial pattern. This starts to repeat, but is broken into by a sudden harmonic shift (to C major); the last half of the piece is a falling-away from this moment.
texture	Largely homophonic—right-hand chords over left-hand melody. However, the right hand plays a counter-melody at one point, and the top notes of the chords outline a subtle melodic pattern as well.
timbre	Piano, with melody in the left hand, " 'cello" range of the instrument.
function	Designed for small scale, intimate performance settings. Also popular as an example for teaching.

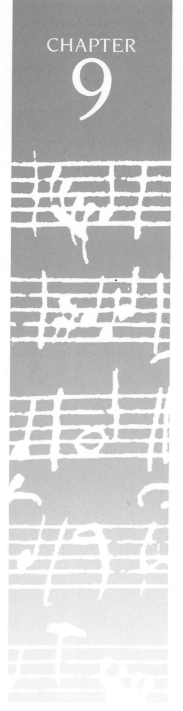

A Concerto: Tchaikovsky's Concerto No. 1 for Piano and Orchestra in B♭ Minor

Public Versus Private Music

Modern technology confuses the old distinctions between public and private music. A stereo system can bring a 100-piece orchestra into a living room or even into an automobile. Microphones and amplifiers can project a single performer's voice to thousands of people in an outdoor arena.

It wasn't always so. Songs and piano pieces were made for private performance in living rooms—"music of the house," in Shakespeare's phrase. Concertos and symphonies were designed for large-scale public performances—concerts.

In a sense it is amazing that, in this age of the stereo, the concert still persists. After all, you can buy an excellent recording of Tchaikovsky's piano concerto for about the same price as a ticket to a concert performance. What does the concert have that the recording lacks? The communal sense of shared experience we receive from the audience surrounding us; the visual immediacy that comes from watching the sounds being made; the sense of danger and chal-

Daniel Barenboim rehearsing a piano concerto with the Cleveland Orchestra.

lenge in watching a performer risk himself or herself in a difficult work; the empathy with the music we can gather from identifying with the performer and feeling as though the music is coming from within us. We pay for concert tickets to receive these experiences; in fact, we pay just for the chance of receiving them, since good performances are never guaranteed.

The Concerto

As a form, the concerto is particularly well-suited for concerts. A solo player performs with a symphony orchestra, giving us both a large sound and a single person to focus on and presenting as well the possibility of dramatic interplay between the two. It is this interplay which sets the concerto apart. It is different in kind from the more familiar solo-with-accompaniment which those who have attended school music contests have heard in such endless numbers. In this format, the instrumental soloist or singer carries the principal melody line, the piano (or other accompanying instruments) supplies the rest. Even when the accompanying instrument is given a moment or two of glory on its own, it is still always clear which is the solo, which the accompaniment. But in the concerto the solo instrument and the orchestra have roughly equivalent stature. Each plays principal themes, each is given vital solo passages, each at times accompanies the other. One might suppose that the solo instrument, in being given a less dominating role in the piece, would appear diminished in importance. In fact the opposite is true. If the orchestra were to play a purely accompanying role—for example, if it were simply to supply a pleasing harmonic background for the soloist—the solo instrument would have nothing to work against. But when the orchestral part is strong and active, the solo part has a partner in its dialogue. And when the solo instrument is seen to hold its own, that is, when the audience recognizes that the single voice can make musical statements with the strength and vigor equivalent to the entire orchestra, then there is a real sense of the power the solo instrument can project. It is as though the solo instrument needed a worthy opponent to prove itself against; in the contrast between the individual voice and the full force of the orchestra, the individual voice can appear heroic in stature. What the concerto gives us is a dialogue between equals, where the equals are apparently mismatched in their resources. Perhaps it is our natural tendency to sympathize with the underdog which helps make us identify with the soloist in this situation. Some authorities think the word "concerto" is derived from the Latin *concertare,* "to fight," others think that it is derived from the Latin *consere,* "to join together." Both meanings fit.

Tchaikovsky

Piotr (Peter) Ilyich Tchaikovsky was born in 1840 and was 34 when he wrote his *Piano Concerto No. 1 in B♭ Minor.* Where Mozart and Beethoven had been composer-performers who wrote piano concerti for concerts which they gave themselves, Tchaikovsky was a composer-teacher and so needed to find a performer in order to get his work before the public. He turned to Nikolai Rubinstein, a noted pianist who was also director of the Moscow Conservatory where Tchaikovsky taught. He played a draft of the piece for Rubinstein, who, according to Tchaikovsky, hated it. Anyone who had heard Rubinstein's comments, Tchaikovsky wrote, would have thought "that I was a stupid, untalented and conceited spoiler of music paper who had the impertinence to show his rubbish to a celebrated man." Of course composers who put their souls into their music are notoriously sensitive to criticism, and it may only be that Rubinstein was not enough impressed with the work to undertake the immense commitment of time and energy needed to learn and perform it.

Tchaikovsky (1868)

Tchaikovsky next turned to Hans von Bülow, second only to Liszt among the great pianists of the day. Von Bülow accepted the work enthusiastically—it is dedicated to him—and gave it its first performance, in Boston, on October 25, 1875.

The "Duel" Between Piano and Orchestra

Tchaikovsky does not wait long to let us know that this is public concert hall and not private living-room music. There isn't a living room in the world, not even in Buckingham Palace, which could comfortably contain the opening measures. These begin with four French horns, in unison, *fortissimo* ("very loud"), proclaiming a motive whose every statement is followed by a full chord from the orchestra, also marked *fortissimo.* The piano enters with a kind of controlled violence—huge chords, both hands together, traversing the length of the keyboard every three beats, played over and against the orchestra's lush melody.

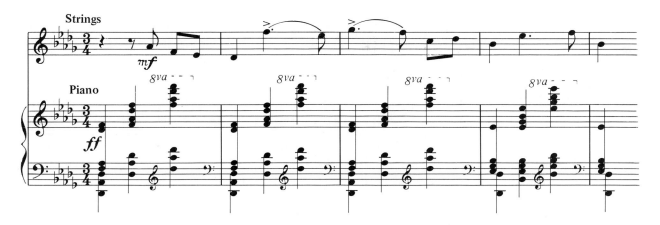

Introductory theme—piano chords against orchestra's melody (measures 7–10)

The orchestra hushes and becomes like a strumming guitar accompanying the piano as it takes over the theme. The piano, as an individual voice, has more freedom and flexibility than can be allowed the communal voice of the orchestra. It doesn't play the melody "straight," but adds its own rhythmic and melodic gestures. Then it seems to seize on one phrase, repeating it higher and higher, until it breaks into a wild **cadenza** (a solo section free from the orchestra), which improvises on aspects of the theme.

In talking about this concerto many writers refer to the "duel" between piano and orchestra. This seems not quite right. At least in this first instance the piano seems to be saying to the orchestra (and to us in the audience), "Look at what passion and possibility are locked inside this theme. Don't be content merely to play on its surface. Explore beneath, and discover its range and its depths." Not dueling, in other words, but teaching. The orchestra and piano then join together for one last version of the theme. This is the introductory section of the concerto—an unusually substantial one—and its theme will not be heard again.

A quiet interlude characterized by repeated sustained notes on the trumpet leads to the first principal theme: a Russian folk dance (based on a tune Tchaikovsky heard in the Ukraine) introduced and led by the piano. This is stated, and we get some sense of its rhythmic vitality, but barely developed before the orchestra comes in with the second theme, a melody strongly characteristic of the Romantic period, full of sighs and longing. The piano echoes this theme on its own, after which the orchestra returns with the third theme. This is a more "optimistic"-sounding melody than the second theme, since it is characterized by an upward-climbing motive and forward-flowing momentum. But the orchestra manages only a tentative statement of this theme before the piano pulls us back to the second theme, and leads the orchestra into a demonstration of what passion, power, and even violence can be developed from it.

First principal theme, based on Russian folk tune (measures 116–17)

Second principal theme . . . "Romantic . . . full of sighs and longing," (measures 194–97)

Third principal theme . . . "more climbing, 'optimistic,' " (measures 206–209)

The orchestra then returns with theme three. After it has been stated in full, we have heard all of the principal melodic ideas the movement contains. Tchaikovsky now begins to work with these ideas, exploring further beneath their surfaces, combining them, placing them in harmony and conflict with one another. As we listen to him develop these ideas, we may recognize fragments of the first, second, and third themes as they occur. What is more important than recognizing these themes, though, is hearing how they are transformed. What was calm becomes hectic, the jovial becomes passionate, the simple complex, the peaceful violent, and back again.

Dramatic Elements

If this piece were a person, we would diagnose it as "manic-depressive," so violent are its swings of emotion. This is not to say that Tchaikovsky was a manic-depressive, only that his aim is to take us on an emotional roller coaster ride. What might be painful in reality can become enjoyable in a piece of music. The analogy to the roller coaster may help explain this. The point of the roller coaster is to give thrills through the illusion of danger. Part of us, presumably some primitive part of our brain, reacts with the symptoms of real fear. But another part of us knows that the sensations are temporary, the situation fundamentally safe and controlled. We can allow a piece of music to take us on an emotional roller coaster ride because we know that here too the sensations are temporary, the situation safe.

Traditional concerto form asks for three movements, whose basic tempo relationship is fast-slow-faster. Tchaikovsky follows this general outline, but introduces a variation on it in the second movement. He gives the movement an ABA, or ternary, structure, where the "A" sections are based on a slow melody treated delicately and simply. This much is traditional. What is not traditional is the "B" section in a strongly contrasting tempo: *prestissimo*. The melody here is based on a French popular song whose title can be roughly translated as "Dance, Laugh, and Have Fun." The combination of a pretty tune, treated simply (that is, *not* explored for its passionate depths) and the French song (whose title characterizes the *prestissimo* section well) gives a needed sense of relaxation from the emotional intensity of the first movement.

The third movement is also characterized by two contrasting principal ideas, the first of which is another energetic Russian folk dance. It is marked by a strong recurring accent on the second beat of every measure.

First theme, final movement . . . folk dance, accent on second beat, (measures 5–7)

Against this physical, dance-inspired folk tune, Tchaikovsky places one of the lilting, lyrical ideas of which he apparently had an inexhaustible supply. It begins:

Second principal theme, final movement . . . "lilting," (measures 57–60)

Although the ideas contrast in character, they are alike in being in "three." The consistent three-beats-to-a-measure pattern helps maintain an outward, physical motion, making impossible the kind of dreamy introspection we heard in the freer rhythms of the first movement.

There is one moment, though, in which Tchaikovsky reminds us of the heights he has taken us to earlier. Near the end of the movement, the orchestra builds up to a piano cadenza which carries us on into a version of the lyrical idea, everyone playing together *fortissimo*. It was always a pretty melody, but here it is transformed into something rich, triumphal, even ecstatic—possibilities we never would have realized lay within it.

For the performer, this is one of the most challenging of concertos. The technical dexterity required, the strength and endurance, the depth of emotional response, plus the sheer mental effort needed to conceive of such a vast work as a whole, not just passage by passage, and the responsibility so often placed on the piano to lead the orchestra and to sustain the texture on its own—all of these factors make the work a difficult one.

Indeed the difficulty is so great that I feel a sneaking sympathy for poor Nikolai Rubinstein, who, in turning down the opportunity to première the work, missed his chance to be immortalized in Tchaikovsky's title-page dedication. And yet these factors are different only in degree, not in kind, from the challenges that face every soloist in every concerto. They are challenges which furnish a large part of the drama which makes the concerto so ideal a form for concert performance.

SUMMARY: *Tchaikovsky's* **Piano Concerto No. 1 in B♭ Minor**

melody	Contrasting types. Tchaikovsky uses rich, Romantic themes of his own invention, themes taken from Russian folk music, and even a French popular song. Tchaikovsky's own melodies tend to stretch out over many measures, taking time to develop; the folk tunes establish their character quickly.
harmony	Although the first and most important movement is in B♭ minor, a great deal of the concerto is in the major mode. The principal introductory theme, for example, is in D♭ major, and the work ends in B♭ major. Folk themes are characterized by relatively simple, static harmonies; Tchaikovsky's own melodies have richer variety in their harmonic progressions.
rhythm	Variable and free in first movement. Dancing folk rhythms are contrasted with free, rhapsodic rhythms, especially in piano cadenzas. Second movement inserts very fast middle section into a generally slow pace, but within each tempo the beat is consistent, not free. Third movement keeps to a strong "three" pattern. Its folk dance theme is marked by a syncopated accent on the second beat of every measure.
form	Tchaikovsky uses the traditional formal structures of sonata form for the first movement, ternary form for the middle movement, and rondo form for the last movement. His treatment of sonata form (*see* Chapters 19 and 20) is very free, and we are conscious less of that structure than we are of the work's changing textures. The ternary (ABA) structure of the middle movement is clearly marked, the B section being a strongly contrasting *prestissimo*. His treatment of the **rondo** form in the last movement is free, but does give the hallmark of that structure—a recurring identifiable theme.

texture	Predominantly homophonic, although piano and orchestra frequently play in counterpoint to one another, occasionally using imitation. Solo passages for orchestra and solo passages for piano alternate with passages in which piano and orchestra work together in concert.
timbre	Piano and large orchestra. The full range of piano timbres is explored, with particular stress on the extremes of high and low, loud and soft.
function	Public concert performance. From its première to the present it has remained one of the most popular piano concertos in the repertory.

A Symphony: Haydn's Symphony No. 100 (*the "Military"*)

Sometime during the nineteenth century, "commercial" music acquired a bad name. It was assumed that if you were a composer who wrote to sell, your music had to be superficial and contrived. Writing "commercial" music meant selling out your ideals, prostituting your art, and corrupting your soul simply to make money. Or so the myth ran in the Romantic era, and it runs right on into our own time, all of which would have been very surprising to composer Franz Josef Haydn (1732–1809)*.

Haydn and Salomon

In 1790 an English impresario—the equivalent of today's producer-promoters—named Johann Peter Salomon approached Haydn with a commercial pro-

*For additional biographical information, *see* Chapter 20.

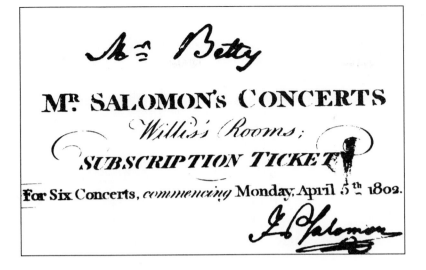

A ticket to English impresario Johann Peter Salomon's concert series of 1802, with his signature.

position. Salomon would put together a series of concerts in London. He would hire the orchestra, rent the hall, take care of the publicity, and print the tickets. Later he would publish scores of the music and market them. For his part, Haydn would write the music, including six symphonies. For the symphonies he would be paid 300 English pounds, plus 200 pounds as his copyright or publication fee.

Or the story could be told a different way: Salomon was a musician, a composer and violinist, who cherished Haydn's music dearly. He desired above all else the privilege of introducing Haydn direct to the London public. Haydn had just retired (at age 58) from service at a Hungarian court and was free to travel and make his music known to the world. The two men, united in their love of music, became good friends, and the period of their joint collaboration was the happiest and most rewarding of both their lives.

Both stories are true, or rather they are the same story told from two different viewpoints. Love of music and love of money—if there is something contradictory in these two impulses, Haydn and Salomon were unaware of it.

And so Haydn came to London in the 1790s with the express aims of writing music to please the London concert-going public, and—not a contradictory impulse—to write the best symphonies he knew how to write. He succeeded in both his purposes. The concerts sold out. The public loved his symphonies. The morning after the second performance of the "Military" Symphony, the London *Morning Chronicle* reported "absolute shouts of applause. Encore! encore! encore! resounded from every seat: The Ladies themselves could not forbear."

In the Hanover Square Rooms, Haydn's first London symphonies were performed. Not even Haydn's music could force fashionable members of the audience to sit down and cease conversation.

Themes and Transformations

Haydn's "Military" symphony begins with an introductory section, initially as slow and stately as a courtly dance. It is *so* calm that tension builds behind it, as we wonder when the smooth surface will be broken. There isn't long to wait. The orchestra expands, we hear the flutes enter, there is a shift to minor, the melody starts down in the low strings, and the timpani enter with a roll which crescendoes to *fortissimo.* These factors all contribute to a new kind of tension in the piece, a sense of held-back foreboding. Then Haydn shows us one of his favorite "surprise" techniques. The texture thins, and the strings state a motive which falls and quietens, letting us think it will fade away, when instead it suddenly finishes off with four blaring chords:

An example of a Haydn "surprise" technique (measures 21–22)

The main part of the movement revolves around two principal themes. The first of these we hear immediately, high in the woodwinds, a bright, quick, almost "chirpy" theme.

First theme . . . "chirpy" (measures 24–28)

The second, stated in the violins, is a country dance, based on a polka-like rhythm.

Second theme . . . "country dance" (measures 94–98)

Both of these themes are light, bouncy, happy-sounding, but the way Haydn develops them is not consistent with this first impression. They are originally heard in relatively high registers, thinly orchestrated, both in major modes, both built around light but rhythmic accents. As the movement develops, we hear heavy orchestration, thicker textures, minor modes, deep pounding accents from the timpani. Against the airy, the ponderous, against the dance, the march, against the frivolous, the purposeful. The result is a movement full of sudden shifts and dramatic contrasts.

One example of "sudden shifts and dramatic contrasts" (measures 235–39)

The second movement started life in another piece entirely. It was a movement labeled "Romance" in a concerto Haydn wrote for the King of Naples. As is fitting for a "Romance," the melody is a simple, lyrical tune, presented in four neatly balanced phrases.

Principal theme of the second movement . . . "four neatly balanced phrases" (measures 1–8)

These phrases are in turn responded to by other balanced phrases, and repeated in varied orchestrations.

The greatest composers often use the simplest techniques. Surely there is no simpler way to change the character of a melody than to change it from major to minor. Haydn needs only to change one note in the first phrase: making the third (an E in the key of C) a flatted, or minor third, instead of a major third.

becomes

Dancers performing the minuet (1735). *(By courtesy of the Board of Trustees of the Victoria and Albert Museum, London)*

This is a simple change, but Haydn does not rely on us to perceive its implications. Instead, he projects its implications beyond anything we would conceive of. He injects drums, triangles, cymbals, and trumpets into the orchestration, turning the tune into a crashing, heavy, almost raucous march. And then he takes us back to the gentle "Romance" treatment of the theme again, and back and forth, until we are in suspense about which we will hear next. Finally a low trumpet fanfare, a real military fanfare which Haydn has borrowed for the occasion, takes us into the concluding measures, still veering between the military and the Romance, but concluding on a triumphant military note.

The third movement is a minuet, heard, as is usual in symphonies, in three-part form: the minuet, a contrasting "trio" section, and the minuet repeated. The minuet is a precise, polite dance form. It originated at the court of Louis XIV of France, and so has aristocratic connotations. The melody Haydn creates has an elegant turn of phrase, suitable for the dance; we can hear in its outlines the graceful bows and hand-gestures which were part of the form. In Haydn's treatment of the tune we can also hear pounding timpani accents on the first two beats of the measure, totally out of place in the polite drawing-room atmosphere we usually associate with the dance.

Minuet melody; timpani accents underneath (measures 1–4)

The trio section is one of the loveliest portions of the symphony; it is built around a gentle, lilting melody. By now you will not need a guide to tell you to look out for sudden shifts into brass and drums and *fortissimos*.

Nor should you need much guiding through the last movement, the finale. Its principal theme embodies a dance rhythm similar to an Irish jig or a Virginia reel; in fact, the theme became popular as a dance, achieving a separate existence as a piece of popular dance music.

Principal theme, last movement . . . "popular dance music" (measures 1–4)

As in the earlier movements, Haydn shifts back and forth between the light-hearted dance and heavier martial connotations. By the end of the movement, the effect is almost like movie editing, as he cuts back and forth between the images of a dancing party and a quick march on the parade ground.

Images of War vs. Peace

The word "images" is used deliberately. Haydn's "Military" Symphony is not a complex essay on issues of war and peace. It is instead a series of brightly-colored pictures. On the "war" side he does not give us a report from the trenches. There were real wars being fought in the 1790s, and real people were dying in them; at the moment Haydn's symphony was being played in London, English soldiers were dying, mostly of disease, in an ill-advised venture against the French in the West Indies. This was not Haydn's concern. He would be serious about religion, but he would leave war to the soldiers and the politicians. His military is the boom of the cannon, the crash of the cymbals, the marching drills, the brightly colored uniforms—the fear, sometimes, and sometimes the triumph, but mostly the spectacle. Against these images he places the images of peacetime: birds singing, peasants dancing, a formal Romance, a courtly minuet, a popular dance. The result is a work full of dramatic contrasts. It is not itself a drama, it does not tell a story, but it is a unified whole.

The Symphony

The symphony is the major orchestral form. Almost every concert by a major orchestra includes one. Orchestras are called "symphony orchestras" simply because they can and do play symphonies. The form of the symphony usually follows the general outline we have seen in Haydn's: a large-scale, four movement work, with a variety of tempi and a wealth of musical ideas, demanding brilliant playing from the orchestra. Its history before Haydn was not quite so glorious. It began in the overtures to operas. These were largely audience-settling devices, and in the eighteenth-century audiences were known to require a great deal of settling. Haydn's great accomplishment was to take this incidental form and make it into something important—something which would take Salomon to Vienna to recruit Haydn to come to London in the sure knowledge that his symphonies would make their concerts into major cultural events. Haydn had elevated a purely instrumental work to an importance which before only large-scale vocal works, such as operas and oratorios, could pretend to. In works like the "Military" Symphony, he demonstrated that such an instrumental work could have both unity and diversity, could maintain both a sense of wholeness and a rich variety of dramatic contrast. As a form, the symphony would undergo further evolution, particularly in Beethoven's hands, but it was Haydn who was largely responsible for giving Beethoven such a mature and well-developed form to work with.

SUMMARY: *Haydn's* Symphony No. 100, *the "Military"*

melody	A variety of melodic types are stated: a "bird song" type, a polka-like dance, a "Romance" theme, a courtly minuet, a quick dance. Each of these themes is developed in ways which transform its character from "peaceful" to "military" connotations.
harmony	The harmonies which accompany the themes' first statements are simple and straightforward, generally consonant and in major keys. As the themes are developed, a number of complexities are introduced, including minor modes and rapid modulations.
rhythm	Rhythmic variety matches the melodic variety discussed above. For example, the second movement begins as a gentle, if polite, love song, which is then transformed into a noisy march.
form	Four movements. First movement in sonata form (*see* Chapters 19 and 20), with introductory section *adagio,* and main section *allegro.* Second movement, *allegretto,* first states and then develops a single theme. Third movement a minuet in traditional ABA form: minuet-contrasting trio section-minuet. Finale movement, *presto,* in sonata form, but based almost entirely on one theme. Use of

"military" motifs—especially with brass and percussion orchestration—serves to unify symphony as a whole.

texture Homophonic. Haydn uses a full orchestral texture for episodes with "military" connotations, a much thinner texture for his more "peaceful" images.

timbre The orchestra for Haydn's London concerts was large for its time, but small by present-day standards. It included 12 to 16 violins, four violas, three 'cellos, and four bass viols, plus pairs of flutes, oboes, clarinets, bassoons, horns, trumpets, and timpani. In addition, the orchestra is increased by triangle, cymbals, and bass drum in the second and fourth movements. Strings provide the basic continuity—woodwinds, brass and percussion are used to vary and transform the orchestral colors.

function Originally designed for performance in concerts of symphonic music, and still used for that purpose.

An Opera: Purcell's Dido and Aeneas

Opera's Patrons and Audiences

Operas tend to be about people in the grip of powerful passions, and people tend to be pretty passionate in their opinions about opera, either loving it or hating it. In fact there are good arguments for loving it, and good arguments for hating it, and sometimes the same argument works for both cases.

To many people, opera means rich, snobbish audiences, interminable performances, melodramatic acting, incomprehensible words (whether in a foreign language or in English), unnatural warbling instead of singing, and lovers who scream in each others' ears and end up stabbed or poisoned. To others, it is the richest possible combination of sight, sound, and action, the drama of great theater multipled by glorious music and superhuman performing ability. Both positions have elements of truth.

Opera has been a rich man's sport. It has almost always required some sort of subsidy, only very rarely supporting itself on box-office receipts. The reasons for this have to do with production expense. An opera production begins with all the expenses of a theater work—actors, sets, costumes, lights—and adds to these the expenses of an orchestral concert, a choral concert, and, frequently, a dance concert as well.

What may be less obvious is *why* rich people, the aristocracy in most of the historical periods we will be looking at, should have supported opera. It was not something they did simply for their own amusement or entertainment. It was instead a form of public display. This is traditionally an important part of the aristocratic role. Pomp is needed to support circumstance, and art is as much a part of aristocratic display as are satins, furs, jewels, and crowns.

Princes or dukes would band together and as part of their aristocratic role sponsor an opera or a season of operas. But display is never successful if no one is there to witness it. Thus, in the case of opera, the old saying "He who pays the piper calls the tune" is not quite accurate. If the audience stays away the display is useless, and for this reason both popular taste and aristocratic patronage are intimately bound together in opera's history. In addition, opera is so very expensive that few have been rich enough willingly to subsidize it entirely, and the art form even on a purely economic level has depended on popular support through ticket sales as well as on aristocratic subsidy. In short, there is good historical reason for connecting opera with snobbism and equally good historical reason for connecting it with populism.

Operatic Conventions

Vocal Qualities

Whether for purposes of display or for purposes of selling tickets, opera has traditionally played in large halls. This simple fact underlies many if not most of the oddities in its style, especially with regard to singing and acting. Imagine for a moment walking out on a stage in front of, say, 2000 people. It is a safe bet that the average person would have a good deal of trouble just talking understandably to so many. But now add a chorus singing behind, someone else singing alongside, and between you and the audience a good-sized orchestra playing energetically, and remember that you are required to project your voice to the upper balcony, row ZZ.

It should be clear that a "natural"-sounding voice, based on a conversational tone, will not work, unless it is helped by a microphone. Unaided by amplification, the voice must be much higher, or much stronger, or much lower, or much more penetrating than the normal voice, simply to satisfy the elementary requirement that it be heard. From this basic physical necessity arises much of the characteristic operatic style. That the opera singer will not use a "normal"-sounding voice is a fact which the general listener must accept as a convention of the art form, just as the viewer of a soccer match must accept the convention that the players will not use their hands.

Elsa and Lohengrin from the San Diego Opera's production of Wagner's *Lohengrin*.

Plots

Other conventions may be more difficult to justify: the nature of the dramas, for example, which tend towards the exaggerated and melodramatic, even in the comedies, but especially so in tragedies. In this context it may be useful to remember the derivation of the phrase "soap opera." These television serials earned the word "soap" from their advertisers and the word "opera" from their plots, which were full of twisted, tangled love affairs, violent deaths, illicit sex, and secret identities—which were, in short, operatic.

Such plots are clearly unrealistic, at least in the sense that they do not represent the texture of average, everyday life. But then everyday life is not populated by characters who sing. It is easy to imagine a realistic play where people stand around and talk about groceries, but how could people stand around and *sing* about groceries? The heightened energy of the form demands heightened drama. If the characters are to sing, the drama must supply something worth singing about.

Acting Styles

As does soap-opera acting, opera acting has its own conventions. These result from a basic practical difficulty: to communicate the essence of a scene to a large house when the words may not be understood. The subtle facial expressions we are accustomed to in film acting are useless in this context, where broader gestures are necessary. This kind of acting can deteriorate into empty posing, and, in the history of opera, it has at times done so. At the present moment, there is a movement towards a more realistic style, which includes making sure the singers physically resemble the characters they portray. Along with this, there is a desire to make the words more easily understandable, by singing them clearly, by performing them in versions translated into the audience's language, or even by presenting the opera with "super-titles," where the translated text appears on a screen above the stage.

Some dedicated opera fans—the word is derived from the word "fanatic"— are not interested in such reforms. Their primary concern, above either drama or music, is for the voices themselves. They love those operatic conventions which tend to make all else subservient to the voice, and it is exactly those conventions which the average listener finds hardest to take—which is how the reasons for loving opera and for hating it can often be similar.

It is not realistic to believe that everyone should love opera, anymore than it is realistic to believe that everyone should love soccer. The point of this discussion is just that it is necessary to understand the conventions of the form, the rules of the game, in order to get a clear view of a particular example of opera.

Henry Purcell's Dido and Aeneas

Dido and Aeneas is an early example of opera (1689), but it includes many of the elements we would expect to find: solo songs and choruses, overtures and dances, nobility and commoners, pity and betrayal, love and death. It is unusual in two major respects: one, it is relatively short, and two, it was written not for a large opera house but for a school performance.

Henry Purcell

Its composer is Henry Purcell (1659–1695). Purcell's career exemplifies the sort of "civil service" approach to music making which has gone out of fashion in our day. Being a composer then could be an official job, justifying a salary paid by the state, in this case the King of England. As a youth Purcell sang in the choir of the King's chapel; later he became organist at Westminster Abbey and composer to the court, meaning that he supplied the music for important state functions and occasions. But with *Dido and Aeneas* he was undertaking an independent commission from one Josias Priest, who kept a boarding school for aristocratic young ladies, and who asked for a work they could perform themselves.

Henry Purcell

Nahum Tate

The words of an opera are called the **libretto,** and their author the *librettist,* in this case a not particularly distinguished writer named Nahum Tate. On the plus side, he was made poet laureate of England in 1692. On the negative side, he is remembered chiefly today for his rewriting of Shakespeare's *King Lear* to give it a happy ending, and for being satirized by the poet Alexander Pope in his *Dunciad* (dunce's epic).

Principal Themes and Episodes

For *Dido and Aeneas* Tate built his plot on a section of a work which every schoolchild in England studied—the *Aeneid* by the Roman author Virgil. The *Aeneid* tells the story of the adventures of the Trojan warrior-hero Aeneas after the fall of Troy, on his way to the founding of Rome. The work was particularly meaningful to the English because they were building their own empire (their holdings in America were just one part of this) and identified themselves with the empire-builders of ancient Rome. In this episode of the story, Aeneas has made his way to Carthage, where he is the guest of Queen Dido. Her guest—and more.

Overture, Chorus, and Aria.   *Dido and Aeneas* opens with an *overture,* an instrumental section whose function is to "frame" the drama with music, to announce the work's presence and to get the audience settled in their seats. Its form is that of the "French Overture"—a slow section with dotted rhythms:

followed by a fast section which uses imitation.

Then enter Dido, her handmaiden Belinda, and her attendants, who form the chorus. Belinda sings to Dido:

Shake_____ the cloud from off your brow.

and we hear an example of word-painting—the musical line makes her voice shake on the word "shake." The chorus chimes in to reinforce Belinda's message: "Banish sorrow, banish care, grief should ne'er approach the fair." Dido responds with the opera's first **aria;** that is, its first major solo song.

It comes at a crucial moment. Up until now the characters have been abstractions, their comments generalizations. Now is when Dido starts to use the word "I," and to let us share her innermost feelings. It is through the expression of these feelings that Purcell must make her come to life—change her from some mythical ancient queen of Carthage into a living, breathing human being.

Dido confiding in Belinda from the Mini Met's production of *Dido and Aeneas.*

Ground Bass.   He creates two musical lines. One is called a "ground bass." It is a bass line which is repeated over and over throughout the aria—twenty-one times, in fact, with only one variation.

Ground bass

Against this Purcell puts a rich, varied, and expressive vocal line, full of doubts and hesitations, rises and falls, as though torn between hope and dejection. I stress the word "against," because the vocal melody is deliberately placed off-center rhythmically, so that it seems frequently out-of-step with the ground bass.

Vocal line phrases

Ground bass phrases

Only at one point does the vocal melody succeed in moving the ground bass. Midway through the aria (where Dido sings "I languish till my grief is known"), the ground bass shifts from being centered on C to the tonal center of G. The original C-based pattern then returns. Dido's final attempt to escape it occurs with the words (below left) when an E natural signifies an escape into the major key. But this is followed immediately by (below right) returning to the E flat which brings us back into minor.

Yet would not,   Yet would not

The ground bass can be seen as a metaphor for the patterns of duty and destiny, Dido's melody as an expression of the individual's yearning to escape from them. If we feel for her, if this aria makes us relate to her situation, Purcell has done his job, and the opera can proceed with a new dimension added.

If the job is done, it is done almost entirely thanks to Purcell the composer, not to Nahum Tate, the librettist. The words for the aria are only:

Ah, Belinda, I am pressed
With torment not to be confessed.
Peace and I are strangers grown.
I languish till my grief is known.

These could easily fall into a sing-song pattern:

/ ◡ / ◡ / ◡ /
Ah, Belinda I am pressed
  ◡   / ◡ / ◡ / ◡   /
With torment not to be confessed.

But Purcell's treatment allows no hint of this to surface.

Recitative.   Belinda and the chorus next tell Dido that she should marry
Aeneas, and his virtues are discussed by Dido and Belinda in the **recitative**
"Whence could so much virtue spring." A recitative corresponds to the portions of the opera which would be spoken if the work were, say, a musical
comedy. Where the *aria* expresses the singer's feelings, her state of mind at the
moment, the *recitative* is concerned with giving conversations, information,
and advancing the plot. In Purcell's hands it has other functions as well. He
doesn't really create a melody in the sense of a highly-patterned, easily-
remembered tune. Instead he allows the voice to follow the inflections of
speech, and in effect he makes himself, as composer, into an actor, since he
determines with his music the kind of inflections to be given to each word. He
word-paints whenever possible, seeming to enjoy the opportunity this gives
him to display his own cleverness as a composer, and at the same time allowing
the singers to display their own vocal virtuosity. To give one example:

How soft, how soft in peace, and yet how fierce how fierce in arms!

From recitative "Whence could so much virtue spring?"

The recitative concludes with Dido expressing her fear at her love for Aeneas.
Belinda and the chorus tell her there is nothing to be afraid of: "fear no danger
to ensue, the hero loves as well as you." Anyone who has watched soap operas,
or movies, or plays, or operas for that matter, could tell Dido that the moment
when your best friend tells you "Go ahead, there's nothing to be afraid of" is
the very moment you should be most afraid. But Aeneas appears, expresses his
love, says he will defy the feeble stroke of destiny, and tells her it will be better
for his empire. The chorus eggs them on, and sends them off, happily, together:

"Go revel, ye cupids, the day is your own." A triumphing dance closes the scene.

The next scene is the witches'. Nahum Tate has been criticized here, on the grounds that the witches seem somewhat unnecessary, and certainly weaker than the god Jove who motivates the action in Virgil's *Aeneid.* But we have to remember that Tate was writing for a girls' school, and witches provide several good female parts. Besides, there is something attractively theatrical about witches. There is nothing attractive about their actions. They plan cold-bloodedly to deprive Dido of her fame, her life, and her love.

Dido, Aeneas, and their company are out hunting (in ancient times, in Purcell's time, and still today an aristocratic sport). The witches conjure up a storm to spoil the hunt, they separate Aeneas from Dido, and they tell him that Jove commands him on to Rome that night. The conjuring scene gives Purcell the opportunity for an unusual vocal effect. The witches sing (below left) referring to their cave, and the chorus, backstage, echoes (below right) giving the illusion of a real echo in a real cavern.

In our deep vault-ed cell   -ed   cell

The witches' plan is carried out, and the first to get the news are Aeneas's sailors, whose reaction is blunt but honest. "Take a bowsey [boozy] short leave of your nymphs on the shore, / And silence their mourning with vows of returning, / Tho' never intending to visit them more." This may seem an unpleasant way to treat your girlfriend, but it prepares us for Aeneas's actions. He returns, apologizes to Dido briefly, blames it all on the gods—saying nothing of his previous vow to defy them—and finally offers to stay if she really wants him to. She, in quick, high, forceful tones, accuses him of weeping crocodile tears, of being a hypocrite and murderer, and of not having the courage even to take responsibility for his own actions.

Thus on the fa-tal bank of Nile, Weeps the de-ceit-ful croc-o-dile; Thus hyp-o-crites that mur der act,

The stage is set for the final aria. It is introduced by a brief recitative in which Dido asks for Belinda's comfort, as she is about to die. The aria itself is begun with the slow statement of a ground bass, reminding us of the one which underlay her opening aria. Above it her melody keeps rising, or trying to rise, like the wings of a dying bird, until it subsides to meet the final G minor of the bass. (*See* music example at the top of page 84.)

The chorus closes the opera. They pick up Dido's dying fall with their own melody, and sing of cupids' drooping wings in a dense imitative texture, which simplifies to a homophonic one for the final minor cadence.

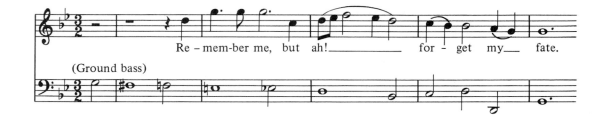

Re – mem-ber me, but ah!_____ for - get my__ fate.

(Ground bass)

The opera does not show her actual death, in which, according to the legend, she immolates herself on a funeral pyre; nor, for the contemporary audience, does it answer the question: why does she have to die? The answer which an audience steeped in the *Aeneid* would know is that her affair with Aeneas had proved her fallible, weak, neglectful of her role as Queen, and therefore unfit to rule. Death was the only avenue through which she could redeem her dignity and strength and that of the throne.

Music Serving Drama, Drama Serving Music

In its concern with large issues like duty, love, fate, dignity, and honor, the opera is typical of its time. Purcell wrote songs for a play by John Dryden—a much greater poet than Nahum Tate—called *The Indian Queen.* It is set, but not very believably, among the Incas of Peru. A typical portion of its dialogue could be summarized as follows:

> Character A: I will sacrifice myself for you.
>
> Character B: No. I will sacrifice myself for *you.*
>
> Character C: Wait. I will sacrifice myself for *both* of you.

And so on, in a way which makes for slow reading today. Yet Purcell and Tate achieved something which remains vital. Why does *Dido and Aeneas* continue to live on stages, while *The Indian Queen* gathers dust in libraries?

Part of the answer lies in the formal rightness of the combination of words and music. Although Nahum Tate has been disparaged, his contribution is not a negligible one. The simple, strong words, with their long open vowels, which he gives to Dido for her final aria: "When I am laid in earth, may my wrongs create / No trouble in thy breast," are an example of his skill as a writer of lyrics. And although the principal contribution is Purcell's, we can see how Tate's drama serves the music. The two main qualities in a long form are continuity and contrast—continuity to hold the work together, and contrast to guarantee against boredom. Plot supplies continuity, with developing action and suspense to carry us from one episode to the next. The conflict which makes the plot run also helps to supply musical contrast. To express the drama, Purcell must write music to express Dido's depression, her love, her joy, her fears, her resignation to death; the witches' infamy, the sailors' exuberance, the chorus's excitement and their grief. Each of these qualities demands and receives from him a different kind of music, ultimately resulting in a work richer in its contrasts than any other from his pen.

The other part of the answer lies with the ability of words and music to make the characters come alive. Dido and Aeneas do not act the way we would—but then, neither do the characters on the television soap opera *Dallas.* It is the art of combining music and words which convinces us of Dido's love, of Aeneas's weakness, of her anger and her final resignation.

This is finally what an opera has to do. It is not a naturalistic art form. It does not have to convince us that its characters are just like the folks next door. But if it can give us the emotional connection we need in order to believe in its characters, it can transport us beyond the world of the folks next door and into another world where passions are grander, hates run deeper, and actions have dramatic (though often unforeseen) consequences. If it does this, and provides us with fabulous spectacle and superhuman singing, it will lose money at the box office, but still continue to thrive.

SUMMARY: *Purcell's* Dido and Aeneas

melody   Ornamented, virtuoso display in recitatives; elsewhere marked by strong, memorable melodic patterns, usually in distinct two-, four- and eight-bar phrases.

harmony   Predominantly consonant; dissonance used for effect (to set words like 'woe,' for instance). Each number has its own strong sense of tonal center, on which it concludes. Strong sense of harmonic rhythm—typically, chords change every beat or two beats, along with bass line movement.

rhythm   Free and flexible in recitatives, elsewhere clearly measured. Dance rhythms in some orchestral numbers and choruses, and, of course, in dances. Rhythmic ambiguity—especially in the sense of conflict between voice and bass line—in Dido's two principal arias.

form   Alternation of orchestral numbers, solo songs, recitatives, choruses and dances. Dido's two ground bass arias, one near the beginning of the opera, one near the end, help to give formal unity.

texture   Usually defined by the relationship between melody and bass line—most obviously in Dido's arias which use ground bass, and in recitatives where only the melody and the bass line were written out, inner parts being improvised. Choruses alternate between polyphonic textures rich in imitation, and homophonic ones.

timbre   Voices, principally female, and small orchestra (strings and harpsichord).

function   Its original role was, in effect, to be a school musical. It survived its original performances and is found in opera houses today, although it remains most popular with student groups partly because of its relatively small scale.

Gregorian Chant and Its Evolution

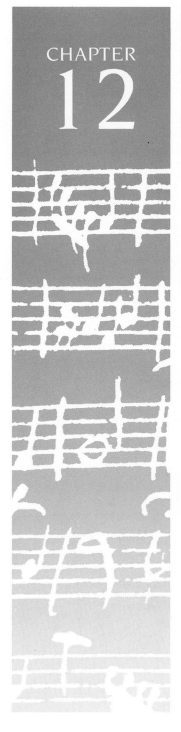

The Mass

For an American, one of the most striking of Europe's aspects is the magnificence of its churches—not just the architecture of the great cathedrals in the major cities, and not just the architecture's beauty, but also the sheer impressiveness of the churches in the villages and towns. Knowing that in the Middle Ages small towns often balanced on the edge of survival, and peasant farmers lived barely above the subsistence level, the visitor is amazed at the magnificence of the structures these Medieval populations managed to create. Of course it is also true that balancing on the edge of survival provides a great stimulus to believe in something eternal and to try to leave something more or less eternal behind.

The size of the churches alone tells something of how important they must have been in the villagers' daily lives. They were the centers of their communities, and contemporary writers describe the noise, talk, business, and socializing which distracted from the almost constant religious services. These included a

Nave of Amiens Cathedral (1220–1236).

Pope Gregory I, regarded as the primary force behind the codification of official church music, is shown here dictating a chant to be used in a religious service.

variety of different services (for example, vespers and matins) for different hours of the day, but the principal ceremony of the church was the Mass.

The Mass is a ritual which re-enacts, on a symbolic level, Christ's last supper. As Jesus informed his disciples then that the bread they ate was his body given for them, and the wine they drank was his blood of the new testament, shed for them, so when the priest eats the wafer and drinks the wine (the congregation did not participate in this act until a much later date), he is performing a symbolic act through which the worshippers can commune with Christ and be changed by his sacrifice.

Music as Prayer

There is much more to the ceremony than the drinking of the wine and the eating of the wafer. There is reading from the Bible, and the opportunity for sermon, but most of all there is prayer: of praise, confession, thankgsgiving, supplication, belief, blessing. Some of these prayers varied from day to day, according to festivals connected with particular saints, or ceremonies for particular seasons. These are called the *proper* of the Mass. Others were said in the same order and form every day and are called the *ordinary* of the Mass (*see* Table 12–1).

Every religion has its own way of praying. Even religions which share the same god can disagree on the question of how to address him. This may seem like a small enough point, a question only of religious practice, not of belief. If you and I should agree on God's identity, how can we disagree on the small point of our different ways of approaching him? Unfortunately, the disagreements are and have been many, and many of them have been violent. Perhaps the point is not such a small one after all; perhaps the manner of the praying is just as important as the matter of the prayer.

Gregorian Chant

The Kyrie

In looking at the music of a thousand years ago, prayer is what we see. There was musical life apart from religious life, but little of it was written down. The church preserved its music. Pope Gregory I (in office from 590 to 604) is traditionally credited with the first systematic organization of the chants used in religious services. The first manuscripts we have date from the 10th century, some three centuries after Gregory's death; however, we still call the music they contain "Gregorian Chant." (The music is also referred to as "plainsong" and "plainchant.") The particular chant we will look at was probably written more than 200 years after Pope Gregory, some time in the 800s. It is a *Kyrie,* with words of the utmost simplicity: Kyrie eleison (sung three times), Christe eleison (three times), Kyrie eleison (three times). Although most of the church service was conducted in Latin, these words are Greek: Lord have mercy on us, Christ have mercy on us, Lord have mercy on us.

ky-ri - e_____ e – le - i -son

First Kyrie statement from "Kyrie IV: Cunctipotens"

————

Table 12–1
The Mass

Proper	Ordinary
1. *Introit* (processional as priest and assistants enter)	
	2. *Kyrie eleison* ("Lord have mercy on us")
	3. *Gloria in excelsis Deo* ("Glory to God in the highest")
4. *Collect* (prayer on behalf of congregation)	
5. *Epistle* (reading from the Bible)	
6. *Gradual* (verse from one of the psalms)	
7. *Alleluia* (from the Hebrew: "Praise ye Jehovah")	
8. *Sequence* (a form of hymn)	
9. *Gospel* (reading from the Bible) and *sermon*	
	10. *Credo* ("I believe in one God")
11. *Offertory* (bread and wine are offered to God)	
	12. *Sanctus* ("Holy, holy, holy")
	13. *Benedictus* ("Blessed is he that cometh")
	14. *Canon and Consecration* (prayers by the priest as bread and wine are made sacred)
	15. *Agnus Dei* ("Lamb of God who taketh away the sins of the world")
16. *Communion* (receiving the bread and wine)	
17. *Post-Communion* (final prayer)	
	18. *Ite missa est* ("Go, the congregation is dismissed")

Gregorian Chant vs Modern Music

As music, this is so different from the norms of our contemporary culture that it is easiest to define it through negatives. There is no beat, no regularly recurring pulse. Instead, the notes are given relatively equal stress. There is no traditional harmony. The music is termed **monophonic** because although there are several singers, there is only one musical voice or line. There are no phrases of the sort we are used to, where a phrase is like a breath, a clause, a sentence in conversational speech. Here each statement (Kyrie eleison, for example) is heard as a single phrase, although it may have some slight pauses within it, and the phrases stretch out over 20 or 25 notes. Where we are used to music which follows speech patterns in giving each syllable one or two notes (**syllabic** style), this music offers us eight or ten notes on a single syllable (**melismatic** style). The melody is not based on a major or minor scale, but on one of the church modes.

D-major scale: two sharps   D-minor scale: one sharp going up, one flat coming down

Dorian mode: from D to D with no sharps or flats

A melody based on a D-major or D-minor scale would have the single tone of D as a tonal center. The chant melody in the Dorian mode revolves around the two principal tones of D and A. For example, in the first Kyrie statement of this chant, the melody begins on A and slowly works its way down to the D. Perhaps the most strikingly different aspect of the music is its timbre: no instruments, no variety of voices; instead, a group of male voices together on the same pitch.

Rhythm without a beat, harmony without chords, melody without major or minor scales, structure without breath-like phrases, texture of only one line, timbre of only one kind of voice—these are qualities which separate Gregorian chant from more modern music. Of course the music is old, and it would be easy to say that it is different simply because it is old. This would be forgetting that the music had a function which *is* familiar, and that is prayer. What we hear when we listen to this chant is the voice Medieval culture thought was the right voice for speaking to God.

This was a culture which saw humankind as poised in the middle between God and the devil, heaven and hell. It saw the individual as split, dual in nature.

Our senses, our appetites, our bodies all ally us with lower forms. But we are more than animals; we have a soul and a mind which is capable of spiritual thoughts. To speak to God, this is the half we must use, the other is the half we must deny. Gregorian chant follows directly from this belief. In negating conversational phrases, the physical responses which rhythm elicits, the sensual appeal of instruments, the chant is trying to remove us from thoughts of the world, the flesh, and the devil. In creating music which floats free from the specifics of the individual voice and from the patterns of human conversation, floats free even (through *melismas*) from the individual words, the chant is giving voice to the spiritual aspirations of the singers and their listeners.

This is what I meant by suggesting that the manner of the prayer might be as significant as its matter. The "matter" of the Kyrie is a simple appeal to God for mercy. Its manner reveals far more of how humanity in Medieval times saw itself in relationship to God.

SUMMARY: *Gregorian chant "Kyrie IV: Cunctipotens" (ca. 800–900)*

form	Follows the structure of the text. Kyrie eleison phrase repeated three times, Christe elesion phrase repeated three times, second Kyrie eleison phrase repeated three times, with an extension on the final phrase.
melody	In the Dorian mode. Exceptionally long phrases. Melismatic treatment of words. Predominantly step-wise motion.
harmony	No traditional harmony, since there is only one musical line, although the sounds do tend to mingle in an echoing cathedral.
rhythm	No strong pulse, no pattern of accents. Notes tend to be even in length.
texture	Monophony: one musical line.
timbre	Male voices in unison.
function	Part of the religious ceremony of the Mass.

The Trope

Gregorian chant is such a perfect statement of Medieval belief that it came to have a semi-sacred status all its own. Nevertheless, there were pressures on it to evolve. In part these were the pressures any art form is subject to from the seemingly innate human desire to elaborate, ornament, experiment, and change. In part the pressures resulted from the fact that this ideal form had to function in a less-than-ideal world.

We can see an initial tendency towards elaboration in the **trope.** This involved the insertion of new music or poetry into the chant to enrich sound and meaning. In the case of the Kyrie used as an example earlier, the trope involves a poetic text designed to fit the notes of the first melisma (extended syllable) in each phrase. Thus:

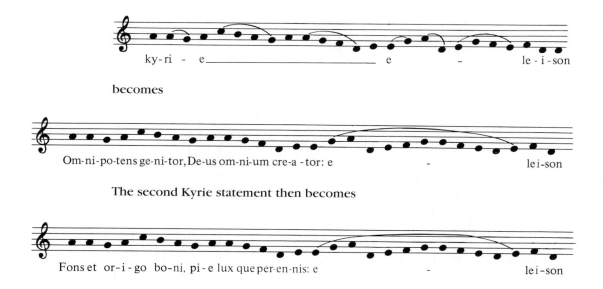

ky-ri - e_____ e - le-i-son

becomes

Om-ni-po-tens ge-ni-tor, De-us om-ni-um cre-a-tor: e - le i-son

The second Kyrie statement then becomes

Fons et or-i-go bo-ni, pi-e lux que per-en-nis: e - le i-son

and so on. To translate, instead of the statement "Lord, have mercy on us," we are given: "Omnipotent Father, Lord master of all: Have mercy on us." To replace the second statement of "Lord, have mercy on us" we are told: "Fount and source of good, kindly light eternal, have mercy on us."

Organum

A further development was the addition of harmonies, in the form of added musical lines. This process was called *organum*. In "organum of the fifth," for example, a second musical line is added five steps below the original. For our Kyrie this would result in

ky-ri - e _____ e - le - i - son

A later development was "free organum," where the second musical line, instead of paralleling the first, moved independently.*

Cun - cti - po-tens ge - ni - tor de - us, om - ni - cre - a - tor, e - lei - son.

*This version, from the 11th century, is troped with slightly different words. It is the first word of this trope, "cunctipotens," which has given the chant its name.

Carved stone statue of the Virgin Mary on the facade of Amiens Cathedral.

We can see some of these techniques combined with others in an anonymously-composed Mass from 13th-century Spain, the *Missa de Sancta Maria* (a mass dedicated to the Virgin Mary, who had become immensely popular as a devotional figure [*see* color plate 1]). As a kind of introduction, the Kyrie eleison is sung in the traditional monophonic style, much as we first heard it. What follows is radically different. The chant melody is still present, but it is no longer dominant. It has become a lower, accompanying voice, which could be played on the organ. Above it is a whole new melody with freshly composed words, praying to God, but relating him to Mary. The chant in its accompanying role is called a "tenor" from the Latin *tenere,* "to hold," referring to the way the individual notes are held out. The new melody above it is called a "discant."

The next Kyrie statement returns to the chant, this time with troped words again directed to God but referring to Mary. The alternating pattern continues throughout—troped monophonic versions of the chant followed by discant.

In terms of plainchant "purity" there is much to be objected to. The discant sections are characterized by the harmony of the voice with the organ, by a definite rhythm with a recognizable beat (a "three" pattern), by clearly marked phrases, by the timbres of instrument and individual voice, and by a sense of freedom and energy these factors combine to produce. There is something spontaneous in the soloist's melody, and it is likely that such passages were originally improvised. As such, the discant sections might be evidence of the church musicians' sheer urge to create. But the fact that such sections were written down and saved for repeated use tells us something more, that there was a felt need for music which would not so entirely deny the physical, sensual side of human nature. If the Gregorian chant in its original form was a perfect statement of Medieval belief, this later version was a better reflection of Medieval life.

SUMMARY: **Missa de Sancta Maria,** *anonymous 13th-century mass from Spain*

form	Follows Kyrie text pattern. Alternates plainchant and two-part polyphony.
melody	Based on Gregorian chant "Kyrie IV: Cunctipotens." Discant voice responds to this melody with a stronger, more active, almost dance-like tune.
harmony	Generally "open"-sounding, preferred intervals being the fourth and fifth.
rhythm	Strong three-beat pattern in discant sections. Chant melody is used to stress first beat of each group of three.
texture	Monophony and two-voiced polyphony alternate.
timbre	An instrument, the organ, is used with the solo voice in the discant section.
function	Part of the religious ceremony of the Mass.
text	

Rex virginum amator Deus, Mariae decus eleison.	King, lover of virgins, God, glory of Mary: have mercy on us.
Qui de stirpe regia clara producis Marian eleison.	Who brought forth Mary from royal stock: have mercy . . .
Preces ejus suscipe dignas pro mundo fusus eleison.	Receive her prayer, a worthy offering on behalf of the world: . . .
Christe Deus de Patre homo natus Maria matre eleison.	Oh Christ, God from the Father, born a man from thy mother Mary: . . .
Quem ventre beato Maria edidit mundo eleison.	Whom Mary gave forth to the world from her holy womb: . . .
Sume laudes nostras Mariae almae dicatas eleison.	Accept our praises, consecrated to thy beloved Mary: . . .
O paraclite obumbrans pectus Mariae eleison.	Oh Comforter, protecting the body of Mary: . . .

Qui dignum facis thalamum corpus
Mariae eleison.
Qui super coelos spiritum levas
Mariae eleison.
Fac nos post ipsam scandere tua vir-
tute, spiritus alme eleison.

Who made the body of Mary a worthy
chamber: . . .
Who raises the spirit of Mary above
the skies: . . .
Make us ascend after her through thy
power, beloved Spirit: . . .

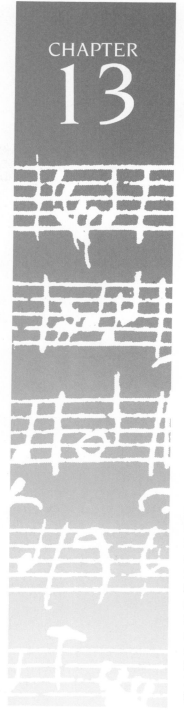

CHAPTER 13

Folk Song and Court Song

Folk Song

Church music was written down, folk music was not. This may seem regrettable, if we are trying to acquire a sense of music's history, but it is also something which is inseparable from the nature of folk music. Where music from the high art tradition can be fixed, dated, and placed at a particular spot and moment, folk music is fluid, constantly evolving, shedding its past skins as it takes new forms. The particular version of the song "False Sir John" which we will look at was recorded in Kentucky, in 1954. Its singer is Jean Ritchie, the most famous member of a family of folk singers who preserved the traditional Scottish ballads better than any who stayed in Scotland. The song has been noted in hundreds of versions, not just in the United States and Scotland, but also in England, France, Germany, Scandinavia, and Eastern Europe. What we know about it today is based only on what has been written down in the past 100 years or so, the tips of the branches on the song's family tree. The whole tree, if it could be seen, must go back through the centuries to some common

The Ritchie Family of Viper, Kentucky, preservers of Scottish folk ballads. (Jean Ritchie is second from left in lower left-hand corner.)

trunk. We must assume that each singer who heard the song and developed a performance of it, altered it, intentionally or not, perhaps forgetting some parts, adding others, until eventually there grew up the variety of versions now known.

The Ballad "False Sir John"

"False Sir John" is a **ballad,** a story song. In this case, despite the title, the story is May Colvin's. Sir John woos her and convinces her to elope. She steals her father's gold (disdaining the silver) and his best horses. Once he has her alone Sir John confides his intention of murdering her as he has murdered seven others. Then comes the pivotal moment. He is greedy; she is clever. He doesn't want to waste her valuable clothes, so asks her to undress. She takes advantage of his pretensions to "gentlemanly" status and asks him to turn his back. As he does, she turns the tables and kills him. Then, in the ballad's strangest moment, her pet parrot voices some suspicions, at which May Colvin, an assertive but not wholly admirable woman, bribes it to silence. There is not much of a moral here. May Colvin is the heroine, and we like her for her toughness and quick thinking, but her casual attitude towards stealing and bribing make her less than ideal as a role model.

The song's melody is typical of folk song melody in its tendency to revolve around a central tone. Through the first three lines of each verse (or **strophe**) that central tone is a D.

Music for first three lines of strophe

Out of 24 total beats, 14 are occupied by that pitch. The principal movement away from the D is to the G above it and the G below it. The effect is an open one, the repeated pulses on the Ds and Gs giving some of the droning quality and rhythmic drive of Scottish bagpipe music or country fiddle music. The last line of each strophe is repeated, to let us know that it usually carries some bit of information with a little extra meaning. Here the music retreats from D as a central tone; instead, the important relationship is between G and B. This is a warmer, more closed sound than the open G-D relationship, and helps to relax and finish off the verse.

Music for last line of strophe

Which brings us to the question: Is this "primitive" music? It is primitive in the sense that its resources are so skimpy—a single human voice. It is also primitive in the sense that it betrays no influence of six centuries of high-art music. If we write out the song's scale we get

the ancient Greek or church mode called the *Mixolydian;* there is no harmony as such, only the drone quality on D and G; the rhythm has a simple, straightforward pulse, accented beat followed by unaccented beat. And yet, it is hard to imagine a better means of remembering and retelling a story, of taking us through this long series of verses with a detached, observer's point of view, delivering amazing and outrageous events with the calm of a radio news report.

SUMMARY: *Folk song ballad "False Sir John"*

form   **Strophic;** that is, the same melody is used for each stanza of the lyrics.

melody   In Mixolydian mode. Follows phrase structure of text. Dwells on notes D and G.

harmony	Monophonic.
rhythm	Two-beat pattern (strong beat, weak beat).
texture	Monophonic.
timbre	Solo voice.
function	Story-telling entertainment within a small community.
text	

False Sir John a-wooing came
To a lady young and fair.
May Colvin was this lady's name
And her father's only heir,
Her father's only heir.

He woo'd her while she spun the
    thread,
And while they made the hay,
Until he gained her low consent
To mount and ride away,
To mount and ride away.

It's bring-a me some of your father's
    gold
And some of your mother's fee.
I'll take thee to some far-off land,
And there I'll marry thee,
And there I'll marry thee.

She's gone into her father's coffer,
Where all of his monies lay,
She's took the yeller and left the
    white
And lightly skipped away,
And lightly skipped away.

She's gone into her father's stables
Where all of his steeds did stand,
She's took the best and left the worst
In all her father's land,
In all her father's land.

She's mounted on a milk-white steed
And he on a dapple-grey
And they rode till they come to a
    lonesome spot,
A cliff by the side of the sea.
A cliff by the side of the sea.

Light down, light down, said false Sir
    John,
Your bridle bed you see,
It's seven women have I drownded
    here
And the eighth one you shall be,
And the eighth one you shall be.

Have off, have off your holland
    smock,
With borders all around,
For it's too costly to lay down here
And rot on the cold, cold ground.
And rot on the cold, cold ground.

Cast off, cast off your silks so fine,
And lay them on a stone,
For they're too fine and cost-i-lie
To rot in the salt sea foam,
To rot in the salt sea foam.

Take off, take off your silken stays,
Likewise your handsome shoes,
For they're too fine and cost-i-lie
To rot in the sea with you,
To rot in the sea with you.

Turn around, turn around, thou false
    Sir John,
And look at the leaves of the tree,
For it don't become a gentleman
A naked woman to see,
A naked woman to see.

Oh false Sir John has turned around
To gaze at the leaves on the tree,
She's made a dash with her tender
    little arms
And pushed him into the sea,
And pushed him into the sea.

Oh help, oh help, May Colvin,
Oh help or I shall drown,
I'll take thee back to thy father's
    house
And lightly set thee down,
And lightly set thee down.

No help, no help, said May Colvin,
No help will you get from me,
For the bed's no colder to you sir
Then you thought to give to me,
Then you thought to give to me.

She mounted on the milk-white
    steed,
And led the dapple-grey,
And rode till she come to her father's
    house
At the breakin' of the day,
At the breakin' of the day.

Then up and spoke that little parrot,
Said, May Colvin, where have you
    been,
And what have you done with false
    Sir John
That went with you ridin',
That went with you ridin'?

Oh hold your tongue my pretty
    parrot,
And tell no tales on me,
And I'll buy you a cage of beaten
    gold
With spokes of i-vor-y,
With spokes of i-vor-y.

Court Song

But what of the rich? Since they were, by and large, members of the nobility themselves, they would not have been amused by the folk song "False Sir John," where a knight mass-murders for profit. It was love songs they were fond of. These were not narratives which told the story of a love, but direct, first-person expressions of a particular kind of love, "courtly love."

Two musicians, one holding a bow, the other a lute, from an illustrated 13th-century Spanish music manuscript.

The "court" the term refers to was an aristocratic social center, the residence of some powerful lord, to which would be attracted other members of the nobility, their families and retinues. (King Arthur's Camelot is an idealized version of one such court.) While there, the lords and ladies did not, of course, work; they could only play games, make love, banquet, dance, be entertained. The "courtly love" which filled their poems and songs was, like Sir Lancelot's for King Arthur's Guinevere, passionate, adulterous, hopeless—or, sometimes, not quite so hopeless. Not much is known about the actual behavior of these Medieval forerunners of the jet set; most of what has survived is their fictions, which tell endlessly of man's desire for unattainable woman. In France during the 12th and 13th centuries, poet-musicians of noble birth, called "troubadours" and "trouvères," composed most of the courtly love poems and songs; there were also "jongleurs" or minstrels, professional musicians employed in noble households.

Machaut's "Quant je sui mis au retour"

The example of courtly love song we will discuss comes from a slightly later date, the 14th century. Its author is Guillaume de Machaut. Only a tiny number of those born, like him, in France in the year 1300 could have survived with him to the year 1377. The intervening years were marked by war between France and England, civil war, bands of pillaging mercenary soldiers, persecutions of the poor and the powerless, conflicts between secular and religious rulers, famines, and most devastating of all, the "Black Death," the bubonic plague, which in some locales caused the death of one-half to two-thirds of the population.

Machaut was fully aware of the horrors of his age. Yet he himself survived and even thrived through it. Educated as a youth (not a common occurrence in the 14th century) he became the secretary to a king, an official of the church, and musician and poet to a number of royal households. Where the composers of previous centuries were content to be anonymous or nearly so, Machaut collected his own works to save them for posterity. He wrote about his own life, including his inner thoughts as well as its outer events. He tells of his despair after the great plague year of 1348, when his friends were dead, and the world seemed turned against itself in bitterness. Later, in his sixties, he tells the story of his reawakening energies under the influence of a passionate love affair with a young noblewoman, Peronne d'Armentières. Since only his version of the story has survived, it is difficult to tell how much of it is true, how much fiction. In the song, he pictures himself as a feeble and timid lover—the romance was conducted mostly by letter—which gives an air of truth to the account, since we would expect a fictional account to glorify its author a little more. Whether truth or fiction, the account, with its mixture of narrative, poems, and letters, is, like much of Machaut's work, far ahead of its time.

He called his song a *virelai,* a popular song-form of the day, although it does not follow the standard pattern of that song-form exactly. Machaut wrote both the music and the lyrics, in which the lover describes the state of his feelings towards his loved one at the very moment when he is traveling away from her. Typically for a courtly love song, he places her on a pedestal; her "high worth" makes him content merely to serve her. In the refrain, he appeals to God to recognize the rightness and blamelessness of his love. Why appeal to God? Surely God would be happy to sanction such a pure love. But perhaps the love is not quite so pure. What is in his memory is her beauty and her gentleness, and it is burning in him, "enflaming" him. This is not a pure or spiritual love. In appealing to God to sanction it, Machaut is mixing the sacred and the profane.

The music to the song can be written in just 14 measures, since it is strophic, each of the three verses fitting the same tune. Machaut notates only the melody. When it was performed at the court, a jongleur or two might have improvised an accompaniment, but this is only a guess, as is any reconstruction of what such an accompaniment might have been like.

The melody flows in gentle, step-wise motion, within a narrow range. The effect is one of closeness and intimacy, as the music describes for us the tender qualities of the lover's feelings. It is divided into even two-measure phrases, except at the point of transition between verse and refrain. Here the music, instead of coming to rest at the end of the verse, flows on through it into the first word of the refrain, "Dieus" (God.) Thus the appeal to the sacred comes in unprepared-for, and the music matches the words in mixing the sacred with the profane.

We cannot help but hear this Medieval song with modern ears, influenced by all the music we have heard. This has conditioned us to the idea of a tonal center, which Medieval music had not conceived of. Nevertheless, there is at least the hint of a tonal center in this song. It is written in a scale called the *Hypodorian* mode, a scale close to the modern A minor:

Hypodorian mode

The "home" chord in this mode would be a chord based on A:

Every phrase in the song either starts or ends on a note from that chord. In the instances where the phrases do not stress notes from the A chord, the stressed notes can be found in a chord based on G:

Thus the first phrase starts and ends on notes from the A chord; the second phrase starts on a note from the A chord but ends on a note from the G chord. This feels like a shift away from the home tonality. The last phrase of the piece starts on notes from the G chord, and ends on notes from the A chord, which feels like a return to the home tonality. Machaut was very much a man of his time. But like his great contemporaries, the poet Chaucer in England and the painter Giotto in Italy, he was also capable of transcending his time. In the work of all these men there are moments which seem to leap forward by the century. The hint of a tonal center in the *virelai* "Quant je suis mis au retour" provides one of those moments.

SUMMARY: ***Guillaume de Machaut's** virelai "Quant je sui mis au retour" (mid-1300s)*

form	Three short strophes, each followed by a short refrain.
melody	Evenly phrased, in step-wise motion, based on the Hypodorian mode.
harmony	Monophonic.

rhythm	A two-beat pattern, not strongly stressed, but with some syncopation towards the close of the phrases.
texture	Monophonic, although it is possible that performances originally included improvised accompaniment.
timbre	Solo voice.
function	Entertainment for an aristocratic, courtly audience.
text	

Quant je sui mis au retour de veoir
  ma dame,
il n'est peine ne dolour qui j'aie, par
  m'ame.
Dieus! C'est drois que je l'aim, de loial
  amour.

When returning from seeing my lady
There is neither pain nor sorrow in
  my soul.
God! It is right that I love her,
  without blame, with a loyal love.

Sa biaute, sa grant doucour
  d'amoureuse flame,
par souvenir, nuit et jour m'esprent et
  enflame.
Dieus! . . .

Her beauty, her great tenderness, with
  the flame of love
In my memory night and day, seizes
  and inflames me.
God! It is right . . .

Et quant sa haute valour mon fin cuer
  entame,
servir la weil sans folour penser ne
  diffame.
Dieus! . . .

And when her high worth cuts my
  sensitive heart,
To serve her with vigilance, to think
  of her without defaming,
God! It is right . . .

Machaut's *La Messe De Nostre Dame*

Machaut was one of the first to compose a complete setting of the Ordinary of the Mass (*see* Table 12–1). He based his composition of the Kyrie section on the same Gregorian chant illustrated earlier (page 91):

Kyrie from *Mass IV: Cunctipotens*

He uses the chant melody as his *cantus firmus,* "fixed song." It will provide the tenor voice around which three other voices will revolve. Machaut also uses a compositional device called "isorhythm" ("iso-" meaning "same"), whereby a single rhythmic pattern is employed throughout the piece. In this case the pattern is as follows:

Combining this pattern with the given chant melody gives:

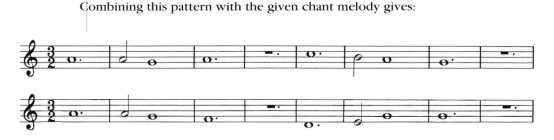

Machaut's next step is to create three other voices to go with this cantus firmus. As was mentioned earlier, the chant melody is in the Dorian mode; its important tones are D and A. For his top voice, Machaut creates a melodic line which is centered around A. Out of 81 half-note beats, 26 are on that pitch; eight are on the pitch D. In the next voice down, the proportions are reversed, creating a line centered on D; six of the beats are on A, while 22 of them are on D. The third voice down is the cantus firmus. The lowest voice is balanced between the two principal tones, with 11 of the the half-note beats on A and 11 on D. The top voice begins on A and ends on A; the second voice begins on D and ends on D; the cantus firmus begins on A and ends on D; the lowest voice begins on D and ends on A. Machaut is not trying to create easily-memorable tunes in these voices; he is instead trying to create a many-voiced or polyphonic texture. The repeated isorhythmic pattern helps to anchor the texture rhythmically, and the open harmonies which result from the four voices all singing on D or A provide the harmonic point of stability.

Opening measures of Kyrie section from Machaut's *La Messe de Nostre Dame*

SUMMARY: *Guillaume de Machaut's* La Messe de Nostre Dame (Notre Dame Mass), *first Kyrie section (mid-1300s)*

form   Follows 3,3,3 pattern of Kyrie text.

melody   Four voices of which one is the plainchant melody. All share the same mode (Dorian) with varying degrees of emphasis on the important tones of D and A.

harmony   Predominantly consonant, although most cadences end on "open"-sounding chords (no thirds.) Some feeling of pull towards a final chord made up of tones of D and A.

rhythm   A three-beat pattern, usually treated as strong-weak-weak. Considerable syncopation: while one voice lands on the beat, another will sing off the beat in contrast. Tenor voice uses isorhythmic pattern.

texture   Four-voiced polyphony. Voices maintain their independence mainly through rhythmic variety — in any given measure there are usually two or three different rhythmic patterns among the voices.

timbre   Male voices. Although Machaut does not specify the use of instruments, it is evident that instruments were often used, probably doubling certain vocal lines or substituting for them.

function   Part of the religious ceremony of the Mass. Its name derives from the tradition that it was first performed at the coronation of Charles V at the Cathedral of Notre Dame in Paris. Although this no longer seems likely, the work was certainly designed for royal religious services.

Stone sculpture of *The Virgin of Paris,* Notre Dame Cathedral, Paris (14th century).

Evolution of the Gregorian Chant

A kind of evolution has been illustrated in the various treatments of the Gregorian chant melody, although I should stress that the evolution of new musical techniques did not out-date the old ones; plainchant was still in use alongside polyphony. First came the plainchant melody alone; then the chant melody with tropes inserted; then harmony in the form of parallel organum; then free organum; then the discant style; and finally this four-voice polyphony. With it, Machaut has created a texture far richer and more complex than the original plainchant melody. The result would for most listeners be an increased sensual and intellectual appeal. At the same time, Machaut's polyphony restores an element of mystery to the chant. The four voices intertwine and overlap, and the texture is not one which the listener can easily disentangle. And yet the parts do combine, fit, and ultimately agree. This was and is polyphony's great virtue as a vehicle for religious music—the ability to convey a sense of mysterious unity.

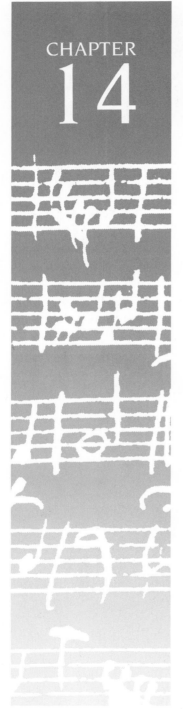

CHAPTER 14

Sacred Aspects

Renaissance Beginnings in Art and Music

Masaccio's *The Tribute Money*

The Renaissance is no longer viewed as a cultural rebirth which occurred overnight. Its roots are evident in the late Medieval period, and certainly many of the traits we think of as Medieval persisted throughout the Renaissance centuries (approximately 1400 through 1600). Nowhere is this more true than in the history of music. Nowhere is it less true than in the history of painting, which arrived in the modern era with stunning speed and completeness in the city of Florence, Italy, in the 1420s, in the person of the painter Masaccio (*see* color plate 2).

His painting *The Tribute Money,* painted in 1427, only a year before his early death at age 27, typifies much of what is conventionally meant by "the Renaissance." It is a religious painting, and was painted on the wall of a chapel, but many of its concerns are secular and modern. Its subject, for instance, is taxes. In the center group, the tax collectors are asking Jesus for money. He solves the problem miraculously by asking Peter to find a silver coin in a fish's

Masaccio: *Tribute Money* (c. 1425) *(Branacci Chapel, Sta. Maria del Carmine, Florence)*

mouth (far left). Peter pays the taxes (on the right). Although the episode is taken from the Bible, it served a contemporary purpose, since Florence was in the throes of a tax controversy when the painting was made (Florence was a semi-democracy, and democracies are prone to tax controversies). More to the point, the space Jesus occcupies is organized according to the rules of perspective, which makes it look like the space we as viewers occupy. His figure is solid like ours and stands on solid ground. The light which models his features comes from a consistent light source, which, if we were standing in the chapel, would be from the same direction as the light which falls on us. He gains his strength not from being over-sized, or from floating on a cloud, but by the simple dignity of his human form, and the power of his personality to make him the automatic center of the group around him, a power which Masaccio indicates by having the lines of perspective meet at his head. This is a figure dealing with tangible human problems. Even the solution, though miraculous, is presented in the most matter-of-fact of ways, with Peter kneeling at the water's edge, opening the fish's mouth. One way of looking at the painting would be to say that Christ is being brought down to a human level. It would be more in keeping with the Renaissance spirit to say instead that everyday human concerns are found to have a place in Christ's world. The fascination with what is human is the great Renaissance preoccupation.

There is some logic to the fact that the new Renaissance ideas found their first expression in visual terms. It was neither feudal lords nor church fathers who were behind such ideas, but rather a new middle-class of men who had acquired wealth and power not by birth but by worth—at least "worth" as they defined it. They were bankers and businessmen, perhaps originally pawnbrokers and gang-leaders, men who believed in what they could see and touch, and who wanted art which could be seen and touched and which represented that which is seeable and touchable.

The chaos of the late Middle Ages stemmed in part from the inability of Medieval institutions to cope with the changes occurring in society. Even the bubonic plague was not just bad luck; it was also the result of bad sanitation, which was incapable of dealing with the newly-grown market towns and cities. Through advances in agriculture and trade there was new wealth in society. Neither the church, which thought usury (the charging of interest on a loan) to be a sin, nor the nobility, still tied to their land and to rent payments in the form of such things as bushels of wheat, was equipped to handle this new wealth. Small wonder that the new middle class which *was* equipped to handle it became pleased and fascinated with themselves, eager to question the old, traditional ideas of Medieval culture.

Josquin Des Prez's Motets

Music still found its principal patronage in the church and in court chapels. The career of Josquin Des Prez is typical, at least in this regard. He was born in the North of France around 1440, and died there in 1521, but spent the greater part of his career in Italy. He was a choirboy at the Milan Cathedral; later he was employed by the Sforzas, the ruling family of Milan. He next went to the Sistine Chapel, the Pope's own chapel in Rome; after this he worked at other courts, then ended his career back in France as an official of the Church. He was the most highly respected composer of his time, and the first composer to have a collection of works published under his own name. Although he wrote some secular music, his principal compositions are his masses and his religious motets.

The Renaissance **motet** was a sacred, polyphonic vocal work. It was sung not as part of the Mass but as part of other religious services, most popularly at vespers, the evening service (*see* color plate 3). The motet by Josquin which we will look at is an *Ave Maria,* a prayer to Mary: "Hail Mary, full of grace . . . " The particular version which Josquin set was in the form of a Latin poem of seven stanzas. He sets each of the stanzas differently, beginning with a **canon.** The word derives from the word for "rule," since the canon is the strictest form of counterpoint, where each voice must enter with the exact same melody as the previous voice. Although the form is strict, it needn't be difficult—"Three Blind Mice," for example, is a canon. The melody in this case is taken almost unchanged from an appropriate Gregorian chant:

To make this phrase into a canon, Josquin devises a rhythmic pattern which will allow the notes of the different voices, when they meet together, to make consonant harmonies.

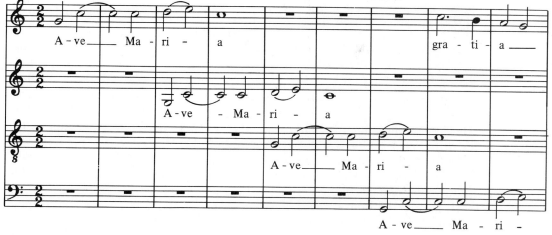

Opening measures of Josquin's motet "Ave Maria"

The result is an even texture, where each voice has equal importance. As the setting of the first stanza develops, the canonic treatment beomes less strict. The second stanza begins with the two voices singing in sixths:

Josquin's "Ave Maria," beginning of second stanza

Medieval theorists had determined that fifths were a "perfect" sort of harmony. This passage, put into perfect fifths, would sound like this:

The effect, compared with the sixths, is a cold and open sound. It also lacks "direction." We begin, in this piece, to feel the pull of a tonal center. At the close of this stanza, the top voice climbs past C and then returns to it. The moment of the return looks like this:

Cadence at end of second stanza of Josquin's "Ave Maria"

Josquin has used his voices to create three chords. First a IV chord (built on the fourth note, F, of the C scale); then a V chord (built on G); then a I chord (built on C.) This is the traditional tonal cadence, pulling us strongly home to the tonal center, or tonic, chord. The I chord is first heard in an open form, but the alto voice soon fills in the third.

Each of the stanzas gets a different treatment; the motet is like a little encyclopedia of polyphonic techniques. One of its most affecting moments comes at the end, and is homophonic rather than polyphonic. The voices lose their independence, and unite in chords to sing "O Mother of God, remember me." "Me," the individual person. In stressing this aspect of the poem, Josquin is revealing a Renaissance sensibility, a human-centered view. In the visual arts, the human-centered view became evident in the use of perspective, which organizes pictorial space in a way familiar to the human eye. In music, the use of tonality organizes the musical space. The sense of progression away from or back towards a tonal center somehow ennables us, the listeners, to center the music on ourselves.

This is not to say that Josquin used a fully-developed tonal system. The kinds of discoveries which caused a new painting style to develop within a very few years, took centuries to evolve in music. Josquin's motet marks a major step in that development.

SUMMARY: *Josquin des Prez's motet "Ave Maria . . . virgo serena" (ca. 1490)*

form	Follows text—a different musical setting is given for each of the poem's seven stanzas.
melody	Based on a Gregorian chant, in the Ionian mode, corresponding to the modern C major. The first stanza's setting uses the chant melody directly; other settings are related to it, a device which serves to unify the work.
harmony	Consonant, with a sense of tonal center reinforced by strong cadences.
rhythm	Evenly-paced, but without a strong rhythmic pulse.

texture
Employs a variety of polyphonic techniques, plus moments of homophony, most notably in the work's final phrases.

timbre
Unaccompanied chorus, soprano, alto, tenor, bass, originally performed with boys on the upper parts.

function
As part of religious service, originally for an aristocratic or papal chapel.

text

Ave Maria,	Hail Mary,
Gratia plena,	Full of grace,
Dominus tecum,	The Lord is with Thee,
Virgo serena.	Virgin fair.
Ave coelorum Domina,	Hail, Mistress of the Heavens,
Maria plena gratia,	Mary, full of grace,
Coelestia, terrestria,	With heavenly and earthly joy
Mundum replens laetitia.	Thou fill'st the world.
Ave cujus nativitas	Hail Thou, whose birth
Nostra fuit solemnitas;	became our feast,
Ut lucifer lux oriens,	As the morning star, a rising light,
Verum solem praeveniens.	Thou precedest the true sun.
Ave pia humilitas,	Hail blessed humility,
Sine viro fecunditas,	Inviolate fecundity,
Cujus annuntiatio	Whose Annunciation
Nostra fuit salvatio.	Became our salvation.
Ave vera virginitas,	Hail, true virginity,
Immaculata castitas,	Unspotted chastity,
Cujus purificatio	Whose purification
Nostra fuit purgatio.	Became our expiation.
Ave praeclara omnibus	Hail Thou, who shinest
Angelicis virtutibus,	With all angelic virtues,
Cujus fuit assumptio	Whose Assumption
Nostra glorificatio.	Became our glorification.
O Mater Dei,	O Mother of God,
Memento mei.	Remember me.
Amen.	Amen.

The Protestant Reformation

The idea of "human-centeredness" was not limited to art and music. It made itself felt in religious practice as well, principally in the Protestant Reformation, which began in 1517 when Martin Luther nailed his 95 theses to the church door in Wittenburg, Germany. Luther's complaints against the religious estab-

Martin Luther burning papal documents a few weeks prior to his excommunication by Pope Leo X.

lishment were largely concerned with the selling of "indulgences," that is, pre-paid penance for sins. His own church as it evolved was different from the Medieval Catholic church in other ways as well. One of these was his require-ment that the Bible be translated from Latin into the vernacular, the language which people spoke. A second was that the congregation be more actively in-volved in the religious service. Towards this end, he instituted the practice of congregational singing of hymns in the vernacular language. An accomplished musician, he wrote some of these hymns himself, in some cases adapting folk songs, art songs, and earlier religious music for his purposes.

Luther's "A Mighty Fortress Is Our God"

"A Mighty Fortress Is Our God" is credited to Luther, although the melody may be one he adapted from an earlier source. It was written in the mid-1520s. The published version of 1533 is different from the one now found in hymnals, prin-cipally because it has more rhythmic liveliness. Although the congregation sang the hymn in unison, without harmony parts, the melody itself reveals a tonal na-ture. Its scale, like the one Josquin used for his "Ave Maria", is based on the *Ionian* mode, which looks like this:

and is what we today call the C-major scale.

In any mode, the note which starts and finishes is likely to be the most important one. In the Ionian mode or major scale this importance is increased by the fact that the next-to-last note is just one-half step below the final tone. This half step tends to lead into the final tone, which is why the next-to-last note is called the "leading-tone." It is impossible to hear the leading tone of the scale (a B in C major) without feeling its pull towards C. This double emphasis on the C is what explicitly "centers" it—makes it the tonal center.

Throughout the hymn we feel the movement away from and back towards the tonal center of C. The first phrase begins with three strong Cs; at the end of the phrase, the melody moves away to the fifth, G. The second phrase takes us back to C, the third phrase away to G, the fourth back to C, and so on:

Luther's "A Mighty Fortress," from a version published in 1533

Ein' feste Burg ist unser Gott,	A mighty fortress is our God,
Ein' gute Wehr und Waffen;	A bulwark never failing;
Er hilft uns frei aus aller Not,	Our helper He, amid the flood
Die uns jetzt hat betroffen.	Of mortal ills prevailing.
Der alte böse Feind	For still our ancient foe
Mit Ernst er es jetzt meint	Doth seek to work us woe;
Gros' Macht und viele List	His craft and pow'r are great,
Sein' grausam' Rüstung ist,	And armed with cruel hate,
Aus erd'n ist nicht sein's Gleichen.	On earth is not his equal.

To measure the strength of the melody's pull, leave off the final tone of one of the phrases ending on C, and listen to the sense of incompleteness which results:

For comparison, leave off the final tone from the Gregorian chant we discussed earlier, and notice how much *less* incomplete it sounds:

Two centuries later, J. S. Bach would use the hymn "A Mighty Fortress Is Our God" in a cantata; in the following century Mendelssohn would use it in a symphony. In the 1520s, however, it was a dissident German church song, and it made little impact on the mainstream of musical activity, which remained Italian, Catholic, and polyphonic.

SUMMARY: *"Ein' Feste Burg ist unser Gott" ("A Mighty Fortress Is Our God"), attributed to Martin Luther (mid-1520s)*

melody	Based on the Ionian mode (identical with our major scale). Organized into short, definite phrases which follow the phrasing of the text.
harmony	Originally sung in unison.
rhythm	Strong, definite beat appropriate to the militaristic images of the text. Original version had livelier rhythms than the one which has come down to us.
form	Strophic (although only the first verse is given here).
texture	Monophonic.
timbre	A mixture of amateur voices.
function	To provide congregational participation in Protestant religious service.
text	First verse based on Psalm 46 ("God is our refuge and strength . . .")

The Counter-Reformation

The world seemed ready for Luther's reforms. Within a few decades, Protestantism had become a mighty force on the continent of Europe. The response of the Roman Catholic church was the Counter-Reformation, many of whose principles were worked out in a series of meetings of church leaders over the years 1545 to 1563, called the Council of Trent. One of the Council's guiding principles was that to oppose the Protestant Reformation successfully, there would have to be a Catholic reformation. That is, the Catholic church would have to undertake its own reforms, which included reforms of musical practices. The Council of Trent objected to the use of secular tunes in religious services, a practice which the Lutherans had adopted whole-heartedly. It also objected to the increasing elaboration of polyphonic music, which was thought to obscure the words of the ceremony. One critic from within the church complained that "boys whine the discant, some bellow the tenor, others gnash the alto, others moo the bass; the result is that a multitude of sounds is heard, but of the words and prayers not a syllable is understood."

Palestrina

The composer Giovanni da Palestrina (ca. 1524–1594) came of age in the midst of these controversies, and his work was influenced by the changing Counter-Reformation ideals. Palestrina began his career as a choirboy, later becoming organist and choirmaster at his local church. He had a stroke of luck when the Bishop of this church became Pope Julius III and brought Palestrina to Rome. His career thereafter included a number of important church appointments in Rome. He lost his wife and two of his sons to an epidemic of plague in 1570. For a while he thought of taking holy orders; then he married the wealthy widow of a fur merchant, and subsequently mixed a business career with his musical one. He wrote the *Missa Assumpta est Maria* (Mass of the Assumption—the taking up to heaven—of Mary) late in his life, probably around 1590.

It is a mass for six voices: two sopranos, alto (the soprano and alto parts would have been sung by boys), two tenors and bass. Palestrina makes use of a chant melody appropriate for the occasion: that which would be sung at the vespers service on August 15th, the feast day of the Assumption of the Virgin:

As - sump-ta est Ma- ri - a   in cael - um___
(Ascended is Mary into heaven . . . .)

Giovanni da Palestrina and his patron, Pope Julius III.

Unlike Josquin and Machaut, Palestrina does not quote the chant melody directly, but refers to it, and develops new melodies out of it. Not melody but texture is the key to his work. He balances six different voices, six separate melodic lines, an amazing enough accomplishment on its own. Each of the voices moves in a smooth, flowing, predominantly step-wise fashion. Each contains considerable rhythmic variety, moving back and forth between sustained and quicker tones. There is a great deal of inter-weaving, especially between the two soprano and the two tenor voices. And yet this complex texture never creates dissonance. If you were to stop the music at almost any given moment, you would find the harmony reducible to simple triads. In measure seven, to choose an example at random, the first beat finds C in soprano and bass, E in tenor II, and G in tenor I. The third beat finds C in tenor I and bass, E in alto, and G in tenor II. The first beat of the next measure finds a G in the alto, a B in the bass, and D in the tenor. In other words, two C triads followed by a G triad. We hear a complexity of voices, with considerable rhythmic movement, within the most even and consonant harmonic texture imaginable.

As a result of this even consonance, there is almost no sense of a pull towards or away from a tonal center. The inter-weaving high voices make the whole work seem to float, without root or center. Only at the beginning of the final Kyrie statement, where Palestrina lines his voices up in a homophonic texture, do we get, at least for a moment, the kind of strong, simple definition which seems to pull music down to earth.

A 16th-century mass celebrated with large musical resources. The inscription says that earthly music made with horns, winds, and voices can lift the mind to heaven.

Palestrina is clearly a Renaissance composer. His writing shows a grace and delicacy and sheer sophistication of technique found in no previous era. What he does not give us is the kind of humanism, the down-to-earth human-centeredness, which was the "advanced" spirit of the age. The spirit of Palestrina's music is that of the Counter-Reformation—a revitalized interpretation of the spiritual ideals of the Medieval church.

SUMMARY: *Palestrina's* Missa Assumpta est Maria *(ca. 1590)*

melody	Related to chant melody. Motion primarily step-wise, in long, flowing phrases.
harmony	Extremely consonant. At almost every moment, voices combine to form triadic, consonant harmonies.
rhythm	Each individual voice displays considerable variety between sustained and quicker tones. The moments of quickness and stillness occur at different times in the different voices, so that at any given moment there is rhythmic variety among the voices. Only at the beginning of the final Kyrie is there any strong sense of beat.
form	One Kyrie eleison section, followed by two Christe eleison sections, followed by one Kyrie eleison section.

texture	Almost entirely polyphonic, but with moments of homophony, notably at the opening of the final Kyrie section. Six voices inter-weave, especially the two soprano and two tenor voices.
timbre	Vocal, with emphasis on the higher, lighter vocal timbres of soprano and tenor. Even in the bass part, the writing is relatively high within that range.
function	As part of religious service; probably first used in celebration of the feast day of August 15th, which is dedicated to the Assumption of the Virgin.

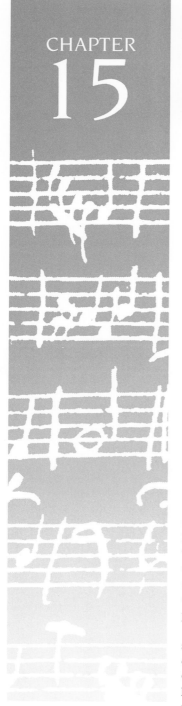

CHAPTER 15

Secular Aspects

Monteverdi

The term "Renaissance" means, literally, "re-birth." To the thinkers and artists of the time, what was being reborn was classical culture, the culture of ancient Greece. Unfortunately—or, as things turned out, fortunately—no one knew exactly what Greek music was like. What the artists and thinkers did have were documents which talked about the theory of Greek music. Many of these discussed the relationship between music and words. The Renaissance thinkers interpreted this to mean that music should express the particular states of emotion which specific words refer to. The composer primarily responsible for putting these new ideas into practice was Claudio Monteverdi.

Monteverdi was born in Cremona, Italy, in 1567. His father was a barber-surgeon (the two trades were combined in those days) and apparently a successful one. Monteverdi studied music with the chapel master at the Cremona Cathedral, but went on to work at the ducal court at Mantua. Although later in his life he became the musical director of St. Mark's in Venice, most of his compositions are secular (not religious) in nature.

It would be hard to get more secular than "Si ch'io vorrei morire," a **madrigal** (a secular polyphonic vocal work) he published in 1603. "Yes, I would like to die," the words say, "now that I kiss at last, dear love,

the beautiful mouth of my heart's
    desire.
Ah, dear sweet tongue,
give me such humors
that from sweetness I may, on this
    breast, perish.
Ah, my life, against thy white breast
press me until I become nothing.
Ah mouth, ah kisses, ah tongue,
    come back to me that I may say
Yes, I would like to die.

Two words here may require some definition. "To die" had two meanings in Renaissance poetry, one the familiar one, the other referring to sexual climax (*see* Chapter 7.) The word "humor" has nothing to do with jokes—it refers to moisture from living things, in this case the moisture of the loved one's mouth.

If Renaissance poets could talk freely about sex, so could Renaissance composers. The madrigal begins with a cheerful statement—all five voices in harmony on a series of major triads, with a lively rhythmic pattern, singing "Yes I would like to die." While it is true that the word "morire" (to die) is lower and more stretched out, the chords and rhythms tell us the death will be a happy one. The musical line ascends with the next line of poetry. Then comes an amazing bit of writing. It is imitative; the voices overlap with closely related patterns; there is dissonance—the first voice enters on an A, the second on a B against the A, the third on a C which is heard against the B and A:

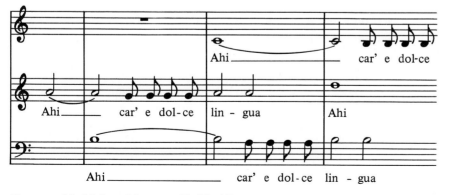

Measures 15–18 from Monteverdi's "Si ch'io vorrei morire"

Two things are accomplished. One, the closeness of the voices symbolizes how close the lovers are, both physically and musically. Two, the closeness of the voices creates dissonance, a harmonic tension which supplies energy for the music's slow climb. Again, symbolism: the closeness of the voices creates harmonic tension just as the lovers' closeness creates sexual tension; in both cases the result is a climbing, increasing, building tension followed by a slow decline and release until: " . . . m'estingua," " . . . (I) perish."

Throughout the madrigal, Monteverdi finds musical equivalents for the physical and emotional states described by the words. In doing this he was fulfilling the Renaissance search for an equivalent to the (imagined) music of ancient Greece. More important, he was giving musical voice to an aspect of Renaissance humanism. This provides a contrast with Palestrina. Although Palestrina was a Renaissance composer, the nature of his work for the church constrained him to music which contemplates the eternal, the spiritual, and the everlasting soul. In writing secular music for private entertainment, Monteverdi is allowed different concerns. His music devotes itself not to the eternal but to the here and now, the present day; in fact, to the present *moment,* the specific sensations of a particular instant. His concern is not with the spiritual and the everlasting soul, but with the body and the emotions. Welcome, this music says, to the modern world.

SUMMARY: *Claudio Monteverdi's madrigal "Si ch'io vorrei morire" (1603)*

melody	A very flexible melodic line, changing to follow the images of the text.
harmony	Also flexible, varying from consonance to dissonance, major chords to minor ones, according to the demands of the words.
rhythm	A fairly consistent half-note pulse, but within that basic pattern there are a great many smaller patterns giving various combinations of quick and sustained notes. There is frequently a sense of syncopation, as different voices enter and each voice places its accent on a different beat.
form	First phrase is repeated as last phrase; other than this, each section of music presents new ideas.
texture	Predominantly polyphonic, but with homophonic episodes.
timbre	Five voices, two female, three male, unaccompanied.
function	Originally written for aristocratic entertainment where it was performed by well-trained amateur or professional singers. The music was also published, in which form it was available to a wider audience.
text	

Si ch'io vorrei morire	Yes, I would like to die,
hora ch'io bacio amore	now that I kiss at last, dear love,
la bella bocca del mio amato core.	the beautiful mouth of my heart's desire.

Sebastiano Florigerio: *Divertissement Musical* (c. 1540) *(Alte Pinakothek, Munich)*

Ahi car'e dolce lingua	Ah, dear sweet tongue,
datemi tant' humore	give me such humors
che di dolcezz' in questo sen	that from sweetness I may, on this
m'estingua.	breast, perish.
Ahi vita mia, a questo bianco seno	Ah, my life, against thy white breast
deh stringetemi fin ch'io venga meno.	press me until I become nothing.
Ahi bocca, ahi baci, ahi lingua torn' a	Ah mouth, ah kisses, ah tongue,
dire	come back to me that I may say
si ch'io vorrei morire.	Yes, I would like to die.

Renaissance Music and the Middle Class

The two centers of music-making throughout the Renaissance remained, as they had for centuries, the church and the court. With works like the Italian madrigals, the French *chansons,* and the English madrigals and lute songs, a new possibility opened up, that of reaching a larger public through publication. In published form, music became available to those who could not afford to hire musicians, but who could buy books and instruments, and who could study and learn to play; in other words, the middle class (*See* color plate 4). The English

New York Pro Musica, a modern Renaissance music ensemble.

madrigal composer Thomas Morley, admittedly doing his best to sell his own teach-yourself-music book, describes a fictional gentleman at a dinner party:

> "Supper being ended and music books (according to the custom) being brought to the table, the mistress of the house presented me with a part, earnestly requesting me to sing; but when, after many excuses, I protested . . . that I could not, every one began to wonder; yea, some whispered to others demanding how I was brought up."

Dowland's "In Darkness Let Me Dwell"

John Dowland's lute song "Lady If You So Spite Me" (*see* Chapter 7) is a typical example, written as a courtly entertainment, but also published for the use of the rising middle class of merchants, civil servants, doctors, lawyers, and so on. The satisfactions and disappointments of love provide the subject matter for most such music. Dowland's "In Darkness Let Me Dwell" is an exception. The composer was a melancholy man, thwarted in his ambition for an appointment at Queen Elizabeth's court. But this song speaks to an emotional state beyond what can be accounted for by melancholy and thwarted ambition.

It begins with a short introduction for the lute. This is not a simple matter of strumming chords, but a rich texture of four distinct musical lines, the top two especially having considerable independent movement. The vocal entrance is slow, low, and of minimal energy, at first rising only one-half step before falling back.

In   dark - ness let___   me _____ dwell

Next the words (their authorship is uncertain) begin to elaborate on the song's central image: that of a tomb in which to live. Its floor will be sorrow, its roof despair, its walls wet with tears. Then, the role of music. It will not console or comfort, but will banish sleep with its hellish jarring sounds. Here Dowland, like Monteverdi, makes music symbolize the meaning of the words. The "correct" way to set a word like "jarring" is to place the accent on the first syllable, since in speech we always deemphasize "-ing" endings. For example, I could write:

Hell – ish, hell – ish, jar – ring sounds.

The trouble with this setting is that it is too smooth; it does not "jar" the ear. So Dowland deliberately sets the word "incorrectly:"

Hell - ish, hell - ish, jar - ring sounds, jar - ring jar - ring sounds

"Thus wedded to my woes," the song continues, "and bedded to my tomb," and then the voice pauses for the lute. It is an unnatural spot for such a pause, since it seems to be in the middle of a statement. Suddenly the voice appears, on the highest note of the song, without build-up, unexpected, unprepared for: "O let me living die." If Dowland had led up to that "O" by writing something like this:

tomb_____ O, let me liv - ing die

what would be missing? The "O" isolated, high, and unprepared for sounds like a cry from the heart, a real cry of pain. Led up to, smoothed out, it would be just another conventional "Alas, woe is me." What Dowland is giving us here is realism—the final element music was slow in evolving in comparison to Masaccio's painting, *Tribute Money* (*see* Chapter 14). Dowland's musical statement follows speech and rings true. It is a cry of pain which gives the illusion of being a real cry of pain. In terms of realism, Dowland has set himself an almost impossible task: to give the illusion that, at the instant of composition, he is *in* the state of depression he describes. Yet it is just this state, in which the only desire is to withdraw from the world, and in which music itself has become hellish, which would make the writing of music impossible.

    The song ends with a restatement of the initial phrase "In darkness let me dwell." The voice this time ends alone, the last note, G sharp, is left hanging without accompaniment. The final cadence should be in A minor. G sharp is the leading tone which approaches the final A. Here the final A never arrives. We want to hear it, our ears are tuned for it, but the music is saying that this state of depression offers no resolution, finality, or release.

SUMMARY: *John Dowland's "In Darkness Let Me Dwell," (1610), to a text probably by Giovanni Coperario*

form	Through composed. The first phrase of the song returns as its last phrase, tying the work together.
melody	Responsive to the emotional states described by the lyrics. Subtle word-painting effects. Emotional realism.
harmony	Strong sense of minor key, strong sense of tonal center.
rhythm	Very slow, drawn out, no strong pulse, but a kind of syncopation in that the singer's melody often seems to lag behind the beat.
timbre	Voice (traditionally the very high male voice called counter-tenor) and lute, often with a low, stringed instrument accompanying on the bass line.
texture	Basically voice and accompaniment, but with a rich contrapuntal texture within the accompaniment part.
function	Lute songs had their original performances as aristocratic entertainment, but were published and thus made available to a more extensive middle-class public.
text	

In darkness let me dwell, the ground
   shall sorrow be.
The roof despair to bar all cheerful
   light from me.
The walls of marble black that
   moistened still shall weep.
My music hellish jarring sounds to
   banish friendly sleep.
Thus wedded to my woes, and bedded to my tomb,
O let me living die, till death do
   come.

Conclusion

In a sense, no two songs could be more different than Monteverdi's "Si ch'io vorrei morire" and Dowland's "In Darkness Let me Dwell." One describes a state of sexual excitement, the other a state of acute depression. Yet they are similar in two important ways. One: they both deal in illusion. They don't try merely to "describe" an emotional state, they attempt to make it seem *real* to the listener, giving not a description of some remembered state of mind, but the illusion that the state of mind exists now as the song is being performed. Two:

they are both fascinated by the particularly human. They do not stop at the level of generality: "a woman loves" or "a man despairs." Instead they set out to explore the shades of feeling, the texture of experience, which can only be found on the level of the intensely personal. Paradoxically, it is at this most personal level that they discover states of mind which are shared and universal. As Renaissance explorers and scientists set out to discover the outer world, Renaissance artists began to discover the inner one. For them the human soul did not have to aspire to Heaven; the plain old human mind and body living here on earth were material enough.

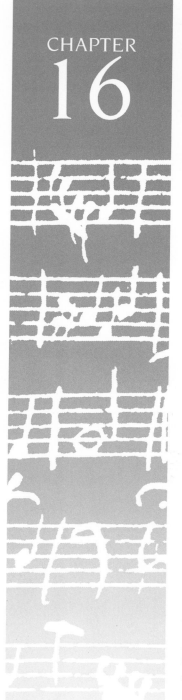

CHAPTER 16

Opera, Ballad Opera, and Oratario

Baroque Opera

The Renaissance loved voyages of discovery, whether anything was discovered or not. Some of the most famous of these were glorious failures. Columbus tried to discover a route west to India, only to find America. Painters and sculptors tried to rediscover the principles of ancient art; instead, they revolutionized their own arts. The search for the principles of ancient music led to the madrigal and revitalized vocal music in the late Renaissance. Some of the people involved with this effort, including Monteverdi, also attempted to revive the traditions of ancient drama. Like Columbus, they were failures at accomplishing their stated aim; what they invented instead was opera.

The invention of opera occurred in the years around 1600, which makes for an awkward problem in naming the period which starts around this time. The madrigals and lute songs of the early 1600s are generally classified as "Renaissance," mostly because they so obviously grow out of Renaissance traditions which began earlier in the 1500s. The operatic tradition, beginning around 1600 and flowering later in the seventeenth and eighteenth centuries, is generally classified as "Baroque." The awkwardness comes when talking about a composer like Monteverdi, who, one morning in 1603, may have been a Baroque composer as he worked on an opera, becoming a Renaissance composer again as he wrote a madrigal in the afternoon. For the purposes of this book, we will follow the conventional pattern and call the period from 1600 to 1750 the Baroque period, while keeping in mind that Renaissance works were still being produced during its early years.

The essential discovery which made opera possible was **recitative,** a way to deliver speech through music. What the early composers and theorists were looking for was a flexible way of writing music, so that it could bend to follow the patterns of the spoken word. Speech has so many expressive intonations and rhythms—our voices sometimes become high and our words come quickly; sometimes the pitch sinks, and the words are drawn out; we hurry or hesitate, our voices climb or dive according to the moment's mood. Song captures some of this, but for a song to have the consistent rhythm and melody we expect from it, it cannot follow all the contours of spoken language. Recitative can. Its melodic line is free, following the ups and downs of speech. Its rhythm also is rarely confined to specific patterns. Its accompaniment is (as a rule) kept simple, so that the accompanists can follow the singers as they act through the music. Here is an example of recitative:

How soft,—how soft—— in peace,and yet how fierce——————how fierce in—— arms!

One instrument (usually a 'cello or related instrument) would play the bass line indicated; another instrument (usually a harpsichord) would play the bass line and also improvise chords above it. Both together are called a **continuo** part. To specify the chords more exactly, composers would put numbers under (or over) the notes, as a guide to the harpsichordist. This is called a *figured bass.*

By 1689, when Henry Purcell wrote his *Dido and Aeneas* (*see* Chapter 11), opera had developed into the form familiar today: the orchestral overture, the choruses, the solo songs, or arias, the dance episodes, and, to carry these along and provide both information and continuity, recitative. Purcell's opera was not part of a flourishing tradition in England; Italy remained opera's heartland. English enthusiasm for the form waited until the early 1700s and the arrival of George Frederick Handel.

George Frederick Handel

Handel was part of an amazing cluster of musicians, the high Baroque generation of composers, all born around the year 1685: Handel, Bach, and Domenico Scarlatti in that year, Vivaldi in 1675, and Telemann in 1681. Handel's birthplace was Halle, Germany, where his father, like Monteverdi's, was a barber-surgeon attached to the court. The father's ambition was for the son to become a lawyer (a common ambition among composers' parents) but Handel's talents so obviously lay with music that his father relented and allowed him to study for a musical career. The church and the court were still the two great social institutions which supplied musicians with work. The church of Handel's Germany was Protestant, and the church musician's duties included playing the organ, rehearsing and conducting the choir, educating young singers, and composing new music for services. This was the career that Bach would choose, and for a time it appeared that Handel would also. In fact, his and Bach's paths nearly crossed when the great church musician, Buxtehude, nearing retirement, began auditioning young composers for his post. Handel and Bach both, at different times, visited Buxtehude. A condition of employment was marriage to Buxtehude's daughter, an aspect which neither of the men found appealing. Handel was also offered the position at the Calvinist church in Halle. This would have been a comfortable and easy choice for him to make. Instead, he chose to leave Halle for Hamburg, where he could study that most difficult and chancy of musical forms—opera. After Hamburg, he journeyed to the source of the operatic tradition, Italy.

Opera's Patronage and Popularity

Throughout this period in his life he benefitted from a form of aristocratic patronage. This was similar to the sort of support a young musician—or, for that matter, a young track star—might receive today: a place to stay, meals, the occasional gift of spending money, an introduction to the next patron in the next town. Handel listened, learned, performed, and composed, and quickly established his own reputation. By 1710, four years after leaving for Italy, he had been offered a number of opportunities, finally accepting the position of court composer to the Elector of Hanover (Germany). Before finally taking up his duties, he visited England. He had with him the score to a newly-composed opera called *Rinaldo*. It was given an elaborate, even flamboyant production, complete with such stage effects as a chariot drawn by dragons breathing fire and smoke, a grove of trees populated by real birds, mermaids dancing in water, waterfalls, thunder, lightning "and amazing noises." The work was an instant success, and Handel, neglecting his Hanover duties, was to spend the rest of his working career in England. The first part of this career was devoted almost entirely to Italian opera. As anyone knows who has had experience with musical theater productions—even just working backstage for a high school musical comedy—these are among the most ambitious of human undertakings. The singing, the dancing, the orchestral playing, the stage effects, the scene painting, the dramatic action, the lighting and the costumes all must be developed separately but simultaneously, and finally put together in the few days before the production opens. Handel was not a composer who sat home scribbling while others did this work. He was in the thick of things, hiring, rehearsing, performing, conducting, even becoming involved with financial dealings (never far from center stage in the opera world).

Handel never did take up his Hanover duties, and found himself in an awkward position when, on the death of Queen Anne in 1714, there was no direct heir, and George, Elector of Hanover, became King George I of England. As king, George continued to support him, and Handel, who had been granted a yearly pension by Queen Anne, eventually saw this raised to 600 pounds per year, the equivalent in today's money of a salary in the $50,000 range. He was still free to earn money from his opera writing, and to lose money through his opera investing, both of which he did at a rate which drove him near nervous breakdown and bankruptcy. Opera has always needed people willing to lose money, and these included the king and the nobility, who sponsored the operatic production companies. But the operas depended on public support through box office receipts as well. Tickets ranged in price from one shilling, sixpence to half a guinea—similar to a price range today of from five to 50 dollars.

Handel's Giulio Cesare

One example of what this public was turning out to see is Handel's *Giulio Cesare, Julius Caesar*. This was an appropriate choice of subject partly because the English—in the midst of building their empire—identified themselves with the ancient Roman empire-builders. The plot of the opera involves Caesar's adventures in Egypt, and thus the always-fascinating Cleopatra, Queen of Egypt. Further, there is rich dramatic incident: for example, Caesar meets with the wife and son of his general, Pompey, with whom he has been feuding. They agree to make up their quarrel, when in walk the emissaries of Ptolemy, who bear a gift for Caesar in a box. He opens it right then and there and finds Pompey's head. One of the emissaries watches Pompey's wife react to this horrible sight, and promptly falls in love with her, deciding that he must have her for his own. Ptolemy installs her in his harem, however, as the plot thickens . . . .

In spite of such colorful action, the opera presents difficulties for a modern audience. These are partly the result of the Baroque period's love of great people, grand scale, public actions, and historical significance. More typical of our own period are dramas like *Death of a Salesman* and *The Glass Menagerie,* where we learn about the private lives of individuals who might otherwise live unnoticed in our midst. When, a few years ago, movie producers tried to do a modern version of Cleopatra's story, it was a dismal flop. The only way we tolerate treatment of great figures is if they are brought down to a personal level. A Baroque dramatist wanting to talk about Robert Kennedy, for example, would personify his ideals in some ancient historical character. A modern dramatist would explore his rumored love affair with Marilyn Monroe. Nevertheless, Handel's operas have had a number of successful revivals in recent years.

Scene from Act I, *Julius Caesar,* New York City Opera.

Aria: "Piangerò"

We can see Baroque dramatic and musical principles at work in Cleopatra's aria, "Piangerò," from *Giulio Cesare.* A section of recitative introduces the aria. The singer is accompanied by widely spaced chords on the harpsichord, giving her the freedom she needs to act out her words through the music. The music itself is broken up into short phrases, and within the phrases the melody is jumpy and angular, fitting her distraught, scarcely coherent state. "Oh God!" she says, after recounting her troubles, "there is no hope left in my life."

The aria which follows begins gently. "Piangerò, piangerò" . . . "I will weep, I will weep." The recitative ended in minor; this melody is in the major key, and it is marked by a rising motive. Where is the sorrow? In the bass line, which moves resolutely downward. This is a typical Baroque texture—strong melodic motives against a strong, moving bass line. Here the idea of the tonal center has reached full maturity. The bass line diagrams the pattern. It starts on E, the tonal center, moves further and further away, and then returns. The movement away creates tension against the melody; the return relaxes it.

Melody and bass line from beginning of aria

In the next phrase the melodic intervals grow larger and the harmonic tension increases, growing more dissonant. Meanwhile, there is more to the texture than just the melody and the bass line, as the violins echo and foretell Cleopatra's lament.

What she is lamenting is her fate. This is typical of Baroque opera. Where we like our dramas "up close and personal," they wanted theirs grand and abstract. In this brief recitative and aria we find Cleopatra talking of "glory," "fate," "death," and "hope." In another Handel aria we can find in the space of six lines references to love, honor, nobility, the soul, and victory. I am not sure exactly what has changed, but it is inescapably true that audiences today have lost their faith in such abstract generalizations. The words sound untrustworthy, like politicians' cant. If a contemporary audience is going to find drama in this aria, it will have to be through the music.

Cleopatra's first gentle statement becomes wilder and more eccentric, as her melody leaps, twists, and turns.

Then it softens, and the orchestra reminds us of her opening phrases as it cadences to close this first section, all of which has been based on just three lines of poetry. The next three form the basis for a new, contrasting section. And when she is dead, she says, her ghost will come back to torment the tyrant. The word she uses is "agiterò," related to the English "agitate," and Handel sets its last syllable with a long melisma of 36 notes, to word-paint the idea, and to convey a sense of Cleopatra's overflowing energy.

The passage has another function, unrelated to the opera's drama, but closely related to its popularity. The technical term for such elaborate decoration is "coloratura;" it is written to show off the sheer athletic ability of the singer's voice. This was a large part of what audiences came to hear. The Italian opera revolved around its stars. Handel himself went on scouting trips to the continent to sign potential stars to lucrative contracts, often worth several times his own. Fans of a particular singer might disrupt a performance by cheering their star, or hissing a rival. Not only did singers display their vocal skill (or "virtuosity") in coloratura passages like this one, but they also improvised other coloratura passages, sometimes lengthy ones amounting to vocal cadenzas. At the same time, we must not lose sight of the fact that while Handel is allowing the singer this display, and even delighting in it, he is making it serve a dramatic purpose. Underneath her singing the orchestra keeps up the feeling of agitation, with trembling inner parts over a strong but quick-moving bass. Handel is creating a powerful contrast between this section and the opening one, to which he now returns.

This kind of aria is called a *da capo* aria, since it goes back to the head ("capo" in Italian) of the page, repeating the first section. It is in the contrast between these two sections that the drama lies, between the slow, tender, lifting phrases of the first section and the frenetic energy in the wild coloratura of the second section. Since both of these sections are Cleopatra's, we must interpret the conflict they represent as one which exists inside her: the inward-directed sorrow of the first section against the outer-directed anger of the second. If Handel succeeds in making us feel this conflict within Cleopatra, he can make us sympathize with her on a personal, human level, thus transcending the more impersonal elements in words and vocal display.

SUMMARY: *"Piangerò" from Handel's* Giulio Cesare

form	Recitative and aria, the aria in da capo form, ABA.
melody	Follows speech inflections in recitative. In A section of aria, melody begins with lifting phrases, then becomes more irregular, with wide leaps and sudden changes of direction. Middle or B section characterized by melismatic coloratura effects.
harmony	Strong feeling of harmonic progression throughout, away from and back towards the tonal center. Dissonance used for "plaintive" effect.
rhythm	Contrast between moderate "three" in A section, fast "four" in B section. Within each section, the beat moves steadily and evenly.
texture	Defined principally in the relationship between melody and bass line. Bass line determines harmonic progression, but also has melodic qualities of its own (which is why it is called a bass "line"). Higher string points provide orchestral responses and counterpoint to vocal line.
timbre	Soprano voice, continuo provided by harpsichord and 'cello, with violins and flute.

function   The aria is designed to reveal Cleopatra's emotional state at a given point in the drama; in a more general sense, the opera itself appealed as entertainment to a large English public, partly because of its subject matter, partly because of its singing, and partly because of the beauty and the drama of its music.

text

recitative

E pur così in un giorno perdo	And do I thus in one day lose
fasti e grandezze? Ahi, fato	power and glory? Ah, cruel
rio! Cesare, il mio bel nume, è	fate! Caesar, my handsome god,
forse estinto! Cornelia e Sesto	may be dead! Cornelia and Sesto
inermi son nè sanno darmi	to are disarmed, and cannot
soccorso. O Dio! Non resta	aid me. Oh God! There is no
alcuna speme al viver mio.	hope left in my life.

aria

Piangerò la sorte mia,	I will weep for my fate,
si crudele e tanto ria	so cruel and evil,
finchè vita in petto avrò.	as long as life remains.
Ma poi morta, d'ogni intorno	But when I am dead, my ghost,
il tiranno e notte e giorno,	everywhere, night and day,
fatta spettro, agiterò.	will torment the tyrant.

John Gay's The Beggar's Opera

Satire in Opera

John Gay, like Handel and Bach, was born in the year 1685. There the similarity ends. He was a literary figure in early eighteenth-century London, not a musical one, but his *The Beggar's Opera* helped to change the course of Handel's career. *The Beggar's Opera* is a satire on both the style and the sentiments of the Italian opera. It is not really an opera at all, having no recitative; rather, it is a form called *ballad opera,* consisting of dramatic dialogue broken up by short songs which Gay made by combining his own lyrics with melodies borrowed mostly from folk and popular music of the day. The story is set not in some far-off time and place, but in houses, taverns, and prisons of present-day (1720s) London. The language is not Italian but colloquial English; the characters are not great historical figures like Caesar and Cleopatra but thieves, fences, prostitutes, and murderers, with names like Filch, Crook-fingered Jack, and Suky Tawdry. They are not much concerned with concepts like love, honor, duty, or justice. Money and sheer survival are their worries. Even sex takes a second place to money and survival. The character Filch, for example, makes love to the women prisoners because they pay him to do it, and they pay him to do it because being pregnant will lessen their chances of being hanged.

Hogarth: *The Beggar's Opera. (Tate Gallery, London)*

The only character who shows much sign of finer feelings is Polly, the daughter of Peachum, a fence who also informs on—"peaches" on—his thieves for further profit. Polly loves Macheath, a highwayman. Peachum opposes the match, then realizes that if he gets Macheath hanged, Polly will become a wealthy widow. Macheath is involved with a string of women, but Polly's main rival for his affections is one Lucy Lockit, the daughter of Newgate Prison's chief jailer. Lucy, of course, is jealous of Polly. She introduces her song with lines that mock the Italian style: "Jealousy, rage, love and fear are at once tearing me to pieces. How I am weather-beaten and shatter'd with distresses!" Cleopatra was torn between two emotions; Lucy goes her two better, being torn by four. This prepares us for a big dramatic aria. What Gay gives us is a song in which she dwells on her inability to sleep at night for thinking about Polly in bed with Macheath. The tune is from a popular song. At the climactic moment, "Revenge, revenge, revenge," where Handel would make his aria explode with notes, Gay gives us just:

In case we still entertain illusions about Lucy's nobility of character, we have her lines at the conclusion of the song:

> I have the Rats-bane ready.—I run no Risque; for I can lay her Death upon the Ginn, and so many dye of that naturally that I shall never be call'd in Question.— But say, I were to be hang'd—I never could be hang'd for any thing that would give me greater Comfort, than the poysoning that Slut.

The Beggar's Opera was a hit. In satirizing the high-flown characters, language, and emotions of the Italian opera, it helped to kill the fashion for Handel's works in that style. The fashion might have declined in any event; it is hard to imagine continued English enthusiasm for such a transplanted art form. As the taste for Italian opera weakened, Handel was forced to look for new outlets. What he found was *oratorio,* which we'll discuss in the next section.

SUMMARY: *Lucy's air "I'm like a skiff on the Ocean tost," from John Gay's* The Beggar's Opera *(1728)*

form	One idea for the first four lines, a contrasting idea for the second four lines, which are then repeated, giving an ABB structure.
melody	Clear, simple, strong phrases, frequently repeated and easily learned.
harmony	Strong sense of tonal center; the harmonies move away from it only to return almost immediately.
rhythm	Consistent two-beat pattern, each beat being subdivided into three.
texture	Vocal line dominant, orchestral part as accompaniment.
timbre	Soprano voice, accompanied by small orchestra with harpsichord.
function	*The Beggar's Opera* was popular London entertainment; popular both because of its effective satire on the Italian opera and because of the vitality and humor of its characters and situations.
text	

I'm like a skiff on the Ocean tost,
Now high, now low, with each billow born,
With her rudder broke, and her anchor lost,
Deserted and all forlorn,

While thus I lye rolling and tossing all night,
That Polly lyes sporting on seas of delight!
Revenge, revenge, revenge,
Shall appease my restless sprite.

A sign of the opera's popularity was that its songs were printed on playing cards.

Handel's Messiah

Oratorio

As a form, the **oratorio** has a history which long precedes Handel. It began in the church—not as part of regular religious services, but as a separate event, with words and music designed both to educate and to entertain the congregation. Handel's oratorios, however, derive chiefly from his experience in opera. Like operas, they have overtures, recitatives, arias, and choruses. Unlike operas, they are not staged, there is no scenery, dance, action, or costumes. The words are in English, the subjects are religious. The principal musical difference is in the choruses, which receive much richer treatment in a Handel oratorio than in one of his operas.

The switch from opera to oratorio allowed Handel to do away with many of the operatic elements which critics had objected to: the extravagant scenic devices, the foreign language, plots and characters derived from unfamiliar sources. Handel found the subjects for most of his oratorios in the Old Testament: Esther, Samson, Deborah, Saul. But the most famous of his oratorios, his greatest work (and, many would say, all music's greatest work), is *Messiah*. Its libretto, by Charles Jennens, a wealthy gentleman-writer, is constructed of quotations from the King James version of the Bible. Just as the English identified their nation with ancient Rome, so they identified their national religion with the words of this particular Bible translation, which happens also to be the most beautiful and poetic of translations. The libretto does not, like those for Handel's other oratorios, tell a dramatic story; it does not recount the life of Christ. Instead it uses a mixture of Old and New Testament quotations to reflect on the idea of the Messiah and what his coming might mean—the possibility of redemption: spiritual salvation and deliverance from sin.

The work's ultimate statement may be contained in its very first sung words: "Comfort ye."

If this is the work's statement, its drama is implied in a phrase which follows soon after:

Where the initial phrase is soft, descending, and gentle in its rhythm, the succeeding phrase is climbing, definite, and stern: this comfort will have to be earned.

How stern the test will be is described in the aria "But who may abide the day of his coming?" where, to describe the power of the Lord, Handel indulges in magnificent word-painting, for example asking the singer to imitate licking flames on the word "fire."

Aria: "He shall feed his flock"

The sense that the Messiah will help his people through such tests is given in the aria "He shall feed his flock." Here Jennens combines the Old and New Testaments. He begins with lines from the Old Testament prophet Isaiah:

> He shall feed his flock like a shepherd: and he shall gather the lambs with his arm, and carry them in his bosom, and gently lead those that are with young.

Jennens then continues with lines from the New Testament Gospel of Matthew:

> Come unto him, all ye that labour, come unto him, that are heavy laden and he will give you rest. Take his yoke upon you, and learn of him; for he is meek and lowly of heart: and ye shall find rest unto your souls.

Handel begins his setting of these words with the simplest of melodies, gently rocking like a lullaby, down the scale and back up again, over simple and consonant harmonies. These shift at the phrase's end from the I chord (based on the first note of the scale) to the V chord (based on the fifth note of the scale.) It is this movement away from the tonal center which makes the melody's continued development feel necessary.

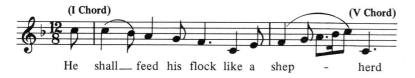

The next phrase begins with the same melody, but sees more active harmonies, as the bass line moves in contrary motion. At the phrase's end, we have been taken further from the tonal center, and another short phrase is needed to bring us back.

Second phrase, showing contrary motion between voice and bass line

This much of the music repeats before a new phrase is introduced. Again we hear the simple beginning, but this time the harmonies underneath are made still more distant, as they take us for a moment into a minor key. The melody's simple descent is interrupted, as it must land on the F sharp instead of an F natural, and it requires the next six measures to find its way back to its tonal center.

Next, the music modulates up four steps to a new key, and the same pattern we have heard is used in the soprano register for "Come unto him . . . "

The word "Baroque" is thought to derive from a Portugese word for "misshapen pearl." As an oyster creates a pearl by accreting layers around an irritant grain of sand, so Handel spirals his melody out of a grain of harmonic tension. With each new phrase the spiral's irregular circle increases. In this case the result is as beautiful as a pearl, misshapen or round.

Chorus: "Hallelujah"

At the end of the second part of *Messiah* comes a chorus which expresses joyful praise that the Lord reigns supreme: the "Hallelujah" chorus. Here the music is not constructed out of a spiralling melody. Instead, it is built from a number of simple and compact melodic-rhythmic ideas. It is in combination that their effects accumulate and become powerful. The four principal "building-block" motives are:

In examining the chorus, we can see how Handel puts these ideas together. It begins with a series of ten "Hallelujah"'s, each statement a short, strong, rhythmic phrase, sung in four-part harmony. The phrases have a sharp, "bitten-off" quality, expressing a rhythmic energy barely contained, and reminding us of a choir of trumpets almost as much as of a choir of voices [1]. For the next phrase in the text, "for the Lord God omnipotent reigneth," Handel puts his singers in unison on a simple, climbing theme [2]. He switches back and forth between these ideas, then combines them. One such combination has the alto and tenor voices singing the climbing melody [2] while soprano and bass have the short "hallelujah" phrase in rhythmic imitation [1].

Measures 29 and 30

After uniting the chorus again in harmony for "The kingdom of this world is become the kingdom of our Lord and of his Christ," Handel begins a new section with an angular, descending line [3]. It is stated first by the basses. Then the tenors imitate. The basses continue with a counterpoint underneath the main melody, concentrating principally on the three-note motive which sets the word "forever." The altos enter with their statement of the angular theme [3] and the sopranos with theirs, the three other parts continuing in counterpoint. Next comes one of Handel's greatest and simplest ideas. "King of Kings," the words say, "and Lord of Lords." Sopranos and altos state this with the plainest theme possible—all the words on one note [4]. The effect is like a blast of heralding trumpets. The tenors and basses discover for us that the phrase "forever" fits with the phrase "hallelujah," and sing both phrases in harmony [1]. The sopranos return to "King of Kings" [4] on their own, and gradually climb with it, up the scale, step by step, while the other three voices sing the short "hallelujah" and "forever" phrases [1]. When the sopranos reach the peak of their line, the other parts join in harmony [4].

Roubillac: Handel monument in Westminister Abbey.

Handel breaks the texture up into theme and counterpoint again before beginning the final series of statements: "King of Kings," still in powerful, plain, repeated notes [4]; "hallelujah" and "forever" as rhythmic counterpoint [1]; the angular "he shall reign" in four-part harmony [3]; and finally the chorus together on short Hallelujah's [1], leading to one final, mighty, slowed-down, "Hallelujah."

This is architectural music. Who would look at those four simple "building-block" motives and imagine that such an edifice could be constructed from them? This is part of Handel's genius, but it is also part of the Baroque style. The switch from opera to oratorio did not mean that he scaled down the size of his enterprise; he still dealt with the greatest of ideas on the grandest of scales (*see* color plate 5).

The third part of *Messiah* follows immediately after the "Hallelujah Chorus." It focusses more directly on the idea of redemption, beginning with the aria which Handel is shown holding in the memorial statue at Westminster Abbey: "I know that my redeemer liveth." Later, in a recitative, we hear the bass sing "Behold, I tell you a mystery; we shall not all sleep, but we shall all be chang'd, in a moment, in the twinkling of an eye, at the last trumpet." Not only is this the grandest of ideas, but it is an idea which spoke directly to the average middle-class audience member in a way which all Cleopatra's talk of duty, honor, and fate could not. I suggested earlier that *Messiah's* ultimate message was one of comfort. Another part of that opening phrase may be significant as well. "Comfort ye," it says, "my people." Although the people Isaiah was talking to were the Jews of ancient Israel, Handel's audience knew that the words were directed to them as well. *Giulio Cesare* talked about the fate of a queen; *The Beggar's Opera* talked about the fate of a highwayman; *Messiah* talks about the ultimate fate of average people. Even if we no longer share Handel's perfect faith in redemption, we can still feel the force of the fact that his message of comfort is directed straight at us.

SUMMARY: *Handel's* Messiah *(1741)*

form   Follows the general format of the operas: overture, recitatives, arias (called "airs"), and choruses. Some arias use da capo form; others do not. An example of an aria which does not follow the da capo form is "He shall feed his flock," which is based on a single melodic idea which is gradually expanded in succeeding statements; then a second section repeats the first section four steps higher, moving from alto to soprano range.

melody   Handel uses an enormous variety of melodic types. In the recitatives, the melody is flexible, following the patterns of speech, but at times including word-painting. Some of the arias include a great deal of word-painting and coloratura passages; others (like "He shall feed his flock") are marked by simplicity and directness of statement. Choruses are usually built around "kernel" or "building-block" ideas—short, strongly-identified motives.

harmony	Generally consonant, with strong harmonic movement based on clear V-I relationships and a regular harmonic rhythm (rate at which the chords change).
rhythm	Often free and irregular in the recitatives, but in the arias and choruses the underlying rhythm provides a consistent and regular pulse, related to the harmonic rhythm. In melodic lines, rhythmic patterns serve expressive purposes. For example, "He shall feed his flock" is based on a gently rocking, lullaby-like rhythm; the rhythms of the various motives in the "Hallelujah" chorus help create their individual identity and meaning.
texture	Vocal parts dominate. The orchestra generally supplies the strong bass line typical of the Baroque; interior parts support and respond to the vocal lines.
timbre	Chorus, soloists, and orchestra with harpsichord or organ.
function	Directed towards a wide public audience. Handel's oratorios were originally designed for performance in theaters; their resemblance to operas made them initially unacceptable for church performance. Today the oratorio is regularly performed in both church and concert hall.
text	Devised by Charles Jennens from brief quotations from the King James version of the Bible, all relating to the coming of the Messiah and the possibilities for redemption which his coming represents.

Secular Instrumental Music

It is a little ironic that most of what is remembered of Baroque Italian opera was written in England by a German, Handel. Italian Baroque composers wrote operas, but their principal accomplishments that come down to us are in the form of instrumental music. People who go to symphony orchestra concerts, or, for that matter, to jazz concerts, see nothing remarkable in the idea of sitting down to listen to instrumental music. But before the Baroque period this was a relatively rare occurrence. Almost all religious music was written around words; court songs required words as well, of course; what instrumental music there was was often designed for dance rather than plain listening. Even the instrumental music which was designed for listening was frequently based on dance forms. For example, the lute song composer John Dowland (*see* Chapters 7 and 15) wrote pieces for the lute alone, based on popular dance forms like the slow *pavane* and the leaping *galliard*.

The Baroque Sonata and Concerto

The Baroque period saw the development of forms designed specifically for instrumental music performance. Two such forms are the **sonata** and the **concerto.** The word sonata originally meant simply that it was a piece to be sounded, or played, rather than sung. It developed into a form created to feature a solo instrument, or a solo instrument with keyboard accompaniment. The concerto also features a soloist, or at times a small group of soloists, heard in combination with an orchestra. Two Italian composers influential in the development of these forms are Domenico Scarlatti (1685–1757) and Antonio Vivaldi (1678–1741). Since Scarlatti wrote over 500 keyboard sonatas, and Vivaldi wrote about 500 concertos, they seem appropriate choices to exemplify these forms.

Scarlatti's patron was a Spanish princess, later Queen. She was also his pupil, and many of the sonatas were written for her to learn to play. They were also used in court entertainments with Scarlatti performing, and some few he published with these prefatory remarks:

> Reader! Whether you be Dilettante or Professor, in these Compositions do not expect any profound Learning, but rather an ingenious jesting with Art, to accommodate you to the Mastery of the Harpsichord.

These remarks speak directly to the teaching function the pieces were intended to have in their published form (a form which made them available to the middle classes.) The closest picture of the function they might have had in court entertainments was given by Robert Browning in his poem "A Toccata of Galuppi's," where he pictures Galuppi, another Italian master, performing his compositions for an aristocratic audience:

> Did young people take their pleasure when the sea was warm in May?
> Balls and masks [masquerades] begun at midnight, burning ever to midday . . .

Browning imagines a woman pausing momentarily to listen, then saying:

> "Brave Galuppi! that was music, good alike at grave and gay!
> I can always leave off talking when I hear a master play!"

Scarlatti's Sonata in D Major

Writing for an audience like this, Scarlatti could not create works which required long attention or deep thought. His sonatas are short, brilliant, and filled with dramatic effects. The D-major Sonata, K. 119, begins with a pounding rhythm under a melody which climbs steadily higher using only the notes from a D-major chord.

First few measures

From here the music goes immediately into an episode characterized by left-hand runs, and then to a passage where the bass line moves slowly downward, while the right hand has a rhythm like that of a flamenco guitar.

Measures 18–21, flamenco-like rhythm

All through this section Scarlatti emphasizes the music's beat and its rhythmic patterns rather than its melodic or harmonic development. It doesn't seem far-fetched to imagine that he was remembering Spanish folk-dance guitar music as he wrote this, transforming the material into patterns idiomatic, that is, ideally suited, for the harpsichord.

A harmonic shift brings the section to a close. The shift is based on a simple action—the introduction of a G sharp. This one note might not seem important when it is first heard. But there is no G sharp in the key of D; G sharp is instead the leading tone of the A-major scale. Scarlatti makes sure that we take the hint. There are ten G sharp's in the next eight measures, and all are found in the chord (a dominant seventh) which provides the strongest possible movement to A major, climaxing with a short cadenza using a four-octave scale based on that chord.

Measures 34–35, cadenza

Seventeenth-century harpsichord similar to one played by Scarlatti. *(Metropolitan Museum of Art, The Crosby Brown Collection of Musical Instruments, 1889)*

We are prepared for the next section to start in A, but it is A minor rather than A major which we hear, and with the shift from major to minor the mood of the sonata changes. The melody now becomes important; it is a delicate melodic line, somewhat dissonant and angular. As it is repeated, the music focusses first on a single phrase from this melody, then on one note as the accompanying texture grows thicker and heavier, to the point where the right-hand chord includes six notes:

Measure 63, six-note chord

(To play this chord with a normal, five-fingered hand, you must place your thumb sideways so it covers the two bottom notes, D and E.) Again, this is writing which is idiomatic for the harpsichord, which, unlike the piano, cannot make a crescendo on a single note. By gradually making the texture thicker and heavier Scarlatti creates the effect of a crescendo on his instrument. He also creates an emotional effect, a feeling of increased tension and foreboding, of storm clouds gathering. In the next instant, the clouds blow away, as the texture thins again, the melody softens, and the harmonies resolve into a pleasant, consonant A major. All this constitutes the first half of the form, and it is repeated.

The second half of the form will also be repeated. In its first section, it goes through a number of different keys: we hear suggestions of D minor, A major, B minor, and E minor as once again the texture thickens. Its tension seems about to resolve back to the starting key of D major, but instead it lands on D minor. Again, the melody focusses down onto a single phrase and then a single note, as the texture thickens, eventually to present us with 11-note chords:

Measure 167, 11-note chord

These do finally take us back to a quick and happy-sounding D major.

The overall form of the sonata can be described as follows:

First Half (repeated)	**Second Half (repeated)**
1. rhythmic motives in D major, leading to the dominant-seventh chord of A.	1. go through several keys, leading to the dominant-seventh chord of D.
2. angular melody in A minor, followed by thick chords and increasing tension.	2. angular melody in D minor, followed by thick chords and increasing tension.
3. return to rhythmic motives, this time in A major.	3. return to rhythmic motives, this time in D major.

Tonal Centers to Create Larger Forms

The structure just described is based on key relationships. Establish a tonal center—in this case, the key of D. Move away from it—in this case ending up five steps away, on A. This marks the end of the first half. In the second half, go through some other keys, and then return to the original key—in this case, D.

A structure of this sort is to some extent a "subliminal" one, one that takes place below the level of conscious attention. It is easy to be conscious of changes in melody and texture, but a well-done modulation from one key to another does not draw attention to itself. A listener can learn consciously to notice modulations, but a composer like Scarlatti would probably not have expected such attention. All he assumes is that the listener will acquire a subconscious sense of the original tonal center, enough so that the modulation will feel like a lifting away, and the later modulations which come back to the original tonal center will feel like a return, a relaxation, a completion of the pattern.

Structures based on key relationships were not possible before the development of the system of tonality, which allowed the composer to establish the sense of one key and then another. The kind of pattern Scarlatti used in his sonatas is a basic one, both in the sense that it is relatively simple, and in the sense that it was to form the basis for much longer and larger structures during the century and a half after his death—in poverty, not because he had been neglected during his career, but because he was addicted to gambling—in 1757.

SUMMARY: *Scarlatti's* **Sonata in D Major,** *K. 119, L. 415*
                  (ca. 1730–1750)

melody	Two basic melody types: rhythmic motives in major keys, melodic motives in minor.
harmony	Moves between major and minor; modulates; is mostly consonant during rhythmic, major episodes, but becomes more dissonant underneath minor melody, and becomes quite dissonant as texture thickens during crescendos.
rhythm	Strong pulse in "three," especially in major sections.
form	"Binary form," since the sonata is divided into two halves. The first half modulates from D major to A major, and is repeated; the second half goes through several keys before returning to D major, and is also repeated. Can be summarized as AABB.
texture	In a few measures, the writing is linear for both hands, but in general Scarlatti gives the right hand the melody, the left hand the accompaniment. The nature of the accompaniment varies considerably, from single-note patterns, to repeated chords, to very heavy, thick chords, and back again to single notes.
timbre	Solo harpsichord; writing style pushes the instrument to extremes. If you were buying a harpsichord, this would be a good piece to try it out on.
function	Principally used as aristocratic entertainment, but also as teaching music for Scarlatti's patron, and for the larger public reached through publication.

Vivaldi

By contemporary standards, Vivaldi's life story can only be called bizarre. He was the son of a barber who was also a professional musician, a violin player at St. Mark's Cathedral in Venice. He became a priest, not an unusual career choice for a serious musician in the seventeenth century, becoming known as the "Red Priest" because of his red hair. He asked for, and was granted, relief from his priestly Mass-saying duties, on the grounds that he suffered from chest pains. He began working for an orphanage and home for unwanted girls, and at the same time began an independent career as virtuoso performer on the violin, composer and conductor of operas, and, eventually, as opera producer as well. His health problems seem not to have hindered his career as conductor, performer, and producer. He did, however, take a nurse along with him on his tours. This nurse was the sister of Anna Giraud, the woman who was his constant companion, and performed the leading female roles in his operas. Priest-composer, singer-mistress, and sister-nurse lived happily together, and Vivaldi enjoyed a long and productive career.

It is the most hum-drum aspect of this colorful life which is most important for a study of his concerto-writing—his employment as music master at the girls' orphanage. The musical schooling there was thorough, and the concerts the girls gave became famous. Vivaldi wrote, and was required to write, concertos to feature many of the different performers, on a wide variety of instruments. Before Vivaldi, the most common kind of concerto was a **concerto grosso,** where a group of string players alternated with the orchestra playing as an ensemble. Vivaldi's pupils were not all string players, however, and he had to develop a solo concerto form which would fit flute, oboe, trumpet, and horn as well as violin. He also wrote concertos for himself to play, for other professional players, and for talented amateurs. But it seems safe to assume that the development of the solo concerto in his hands resulted principally from the need to provide them (at a rate something like two per month) for the concerts given at the girls' school.

The twentieth-century Italian composer Luigi Dallapiccola accused Vivaldi of writing "a single concerto 600 times." Perhaps Dallapiccola was a little envious. The modern composer is expected, when writing a concerto, to produce a substantial work which fully utilizes all the resources of the modern orchestra, and which gives constant evidence of originality. Vivaldi, like other Baroque composers, out of practical necessity used formulas in his writing. With a few strong musical ideas, he could spin out a concerto according to certain well worked-out forms—he boasted that he could write a concerto faster than a copyist could copy it. He did use formulas, then, but he controlled them, and varied them, and made them servants to the amazing range of his musical ideas.

Vivaldi's "Il Cardellino"

Vivaldi's Flute Concerto in D Major, called "Il Cardellino" ("The Goldfinch") provides a good example of his concerto-writing style. It opens with a strong, rhythmic theme, played in unison by the small string orchestra, interspersed with some arpeggios from the flute. This theme is called the **"ritornello,"** the "little return." It is a theme which stays identified with the orchestra; it will return in one form or another several times throughout the movement.

Beginning of ritornello theme

Next comes the flute's first solo passage. It takes the form of a cadenza in which Vivaldi runs through an array of musical bird-like songs, illustrating the flute's ability to imitate or improve on nature, and also the player's virtuoso ability on the flute.

The orchestra returns with the ritornello, this time in shortened form. Then the flute again, this time heard with a fuller orchestral accompaniment. Two characteristic Baroque devices appear here. One is the **sequence.** A melodic idea is played, then repeated, a step or two down (or up), then repeated once or twice more, each time moving further in the same direction. In the accompaniment we hear the kind of rhythmic pulse which is sometimes called "motoric"—an even, constantly throbbing, forward-moving pulse.

(Sequence pattern starts)   (First repeat of pattern, one step down)

("Motoric" rhythm in accompaniment)

Another brief ritornello from the orchestra, this time in a minor key, and the flute introduces new solo material, more lyrical this time, and with some imitation from the accompaniment. This is the longest solo section, and after it the orchestra returns for the final ritornello, which closes the movement.

For the second, slow movement, Vivaldi thins out his texture to the barest minimum of melody and bass line. The rhythm is that of a slow and stately dance, derived from a Sicilian folk dance and thus called a *siciliana.* The harmonies are simple and consonant, the harmonic movement slow. The movement is binary in form, like a Scarlatti sonata: the first half (repeated) starts in D, and modulates to A. The second half (also repeated) goes into a minor key before returning to D. But what is most striking is the aspect most typically Baroque—the musical energy generated in the relationship between melody and bass line. The bass line creates a feeling of harmonic progression as it goes

This mid-18th-century German engraving shows a typical Baroque orchestra with the 'cello and harpsichord in the foreground and the other performers arranged behind the harpsichord.

along, yet at the same time it has a line, a melodic shape, of its own; against this plays a melody which is tied to it and yet soars free from it. This relationship between melody and bass line can also be heard in Dido's lament from Purcell's *Dido and Aeneas* (*see* Chapter 11) and in Cleopatra's aria from Handel's *Giulio Cesare* (*see* Chapter 16). It is most evident in the closing measures of Vivaldi's slow movement:

This isn't just Baroque; it's boiled-down essence of Baroque. The disgruntled Dallapiccola could say that Purcell, Handel, and Vivaldi were all using the same formula, which is in a sense true. What it illustrates is an important difference between science and music. In science, a good formula produces the same result every time. In music, a good formula allows the results to be different.

The third movement goes back to the ritornello form and allegro tempo of the first movement. The ritornello theme is characterized by a quick, rhythmic scale:

Ritornello theme, third movement

while the flute is once again given melodies reminiscent of bird songs. In developing this pattern—first movement fast and virtuosic, second movement slow and lyrical, third movement fast and light—Vivaldi determined the pattern of concerto-writing for generations to come.

SUMMARY: *Vivaldi's* **Flute Concerto in D,** *"Il Cardellino"* *(ca. 1720–1730)*

form	Three movements: fast-slow-fast. First and last movements use *ritornello* form; slow movement is in binary form.
melody	Variety of types. Flute solos are virtuosic and imitate bird songs. Orchestral *ritornellos* are defined by their rhythmic character as well as by their melodic shape.
harmony	Consonant. Harmonic movement largely based on V-I relationship. Modulations used to give energy to the formal structures.
rhythm	Always regular, with a constant pulse running through each movement, except during the brief flute cadenza. A "motoric" quality in the first and last movements.
texture	Usually characterized by one or two strong lines. Frequently the entire ensemble plays in unison; another favorite device is to have two melodic ideas working against each other while another instrument or section marks time with a constant pulse. The slow movement in particular is characterized by the simplest and clearest of relationships between melody and bass line.
timbre	Originally written for flute, oboe, violin, bassoon, and continuo (harpsichord and 'cello). Later version, revised for publication, replaces oboe and bassoon with strings. (*See* illustration, page 152.)
function	Probably intended first for public concert performance, later published. The public concerts would have had a select and largely aristocratic audience. In published form the work would have been available to small amateur groups as well, since it could be performed with just five or six players.

J.S. Bach

Genius and Practicality

Today our idea of behavior befitting a genius includes eccentricity, if not actual craziness. The Baroque composers we have looked at so far fit this mold at least to some extent. Handel worked in bouts of furious creativity, although he also engaged in such ungenius-like activities as investing in the stock market. Scarlatti's career was a secure and stable one, much of it devoted to one patron, but he did have the eccentricity of his gambling addiction. Vivaldi's life was unusual by any standard. But Johann Sebastian Bach, perhaps the Baroque's greatest genius, had the most conventional of lives and careers.

He was born in 1685, the son of a town musician. Music was the traditional profession of the Bach family. For over two centuries the family supplied musicians for their part of Germany; of 60 male Bachs known from this time only seven were not musicians. This goes some way towards explaining Bach's no-nonsense attitude towards his art: as well as being art for him, it was also trade and craft. By the time he was 18 he was working as a church organist. After his first marriage, he became court musician to the Duke of Weimar, his main duty being that of organist for the palace church. Then in 1717 he was offered a court musician's post, as musical director for Prince Leopold of Cöthen (a small city near Leipzig). Here he composed chamber music in various forms, including sonatas and concertos, and began his great teaching work, the *Well-Tempered Clavier* (*see* Chapter 5). In 1720 his wife died, leaving him with four children (three others had died in infancy). A year later, he married again. His second wife, Anna Magdalena, was the daughter of a musician, herself a singer. They were to have thirteen children together, only six of whom survived infancy. Five of the six sons from the two marriages continued the family tradition, becoming musicians themselves.

St. Thomas's church in Leipzig, Germany, where in 1723 Bach became cantor.

In 1723, Bach became Cantor of St. Thomas's church in Leipzig, one of Germany's most important Lutheran churches. His duties as Cantor were strenuous. He taught at St. Thomas's school, training boys in singing, playing, theory and composition. He was expected to use these students in supplying music for four different churches. Not all the churches conducted services on an equally grand scale—one church got only the benefit of the least capable boys singing hymns. But the two principal churches featured elaborate musical settings in their religious observances. This responsibility was Bach's from the ground up. He wrote the music, copied the parts (a task his wife helped with), trained the singers and instrumentalists, rehearsed with them, and led the choir and orchestra through the performances.

Today a church musician relies largely on published works. In Bach's time, publications were few, and church services elaborate. A typical service might begin with organ music, followed by a short choral piece. Then, after a reading from the Bible, the organist played a prélude based on the chorale of the day, followed by the singing of the chorale. A further Bible reading preceded the first part of the main musical work, the *cantata,* which was like a miniature oratorio, with recitatives, arias, and choruses. It was based not on the Bible but on a poetic religious text, often devised for the particular day being celebrated. After the first part of the cantata came the sermon; after the sermon, the congregation would join in singing hymns. Then came the second part of the cantata. Finally, the choir might sing chorales, alternating with the organist playing préludes based upon them, during the taking of communion.

Bach's main responsibility as a composer was to write the cantatas—he composed about 150 of them during his first four years at St. Thomas's. Eventually, he wrote five complete yearly cycles, over 300 works, some of which have been lost.

There is an irony here. We devote time and study to the preservation of music from the past, and as a result Bach's works are performed in concert halls and churches, on radio and record, and are written about in books like this one. Yet the works exist partly because Bach's own society cared so little for past music, instead demanding an almost constant stream of new compositions from its musicians.

Bach held his position as Cantor from 1723 until his death in 1750. As might be expected in any such long relationship, continuous harmony did not prevail. The amount of discord between him and his employers, the town council, may be exaggerated in our eyes, since it is only matters of complaint and controversy which get preserved in council records; nobody writes angry letters when things are running smoothly. Anyone who has lived in a town with a high school and a school board would find these controversies familiar. The council appoints a young administrator; Bach resents his attempts to exert authority. On another occasion Bach complains because he is being given students who aren't talented, bright, or capable enough. A small controversy outside of school matters arises when a gentleman of Leipzig marries in an out-of-town church. Bach and two of his colleagues write to the town council demanding that the man be required to pay the standard music fees anyway (which in fact the council eventually made the man do.) This controversy does not show Bach in a particularly flattering light, but it is significant for what it reveals about his relationship with the community. Simply put, he was part of it. Supplying music for weddings and funerals (especially funerals) was a large portion of his income. His music was a major part of the community's life. Although he became relatively famous, especially for his organ playing, and could have taken other posts, and did once threaten to take another post, the evidence indicates that he was content in his work.

This leaves the question about his genius. Bach was a hard-working, practical musician, a good father, affectionate husband, sound teacher—but so were other men. Most of his music he wrote as occasions demanded him to. In com-

Bach performing at the organ.

posing a cantata he was not thinking of us, two and a half centuries to come; he was thinking of a specific church, of specific singers on a specific Leipzig Sunday. We could say that he was also thinking of God, and he was, but other composers thought of God, and their music did not turn out divine. What can we conclude from this? First, that there is something wrong with our penchant for seeing genius as related to eccentric or aberrant behavior. Bach proves that genius can be calm, middle-class, and conventional, and still be genius. Second, that a culture's demand for music is not sufficient cause for genius to occur. Bach's works were a hundred times better than they needed to be. Were they one-hundredth as good, he could have had the same degree of material success—as indeed, many of the less-talented members of his family did. Third, that while a culture's demand for music is not sufficient to cause genius to exist, it still is necessary if that genius is to flourish. If Bach had been born into a society which did not demand a new cantata every Sunday, he would not have been Bach.

"Little" Organ Fugue in G Minor

It was probably around 1709, during his time as organist and court composer to the Duke of Weimar, that Bach wrote his *Fugue in G Minor for Organ* ("The Little"). It illustrates his, and the Baroque's, solution to the problem of polyphonic writing.

As detailed in this engraving, air was supplied to the organ by three bellows operated by pulling down and releasing long wooden handles.

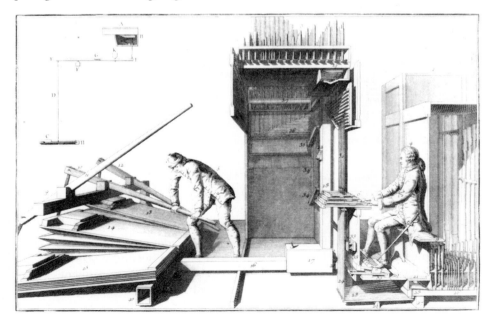

The great difficulty with writing in a many-voiced texture is to give the listener the sense of hearing a number of independent musical lines concurrently but not chaotically. As we have noted earlier, polyphony, if it occurs in real life, does not occur in an understandable way; we can't make sense of four conversations going on at once, or, for that matter, of four mockingbirds singing at the same time.

To this typical problem of writing polyphony the Baroque period adds another. Not only do the several voices have to be heard at the same time, each one maintaining its identity while mixing comfortably with the others, but also their combination must create a sense of harmonic movement, of a progression of chords. For example, in a given measure the notes which occur on beat two might have to add up to the sound of a V chord, which would mean that the notes on beat three would probably have to add up to the sound of a I chord.

Measure 52 of G Minor Organ Fugue,   The chords created by beats two and
beats two and three   three (V-I in C minor)

Each of several voices must, then, have independence along the music's horizontal paths, its melodies, while lining up into progressions of chords along the vertical axes of its harmonies.

Bach's organ fugue begins with a solitary statement of a melodic idea, called the *subject*. It is a "spiralling" Baroque idea, starting with a simple phrase

which creates just enough tension to demand a continuing, longer phrase

which in turn demands a longer response, finally leading to a quick and energetic running passage which climaxes in the entry of the second voice.

Since the Baroque fugue must have regular harmonic movement, Bach creates a subject with nice clear harmonies already embedded within it. For example, the first phrase is made of the notes of the G-minor chord (I); the second phrase ends with the notes of the D-major chord (the V chord in G minor.) The continuing phrases are also full of V-I implications.

In addition, the subject makes a rhythmic statement. Its beat is stated with strength and clarity in the opening phrase, and it gradually picks up steam towards the kind of "motoric" movement so often characteristic of Bach fugues, and of Baroque style in general.

The second voice enters in imitation of the first, but a fourth lower, while the top voice continues in counterpoint (this counterpoint is called the counter-subject).

Second voice enters, playing subject four steps down; first voice continues in counterpoint

Next the third voice enters, playing the subject on the same pitches as the first statement, just an octave lower. Above it, the two top voices continue in counterpoint. Then the lowest voice enters, while two of the other three play the counterpoint. With this last entrance, which Bach cuts a little short, we have heard the *exposition* section. It is followed by an *episode,* a little breathing space in the structure, where Bach gives us a few simple sequences. We hear the subject again, in what would be the alto voice; it is discontinued but picked up by the soprano, while the bass holds a tone for three measures. This is called a **pedal tone,** named for the foot pedals of the organ, although the term can be applied to a note in any voice which is held while other voices change their harmonies. Looking back at the original subject, we can see that the pedal tone implication is another factor which Bach had built into it:

Measures three and four of the subject, showing repeated Ds

After this pedal tone, there is a change of mood, as the fugue shifts into B-flat major. The alto voice begins to state the subject; the tenor voice picks it up. There is another episode before the bass voice plays the subject, still in B-flat major. But now the texture is growing denser. After another episode, the subject returns to the soprano, back in a minor key. Bach uses the episode after this statement to increase markedly the harmonic tension in order to build up to the final return of the subject, in the bass voice, in the home key:

Final episode, leading into last return of subject

In a longer fugue, Bach would have returned with full expositions after each episode, taking the returning subject through all four voices. But even in this "Little" fugue we can hear the Baroque combination of the horizontal and vertical: writing which gives a strong sense of independent melodic lines while at the same time conveying a strong sense of the movement of harmonies. As a device for achieving this combination, the Baroque fugue is the most sophisticated form music has invented, and Bach is universally recognized as its greatest practitioner. Whenever the technique is taught today, his are the examples which are studied. Students struggling with the form can generally take some comfort from the fact that Bach almost always broke a rule or two himself; he believed in learning the rules, but not in following them slavishly.

SUMMARY: *J. S. Bach's* "Little" Organ Fugue in G Minor *(ca. 1709)*

melody	An energetic Baroque melody which mixes conjunct and disjunct motion, "spiralling" from an initial idea. It contains harmonic implications within it, including V-I relationships and pedal tones.
harmony	Strong sense of harmonic motion, usually based on V-I relationships; modulations away from and back to original key.
rhythm	Strong quarter-note beat continues from beginning to end. Bach increases rhythmic energy by "filling-in" the spaces between the beats with eighth notes and then sixteenth notes.
form	A shortened version of the fugue form. One complete exposition at the beginning (subject treated in all four voices); then episodes alternate with expositions, but the expositions are incomplete in that the subject is usually stated in only one voice.
texture	Four-voice polyphony.
timbre	Pipe organ.
function	Probably first used as an organ introduction to a church service—a kind of prélude or overture to the service. Still used for similar purposes today but also as a concert piece for organ.

St. Matthew Passion

The church required a cantata for every Sunday, but in addition certain special days demanded special music. One of these was Good Friday, the Friday before Easter. Since this is the day which commemorates the day of Jesus's crucifixion, the appropriate text is from one of the gospel accounts of the suffering and death of Jesus, called the "Passion."

The Passion has a long history of musical settings, back into the period of plainchant. By Bach's time, what had begun as a recitation of words from the Bible had grown into a more dramatic, oratorio-like form, with arias and choruses inserted into the Biblical passages. Bach composed his "The Passion of Our Lord According to St. Matthew" in 1729 (some say 1727), at a time when he had built up his cantata repertory to the point where he no longer needed to compose a new one every week. At the same time, his cantata writing experience had prepared him well for this monumental project, since it called for the development and expansion of many of his cantata-writing techniques. We will look at just one small section of the work, the numbers surrounding the crucifixion itself, beginning with the alto recitative "Ah, Golgotha."

The recitative is based on an interpolated text, words not found in the Bible, but written by Bach's literary collaborator, Picander. "Ah, Golgotha," it begins, "Unhappy Golgotha!" referring to the hill (the name means "place like a skull") where Jesus was crucified. The alto is singing a kind of personal reflection—what Golgotha means to me—which helps to provide a guide or interpretation of the Biblical text. It is an accompanied recitative; in addition to the continuo part ('cello plus organ) there is instrumental accompaniment by two oboes.

The particular oboe timbre seems an essential part of the musical texture. They repeat their pattern over and over again, with only slight variation:

The repetitions create a kind of drone which seems appropriate to this bleak place; in addition, they may be marking time for us, reminding us that Christ's life is ebbing away as we listen. Perhaps accidentally, the oboes as instruments have a Middle Eastern connotation, and thus seem appropriate to the atmosphere of this particular Middle Eastern spot. (I say "perhaps accidentally" because it seems unlikely that Bach or his audience would have had much acquaintance with Middle Eastern music.) On a more general level, Bach associates woodwinds with the human and strings with the divine, throughout the work.

The bleak recitative turns into a joyful aria. In the aria the alto reinterprets the image of the crucifixion. Where it had been the cause of grief, it now becomes the image of hope, as Jesus's outstretched arms become symbols of welcome and acceptance, not a means of death. The two oboes continue, but now are not locked so securely in tandem, but chase each other with a lively and upward-climbing theme:

The alto asks us to come and find rest in Jesus's arms. This could be a merely rhetorical request, but it is given dramatic life by the sudden interjections from the chorus: "Where?" the chorus asks. "In Jesus's arms," the alto replies. Her line becomes rich and decorated, with long melismas, yet they are not the virtuoso coloratura passages Handel was so fond of. Perhaps this is because Bach was working with his own singers and students—the alto part would have been sung by a boy—and not with professional opera singers.

We hear next the voice of Matthew. These are the words he speaks in the Bible, recounting with simplicity and directness the fateful moments leading up to Jesus's death. Bach sets them in recitative *secco;* that is, "dry" recitative, accompanied only by the continuo part. "And at the ninth hour," Matthew says, (around three in the afternoon) "Jesus cried aloud, and spoke." Here Bach gives us the voice of Jesus, as he cries "My God, My God, why hast thou forsaken me?"

Jesus has spoken before in the Passion, always accompanied by a "halo" of strings. Here at his weakest and most human of moments, there is no halo, only the sustained tones of the continuo underneath.

It is not a wild or uncontrolled outcry. Its anguish comes from its dissonance against the accompanying harmony, especially in the second phrase. The words are, as in the Bible, given first in Jesus's Hebrew, giving them a Jewish flavor which may carry over into the melodic line as well. The melody is certainly far

removed from the plainchant setting which earlier Lutheran composers had
adopted:

Matthew translates these last words into German and then goes on to describe
the crowd's reaction. But it is not really a description in Bach's setting, for he
gives us the crowd's reaction, making the chorus become the crowd as they
shout out "He calls for Elias!" And then, after one of them offers Jesus some
vinegar (thought to reduce pain), the rest say "Stop, stop, let's see if Elias will
come to help him." Bach does not turn this moment into a morality play, a
chance for the congregation to feel self-righteous. The crowd is not portrayed
as evil, merely human; bystanders to an event which they do not understand,
but which fills them with the nervous excitement conveyed in the violins:

God of course does not descend, and Matthew reports Jesus's death in simple
recitative. Bach's response to the event is a chorale. This is outside the text and
outside the drama. It is a Lutheran hymn, and follows the same form heard in "A
Mighty Fortress Is Our God." Here it is set in four-part harmony. It is one of
Bach's favorite hymns, judging from how frequently he used it, and he uses it
five times, with different words and harmonizations, in the Passion. It comes
back to us with the weight of these repetitions. For a member of Bach's congregation, the hymn also carries the weight of its connection with the Lutheran
church—not just familiarity, but a sense of possession, an identification of this
music with their church. Indeed, the congregation may have sung with the
melody (although the words Bach uses here are from the hymn's ninth stanza,
so it is difficult to imagine many people knowing them.) In effect, then, the
music steps outside the action, allowing the congregation to commune in a moment of consolation which relates Christ's death to their own: "At my moment
of death," the verse says, "help release me from my anguish."

Then, back to the drama. "And behold," Matthew continues, "the veil of the
temple was torn in two, from the top to the bottom, and the earth quaked, and
the rocks split open." He sings of these events with a phenomenally active vocal
line, while the organ word-paints beneath him. Then, the Roman guard and
those who were with him are filled with a new awareness. The chorus plays
their part, supported by the orchestra. The moment is a brief one, only two
measures long, with four independent parts creating a dense contrapuntal tex-

ture. But the texture is as clear as the light which has struck them: "Truly, this was the son of God."

Wahr-lich, die — ser ist Got - tes Sohn____ ge-we - sen.

Wahr-lich, die — ser ist Got - tes Sohn__ ge - we — sen.

Wahr-lich, wahr-lich, die - ser ist Got — tes Sohn ge - we — sen.

Wahr-lich, die — ser ist Got tes Sohn__ ge - we — sen.

Polyphony has a traditional and functional relationship with religious music; it seems to illustrate that the whole is greater than the sum of its parts, that separate strands can mysteriously unite. There is an additional dramatic element in this instance. If Bach had written these measures in a homophonic texture, like a chorale, they would seem to express an axiom, a given truth.

Not Bach's version—"Truly, this . . . " in homophonic texture

The polyphonic texture, by contrast, gives a sense of the different voices gradually finding their way to this realization, taking separate paths to the same conclusion. There is more drama in watching the realization dawn than in seeing it already known.

Bach was fond of using hidden symbolism in his scores. For example, he occasionally used a theme based on the letters of his name ("H" in German stands for "B-natural"). One authority claims that the bass part in this choral episode also stands for Bach's name, since by simple number code (A = 1, B = 2, etc.) the letters in his name add up to 14, and there are 14 notes to the voice part. Of course there are 14 notes in many melody lines, including for example the Beatles song "If I Fell" ("If I fell in love with you would you promise to be true") and I could use the same sort of symbolism to prove that Bach was writing about my cat (the letters in "Foxy" add up to 70, and there are 70 notes in the orchestra part.)

More important than number symbolism is dramatic content. Bach's efforts are directed towards bringing the drama home to his listeners, at making the events both real to them and meaningful. The alto's recitative creates the scene's atmosphere; her aria illuminates its significance; the choral interjections bring the listeners into the dialogue. We see Jesus at his most vulnerable, the crowd in its wild excitement, and Matthew, reporting on events and feeling their import himself. The chorale brings the congregation into the middle of the piece, Matthew recounts the events after Jesus's death, and the chorus responds with its moment of enlightenment.

All of this occurs in just a small (although certainly crucial) section, approximately one-twentieth of the work as a whole. The *St. Matthew Passion* is truly monumental—Bach, like Handel, shares the Baroque fondness for great subjects on a grand scale. But where *Messiah's* great subject is the possibility of redemption, Bach's great subject is the death of Christ. The subjects, though related, are distinct. The opening "Comfort ye" of *Messiah* sets the general tone of the work. Bach's *St. Matthew Passion* is far less comforting or comfortable. "Come daughters, share my mourning," are its first words, and the minor key, the bass pedal tones, and frequent use of diminished harmonies support this sentiment and continue to do so throughout the work. More significant are the next words: a command to "See Him." This is surely Bach's aim, to make the events real enough for us to see and feel them. There are moments of happiness and peace to be found, but we are never allowed to look away for long. *Messiah*, written for a general public, transplants much easier into the concert hall or (via technology) the living room than does the *St. Matthew Passion*. This is not a criticism of Bach's work. Rather it illustrates the degree to which the work was committed to its subject matter and to its audience.

From the Medieval through the Renaissance periods, the church was a dominant force, often the principal patron of music. In Bach's time this influence was waning. One way of looking at his music is to see it as a culmination of the religious tradition—of the polyphonic writing that began in the late Middle Ages and continued through the times of Machaut, des Prez, Palestrina, and on into Bach's own time. This is a view which is commonly held today, and it is a correct one, but not complete. Another way of regarding Bach's music is to concentrate on its capacity for dramatic and emotional realism, and for direct and immediate appeal to its audience. In this respect Bach's style looks forward, not back, predicting trends which would develop in the century after his death.

SUMMARY: *J. S. Bach's* The Passion of Our Lord According to St. Matthew *(1727 or 1729)*

melody	Several different melodic types. As usual, the most flexibly expressive melodies are in the recitatives. In the chorales, Bach uses the traditional Lutheran tunes, giving them his own harmonizations. In arias and especially in choruses, he likes to create melodies with their own rhythmic "signatures," rhythmic patterns which are repeated throughout the number.
harmony	Minor keys heard more often than major. Harmonic tension created by the use of diminished chords and pedal tones.
rhythm	Except in *secco* recitatives, the rhythmic pulse tends to be strong, steady, and even.
form	Some of the same elements found in opera and oratorio: instrumental episodes, recitatives, both *secco* and accompanied, arias, and choruses. In addition, Bach includes chorales—choral settings of Lutheran hymns. By bringing the same chorale tune back several times, in different keys and harmonizations, he uses it to create structural unity.
texture	Generally polyphonic in choruses, homophonic in chorales, recitatives and arias characterized by strong bass and melody lines.
timbre	Designed for two choruses, each with its own small orchestra and continuo accompaniment, plus solo singers. The orchestras include two flutes, two oboes, violins and violas. The continuo is supplied by organ and 'cello.
function	Designed for Good Friday services.
text	Three sources: St. Matthew's words in the Bible; new text written by Picander; words to the Lutheran hymns.

ALTO RECITATIVE:

Ach, Golgotha, unsel'ges Golgotha! Der Herr der Herrlichkeit muss schimpflich hier verderben, der Segen und das Heil der Welt wird als ein Fluch an's Kreuz gestellt. Dem Schöpfer Himmels und der Erden soll Erd' und Luft entzogen werden; die Unschuld muss hier schuldig sterben. Das gehet meiner Seele nah; ach Golgotha, unsel'ges Golgotha!

Ah, Golgotha, unhappy Golgotha! Here the Lord of Glory was vilely rejected. Here the blessed Saviour of the world hangs upon the accursed tree. The God who created heaven and earth, from earth and sky must be taken, though innocent must die as though guilty. Ah, how this grief afflicts my soul. Ah, Golgotha, unhappy Golgotha.

ALTO ARIA:
Sehet, Jesus hat die Hand,
uns zu fassen ausgespannt,
Kommt [Wohin?], Kommt [Wohin?]
in Jesu Armen such Erlösung,
nehmt Erbarmen, suchet!
Lebet, lebet,
sterbet, ruhet hier,
Ihr verlass'nen Küchlein ihr,
bleibet in Jesu Armen.

See Jesus's outstetched hands! He
draws us to Himself! Come [Come
where?] In Jesu's bosom. Seek
redemption, seek mercy. Live, die,
rest here, you who are abandoned
and rejected, rest in Jesu's arms.

ST. MATTHEW:
Und von der sechsten Stunde an
ward eine Finsternis über dan
ganze Land, bis zu neunten
Stunde. Und um die neunte
Stunde schreie Jesus laut, und
sprach:

And from the sixth hour there was
darkness over the land until the
ninth hour. And about the ninth
hour, Jesus cried aloud, saying:

JESUS:
Eli, Eli, lama, lama
asabthani!

"Eli, Eli, lama sabachthani."

ST. MATTHEW:
Das ist: Mein Gott, mein Gott,
warum hast du mich verlassen?
Etliche aber, die da standen,
da sie das höreten, sprachen sie.

That is: "My God, my God, why hast
thou forsaken me?" Some of them
that stood there, when they
heard this, said:

CHORUS:
Der rufet den Elias

He calls for Elias!

ST. MATTHEW:
Und bald lief einer unter
ihnen, nahm einen Schwamm, und
füllete ihn mit Essig, und
stekkete ihn auf ein Rohr, und
tränkete ihn. Die andern aber
Sprachen:

And straightaway one of them ran,
and took a sponge, and filled it
with vinegar, and put it on a reed,
and gave it to Him to drink. The
others said:

CHORUS:
Halt, halt, lass sehen, ob
Elias komme, und ihm helfe.

Stop, stop, let us see whether Elias
will come to help him.

ST. MATTHEW:
Aber Jesus schreie abermal
laut, und verschied.

But Jesus cried aloud again, and
was gone.

CHORALE:
Wenn ich einmal soll scheiden,
so scheide nicht von mir!
Wenn ich den Tod soll leiden,
so tritt du dann herfür!
Wenn mir am allerbängsten
wird um das Herze sein,

When comes my hour of parting,
O, part thou not from me!
To my aid come flying,
Lord, and set me free!
And when my heart must languish
In death's last awful throe,

so reiss mich aus den Ängsten
kraft deiner Angst und Pein!

ST. MATTHEW:

Und siehe da, der Vorhang im
Tempel zerriss in zwei Stück,
von oben an bis unten aus. Und
die Erde erbebete, und die
Felsen zerrissen, und die
Gräber taten sich auf, und
standen auf viel Leiber der
Heiligen, di da schliefen; und
gingen aus den Gräbern nach
seiner Auferstehung, und kamen
in die heilige Stadt, und
erschienen vielen. Aber der
Hauptmann, und die bei ihm
waren, und bewahreten Jesum, da
sie sahen das Erbeben, und was
da geschah, erschraken sie
sehr, und sprachen:

CHORUS:

Wahrlich, dieser ist Gottes
Sohn gewesen.

Release me from my anguish
By Thine own pain and woe.

And behold, the veil of the temple
was torn in two, from top to
bottom, and the earth quaked, and
the rocks split open. And the graves
were opened, and there arose many
bodies of the saints which had
slept, and came out of the graves
after His resurrection, and went
into the holy city, and appeared
unto many. Now when the
captain and
those who were with him, watching
Jesus, saw the earthquake and those
things that were done, they feared
greatly, saying:

Truly, this was the Son of God.

Mozart and the Classical Style

"Classical" is a vexing word. It is used in a hundred different ways. In its root meaning it refers to the culture of ancient Greece, which produced art and architecture of such beauty, balance, and perfection of form that it has had a continuing and profound influence on Western culture (*see* color plate 6 and 7). At the same time, someone may talk about a "classic car," implying that the car's design possesses the kind of perfection of form which will earn it enduring respect. Or someone might refer to a "classic joke," meaning that it is absolutely typical, the type after which all other such jokes could be patterned. Similarly, baseball players have "classic swings" and tennis players "classic backhands." In architecture the use of a few grooved pillars can earn the term "neoclassical;" in literature, any novel still read after 20 years or so gets called a "classic." In music, practically everything associated with high-art performance has come to be called "classical." My local radio station which plays high-art music from the Medieval right through the modern periods calls itself "your station for the Classics."

In this book, however, I am going to attempt to use the term in a much more restricted way, letting "Classical" refer specifically to the style which dominated music from 1750 until 1825. It is called Classical not just because it is a style which has endured, but also because the elements of the style share distinct qualities with the style of ancient Greek art: fondness for balance, symmetry, evenness, and for rational, well-thought-out design.

The three great composers of the Classical period are Haydn (1732–1809), Mozart (1756–1791), and Beethoven (1770–1827.) Although Haydn was the first born of these three, I will depart from strict chronology and begin with Mozart, because I think his works present the clearest introduction to the Classical style and to the ways the great composers treated it.

Mozart's Life

Mozart was born in 1756. His father, Leopold, a violinist, composer, and conductor at the court of the Archbishop of Salzburg, married Mozart's mother, Maria Anna, in 1747. In a pattern common in the eighteenth century, their first child was born in 1748 and died six months later; their second child was born in 1749 and died six days later; their third, born in 1750, lived ten weeks; their

In a high-ceilinged salon typical of the mid-18th century, eight-year-old Mozart plays the harpsichord at a tea party despite the obvious inattention of the guests. *(The Louvre, Paris)*

> To all Lovers of Sciences.
> THE greatest Prodigy that Europe, or that even Human Nature has to boast of, is, without Contradiction, the little German Boy WOLFGANG MOZART; a Boy, Eight Years old, who has, and indeed very justly, raised the Admiration not only of the greatest Men, but also of the greatest Musicians in Europe. It is hard to say, whether his Execution upon the Harpsichord and his playing and singing at Sight, or his own Caprice, Fancy, and Compositions for all Instruments, are most astonishing. The Father of this Miracle, being obliged by Desire of several Ladies and Gentlemen to postpone, for a very short Time, his Departure from England, will give an Opportunity to hear this little Composer and his Sister, whose musical Knowledge wants not Apology. Performs every Day in the Week, from Twelve to Three o'Clock in the Great Room, at the Swan and Hoop, Cornhill. Admittance 2s. 6d. each Person.
>   The two Children will play also together with four Hands upon the same Harpsichord, and put upon it a Handkerchief, without seeing the Keys.

Press notice in the London *Public Advertiser,* July 11, 1765, for a harpsichord recital by Mozart and his sister. *(by permission of the British Library)*

fourth, a girl, Nannerl, born in 1751, was the first to survive. The fifth child, born in 1752, lived three months; the sixth child, born on January 27th, 1756, was Wolfgang Amadeus Mozart.

His older sister showed musical gifts, and her father began teaching her harpsichord. But he made a note in her music book, beneath a piece she had been studying: "This piece was learnt by Wolfgang on 24 January 1761, 3 days before his 5th birthday, between 9 and 9:30 in the evening." Musical prodigies—children who show astonishingly mature and seemingly effortless musical abilities at an early age—are rare, but a few of them turn up in every age, including our own. What made Mozart different from most was his ability to compose. For a child of six, seven, or eight to be able to play the piano or harpsichord beautifully is certainly wonderful, although far from unknown. Mozart at this age could sit at the keyboard and improvise; that is, he could compose extemporaneously in front of an audience, for an hour at a time.

And he did display his gifts in front of audiences. Leopold Mozart took Mozart and his sister on extensive tours to the courts and great cities of Europe to play for royalty in their palaces and for the public in concerts. In London in 1765 he advertised young Mozart's presence in the newspapers:

> . . . Those Ladies and Gentlemen who will honor him with their company from twelve to three in the afternoon, any day of the week, except Tuesday and Friday, may, by taking each a ticket, gratify their curiosity, by giving him any thing to play at sight, or any music without bass, which he will write upon the spot, without recurring to the harpsichord.

The tickets were half a guinea each, a healthy sum in those days. But it is the word "curiosity" which rankles. Was Leopold Mozart exploiting his children, exhibiting them like circus freaks? The short answer is "no." Leopold Mozart was dedicated to his children, to their abilities which so far exceeded his own, and to their futures. What he exploited was not his children, but their situation. He saw it as a potentially profitable one—profitable in the sense of immediate money-making, but also profitable in that it might provide young Mozart with a richer musical education than could ever have been his in Salzburg, and in providing him with the fame which would make it easier for him to acquire a secure court appointment once his days as a "curiosity" were over.

Leopold's plan was largely successful. They did make quite a bit of money, and Mozart did acquire a wonderfully sophisticated musical education along with a considerable degree of fame. He also acquired some ideas about himself and his station in life which were to bring him into conflict with his father's plans.

It is hard for us, now, in America, really to have a feel for the idea of rank as it existed in the eighteenth century. The notion that someone's birth automatically entitles him or her to our respect and deference, the idea that we should feel humble before such a person, is not an idea we are comfortable with. Even after we *elect* someone to high office, we tend not to feel humble before the person. Leopold Mozart was comfortable with the idea of rank; he believed that society had its ranks and niches, including a particular spot for the court composer. That was the system which was then in operation, and he wanted Mozart to work within the system. It is likely that Mozart could have done so. But he had learned more than musical sophistication, more even than intellectual sophistication, in all his touring. He learned just how uniquely gifted he was; he acquired a healthy disrespect for those born to high rank; and he learned, along with the rest of the intellectual elite of his generation, to challenge accepted ideas about society. It was, after all, this generation which fought and overturned the European system of rank and privilege in the French and American revolutions. That "all men are created equal" is not an idea which Leopold Mozart would have found congenial. Nor, to be fair, could we say that Mozart would have found it congenial either. But he certainly learned to regard *himself* as equal or superior to those born to high rank.

It is easy to see why such an attitude might not lead to a happy life as a court composer. There, his status would have been on approximately the same plane as that of the chef. Mozart did take a brief appointment with the Archbishop of Salzburg, but it ended quickly and acrimoniously. Instead, in 1781, he went to Vienna to be an independent musician and composer. He married and had two children. He gave concerts of his own music, wrote operas and conducted them, gave lessons, sold his music through publication, and wrote music on commission. He was his own master, no one's employee, no one's servant. Perhaps for someone who at the age of six had been fussed over by the Empress of Austria, and who at 12 knew himself to be the equal of any musician in Europe, this was the only career choice possible.

Naturally, being a free-lance composer was a much riskier business than being a court composer—independent employment is often undependable. Nevertheless, Mozart was successful at it. During his best years his income reached 10,000 gulden. By comparison, a maid earned 12 gulden a year (room and board supplied, of course); a violinist in the court orchestra might earn 400 gulden; the chief surgeon at the hospital 1200; the hospital's director, 3,000 gulden. In 1787 Mozart was given a court "appointment," which granted him a salary, but no real duties, for 800 gulden a year. His father, at Salzburg, had earned 300 gulden a year.

Yet when he died in 1791, only 35 years old, Mozart was penniless. His wife Constanze was left with more debts to pay than his entire estate was worth. A major item in his debts was his tailor's bill; a major item in his estate was his billiards table. The two items taken together may help explain his situation. For Mozart was not content merely to survive as an independent musician. He knew himself to be an aristocrat among musicians, and he wished to live as an aristocrat among men. To explain his indebtedness one authority suggests that it may be necessary to add gambling to his aristocratic tastes. Perhaps he gambled because it was part of the aristocratic style of life, or perhaps he was like the great nineteenth-century novelists Balzac in France, Dickens in England, Dostoyevski in Russia, Twain in the United States, who made fortunes with their art, then gambled them away in games or in business ventures, as though compelled to put themselves under enormous pressure to create more art.

Mozart family portrait (c. 1780): Mozart with his sister and his father, and, on the wall, a portrait of his mother. *(Mozart Museum, Salzburg)*

At any rate, a neglected genius he was not. If we have to give up this romantic image, what can we put in its place? He was small, as is well known, perhaps as a result of a serious childhood illness; intelligent, as is obvious from his letters as well as from his music; vain, as we might gather from the above-mentioned tailor's bill; and, like the other members of his family, fond of dirty jokes. His father was his great teacher, but before Mozart reached his teens he knew himself to be the family breadwinner, while he saw his father reduced to copying out his scores. It is around this time that he writes home to his mother, jokingly referring to himself as a fool and an idiot, as though begging still to be treated as a child. If in later years he could behave childishly, perhaps it was because he had been thrust out of a child's role so soon. He was also ill a great deal, suffering under the increasing and multiplying burden of illnesses that brought about his early death.

Visitors to his home would find him preoccupied, thinking about music, drumming his fingers on the tabletop as though it were a keyboard. This must be the ultimate fact about Mozart: not his debts, his vanity, or his home life, but his *musical* life. For him to have written music in the amazing quantity and quality he did, music itself—thinking about it, writing it, rehearsing it, producing it, performing it—must have provided the real texture of his life. Whatever might be said about his life's other aspects, in this aspect it was an unqualified success. Its only tragedy is that it ended so soon.

C-Major Piano Sonata

His *C-Major Piano Sonata* is well-known as a student piece. I won't attempt a complete analysis of the work here; I only want to indicate a few of the ways in which it is typically Classical and typically Mozart. For example, the opening melody is typically Classical in that it begins with a statement of the I chord, in this case the C-major triad, C-E-G:

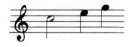

The accompaniment is typical in that it is an "Alberti bass," an accompanying pattern extremely popular in the Classical period. To create one, you take a chord and break it up as follows:

There is no strong bass line here of the sort we associate with the Baroque style. A Baroque composer treating this melody might write something like this:

Fictional "Baroque" setting of melody. This example expects the middle part between the bass and melodic lines to be improvised, according to the rules for playing figured basses.

The Classical composer de-emphasizes the bass line and writes out a livelier middle part. The melody, as noted earlier, begins with a statement which spells out the chord. This strong, disjunct motion is followed by softer, stepwise motion, involving a "turn." In the Classical style, the first phrase seems incomplete, and demands a balancing, answering phrase. Again, strong, disjunct motion is followed by gentler, conjunct movement.

First two phrases of sonata

Just this much—the sonata's first four bars—may be enough to indicate some of the sources of stability and equilibrium which are so important to the style. One melodic phrase is balanced against another, in a "question–answer" pattern; the Alberti bass itself, in its "tick-tock" sort of motion, seems to revolve around a stable mid-point; and the harmonies which the melody makes in conjunction with the accompaniment are themselves very stable: I-V-I for the first phrase, in the second phrase IV-I-V-I.

The balance, however, is not quite complete. At the end of these first four bars we are left hanging just a bit and feeling the need for another musical statement to balance what we have just heard. It is not hard to imagine a second four bars which could fulfill this need.

Not Mozart's completion of the initial statement

However, this is not what Mozart gives us. What we get instead is a sequence of quick runs. Their downward energy takes them past the expected resting place of C major (the tonal center) in the eighth bar and to the expectation of a new key (you can recognize this by the accidentals).

Mozart's completion of the initial phrase

Throughout the rest of the movement, Mozart continues this alternation between stating a theme and developing it with rapid passages of scales and arpeggios. There is a structure behind what he does, called sonata form, which we will examine more carefully later in this chapter; the feeling of balance in the score can be sensed even without knowing the exact nature of the structure. Mozart is like someone who can use polite language to say outrageous things. Listen only for the equilibrium and you will hear the Classical style; listen for the ways the equilibrium is toyed with and challenged, and you will hear Mozart.

SUMMARY: *Mozart's* C-Major Piano Sonata, *K. 545, first movement (1788)*

melody	Thematic statements characterized by strong disjunct motion followed by gentler stepwise motion. Development of these is characterized by rapid scale passages and arpeggios in both hands.
harmony	Predominantly consonant. Relies on such basic harmonic progressions as I-V-I, IV-I-V-I, and so on, but modulates through a number of keys.
rhythm	Measured, strict, consistent 4/4 pattern.
form	Modified sonata form. (When the first theme returns in the recapitulation it is in the IV key rather than the I key. *See* pages 184–88.)
texture	In thematic statements there is a clear melody-accompaniment relationship, where accompaniment fills in the middle ground rather than defining a clear bass line. In development of the themes, the melody-accompaniment distinctions break down, as both hands use scales and arpeggios.
timbre	Harpsichord or piano. Located almost entirely in middle range of instrument (approximately two octaves below middle C and two and one-half octaves above).
function	Original purpose was to serve as a piece for students or for small-scale (living-room scale) performing situations; these are still the work's principal uses today, although it is also used in concert repertoire.

"Là ci darem la mano" from Don Giovanni

To see Mozart at work on a larger scale, we will look at his opera *Don Giovanni,* written in 1787. His librettist was Lorenzo da Ponte, an Italian who was serving as official poet—a kind of writer-in-residence—to the Emperor's theaters in Vienna. They created the work on a commission from the state opera house of Prague, Czechoslovakia, where their previous collaboration, *The Marriage of Figaro,* had been a huge success the year before. Although the opera is set in Spain and was written in Vienna for performance in Prague, the language its characters speak is Italian. This is because Italian was viewed as the appropriate language for opera, just as English—Black American English, to be exact—is the appropriate language for rock 'n' roll. If a Swedish rock group performs in Germany, most of their songs will be sung in English, which has become as much the international language of popular music as Italian in the eighteenth century was the international language of operatic music.

"There we'll join hands, there you'll say yes" sings Don Giovanni, the legendary Don Juan, to the peasant girl Zerlina, only a few hours before she is to be married to the young peasant Massetto. Don Giovanni is rich, powerful, a Spanish nobleman (as the title "Don" indicates), and a seducer of women.

In fact, seducing women is his main occupation in life. Although he has certain preferences, notably for young virgins, he really loves all women—young, old, thin, fat, poor, rich, it doesn't matter—until the moment when the seduction is complete. Then he is bored, and it's on to the next challenge. In this song, we are getting a sample of his technique.

"Look," Don Giovanni continues, referring to his palace, "It isn't far, let's be off from here, my love." The musical phrases are typically classical: smooth, elegant, balanced. One rises like a question; the next falls like an answer. If we take the melody of this opening statement and mark the line of the tonal center, A, we can see how the melodic line revolves around it, rising, falling, passing through, but always returning to it:

Mozart is making the style work for him, dramatically; like the Classical style, Don Giovanni's line seems balanced, even-handed, and therefore *reasonable*.

Zerlina's response tells us her thoughts: "I want to, and yet I don't; my heart is beating faster. It's true I would be happy, but he might still be tricking me." Musically, she echoes Don Giovanni's melody, almost note for note (although of course in the soprano as opposed to the baritone range), until the moment where the melody should make its return to the tonal center of A. Here, instead of coming to rest on the tonic note, her voice flies upwards, communicating her fear and doubt, and demanding a repetition of the words before it settles down again.

ma___ puo bur-lar - mi an - cor___   ma   può___ bur - lar - mi an - cor!
(But he might still be tricking me!)

Don Giovanni senses that she is susceptible but frightened, and decides that a more dominating approach is called for. His melody becomes angular and forceful:

(8ᵛᵃ lower) Vie - ni, mio bel di - let - to!
(Come, my pretty delight!)

Zerlina's response, by contrast, is made of wavering, indecisive little steps:

Mi   fa___ pie - tà___ Ma ___ set - to!
(I feel pity for Masetto!)

Giovanni returns with his forceful tune, promising to change her fortune, and when she stretches out her wavering melody over four measures, confessing her weakness, he becomes even more insistent:

Don Giovanni and Zerlina in the duet, "Là ci darem la mano" from Act I of a Metropolitan Opera production of *Don Giovanni*.

(8ᵛᵃ lower) Vie-ni!   Vie - ni!
(Come!   Come!)

Now their dialogue gets more urgent. He knows that she is ready to give in, but he wants her willing assent. No new words are added; Mozart will construct the drama out of materials already given. He returns Don Giovanni to his opening statement. But where before Don Giovanni sang four phrases, he now sings only one. The answering phrase is Zerlina's. Giovanni responds with insistence:

(8ᵛᵃ lower) Là mi di-rai di   sì
(There you'll say yes)

And after her reply, he uses the same notes to make even more insistent his urging their departure. Suddenly her voice appears high and then quick, conveying her fear:

ma_____ puo bur-lar - mi an-cor.
(He might still be tricking me.)

He does not even wait for her to finish before insisting again, and yet again, entering over the ends of her phrases. And then we hear her wavering melody for the last time. She is repeating words she has said before, but we don't even need the text: the message is in the music. As it falls, she is falling.

"Andiam! Andiam!"—"Let us go! Let us go!" concludes Don Giovanni, and Zerlina answers "Andiam." This phrase becomes the refrain for the conclusion of their duet, as they sing together, happily, in harmony. "Let us go, my dearest, to ease the pain of an innocent love." It is obvious, I hope, that the way to ease the pain of an innocent love is to make it not-so-innocent anymore.

In a typical opera before this time, and indeed in most musical theater works including those of our own time, arias and duets are not used for dramatic action. The average composer, faced with a seduction scene like the one we have just looked at, would develop the changing relationship between the two in recitative or dialogue. Once the relationship had changed, the characters would sing about the new state they had arrived at. (This is as true of musical comedies as it is of the operatic tradition.) Mozart disdains the static approach. He starts the duet almost at the very beginning of the relationship and uses the music to develop the relationship through shifting states, finally taking the characters to their happy agreement and changing them to lovers.

But it is fair to ask how this propensity for dramatic development fits with the Classical style, so strongly characterized by balance, symmetry, and stability. The only answer I can offer is that the mature Classical style, as exemplified by this duet of Mozart's, encompasses both stability and change. In fact, I would go so far as to claim that it is the Classical period's desire to accommodate both stability and change which led to the pre-eminence of the formal structure best equipped to accomplish this: sonata form. This was a structure used not just in the first movements of sonatas, but also in symphonies, overtures, concertos, and—the specific instance we will be examining—in a vocal ensemble which occurs a little further on in *Don Giovanni.*

"Ah, taci, ingiusto core" from Don Giovanni

All through the opera, Don Giovanni is wonderfully successful at getting women to fall for him. He has been having bad luck, however, at actually getting them to fall into bed with him. His problem at the end of his duet with Zerlina is the arrival of Donna Elvira. She is a woman (a noblewoman) whom he had pretended to marry sometime previously. He stayed with her for three days, which was after all a long relationship in his terms, but now she is pursuing him, demanding either vengeance or his return, she's not sure which. In the scene just looked at she does exact a sort of vengeance in leading Zerlina safely away. Later in the opera we see her, at night, on the balcony of the house she has taken. Unbeknownst to her, Don Giovanni and his servant Leporello are also on the scene. Don Giovanni has earlier caught sight of Donna Elvira's maid, and thinks her pretty. His strategem is to exchange hat and cloak with Leporello, so that he can approach the maid as a fellow servant.

Elvira's song is introduced by a tune from the orchestra:

With its quick little run, and repeated staccato notes, it conveys a sense of lightness and humor inconsistent with her first statement: "Ah, be silent, my unjust heart!"

The orchestra returns, even lighter, quicker, and bouncier in effect, perhaps mimicking the beating of her heart:

It is easy to imagine a context in which Donna Elvira would be taken more seriously. A minor key instead of a major one, slow accompanying melodies, deep sustained tones instead of high quick ones—these might produce such a context.

Not Mozart's version

But it is obvious that this is not at all what Mozart wants. The more serious Elvira becomes, calling Giovanni "ungodly," and "a traitor," the more the orchestra laughs at her.

In effect, the orchestra is telling us how to feel, saying: the woman is being ridiculous.

Leporello and Don Giovanni now enter the picture. They whisper to each
other, using a little theme which seems like an undertone to the action:

(8ᵛᵃ lower)

"Undertone" theme

Giovanni is hatching his plot. He will stand behind Leporello, to whom he has
given his hat and cloak, and wave Leporello's arms for him, and sing for him,
with the ultimate aim, first, of making Donna Elvira think that Leporello *is* Don
Giovanni, and second, of making her think that Don Giovanni still loves her.

Musically, the end of the "undertone" theme takes us into a new key, modulating from the A major up five steps to E major. The melody is the same as it

was at the beginning, just lifted up into the new key, but now the orchestra's dialogue is with Don Giovanni, not Elvira. It still laughs, and the singer is still serious, but this time we know that it is a totally false sincerity we are hearing as Don Giovanni sings, "Elvira, idolo mia!"—"Elvira, my idolized one!" The theme which was used for the undertone conversation now has a new role. The two singers are Donna Elvira and Leporello. Their musical lines overlap as Elvira remarks on the strange feeling coming over her, and Leporello registers his amazement.that she is actually going to believe Giovanni. Again, at the end of the section, there is a modulation, this time leading us to a totally new theme, in C major. It is Don Giovanni's love song. He still sings from behind Leporello, forcing his servant into the appropriate gestures. One gathers that it is a sort of all-purpose love song that Don Giovanni has found effective before. (A little later he serenades the maid with a related theme.)

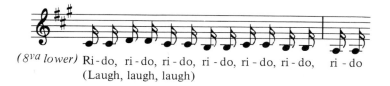

(8va lower) Di - scen - di,o gio - ia   bel-la,   o   gio -   ia   bel - la!
(Come down, oh lovely joy, oh lovely joy)

Elvira responds with an angular, forceful melody, making it clear that she doesn't intend to be fooled by him once again. Don Giovanni replies with equal force: "Believe me, believe me or I'll kill myself." Their melodies overlap, the orchestra's chords grow denser and denser—and then the texture shifts. Don Giovanni continues to exert his force, but Elvira falls silent, and Leporello threatens to laugh:

(8va lower) Ri-do, ri-do, ri-do, ri-do, ri-do, ri-do, ri-do
(Laugh, laugh, laugh)

Underneath, the harmonies are relaxing, resolving back into the original key, and the orchestra returns with its initial melody:

Instead of a solo voice in dialogue with the orchestra, we hear all three singers. They sing together, but their sentiments are diverse. Elvira asks the gods to protect her credulity—her willingness to believe. Leporello calls it her gullibility—her willingness to be fooled. Don Giovanni remarks on his own fabulous gifts. This time there is no modulation, and the trio continue in A major until the end, which we expect to be comic, but which is not.

Mozart made Elvira look ridiculous at the start. He turned her from defiant hater to gullible lover. He accomplished all of Don Giovanni's crafty scheme, and Elvira does indeed, completely fooled, come down from the balcony to go off with the disguised Leporello. But just here, at the end of the trio, the comedy lifts for a moment. She is credulous and gullible—but in their quiet and respectful music, Leporello and Don Giovanni seem to recognize that it is the power of love which makes her so—and there is something not laughable but wonderful in a love so misplaced and yet so strong.

As in the duet between Giovanni and Zerlina, Mozart has developed dramatic action through the music. Here, though, he has employed the Classical period's favorite device for balancing dramatic development with structural stability: sonata form.

Sonata Form

Fifty years ago, it was common to think of sonata form in terms of melodies, and much of the vocabulary we use in discussing it is still couched in melodic terms. But we now see sonata form as based principally on certain fundamental harmonic shifts. This is partly the result of seeing sonata form as a development from the "binary" form of works like the Scarlatti keyboard sonata discussed in Chapter 17. The first half of that sonata saw the harmonies shift from the I key to the V key; the second half saw the harmonies take a path back to the I key. A similar, though more fully worked-out process, occurs in sonata form. (A reminder about terminology: sonata form is named after the sonatas which were its ancestors. But not all sonatas use sonata form, and sonata form is used in many musical types which are not sonatas.)

The first thing the composer working in sonata form must do is establish the sense of the I key, the home key or *tonic,* in the listener's mind. It is for this reason that so many pieces in the Classical era begin by spelling out the tonic chord. Suppose we want to write a piece using sonata form, and we want our tonic key to be D. The D-major chord looks like this:

To establish its centrality in the listener's mind, we might write something like this:

spelling out the D-major triad before going on to a scalar passage based on a D-major scale. The next thing we would do, still working to solidify the sense of the tonic for the listener, is to cadence on the tonic chord. If we were writing in the key of D, we would—perhaps several times—end phrases with the harmonically strong movement of V to I. That is, we would move from a chord based on the fifth step of the D scale (D, E, F#, G, *A*), called the dominant chord, to a chord based on the first step, the tonic.

V – I

Cadence on D-major chord

Now that we have stated the tonic strongly and cadenced on it, we can feel confident that we have established it in the listener's mind. Again, this does not mean that the listener has to be consciously aware that the tonic is D. Unconsciously, he or she should simply have a feeling that a home key has been established.

Once it is established, our next step is to modulate away from it. This is an important moment in the form. Lifting the music into the new key creates a kind of potential energy. The modulation is like a pump, lifting the music to a higher level, from which it can flow down through the rest of the piece. Technically, the modulation is accomplished as follows: we find a chord which is held in common both by the old key and the new one. For example, a B-minor chord is the VI chord of D major (D, E, F#, G, A, *B*) and it is also the II chord of A major (A, *B*). Having come to it from D, we can leave it heading for A. Typically, we do this with a transition theme, which might look something like this:

Key of D: VI
Key of A: II   –   VII   –   V   –   I

The V-I cadence at the end of the transition theme establishes A as the new key.

The modulation, usually from the I key to the V key, signals the end to what is called the first theme. The second theme will start in the new key. This could be a new melody, as the term "second theme" implies. For example, we could write something like this:

But what defines the second theme section is not a new melody, but the new key, and it is not uncommon to bring back the first melody in the new key. To do this we would write:

The first theme portion and the second theme portion together constitute the *exposition*. Frequently, the composer asks that the exposition be repeated, although performers generally regard this as optional.

Next comes the *development*. Here we will go through a number of different keys, rarely resting in one key for long, often not even stopping to cadence, but simply moving through different tonal centers. We may introduce new melodies as well as variations and fragmentations of the melodic material from the exposition.

Towards the end of the development, the pace of the harmonic changes will usually quicken. Typically, the composer will use diminished seventh chords, characterized by tension and instability, until finally allowing the texture to relax back into the *recapitulation*.

The recapitulation is, as its name implies, a restatement of the material introduced during the exposition. The crucial difference is that there is no modulation in the recapitulation: the original tonal center, the original tonic key, is maintained thoughout the section.

The basic structure of sonata form can, then, be summarized as follows:

Exposition	first theme in I key; transition theme to modulate; second theme in V key
Development	various melodic ideas; various keys; increasing tension and instability
Recapitulation	return to first theme in I key; transition theme does not modulate; return to second theme, this time also in I key

In effect, the strong elements of repetition between the exposition and the recapitulation create the stable foundation of the structure. The modulation in the exposition helps supply the energy which leads to the contrasts and changes of the development section. Thus, sonata form is a device which provides for structural stability but also allows for dramatic development. As such, it is

ideally suited to Mozart's purposes in the trio from *Don Giovanni.* We can see
how the trio fits into the sonata form scheme:

Exposition first theme in I key: *Elvira opens her heart while the orchestra laughs at her.*

transition theme to modulate: *Don Giovanni and Leporello hatch their plot in undertones.*

(8 va lower)

second theme in V key: *Giovanni lies about his love for Elvira; she claims not to trust him; Leporello is amazed.*

Development various melodic ideas; various keys; increasing tension and instability: *Don Giovanni sings his love song; Elvira is angry; Don Giovanni is forceful; Leporello laughs, introducing the return.*

(8 va lower)

Recapitulation return to first theme in I key; transition theme does not modulate: *The three characters state their diverse views in harmony.*

Recapitulation *(continued)*	return to second theme, this time also in I key: *The ending (although not a complete statement of the exposition's second theme section) stays in the home key for the hushed conclusion; Elvira is back in love; the two men find the spectacle not laughable but wonderful.**

A *Final Note on* Don Giovanni

These two ensembles, the duet and the trio, do not represent the whole of Don Giovanni. He is more than a womanizer. In the opera's opening scene, he tries to force himself on a young woman, is discovered by her father, duels with the old man, and kills him. While Donna Elvira is pursuing him to avenge her lost honor, the young woman, her fiancé, and, eventually, her father's ghost—in the form of his statue come to life—are pursuing him to avenge the murder. At the end of the opera, Don Giovanni has invited the statue to dinner. When the statue returns the favor by asking Don Giovanni to dine with him in hell, the Don is unafraid.

He is arrogant, violent, and unfeeling. We should despise him for everything he does. But he is larger than life, and so full of life that we end up admiring him for what he is: for the sheer size of his appetites, for his passions, and for his courage. There really is nothing admirable about him *except* for the greatness of his human capacities, but somehow these fill us with a gratifying sense of the human capacity for greatness. Critics have argued whether Mozart and Da Ponte created a comedy with tragic overtones or a tragedy with comic overtones. In my experience, productions which stress the comic are more successful. Ultimately it is not even fair to say that *Don Giovanni* mixes comedy and tragedy; this is a work in which comedy and tragedy are often the same thing. As Don Giovanni descends into hell there is tragic grandeur in the courage with which he meets his fate, spurning the opportunity to repent. There is also comedy in the spectacle of a man who thinks nothing of betraying a woman or dishonoring a girl, but for whom a politely returned dinner invitation from a fellow gentleman is virtually a moral imperative.

SUMMARY:	*The duet "Là ci darem la mano" and the trio "Ah, taci, ingiusto core," from Mozart's* **Don Giovanni** *(1787)*
melody	Simple, balanced phrase structures, which are still flexible enough to allow expression of a multitude of different inflections of meaning.
harmony	Consonant, based largely on IV-V-I relationships; modulations used to create harmonic tension over the larger structure.
rhythm	Tempos in general are moderate and regular. Mozart switches from a moderate "two" to a quick "three" in the duet, as his characters

*For the connection between Mozart's trio and sonata form, I am indebted to Joseph Kerman in his *Opera as Drama.* (New York: Vintage, 1956.)

move from arguing about love to doing something about it. The trio is in six-eight time. Although the pulse is regular, Mozart puts a wide variety of contrasting patterns over it.

form	The duet: A-A'-B. The trio: sonata form.
timbre	Voices and orchestra; Zerlina and Donna Elvira are both sopranos, Don Giovanni a baritone, Leporello a bass. Strings dominate the orchestral timbres.
texture	Largely homophonic; however, Mozart uses counterpoint to put the voices together, especially in the trio.
function	Commissioned by the state opera house in Prague, Czechoslovakia. Support for opera in Mozart's time came both from aristocratic patronage and from the larger public who filled the halls.
text	

"Là ci darem la mano"

DON GIOVANNI:
Là ci darem la mano,　　　　　　There we'll take hands,
Là mi dirai di sì.　　　　　　　There you'll tell me "yes."
Vedi, non è lontano,　　　　　　Look, it isn't far,
Partiam, ben mio, da qui.　　　　Let's be off from here, my love.

ZERLINA:
Vorrei e non vorrei,　　　　　　I want to, and yet I don't;
Mi trema un poco il cor.　　　　My heart is beating faster.
Felice, è ver, sarei,　　　　　　It's true I would be happy,
Ma può burlarmi ancor.　　　　But he might still be tricking me.

DON GIOVANNI:
Vieni, mio bel diletto!　　　　Come, my pretty delight!

ZERLINA:
Mi fà pietà Masetto.　　　　　I feel pity for Masetto!

DON GIOVANNI:
Io cangierò tuo sorte.　　　　I will change your life!

ZERLINA:
Presto non son più forte.　　Soon I won't be able to resist him.

DON GIOVANNI:
Vieni, Vieni!　　　　　　　Come, Come!
[words repeat]

DON GIOVANNI:
Andiam!　　　　　　　　Let's go!

ZERLINA:
Andiam!　　　　　　　　Let's go!

BOTH:
Andiam, andiam, mio bene,　　Let's go, let's go, my dearest,
A ristorar le pene　　　　　　To ease the pain
d' un innocente amor.　　　　Of an innocent love.

"Ah, taci, ingiusto core"

ELVIRA:
Ah, taci, ingiusto core!
Non palpitarmi in seno!
E un empio, è un traditore,
E colpa aver pietà.

Ah, be silent, my unjust heart!
Don't beat so in my breast!
He's ungodly, a traitor,
It's wrong to feel pity.

LEPORELLO:
Zitto! di Donna Elvira,
Signor, la voce io sento!

Shhh! It's Donna Elvira,
My lord, I hear her voice!

DON GIOVANNI:
Cogliere io vo' il momento,
Tu fermati un po' là!

I'll take advantage of this moment.
You stand there!

DON GIOVANNI:
Elvira, idolo mio!

Elvira, my idolized one!

DONNA ELVIRA:
Non è costui l 'ingrato?

Is it the ingrate?

DON GIOVANNI:
Si, vita mia, son io,
E chiedo carità.

Yes, my love, it is I,
Begging for your mercy.

DONNA ELVIRA:
Numi, che strano affetto
Mi si risveglia in petto!

God, what a strange feeling
Is awakening in my breast!

LEPORELLO:
State a veder la pazza
Che ancor gli crederà!

Watch, this madwoman
Is going to believe him!

DON GIOVANNI:
Discendi, o gioia bella,
Vedrai che tu sei quella
Che adora l' alma mia,
Pentito io sono già.

Come down, oh lovely joy,
And see that you are the one
Adored by my soul,
And I am truly penitent.

DONNA ELVIRA:
No, non ti credo, o barbaro!

No, I can't believe you, you
barbarian!

DON GIOVANNI:
Ah credimi, o m'uccido!

Idolo mio, vien quà!

Ah, believe me, or I'll kill
myself!
My idolized one, come here!

LEPORELLO (TO GIOVANNI):
Se seguitate, io rido!

Keep on like this, and I'll laugh!

DONNA ELVIRA:
Dei, che cimento è questo!
Non so s'io vado o resto!
Ah proteggete voi
La mia credulità.

What a risk this is!
I don't know what to do!
Lord, please protect
My credulity!

DON GIOVANNI:
Spero che cada presto!
Che bel colpetto è questo!

I hope she yields quickly!
What a nice little coup this is!

Più fertile talento
Del mio no non si dà!

LEPORELLO:
Già quel mendace labbro
Torna a sedur costei,
Deh proteggete, o dei!
La sua credulità!

A more fertile talent than mine
Could not be found anywhere!

Already his lying lips
Have seduced the poor woman again,
Protect her, dear God,
From her own credulity!

Haydn

Haydn's Life

Franz Josef Haydn was born in 1732, 24 years before Mozart, and lived until 1809, 18 years after Mozart's death. His career typified exactly the sort of success that Leopold Mozart would have wished for his son. This success of Haydn's stands in stark contrast to his early poverty.

His father was a wheelwright. The musical ability which Haydn showed while still a child seemed to his parents to present a possible path out of poverty. They had a cousin who was a schoolmaster, and they sent Haydn to live and study with him. The boy was only six years old. In effect, his first six years were his only real experience of family life. After two years with the schoolmaster, a visiting choirmaster from St. Stephen's cathedral in Vienna heard his voice, and offered him a position there. This was a kind of work-study arrangement; his singing in the choir entitled him to room, board, and schooling.

When this employment ended, he was about 18 and on his own in Vienna. He lived then as many young musicians trying to make their way live in cities today—staying with friends or in cheap rooms, studying, practicing, giving lessons, accompanying, performing, composing the occasional commission.

Finally, in 1759, he achieved his first regular position, as music director to a Count Morzin, and on the strength of this relative security married Maria Anna Kellar, three years older than he, the daughter of a wig-maker. She was, from every account, an awful woman. Together they endured forty years (she died in 1800) of unhappy marriage. They had no children.

Count Morzin lost his fortune and disbanded his orchestra, but not before one of the wealthiest and most powerful princes in the Austrio-Hungarian Empire, Prince Paul Anton Esterhazy, had the chance, while visiting Morzin, to hear Haydn's music. He asked Haydn to come and work for him. A year later, in 1762, Nikolaus Esterhazy succeeded his brother as Prince.

At just the time when, in America, events were building towards a revolution which would establish a form of government dispensing with aristocracy, and when, in France, events were building towards a revolution which would remove not just aristocratic power but also aristocratic heads, it is ironic that there blossomed one of history's most productive relationships between artist and aristocrat, that between Haydn and Esterhazy.

Franz Josef Haydn

Concert room in Esterhazy Palace. Haydn was employed as composer, director, conductor, and performer at the palace for 30 years.

Prince Esterhazy and Aristocratic Patronage

Prince Nikolaus Esterhazy loved music, was himself a fair musician, loved Haydn's work, and was immensely rich. In the later 1760s he moved his establishment to a new palace he had constructed on his ancestral estates in Hungary. It cost approximately 13 million gulden—the equivalent of something like a third of a billion dollars today. This was the Prince's summer residence. But of course it was more than just that. It was a whole community, supporting the Prince, his family, and large numbers of guests for all but the winter months. There were a chapel and two theaters, in addition to ballrooms and dining and living rooms on a grand scale, all of which were used as venues for music making. The list of a year's cultural events at this court—operas, plays, puppet theater, symphonies, and chamber music—was equal to that found in a good-sized American city today. Haydn was involved, as composer, director, conductor, and performer, with most of this. He had his own small orchestra and cast of singers (one of whom was reputed to be his mistress) hired on a permanent basis, as well as visiting artists to work with. "My Prince was content with all my works," he stated later. "I received approval, I could as leader of an orchestra make experiments, observe what enhanced an effect, and what weakened it,

Haydn usually conducted from the harpsichord, as in this performance of his opera *L'Infedelta Delusa* in 1773.

thus improving, adding to, cutting away, and running risks. I was set apart from the world, there was nobody in my vicinity to confuse and annoy me in my course, and so I had to be original." And since the guests included many of the world's illustrious and powerful people, the music he wrote and performed became famous far beyond the confines of the Esterhazy estates. When Prince Nikolaus died in 1790, Haydn found his works in demand throughout Europe. While retaining his connection with the Esterhazy family, and receiving from them an excellent pension, he now became an independent musician, traveling, giving concerts, and writing commissions (*see* Chapter 10 for discussion of a symphony written during this period); only at the very end of his life did he settle down to a quiet retirement.

The aristocratic patronage system had never worked better. But there were drawbacks. Haydn's status while working for Esterhazy was that of a servant. He was, to be sure, an "upstairs" servant, and a generously rewarded one, but still in aristocratic eyes a servant. One symbol of this was the requirement that he wear a uniform. Another, perhaps more meaningful, was that he had to request permission for any sort of independent travel. Another may seem even stranger to our contemporary point of view. When the Prince spoke to Haydn, or to anyone of Haydn's rank, he used not the second person, but the third. That is, he would not address Haydn to his face as "you," but as "he." "He did an excellent job leading the orchestra through the quick movement," I can imagine Esterhazy saying to Haydn. "His new symphony proved quite pleasurable."

Title page for the collection which includes Haydn's *Sonata in F Major,* which the composer dedicated to his employer, Prince Esterhazy. Note the small type for Haydn's name, the large type for Esterhazy's.

SEI
SONATE
DA
CLAVI-CEMBALO
CHE
A SUA ALTEZZA SERENISSIMA
DEL
SACRO ROMANO IMPERO
PRINCIPE
NICOLO ESTERHAZY DI GALANTHA
&c. &c.
D. D. D.
L' AUTORE
GIUSEPPE HAYDN
MAESTRO DI CAPELLA DELLA PREF. A. S. SER.

Sonata in F Major

Haydn composed his keyboard *Sonata in F Major* (Number 23) in 1773 and dedicated it to Prince Nikolaus. It was probably intended originally for performance on the harpsichord, although it may have been performed on an early version of the piano. The work is intimate in scale, and it is easy to picture Haydn playing it for the Prince and some of his family and guests in one of the palace's living rooms.

First Movement

The work is in three movements, fast—slow—very fast *(Allegro moderato—Larghetto—Presto)*. Both of the fast movements conform to the pattern of sonata form. The first movement begins with a kind of rhythmic game. All of the phrases in the first theme section start on a higher note and move lower.

First statement of first theme

Our automatic tendency when we hear a phrase with this sort of movement is to identify the higher, starting note as the place where the beat lies. But Haydn brings in the left-hand chord with the lower, bottom note of the phrase, making that note the place of the strong beat (this is also indicated by the bar line which makes it the first beat of the measure). The listener is thus pulled in two directions, and Haydn has created a kind of syncopation which gives the piece rhythmic energy and vivacity. To see this effect better, we can re-compose the section, either by lining up the left-hand beats with the higher notes

or by making the melody go up to the strong beats.

By doing either of these things, we could remove the rhythmic ambiguity, and most of the rhythmic life, from the piece.

A transition theme modulates to the second theme, which is in the dominant (or V) key, C major. The theme is built on a C scale, and adds another kind of excitement—sheer speed. The runs are in thirty-second notes, eight notes to each quick beat, but they are so nicely written to fall comfortably under the fingers that they sound more difficult to play than they really are.

Second theme, in C major

The development section plays a bit of the first theme in C major; then breaks it up into fragments; then gives us the theme in a minor key; and then embarks on a cadenza-like passage which builds in tension, arriving at a series of fast arpeggiated diminished-seventh chords:

(again, a passage made to play easier than it sounds) before hinting at, and then finally arriving at the recapitulation, back in the tonic key of F. To summarize this movement in terms of sonata form:

Exposition   first theme in I key:

transition theme to modulate:

second theme in V key:

Development   various melodic ideas; various keys; increasing tension and instability (initial theme fragmented, and put into minor key; extended cadenza-like section)

Recapitulation   return to first theme in I key:

transition theme does not modulate (Haydn simply omits the transition theme for the recapitulation)
return to second theme, this time also in I key.

Second Movement

The second movement contrasts in character. Where the first movement is quick, rhythmic, and major, this movement is slow, lyrical, and predominantly minor. The dramatic contrast is between two themes. The first is an F-minor idea. Simply stated, it is a trill, followed by a brief, upward-climbing motive:

We hear it three times in the opening measures. Untypical for a Classical piece, each of the statements seems like a question, with the music supplying no immediate answer. But the balancing phrase is not far behind. It is in F minor's relative major, A♭, and is made of downward-moving, quicker, more certain-sounding phrases:

The piece becomes a dialogue between these two ideas—the one slow, sad, wistful, the other active, positive, optimistic. If it is a dialogue, it becomes a passionate one, and one whose outcome is uncertain until the last four measures, which are dominated by the F-minor key and mood.

Third Movement

As soon as the last movement begins, we realize that this is what the lowered mood of the slow movement has set us up for. It is back in F major, very fast and very rhythmic. Its rhythm is not the playful syncopation of the first movement, but the straight-ahead, definite beat of a folk dance. We know that composers in the Classical period were fond of using actual folk themes, but since the folk music itself was not written down and preserved separately, it is impossible to prove just what melody came from where. Perhaps Haydn borrowed the tune from a dance which was popular among the peasants in one of the local villages. Or perhaps it is entirely Haydn's own invention, merely designed to capture some folk-dance flavor. In the twentieth century, scholars, including the composers Bartók and Kodály, have written down Hungarian folk songs, and rhythms similar to the one Haydn uses can be found in their collections.

Haydn's rhythm

Folk-song rhythm

After eight bars, the folk song repeats its rhythm. Haydn takes the rhythmic idea and develops, changes, and elaborates on it. The energy of the original folk idea is still present, but we are also conscious of the sophisticated, high-art techniques Haydn has used in developing it.

Haydn is like Mozart in this respect; the even consistency of their Classical style can blind us to the contrast and conflict going on beneath it. In his F-Major Sonata he gives us a first movement full of rhythmic ambiguity and virtuoso display; the second movement is full of emotionally-charged melodies; the third carries the physical energy of folk dance into the sonata.

I say he gives "us" these things. It might seem more correct to say that he gave them to Nikolaus Esterhazy, and it is true that Esterhazy was their first and most important listener. But within a year of their composition they had been published and reviewed. Haydn had not just his patron in mind, but the larger public—"us"—in mind as well.

SUMMARY: *Haydn's* Sonata in F Major, *Number 23 (1773)*

melody	In the first movement, the melodies are identified principally by their rhythmic patterns and their harmonic functions. The first theme is angular and rhythmic, the second is based on running scale passages. The second movement's theme is lyrical and song-like. The third movement's melody is angular and "bouncy," suitable to its folk-dance flavor.
harmony	Outer movements major, middle movement minor. Harmonic motion in general governed by basic V-I and IV-V-I progressions.
rhythm	Rhythmic tension in first movement, created by an ambiguity between the implied beat of the melody alone and the actual beat of the melody in its setting. The second movement is cast in a slow 6/8 rhythm. The accompaniment subdivides each beat into a group of three, over which the melody extends in long-held notes. The third movement is characterized by a quick, strong, two-beat pattern.
form	Three movements of contrasting types. First movement rhythmic and virtuosic, in sonata form; second movement slow and lyrical; third movement quick and energetic, with folk- dance quality.
timbre	Probably originally intended for harpsichord, although it is an equally effective piece on the piano.
texture	Almost entirely homophonic, the right hand supplying the melody, the left hand supplying the accompaniment.
function	Originally intended for the private entertainment of aristocratic patrons. At the same time, publication made the work available to a much wider audience.

Beethoven

Beethoven's Early and Middle Life

If Ludwig van Beethoven matches our idea of what a musical genius should be, it is partly because he is the single person most responsible for creating our image of such a figure. He was born in 1770, in Bonn, and died in 1827, in Vienna. Now the capital of West Germany, Bonn in 1770 was a relatively minor provincial court. Beethoven's grandfather had been musical director *(Kappelmeister)* at the court, his father the principal tenor singer there. Beethoven showed talent at an early age, including a love of improvisation. A friend of their family later remembered hearing the father chastise the son for improvising, telling him that he could only learn from practicing the notes.

A somewhat half-hearted attempt was made to market young Beethoven just as the young Mozart had been; his father apparently lied about Beethoven's age to make him appear more of a prodigy. But Johann van Beethoven did not have Leopold Mozart's energy and ability. What he had instead was a serious

Ludwig van Beethoven
(c. 1803)

drinking problem which eventually forced Beethoven into the role of head of the family, taking upon himself the responsibility for his two younger brothers.

He received a salary from the court for playing the organ in the chapel and the viola in the court orchestra. This salary was extended for a time to help support him when he went to further his musical education in Vienna, the musical, cultural, and political capital of the Austrian Empire.

He was in Vienna for a short time in 1790, moving there permanently in 1792. He studied briefly with Mozart, longer with Haydn. Although he was certainly influenced by their music, his studies with these great men were not themselves of great importance to him. His sense of his own style and direction was already so strong that he was able to benefit more from purely technical work with much lesser composers.

Vienna seems to have been crowded with wealthy, music-loving aristocrats. Some had their own orchestras or chamber groups, some sponsored musical activities on a regular basis, many were themselves skilled performers. Beethoven's patronage from this group was unlike that of Haydn, Mozart, or any other previous composer. He became for a time a kind of exalted "society pianist" by playing in their homes, by giving lessons to them or to their children (it was particularly the fashion for women to learn to play the piano, and Beethoven acquired a number of countesses as pupils), and by participating in their concerts. What is so unusual is that he did this not as hired help but as a social equal; not by being charming and deferential, but by—or in spite of—being brash, stubborn, outspoken and egocentric.

In a popular novel of the time, Goethe's *The Sorrows of Young Werther,* the hero goes to a dinner dressed somewhat casually and talks to an aristocrat without showing proper respect; society condemns him for committing these grave sins against its rules. Beethoven constantly broke such rules. While playing some duets at the home of a Count Browne, he was bothered by a young nobleman who continued to converse across the room. He lifted his companion's hands from the keys and said "I play no longer for such swine," and in fact played no more that evening.

The great experience was to hear him improvise. His audiences were not merely amazed at the speed and power of his playing and inventiveness—they were moved by these performances, sometimes to tears. This was a reaction which seemed to embarrass him—he would laugh and call them fools and children.

The aristocracy happily tolerated his insubordinate behavior. A publication from 1795, when he had been in Vienna only three years, includes a list of subscribers which is like an aristocratic "Who's Who." According to the traditional saying, "he who pays the piper calls the tune." It is clear, however, that Beethoven called his own tunes. It may be accidental, but his first Viennese publication makes specific reference to this subject. It is a set of variations on a theme by Mozart, from an aria, "Se vuol ballare," in his opera *The Marriage of Figaro.* In the aria, Figaro, the barber, mocks his employer, the count (not, luckily, nearby to hear him), saying "If you want to dance, Signor Count, I'll play the tune."

The Viennese nobility continued to support Beethoven throughout his career. They paid for lessons, sponsored concerts, commissioned compositions, and paid for dedications. Eventually, the Archduke Rudolph, Count Kinsky, and Prince Lobkowitz joined together to offer him a guaranteed income for life. At the same time, he was developing more widely-based means of support. One of these was through public concert-giving; another was through music publication, an activity gradually becoming more important as more and more middle-class people acquired musical interests, instruments, and skills. Beethoven developed ways of merging these various sources of support. He would compose a piece; then try it out for his aristocratic patrons, benefitting from their orchestras and chamber groups as well as from their responses; then perhaps offer to sell the completed work in manuscript to one of them, so that they would have exclusive rights to it for six months or a year; then use it in a public concert; and then finally sell it to one of the five or six publishers he worked with.

Another set of variations from early in his career is based on a Handel aria, "See the Conquering Hero Comes." Again, the choice of words may be accidental, but it is pertinent. The idea of the "heroic" is a central one for Beethoven. It surfaces most explicitly in his third symphony, which he titled "Sinfonia Eroica"—"Heroic Symphony." It was originally designed as a tribute to Napoleon, a real conquering hero whom Beethoven admired as a champion of the rights of the common man and as a man of common origin who had risen to greatness. When Napoleon declared himself Emperor, claiming for himself the privileges of aristocracy, Beethoven was disgusted and destroyed the dedication, changing it to "the memory of a great man." Surely Beethoven saw something Napoleonic in himself—a man whose genius alone ennables him to rise to eminence.

If a hero is someone who can triumph over adversity, Beethoven was indeed a hero. When he was about 30 years old he began to notice some loss of hearing. By 1802 he could sense that his hearing was gradually and steadily getting worse. He despaired—a despair which was surely justified. The world had seen many blind musicians, but never a deaf one. "Deaf musician" is a contradiction in terms. Spending the summer in Heiligenstadt, a little town in the country near Vienna, he wrote a will, called the "Heiligenstadt Testament." In it he tells his brothers:

> how humiliated I have felt if somebody standing beside me heard the sound of a flute in the distance and *I heard nothing* . . . . Such experiences almost made me despair, and I was on the point of putting an end to my life. The only thing that held me back was *my art.* For indeed it seemed to me impossible to leave this world before I had produced all the works that I felt the urge to compose . . .*

It was his despair which he had to conquer; once it was defeated he could go on to conquer his deafness, or at least reconcile himself to it. He found that he could still compose, could still hear the music inside his head and write it

*Translation by Emily Anderson: *The Letters of Beethoven,* St. Martin's Press, 1961.

down, even when so deaf that he could not hear thunderous applause. At the performance of his Ninth Symphony, he had to be turned around so he could *see* the audience's reaction.

It is always dangerous to draw too-close parallels between a composer's life and his music. Nevertheless, Beethoven's accomplishments in conquering his own despair and fighting through the effects of deafness on his career really are heroic ones, and it is in his music from this "middle period" of his life (approximately 1802 to 1814) which expands in scale, challenges conventions, and imposes a new dramatic and personal style upon the Classical forms. It is as though his personal victories gave him the confidence to re-shape music to reflect his own personality.

"Appassionata" Sonata

One such middle-period work is the *Piano Sonata in F Minor,* Opus 57 ("opus" means "work;" the opus numbers usually refer to the order in which works were published), known as "The Appassionata" (not Beethoven's title.) Like other Classical sonatas we have looked at, it begins by outlining the tonic chord:

Opening statement of "Appassionata"

This opening is similar to that with which Haydn begins his *Sonata in F Major* (*see* Chapter 20).

Opening statement of Haydn's F-Major Sonata

The difference between what the two composers do with this initial statement illustrates the development wrought by Beethoven in the Classical style. The first phrase of Haydn's sonata involves close, quick movement in the middle range of the keyboard; its harmonies go from chords I to V and back to I almost immediately.

Beethoven separates the hands, sending the left hand deep down the piano keyboard. And it is clearly a *piano* keyboard; all through the work Beethoven will be exploring deep piano sonorities, timbres unavailable on the harpsichord and only barely possible on the pianos of his own day, whose capabilities he stretched to, and beyond, their limits. He pauses at the bottom of the chord, then brings both hands up, through the chord, taking two measures to arrive at the V chord with which, after a trill, the phrase ends.

Opening measures of "Appassionata"

The trill is not a new device; it is a typical Classical ornament, a polite and elegant gesture which neatly finishes off the phrase. (Mozart uses a trill to similar effect in the opening phrases of his C-Major Piano Sonata [*see* Chapter 19].) Unlike Haydn, Beethoven offers no immediate return to the tonic (I) chord. Instead, he lifts the whole pattern up one half-step, as though we were suddenly in the key of G♭ instead of F minor. Another trill brings us back to the V chord. Then a little rhythmic figure is introduced:

Another trill increases tension by ending on a diminished-seventh chord. The little rhythmic pattern is repeated low, then high, then low, then high again before suddenly bursting into a cadenza-like passage still on the V chord; only after this does the music return to the I chord. What in Haydn's structure required only two measures, in Beethoven's requires 16. Where Haydn's two measures range over two octaves, Beethoven's 16 use five and one-half.

After introducing his first phrase and providing an answering phrase to it, Haydn presents a variation on the original statement, beginning:

Beethoven also presents a variation on his original statement. It begins, *pianissimo,* like an exact repetition, before erupting into a tremendous series of *fortissimo* chords:

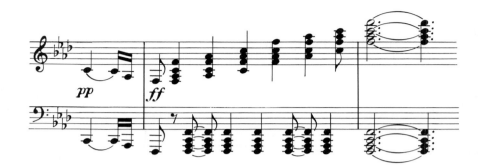

He goes back to the opening pattern and again interrupts it with chords. Again he returns to the opening theme at the point where a trill finished off the opening phrase. As noted above, this trill is so typical of Classical politeness and elegance, that it makes Beethoven's third series of powerful chords seem particularly disruptive.

The opening section has many long-held notes and pauses for rests, which, coupled with the low piano timbres and the minor key, help to create a sense of preparation, even foreboding. But the opening section does not prepare us for these violent disruptions by powerful chords. They open up the structure, thus creating conflict and tension which demand to be resolved. The first result of this demand is a series of quick repeated notes in groups of three, rhythmic energy which flows out of the structure like lava from a volcano. This is the modulating section, which, in Classical sonata form, is slightly different when the first theme is in a minor key.

Normally, in sonata form, the composer moves from the I key to the V key. When the I key is minor, however, the most closely related tonal center is not V, but III. The III key shares a key signature—the same sharps and flats—with the minor I key, and for this reason is called the "relative" major of the minor I key. If the sonata were in A minor, the relative major would be C major. In this case, F minor, the relative major (and the destination towards which Beethoven is modulating) is A♭.

The second theme section is related to the opening theme. Where that theme begins on a C and moves downward to outline the F-minor chord, this theme begins on a C and moves upward to outline the A♭-major (III) chord.

Beginning of first theme—
outlines F-minor chord

Beginning of second theme—
outlines A♭-major chord

The second theme develops a lilting character before showing us another aspect, as it moves into A♭ minor, where the melody changes to one with tremendous energy and building force. It is now cast in sixteenth notes:

Measures 51 and 52

although a simpler pattern arises out of these:

Melody heard in measures 51 and 52

Continuing along the lines provided by Classical structure, Beethoven next begins the development section. He combines melodies from the first and second theme sections with challenging virtuoso passages, going through a number of keys before arriving at an extended passage built on a diminished-seventh chord. This passage lasts nine measures (on one chord) before the pattern

is used to relax the tension in the chord and take us back to the recapitulation.

Following Classical structure again, the recapitulation begins with the opening theme. This time, however, the theme is accompanied by an undercurrent of repeated three-note groupings. Although this rhythmic pattern has not been constantly present, the rhythmic energy it represents has continued from the moment of its introduction. The powerful "interrupting" chords are given this time in F major, preparing us for the second theme to stay in that key, instead of going to Ab as it did in the exposition. The recapitulation section ends back in F minor, and we are prepared for the piece to draw to its close. Instead, it starts up again. Where Beethoven *could* have given us the music shown at the top of page 208, he instead continues the bass line back up, as shown in the second musical example on page 208, leading us into a **coda** section. ("Coda" in Italian means "tail.") This begins somewhat like a second development section, but it becomes something closer to a cadenza—a freely structured, exuberant display of piano virtuosity. Then, back to the recapitulation: the second theme in F minor, one last great build-up of rhythmic chords before the opening statement returns high and sinks down through five octaves to the movement's closing notes.

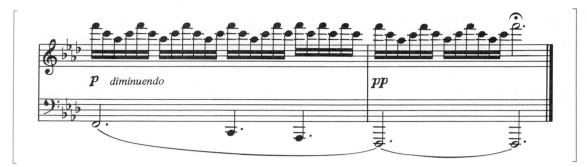

Measures 205–206 turned into an ending

Bass line to measures 206–208

All of the great Classical composers challenge the even balance of the Classical style. There is little energy or excitement in pure balance, absolute equilibrium. But it is clear that Beethoven's challenges go much further than either Mozart's or Haydn's. At times he seems actively to attack the style's conventions. This has led many historians to view him as a composer who left the Classical style and became a Romantic. Those who, like me, regard him as a Classical composer have four principal arguments. One, that clarity of form is a crucial attribute of the style. A work like the first movement of the "Appassionata" carefully marks off first and second themes, their key relationships, the sections of exposition, development and recapitulation. Two, that the Classical style's favorite device of sonata form allows for, even demands, dramatic development, which is certainly an essential aspect of the "Appassionata"'s first movement. Three, the style does not mind violent departures from that equilibrium, as long as equilibrium is finally restored. This movement certainly stretches the idea of "equilibrium" to the breaking point, but the still calm center with which the piece begins is also the point to which it at length returns. Four, that the Classical style is much less concerned with representing emotional states than is the Romantic style. This is, obviously, a very subjective area. But my own conclusion is that the "Appassionata" offers us a picture of Beethoven's personality, not a catalogue of his emotions. Beethoven tells us not "how I feel" but "who I am." If the work's title has any accuracy, it is not because it tells us what Beethoven's passions were, but because it tells us how deeply impassioned a man he was.

Color Plate 1 *Madonna and Child on a Curved Throne,* Byzantine. Tempera on wood panel, 32⅛ × 19⅜″. National Gallery of Art, Washington (Andrew W. Mellon Collection).

Like Medieval religious music, this painting asks the viewer to concentrate on spiritual as opposed to physical values. It hides the physical aspects of its figures beneath its bright, flat, weightless patterns.

Color Plate 2 MASACCIO, *Expulsion from the Garden,* ca. 1425. Fresco. Brancacci Chapel, Santa Maria del Carmine, Florence.

In contrast to the Medieval image in Pl. 1, this Renaissance painting by Masaccio makes the physical nature of its figures seem solid and real. Even at this moment of ultimate shame, their bodies convey the Renaissance sense of human strength, dignity, and beauty.

Color Plate 3   HUBERT AND JAN VAN EYCK, *The Ghent Altarpiece* (detail), ca. 1425–32. Tempera and oil on panel, 11′6″ × 14′2″. Cathedral of Saint Bavon, Ghent.

The Northern Renaissance artist Jan Van Eyck gives his choir of angels a quirky, human individuality. So careful is Renaissance observation of reality, that scholars are able to use works like this to study contemporary techniques of singing.

Color Plate 4   JAN STEEN, *The Family Concert,* 1666. Oil on canvas, 86.6 × 101.0 cm. Gift of T.B. Blackstone, 1891.65. © 1987 The Art Institute of Chicago. All Rights Reserved.

Steen shows relaxed, informal music-making as part of middle-class household life—the kind of situation that called for the growth of music publishing. Although the scene is a homely one, a flair for the dramatic appears in the theatrical lighting.

The religious background to this work is Italian and Catholic, a world apart from the German Protestantism that Bach and Handel knew. But it is similar to their works in its Baroque grandeur and majesty and in its vision of religion as an uplifting and transforming experience.

Color Plate 5   BACICCIO (Giovanni Battista Gaulli), *Triumph of the Name of Jesus,* 1676–79. Ceiling fresco. Il Gesù, Rome.

Color Plate 6   ACHILLES PAINTER,
Muse Playing the Kithara,
ca. 445 B.C. Vase painting.
Private Collection, Lugano.

This work from ancient Greece shows the clarity, balance, grace, simplicity, and elegance associated with the Classical style—Mozart's Classical style as well as ancient Greece's.

Color Plate 7   JACQUES-LOUIS DAVID,
Madame de Pastoret and Her Son,
1791/92. Oil on canvas, 129.9 ×
97.1 cm. Clyde M. Carr Fund and
Major Acquisitions Fund,
1967.228. © 1987 The Art
Institute of Chicago. All Rights
Reserved.

David, working in the year after Mozart's death, imitates not just the pose but also many of the stylistic elements of the Greek vase painting (Pl. 6). At the same time, he is arguing a contemporary point, telling us that this aristocratic woman does her own knitting and nursing and is really just a simple citizen—an argument which may have helped save her from the Revolutionary guillotine.

Color Plate 8   THOMAS EAKINS, *The Pathetic Song,* 1881. Oil on canvas, 45 × 32½″. In the collection of the Corcoran Gallery of Art. Museum Purchase, Gallery Fund, 1919.

Eakins shows Romantic music in a typical setting—a parlor performance. The word "pathetic" in the title means "full of feeling," not, as in today's usage, "pitiful." But there is something modern about Eakins's painting, in that he reports on the scene, but does not, as a Romantic singer would, inject his own feelings into it.

Color Plate 9   EUGÈNE DELACROIX, *The Abduction of Rebecca,* 1846. Oil on canvas, 39½ × 32¼″. The Metropolitan Museum of Art, Wolfe Fund, 1903 (Catherine Lorillard Wolfe Collection, 03.30).

Delacroix, the friend of Chopin and George Sand, here creates a typically Romantic image. He tells a story (borrowed from the novel Ivanhoe *by Sir Walter Scott) about an attempt to corrupt innocence, and tells it in a style full of freedom and spontaneity.*

Color Plate 10 CASPAR DAVID FRIEDRICH, *Monk at the Seashore,* 1808. Oil on canvas. Schloss Charlottenburg, West Berlin.

Friedrich's image captures the Romantic vision of the lonely individual, looking to nature to find a mirror for the soul. The fact that the individual is a monk makes the story even more pointed: where are his brothers, where is his church? They have been replaced by solitude and nature.

Color Plate 11 OSCAR CLAUDE MONET, French, 1840–1926, *Rouen Cathedral at Dawn,* 1894. Oil on canvas, 41¾ × 29⅛″. Tompkins Collection, Courtesy, Museum of Fine Arts, Boston.

Monet painted Rouen Cathedral over and over again because what he was painting was not the stones of the building, but the sensory impressions made by the changing lights and atmospheres through which the building was seen. It is on this level that Monet's Impressionism is similar to Debussy's. Both are concerned with sensory impressions—with the sensations caused by a particular quality of light or by a particular timbre of the piano.

Color Plate 12   OTTO DIX, *Großstadt*, Triptych (middle panel), 1927–28. Oil on canvas, 181 × 201 cm. Museum of the City of Stuttgart.

Jazz (or imitations of it) became popular in Europe in the 1920s. For artists of the time, including the composer Kurt Weill as well as the painter Otto Dix, it seemed to have the vitality of a new culture, providing bitter contrast to what they saw as the decayed or dying values of their own.

Color Plate 13   JULES OLITSKI, *High A Yellow,* 1967. Synthetic polymer, 89½ × 150″. Collection of the Whitney Museum of American Art (gift of the Friends of the Whitney Museum of American Art, Acq. No. 68.3).

Painters like Olitski throw away traditional rules for composition. Instead of forms, they present fields of color. The only tension in the work is between the field and its edges. Olitski's work minimizes conflict; instead, it emphasizes the process of seeing, just as Steve Reich's works emphasize the process of hearing.

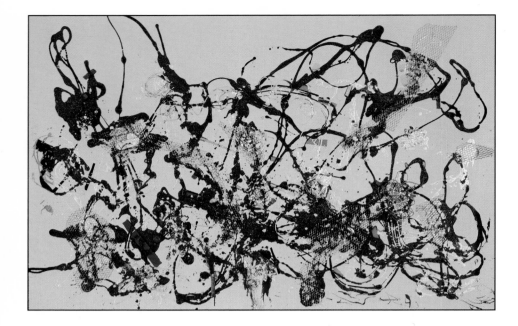

Color Plate 14 JACKSON POLLOCK, *No. 29*, 1950. Oil and other materials on glass, 121.9 × 182.9 cm. National Gallery of Canada, Ottawa.

Pollock's career in painting paralleled Charlie Parker's career in jazz. Both came to New York City, led revolutions in their artforms, and were famously self-destructive in their lifestyles. Beyond this, their works share a love of freedom, of improvisation, and of curving, swirling lines.

Color Plate 15 ANDY WARHOL, *Marilyn,* 1963. Acrylic and silkscreen enamel on canvas, 60″ × 40″. Private Collection.

Pop Art took popular culture into galleries and museums. For the Pop artist Warhol, the most important reality was not the physical material world, but the world of mass media images. When he painted Marilyn Monroe, he painted not her person but her image, and to do so he imitated the mass-media style—reduction and repetition. Her image turns up again on the Pop Art-influenced cover to Sgt. Pepper.

SUMMARY: *Beethoven's* Sonata in F Minor, *Opus 57,*
"*Appassionata," first movement (1805)*

melody	Two principal themes. First theme outlines F-minor chord, using a "long-short-long" rhythmic pattern; second theme uses a similar rhythmic pattern to outline an A♭-major chord, but then develops a more lilting character.
harmony	Modulations follow the pattern decreed by sonata form, but within this there are many shifts between minor (which dominates) and major tonalities. Harmonic motion tends to be slow, with long stretches based on a single harmony.
rhythm	Strong, identifiable rhythmic patterns imbedded in melodies. The characteristic rhythmic pattern which runs underneath much of the movement is four strong beats, each beat subdivided into a group of three.
form	Sonata form with the addition of a coda, which in this work acts somewhat as a cadenza would in a concerto.
timbre	The work is explicitly designed for the piano. Where Mozart's C-Major or Haydn's F-Major Sonatas could be played on the harpsichord, this work could only be performed on the piano. It exploits the piano's wide range, its various levels of volume, and especially its ability to let sounds ring and accumulate.
texture	Homophonic. Any given moment in the piece is likely to find a melodic pattern and an accompanying figure, but their relationship is never static; that is, the melody and accompaniment intertwine as they range up and down the length of the keyboard.
function	First performed for Beethoven's aristocratic patrons and dedicated to one of them, Count Franz von Brunswick. Made available to a wider audience through publication. Popular as a concert and recital piece from that day to this.

The Fifth Symphony

In December of 1808, about four years after completing the "Appassionata" Sonata, Beethoven gave an amazing concert. This was not a private entertainment in an aristocrat's palace, but an event open to the public. The program included: his Sixth Symphony (first performance), an aria, his Fourth Piano Concerto, two movements from a Mass, the Fifth Symphony (first performance), a piano improvisation by Beethoven, and, because he didn't think that the program was full enough with all this, a choral fantasia involving the chorus, orchestra, and piano. This choral fantasia was finished only at the last minute; the orchestra was in general under-rehearsed; all of the different performers had never rehearsed together in a proper run-through; the hall was cold; the concert lasted four and one-half hours.

Klober: *Ludwig van Beethoven* (1818)

A wise friend would certainly have counseled Beethoven to cut a few numbers from the program. The friend would have been wrong. No piece of music is fully born until it has been performed. The birth these works received may have been a difficult one, for artists and audience alike, but the concert succeeded in its delivery, and within a few months the particular work we will be looking at, the Fifth Symphony, was known, published, and being performed elsewhere in Europe. It is probably safe to say that the sun never sets on the Fifth Symphony—today and every day, somewhere in the world some group is rehearsing or performing it.

It begins with the most famous four-note motive in music:

The strings and clarinets play this in unison, plus a following phrase, held out a little longer:

Beethoven isolates the motive and states it as simply and directly as possible. He is like a magician rolling up his sleeves to show that nothing is hidden—these simple materials are all he needs. There is nothing obviously magical in the theme itself; it is a simple, basic idea which could have occurred to anyone. One difference between Beethoven and "anyone" is that Beethoven realizes the energy locked in the theme and knows how to release it. Although the symphony's first movement is in sonata form, with its conventional exposition, development, and recapitulation (plus a coda), there is a sense in which these first five measures are the exposition; everything else in the movement develops them.

The process begins with the motive being traded off among the strings, moving quickly from the second violins to the violas, then to the first violins, back to the seconds, to the violas, and so on. In the process some subtle shifts take place. We learn that the theme retains its identity with its edges rounded:

and even when reversed:

After a cadence on the V chord (G major) the entire orchestra states the theme *fortissimo.* Then the theme begins to move around the orchestra again, and we find that it retains its identity when played on a single note:

when used in a rising pattern:

and when made part of a broken chord:

This motion is leading to the entrance of the second theme, which will be in the key of E♭ major (C minor's relative major).

The second theme is introduced by the horns. They begin with a variation on the first theme, a kind of "fanfare" which involves a longer fall in the melodic pattern. Where the first-theme statement gave us:

this introduction to the second theme gives us:

The second theme itself is like a rebound from the falling motion of the horn fanfare, rising up through the same notes:

The first theme itself is never out of mind. As the second theme develops its own momentum and begins to climb in volume, range, and intensity, the first theme is always present as basses and violas play patterns like:

and:

At the climax of this section, the first theme takes over completely again, taking us back to the beginning for a repeat of the exposition.

As we have seen, development sections in the Classical period frequently lead to fragmentation of thematic material. But how, one might ask, do you fragment themes which only have a few notes to begin with? One method Beethoven chooses is through orchestration, as he sends the theme around the orchestra, presenting it in a variety of timbres. This motion, plus the movement through different keys, leads to a climactic statement of the "fanfare" melody which introduces the second theme:

After stating it and using it to build more energy, Beethoven subjects it, short as it is, to a literal fragmentation. First he cuts off its last note:

Then its first three notes, leaving:

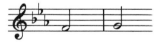

Finally, he reduces it to just one note, traded back and forth between winds and strings. After all of the preceding activity, this reduction to a single note creates an enormous amount of tension; energy seems to build up behind it, and we wait for it to burst forth. Then the first theme begins its return, on the top two notes of a diminished-seventh chord. It is played eight times on these notes before finally relaxing into the recapitulation's return to the opening theme.

There are a number of changes between the exposition and the recapitulation, the most striking of which is the introduction of a brief, slow passage for solo oboe. Another double reed, the bassoon, introduces the second theme section, which follows sonata form rules by simply shifting into C major, instead of modulating up to E♭ as it did in the exposition. This is a logical place for the piece to end; but as the woodwinds and the first violins hold their C, the lower strings shift underneath to a totally unexpected F-minor chord, sending us into a coda which is the equivalent of a second development section.

A version of the "fanfare" theme is heard in the bassoon, a version closely related to the movement's first theme:

First theme   "Fanfare" statement from coda

Now Beethoven takes the last three notes of this theme and turns them into a long downward "stair-step":

When this "stair-step" reaches the bottom of its run, it turns around and begins to climb:

Beethoven then begins to fragment this "climbing" theme:

Flute   Violin   Flute   Violin

As this outline shows, the melodic material he is now using has derived directly from the very first, opening statement of the first theme. Each step away from that theme has felt like a natural and logical development. But it has gone through so many transformations that its connection with the first theme now seems tenuous, leaving us as listeners feeling uncertain where we are. This of course is exactly where Beethoven wants us at the moment just before he brings back the opening statement one final time. For a second it seems that this opening statement is going to take off again, and then it interrupts itself with the series of chords which closes the movement.

Earlier I spoke of the "heroic" qualities connected with middle-period works like the Fifth Symphony. Certainly the world had never heard a work which so completely demonstrated the sheer force and power of an individual personality. While it is only natural to think of the work in terms of the personality of its creator, it is also fair to think about the work's relationship to the world. This is a public work. Not just because it was originally intended for public performance, but because its sheer scale forces it outside the aristocratic music rooms. It may be significant that Beethoven was originally going to sell the work to a Count Oppersdorff, but changed his mind and sold it to a publishing firm instead. He must have realized from the beginning that this music which reflects his own personality—stormy, embattled, grand, stirring, victorious—is also capable of speaking directly to a vast audience.

SUMMARY: *Beethoven's* Symphony No. 5, *first movement (1808)*

melody	A series of developments and transformations from an initial four-note theme.
harmony	The harmonic relationships are usually simple, strong, and clear, often based on movement from V to I. The modulations carry an element of surprise.
rhythm	The typical "short-short-short-long" pattern appears throughout the movement. It is as important to the movement's sense of unity as the melodic patterns.
form	Sonata form: exposition (repeated); development; recapitulation; coda.
timbre	An orchestra of strings plus woodwinds, brass, and timpani.
texture	Predominantly homophonic, but there are strong polyphonic elements as well, in that accompanying figures frequently have a good deal of important melodic content. In addition, the sense of a single melodic line of the sort traditionally associated with homophony is challenged by Beethoven's tendency to move the melody around among a variety of different orchestral timbres.
function	Originally presented in public concert and popular in that medium ever since.

Beethoven's Later Life

The last period of Beethoven's life (the period from about 1813 to his death in 1827) was an unhappy one. His deafness, which became total, proved more of an affliction in his personal life than in his musical one. Most people think that blindness would be the harder loss to bear, but according to people who have suffered both, deafness is much worse. Blindness may isolate you from the visual world, but deafness isolates you from other people. As Beethoven's deafness increased, he was reduced to using "conversation books"—notebooks in which his companions would write their conversation. Other illnesses troubled him as well, and he was tormented by family problems. These revolved for the most part around the family of a brother who died, leaving a son named Karl, and appointing his widow and Beethoven as joint guardians. Beethoven disapproved of the widow's morals and initiated a bitter court battle for custody of the boy. The composer won, but it would have been a far better thing for all concerned had he lost. He was jealous, possessive, demanding—hopelessly ill-equipped to be a parent. Karl's desire to escape the pressures of the relationship eventually contributed to his attempted suicide. (Later, he became an army officer, finally retiring a wealthy man in large part due to his inheritance from Beethoven.)

As a man of passionately-held democratic beliefs, Beethoven was distressed by the turn of political events during this period, as, in the aftermath of Napoleon's defeat, Europe suffered through a period of reaction and political repression. In this harsh political climate, the Viennese public was in the mood for light, escapist entertainment, not works of grand seriousness. At the same time, many of Beethoven's aristocratic patrons had lost holdings and rents during the years of war and so were less equipped to support his music.

On all these fronts—his health, his family, his social life, politics, his relationship with his audiences—Beethoven felt battered and defeated. These feelings are present in his letters, and we might expect to find them in his late-period music. But there is in fact more calm and peace, more joy and enjoyment of beauty in these works than in the works from his middle period.

The "Cavatina" Movement

His very last works were a series of string quartets, compositions for the basic string ensemble of two violins, one viola, and one 'cello. The string quartet represents a "pure" kind of music. That is, it does without the contrasting instrumental timbres found in other ensembles; it lacks the capacity for sheer volume found in larger groups; it does not focus on individual performers and their virtuosity; it lacks the extra-musical references found in vocal works. It is chamber music; that is, music designed to be played not in a concert hall but in a chamber, a room in a house. In short, the string quartet is ideally suited for a small group of listeners seriously committed to music. Beethoven had such a group of listeners in his circle of aristocratic patrons.

The *String Quartet in B♭ Major,* Opus 130, is unusual in having six movements rather than four. The fifth of these movements Beethoven labeled "Cavatina," a word usually used to describe a short song in an opera. Beethoven is saying, in effect, that this is a song without words.

As the movement begins, the first violin has the melody, or the "singer's" part. The other three instruments are not limited to simple accompaniment, however. Each voice has its own melodic content, and the texture Beethoven creates results from weaving the voices together. The first violin's melody is the principal one, but the final texture is as much polyphonic as homophonic.

A second theme appears in the second violin and is taken up by the first. It is characterized by a repeated falling motive:

Second violin   First violin

A melody like this is not much subject to analysis. Beethoven states it, and then repeats it. There is no intricate working-out, no complex transformation of ideas in a development section. Beethoven is more famous for his stirring drama than for his lyrical melodies, but the fact is that his slow movements are often graced by tunes like this one: slow, simple, inexplicably beautiful. Directly after it comes another short section, just eight measures, which is among the strangest of Beethoven's conceptions. The three lower strings set up a triplet rhythm, *pianissimo*. The first violin enters, with the instruction "Beklemmt" (meaning "oppressed"). As the even triplet rhythm proceeds beneath, the first violin's melody hesitates, stutters, jerks along, with no regular pulse, totally "out of synch" with the accompaniment, based as it is on groups of four against the accompaniment's groups of three:

First violin

Second violin

"Beklemmt" melody

The effect is that of human utterance of a particular sort—a voice overwhelmed by emotion, struggling to articulate. A parallel can be found among Beethoven's own letters. The most famous of these was discovered, unmailed, after his death. No one knows for certain to whom he was writing. He calls her "My immortal beloved," and that is how the letter is still identified. It ends with the same kind of inarticulate speech Beethoven uses in the Cavatina:

"Be calm—love me—Today—yesterday—what tearful longing for you—for you— you—my life—my all—all good wishes to you Oh, do continue to love me—never misjudge your lover's most faithful heart. ever yours ever mine ever ours"*

The movement closes with a return to the first theme. As a whole, its structure is a balanced one, and the melodies arrive in classically balanced phrases. Nevertheless, the end result is not purely Classical. The English Romantic poet William Wordsworth defined his poetry as "powerful emotion recollected in tranquillity." That phrase could serve as a fairly accurate description of the "Cavatina." If its ultimate effect seems more Classical than Romantic, that is only because there is such a sense of balance, of formal neatness. The letter to the "Immortal Beloved" has no such sense of form; it is raw emotion. In the "Cavatina" the emotion has been filtered, refined, made beautiful and perfect. Though not raw, it is still real.

That Beethoven helped create our image of a musical genius was not an intentional effort on his part; given the enormous influence his music had on

Beethoven (lower left) lost in thought on one of his famous walks around Vienna, is oblivious to the greeting of fellow composer Schubert (foreground, bowing).

*Translation by Emily Anderson: *The Letters of Beethoven*, St. Martin's Press, 1961.

Lyser: *Ludwig van Beethoven*
(first published in 1833).

succeeding generations, it was inevitable that his personality would continue to exert influence as well. Perhaps if he had been a thoroughly conventional type, like, for example, his pharmacist brother, with a wife and children and a house in the country, with a carriage and horses and the right sort of clothes for every occasion, then that image might have become the popular one for the gifted composer. In fact, of course, he was not very conventional and became less and less conventional in his behavior as he got older. He was fond of taking long walks around Vienna, a short stocky figure with long unruly hair, heedless of his dress, not noticing a rip in his coat, pausing now and then to take out a notebook and write some bit of music in it. His apartments—he never stayed long in any one of them—were a mess, littered with stacks of books and piles of music manuscript, half-drunk bottles of wine, yesterday's breakfast, even perhaps last week's breakfast. He was often charming, often rude even to his closest friends. To servants and people who saw him on the street he sometimes seemed mad. All of this fits with a certain idea of the genius who works from inner inspiration, not caring for the rules of the world. It is true that Beethoven did not bother much with the rules of the world. But in the most important aspect of his life—his music-writing—he did not depend solely on inspiration. He worked more slowly and more carefully than any composer before him. Although he was a gifted improviser, he did not, even when he had his hearing, work at the piano. He worked with notes written down in sketchbooks, rewritten, rewritten, rewritten again, sometimes working with different versions of an idea for years before finally deciding on the right one. The most trusted and organized pharmacist could not be more careful with his medicines than Beethoven was with his music.

SUMMARY: *Fifth movement, "Cavatina," from Beethoven's* String Quartet in B♭ Major, *Opus 130 (1826)*

melody	The two principal melodies are built on long, lyrical, singable phrases. A third section (the "Beklemmt" section) includes a melody broken into short fragments.
harmony	Based on slow, regular, consonant, major progressions, at times almost like the harmonies of a hymn.
rhythm	Slow *(Adagio molto espressivo)*, regular, three-beat pulse. In the "Beklemmt" section this pulse is divided in two different ways: the melody's fragmented notes are based on beats subdivided into four parts, while the accompaniment's beats are subdivided into groups of three.
form	First theme, second theme, "Beklemmt" theme, return to first theme, summarized ABCA.
timbre	Two violins, viola, and 'cello, generally kept to the lower portions of their ranges.
texture	First theme is set with a largely polyphonic accompanying texture; the second theme's texture is simpler and more homophonic; the

"Beklemmt" section is simply melody in the first violin, accompaniment from the three other strings.

function   Commissioned by the Russian Prince Galitzin for his private entertainment, and originally performed in aristocratic homes, but also intended for publication.

Romantic Themes in Song

The dates conventionally given for the Romantic period are 1825 to 1900, making a neat 75-year span to balance the Classical period's 75 years, 1750 to 1825. In reality, the period doesn't fall quite so neatly into these boundaries. Romantic traits had developed before 1825, especially in literature, and continued after 1900, especially in popular culture.

But the years 1825 to 1900 do mark an age, a richly productive age for music—even, in retrospect, a golden age. The middle-class public which had first appeared in the Renaissance was now large and growing, eclipsing aristocratic patronage. It was a public which was passionate about music. It bought pianos, took lessons, purchased sheet music and scores, went to concerts, and performed at home in the parlor. It was not passive. It read, talked, and argued about music, and not just about whose music was best or who played it best but also about what the music meant. Music was not simply polite entertainment for this audience; in Browning's phrase, the music "told them something." If the audiences were passionate, so was the music. In the most general terms, it can be called "Dionysian," after the Greek god of wine. Its aim was to sweep you away, release your passions, talk soul to soul, not mind to mind.

The word "Romantic" itself comes from an Old French word for "courtly story." (In the popular literature of today the "Romance novel" is often still a courtly story concerned with well-born heroes of some past time.) Romanticism as a style has many elements, but this is a basic one: the fondness for stories. In the examples which follow, we will see that these stories tend to center around certain themes, like the theme of unrequited love, for example, or that of the corruption of innocence. The fondness for stories shows also in Romantic forms. While the Classical age was dominated by abstract forms like the symphony and the sonata, the Romantic period gives us descriptive piano pieces with titles like "Scenes from Childhood," orchestral works with plots (called "tone poems"), and, above all, songs.

Schubert

The first and probably the greatest song writer of the Romantic era was Franz Schubert. One remarkable thing about Schubert's career is that he was such an amateur. "Amateur" comes from the word for "love," and includes the implication that the amateur does what he does for love rather than money. Not that Beethoven, Mozart, Bach, or Handel didn't love what they were doing; nevertheless, they were professionals. Their performing, conducting, teaching, and composing were all done on a professional basis, and they expected to be paid for it. They often worked *for* amateur musicians, since music-making was a favorite hobby of the upper classes. But they would no more have thought of writing, performing, or teaching music just for the love of it than a lawyer would think of arguing a case just for the love of it. A lawyer might enjoy being a lawyer, might find it fulfilling, might love the law, but he or she would generally expect to be paid for the work. Not so Schubert.

He was born in Vienna in 1797, and died there in 1828. His father was a schoolmaster and not a very well-paid one; his mother was formerly a servant. Four children survived out of the 12 who were born to the couple. The family was fond of music-making, and Schubert began to learn piano, violin, and viola from his father and elder brothers. When it became obvious that his musical talents were beyond the ordinary, he was sent to the Imperial choir school, which today is the organization that produces the Vienna Boys' Choir. In 1813 he was offered a scholarship to continue his studies, but turned it down in order to train as a teacher, and then went home to assist at his father's school. The school teaching itself (comparable to teaching at a boys' grade school today) was not particularly pleasant for him, but he did find time to compose. Between 1814 and 1816 he wrote five symphonies, four Masses, three string quartets, three piano sonatas, and some 300 songs. No one commissioned this work; no one published it or paid for it. He and his family and friends performed some of it for their own enjoyment; some of it he stuck in a drawer and never thought about again. He may never have heard music which we now consider among his greatest masterpieces.

Reider: *Franz Schubert (Historisches Museum der Stadt, Wein)*

Bohemian Lifestyle

In the autumn of 1816 he gave up his teaching career and began a new style of living which he would continue until his death. The best single word for it is "Bohemian." The word refers to Bohemia (now a part of Czechoslovakia) because that was thought to be the homeland of the gypsies. Young artists, poets, or musicians, who lived in the middle of the city, who held no regular jobs but who survived through the occasional sale of their work and through the generosity of families and friends: these were the Bohemians. For an artist to live like this at the beginning of a career became almost standard practice. In 1849 a novelist named Henri Murger wrote a book called *Scènes de la vie de Bohème—Scenes of Bohemian Life*, which later formed the basis for an opera by Puccini called *La Bohème.* The story centers on a poet, a painter, a musician, and a philosopher who share a Parisian attic. A century or so later, in America in the 1950s, being a poet or a painter meant living in Greenwich Village, New York, in a loft apartment. The trend has fallen out of fashion recently, perhaps because cheap garrets have become expensive condominiums. But in 1816 an apartment above an inn was cheap, especially if shared with friends. They would meet in coffee houses in the afternoon, sit and talk about art, philosophy, and politics for hours, then go to an inn to drink and dine. This is a pleasant enough kind of life, and has produced many more people skilled at posing as artists than people skilled at making art. Sheer hard work is not an essential part of the Bohemian lifestyle, but it was part of Schubert's. He began to write music as soon as he awoke in the morning and continued straight through until the middle of the afternoon. It is said that he slept with his spectacles on so that he could get a quicker start. When he finished one piece, he began another. Still no one was commissioning his works; no one was offering to publish them; there were no plans for commercial performances.

But he did begin to have some success. A singer named Michael Vogl began to perform some of his songs. He and Schubert would play and sing at friends' houses. These friends were neither aristocrats nor Bohemians, but simply middle-class music lovers. The performances even acquired a name: "Schubertiads." Eventually Schubert began to establish his reputation. Some of his friends helped to sponsor the publication of a few of his early songs. As his work became known, publications increased. A local print shop advertised portraits of Schubert for sale—a good sign of fame. He gave a concert, the only public, commercial concert of his career, in March of 1828. It was a great success, musically and financially. But by November he was dead, at age 31.

Schubert had syphilis. It was practically an epidemic in the nineteenth century, especially among young artists. This, of course, is the other side of the Bohemian lifestyle. Bohemianism is part of middle-class culture. It occurs when the middle-class can afford its own revolutionaries—when the cast-offs can survive on hand-outs. In any previous age, a young composer needed aristocratic support. Now the middle-class was buying published music, going to concerts, taking piano lessons, sponsoring musical evenings, and giving a struggling musician a place to stay from time to time.

A "Schubertiad" at the home of Joseph von Spaun, who is seated to Schubert's left at the piano. To his right is the singer Michael Vogl. Another friend, Moritz von Schwind, did the drawing. *(Historisches Museum der Stadt, Wein.)*

Although the Bohemian artist comes from a middle-class background, and is maintained by middle-class society, he or she is also in rebellion against it. Certain middle-class values (like the value of having a steady job) are rejected, and as a result certain privileges (like having a family and house in the suburbs) are denied. This is the tacit bargain between the Bohemian artist and middle-class society. The artist has independence and freedom the like of which aristocratic patronage was unwilling to grant. The price is to remain an outcast, excluded from the safety and comfort of *bourgeois* existence.

It would be an exaggeration to call Schubert an "outcast." He enjoyed a close relationship with his family, especially his brothers, throughout his short life. But when, a year before his death, he wrote a series of songs to poems by Wilhelm Müller, called *Die Winterreise, The Winter's Journey,* the theme of the outcast was on his mind. The hero of these songs has fallen in love with a girl, his love has been returned, but then rejected because he is not rich enough. His journey is a grief-stricken wandering through winter landscape and ends outside a town where a lonely hurdy-gurdy man grinds his songs for no one. "I envy you, old man," he says. "Can I go with you? Will you grind my songs?"

Speaking directly about himself, Schubert wrote in a letter:

Think of a man whose health can never be restored, and who from sheer despair makes matters worse instead of better. Think, I say, of a man whose brightest hopes have come to nothing, to whom love and friendship are but torture, and whose enthusiasm for the beautiful is fast vanishing; and ask yourself if such a man is not truly unhappy. [Here Schubert quotes one of his own songs:] "My peace is gone, my heart is heavy; never, never again will I find rest."

As a Romantic story, this would all be a little more perfect had Schubert actually died of syphilis. The fact is that although the disease may have weakened him, it is far from being a virtual death sentence. What killed Schubert was an infection, probably typhus, which might have struck anyone in those days of poor public health.

Once again we are faced with myth and reality to disentangle. Schubert was not a neglected genius. He was anything but aggressive in pushing his own work, yet was acquiring considerable fame and success at the time of his death. In giving up the profession of schoolmaster for the Bohemian life, he had cut himself off from certain privileges of middle-class life. He was glad to trade these for the privilege of being allowed to immerse himself in his one great, overriding love—writing music. He was part of a warm circle of family and friends who were a sensitive, appreciative, and enthusiastic audience for everything he wrote. He was a phenomenally hard worker with a phenomenally fertile imagination, and the list of his works is immense despite the shortness of his life. He contracted syphilis perhaps as a consequence of his Bohemian lifestyle, but it was probably a less symbolic disease which killed him.

"Erlkönig"

The music we will examine was written for Johann Wolfgang von Goethe's "Erlkönig," "The Erl-King" (or "Elf-King"), one of the great German Romantic poems. It is also, on one level, a sentimental tearjerker.

"Erlkönig"	"The Erl-King"
Wer reitet so spät durch Nacht und Wind?	Who rides so late through the night and the wind?
Es ist der Vater mit seinem Kind;	It is the father with his child.
Er hat den Knaben wohl in dem Arm,	He holds the boy in his arm,
Er fasst ihn sicher, er hält ihn warm.	grasps him securely, keeps him warm.
'Mein Sohn, was birgst du so bang dein Gesicht?'	'My son, why do you hide your face so anxiously?'
'Siehst, Vater, du den Erlkönig nicht?	'Father, do you not see the Erl-King?
Den Erlenkönig mit Kron und Schweif?'	The Erl-King with his crown and tail?'
'Mein Sohn, es ist ein Nebelstreif.'	'My son, it is only a streak of mist.'
'Du liebes Kind, komm, geh mit mir!	'Darling child, come away with me!
Gar schöne Spiele spiel ich mit dir;	I will play fine games with you.
Manch bunte Blumen sind an dem Strand,	Many gay flowers grow by the shore;
Meine Mutter hat manch gülden Gewand.'	my mother has many golden robes.'
'Mein Vater, mein Vater, und hörest du nicht,	'Father, Father, do you not hear
Was Erlenkönig mir leise verspricht?'	what the Erl-King softly promises me?'
'Sei ruhig, bleibe ruhig, mein Kind:	'Be calm, dear child, be calm—
In dürren Blättern säuselt der Wind.'	the wind is rustling in the dry leaves.'

Engraving from the title page of the first published edition of Goethe's "Erlkönig."

'Willst, feiner Knabe, du mit mir gehn?
Meine Töchter sollen dich warten
schön;
Meine Töchter führen den
nächtlichen Reihn
Und wiegen und tanzen und singen
dich ein.'

'Mein Vater, mein Vater, und siehst du
nicht dort
Erlkönigs Töchter am düstern Ort?'
'Mein Sohn, mein Sohn, ich seh es
genau:
Es scheinen die alten Weiden so grau.'

'Ich liebe dich, mich reizt deine
schöne Gestalt;
Und bist du nicht willig, so brauch ich
Gewalt.'
'Mein Vater, mein Vater, jetzt fasst er
mich an!
Erlkönig hat mir ein Leid's getan!'—

Dem Vater grauset's, er reitet
geschwind
Er hält in den Armen das ächzende
Kind,
Erreicht den Hof mit Müh und Not;
In seinen Armen das Kind war tot.

'You beautiful boy, will you come
with me?
My daughters will wait upon you.
My daughters lead the nightly round,
they will rock you, dance to you, sing
you to sleep!'

'Father, Father, do you not see
the Erl-King's daughters there, in that
dark place?'
'My son, my son, I see it clearly:
it is the grey gleam of the old willow-
trees.'

'I love you, your beauty allures me,
and if you do not come willingly, I
shall use force.'

'Father, father, now he is seizing me!
The Erl-King has hurt me!'

Fear grips the father, he rides swiftly,
holding the moaning child in his arms;
with effort and toil he reaches the
house—
the child in his arms was dead.

It is a ballad; that is, it is in the form of a folk-song ballad like "False Sir John"—a series of verses which tell a story (*see* Chapter 13). Also folk-like is the presence in the tale of the supernatural character of the Erl-King. In addition, the way the story is told, with an objective narrator who simply reports on the events, is similar to the method of many folk ballads. The relationship between father and son is never stated. Instead it is allowed to show itself through their conversation. The son is trusting in his childish appeals, "Mein Vater, mein Vater!," obviously at ease with his parent; the father tries hard to be gentle and comforting. Perhaps this is the point at which Goethe begins to depart from his folk-tale model. The conversations are rendered so believably that the characters acquire a heightened realism for us. It is this realism which produces the poem's mystery: Is the Erl-King real, or the figment of the child's fevered imagination? The realism of the child's desperate plaints make us believe that his illness is behind what he sees; the realism of the Erl-King's appeals make him seem the supernatural cause of the child's troubles. As in all the best ghost stories, the mystery is left unresolved.

A sense of realism is further heightened by the immediacy of the setting. A folk tale would begin with a general sort of statement about the time of year and gradually work its way into the story, but Goethe's poem flashes immediately on the scene of father and child riding through the night.

This immediacy of interest is the first aspect of the poem which Schubert captures. The pattern with which he begins, a series of repeated notes in groups of three, is reminiscent of Beethoven's "Appassionata" Sonata.

Accompaniment from opening measures of "Erlkönig"

From Beethoven's "Appassionata" Sonata

But where Beethoven carefully worked up to this state of heightened energy, Schubert leaps directly into it. The quick repeated notes communicate not just the excitement of the moment but also, on the level of scene-painting, the image of the galloping horse. Further scene-painting is present in the left-hand part: a quick, rising, minor key run.

This may refer to a sudden gust of rain and wind, but, more importantly, it helps create an atmosphere of urgency and foreboding.

Above this accompaniment texture the singer's line follows the emotional states of the three characters and the narrator. The narrator is calm and detached, his phrases balanced. The father initially expresses some worry as his melody rises up:

"My son, why do you hide your face so anxiously?"

Then, in response to his son's questions, he attempts to comfort with calming, lower tones, whose harmonies shift into the major key.

Next the Erl-King himself speaks, and the melody becomes lilting, almost caressing. The son's next appeal to his father shows increased tension as his voice climbs higher and is more dissonant against the accompaniment. Again the father attempts to comfort, again the Erl-King responds, this time with a sweet, major-key tune, given a dancing rhythm, and a singing lilt to match the temptations carried in the words. Even the accompaniment quiets for a moment, exchanging its repeated notes for gentler arpeggios. (This is, incidentally, a welcome moment for the accompanist, whose right hand gets a brief relaxation.)

"Darling child, come away with me!"

The son's response climbs another note higher. The father's reply this time cannot conceal his anxiety: it stays in a minor key. Now the Erl-King becomes forceful. Instead of tempting, he commands:

"And if you do not come willingly, I shall use force."

The son responds immediately with a real cry of pain: "Father, Father, he is seizing me!"

At this point the piano's repeated notes, which began here:

have climbed to here:

Against this F, the voice sings a G♭, just one half-step away, with the E♭ in the bass one whole step away.

Mein   Va - ter,   mein Va - ter,   jetzt   fasst   er   mich an!

"Father, Father, he is seizing me!"

This is an extraordinarily dissonant sound, and Schubert was criticized for going too far in allowing it. But it is essential to the climactic moment. It is the last we hear from any of the characters. The music, along with the narrator, describes the last rushed moments home, even permitting a glimmer of hope as the pace finally slows on to a major chord:

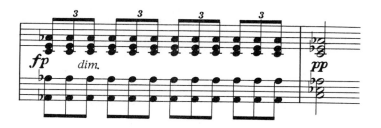

But the major chord is unrelated to the home key, just as the hope is false. The narrator returns to dry commentary which the accompaniment punctuates with simple chords that return to the opening minor: "In his arms the child was dead."

SUMMARY: *Schubert's song "Erlkönig" (1815)*

melody	Different melodic types used for the different characters.
harmony	Considerable dissonance for expressive effect, climaxing with the

	final "Mein Vater, mein Vater!" Frequent modulations contribute to gradual increase in tension; at end, returns to original key.
rhythm	Consistent running triplet pattern which continues without let-up until the final measures.
form	Through-composed. Although the original poem is divided into stanzas, the music's structure obscures these. The strongest sense of repetition comes from the repeated melodic patterns associated with the different characters.
timbre	Voice (originally written for tenor) and piano.
texture	The triplet pattern predominates in the middle range of the piano; voice and bass line contrast above and below this.
function	Used in private entertainments by Schubert and his circle of friends; played occasionally in public concerts; published for a middle-class audience. Schubert's songs remain popular today in concert, recital, and recorded performances.
text	By Johann Wolfgang von Goethe. (*See* pages 224–25.)

"Gretchen am Spinnrade"

"Erlkönig" was Schubert's first published work, so is listed as Opus 1. The publication took place in 1821, but the work was written in 1815, when he was 17 years old. His Opus 2 was actually written even earlier, when he was just 16. It is another setting of a Goethe poem, this time one taken from Goethe's famous drama, *Faust.* The play has a number of songs interspersed in the dialogue, including one which the heroine, Gretchen, sings while alone at her spinning wheel. (Thus the title "Gretchen am Spinnrade," "Gretchen at the Spinning Wheel.") She has met the scholar Faust and fallen in love with him. What she doesn't realize is that Faust has made a pact with the devil, represented by Mephistopheles, and it is the latter who has caused her infatuation. Goethe's *Faust* was well enough known that the average listener would have been aware of the story's tragic ending: after Faust seduces her, she gives birth to a child which she kills in her shame, and is herself condemned to death. At the moment of the song all she knows is that she feels a terrible longing for Faust; a feeling she is unprepared for and ill-equipped to understand. "My peace is gone, my heart is heavy; never, never again will I find rest . . ." These are the words he will use to describe his own situation nine years later.

"Gretchen am Spinnrade"

Meine Ruh ist hin,
Mein Herz ist schwer
Ich finde sie nimmer
Und nimmermehr.

Wo ich ihn nicht hab
Ist mir das Grab,
Die ganze Welt
Ist mir vergällt.

"Gretchen at the Spinning Wheel"

My peace is gone,
my heart is heavy;
never, never again
will I find rest.

Where I am not with him
I am in my grave,
the whole world
turns to bitter gall.

Mein armer Kopf	My poor head
Ist mir verrückt,	is in a whirl,
Mein armer Sinn	my poor thoughts
Ist mir zerstückt.	are all distracted.
Meine Ruh ist hin,	My peace is gone,
Mein Herz ist schwer,	my heart is heavy;
Ich finde sie nimmer	never, never again
Und nimmermehr.	will I find rest.
Nach ihm nur schau ich	I seek only him when I look
Zum Fenster hinaus,	out of the window,
Nach ihm nur geh ich	I seek only him when I leave
Aus dem Haus.	the house.
Sein hober Gang,	His noble gait,
Sein' edle Gestalt,	his fine stature,
Seines Mundes Lächeln,	the smile of his lips,
Seiner Augen Gewalt,	the power of his eyes,
Und seiner Rede	and the magic flow
Zauberfluss,	of his speech,
Sein Händedruck,	the pressure of his hand,
Und ach, sein Kuss!	and oh, his kiss!
Meine Ruh ist hin,	My peace is gone,
Mein Herz ist schwer,	my heart is heavy;
Ich finde sie nimmer	never, never again
Und nimmermehr.	will I find rest.
Mein Busen drängt	My bosom yearns
Sich nach ihm hin.	towards him.
Ach dürft ich fassen	If only I could seize him
Und halten ihn,	and hold him
Und küssen ihn,	and kiss him
So wie ich wollt,	to my heart's content—
An seinen Küssen	under his kisses
Vergehen sollt!	I should die!
[Meine Ruh ist hin,	[My peace is gone,
Mein Herz ist schwer . . .]	my heart is heavy . . .]

In the world of popular music the word "hook" refers to some element of a song that sticks in the memory. Schubert's songs are filled with hooks. The accompaniment of "Gretchen," for example, begins with one of music's most famous scene-paintings. The right hand spins like the wheel of the spinning wheel at which she is seated; the left hand imitates the movement of the pedal—the treadle which makes it go.

This accompaniment communicates something else as well: the anxiety which underlies the girl's words. The tension in the chords projects this, and the constant repetitions of the "treadle" movement in the left hand; in addition there is also a subtle rhythmic tension. We tend to hear the left-hand "treadle" pattern as groups of three beats, whereas the right-hand "spinning" pattern resolves into groups of two:

Left-hand "treadle" pattern   Right-hand "spinning" pattern

The rhythmic tension between these two patterns contributes to the sense of unease. Over this the melody stretches in long, uneven phrases. Its most characteristic pattern:

is typically Schubertian in its unforced and singable lilt. This melodic idea forms the basis of the refrain (the "My peace is gone . . . " verse) and also provides the starting point for the music in the sections between the refrain-verses. The refrain begins the song. The next two verses take the singer higher and into tenser harmonies, as the words make clear the connection between the spinning wheel and her mental state: her "head is in a whirl . . . " After the second refrain, Schubert combines the next three verses into one musical unit. Gretchen starts remembering Faust's attractions, and for a moment her anxiety seems to leave as she loses herself in dreams of him. The accompaniment is quiet and the anxious "treadle" movement silent. The melody climbs in intensity until suddenly she remembers: "and oh, his kiss!" The spinning wheel has stopped, and the chord on "kiss" changes into a harsh, tense diminished seventh:

Her mind has led her back to the sensual desires she is so unprepared to face. With these chords she has stopped her spinning. She begins again, but only hesitantly, after two false starts:

After a refrain, a third verse climbs in intensity once more, telling us that desire is thoroughly awake in her—"If only I could seize him / and hold him / and kiss him . . . " This is followed by a final, incomplete refrain, added to the poem by Schubert.

Gretchen is a young girl suffering through the experience of sexual desire and sexual guilt. It is not surprising that the sixteen-year-old Schubert could empathize with her feelings, but it is astonishing that a sixteen-year-old could convey these feelings so succinctly through his art.

Schubert sent his settings of these songs to Goethe, who noted in his diary that he had received them. If he ever looked at them or listened to them, he left no sign of it, and sent no acknowledgement to Schubert. Goethe was at this time an elderly and established figure, busy and famous. Schubert was young and little known outside Vienna. The irony is that for most of the world today Goethe's poems continue to exist mainly through the medium of Schubert's songs.

SUMMARY: *Schubert's song "Gretchen am Spinnrade" (1814)*

melody   Each section begins with a gentle step-wise motion which then develops and expands.

harmony   Sometimes marked by an *ostinato* effect (same harmonic pattern held over several measures). Modulations and tense harmonies including diminished-seventh chords are used to describe the girl's tormented mental state.

rhythm   The pattern in the melody is regular and straightforward, marked by sustained notes. The accompaniment creates rhythmic ambiguity between the fast "spinning" motive and the repeated "treadle" motive.

form	Schubert develops a tune for the refrain-verse, then departs from it in differing directions for the sections between the refrains. These include two or three verses of poetry, but are through-composed almost as if each were one long verse. Calling the refrain "A" and the sections between refrains "B" gives a structure which looks like this: A B A B′ A B″ 1/2A.
timbre	Voice and piano. Schubert uses the piano's capabilities to get a "blurred" effect appropriate for the whirling spinning wheel.
texture	On the bottom, a bass line played in single sustained notes. In the middle, the "treadle" and "spinning" effects. Above, the vocal melody.
function	Like "Erlkönig," used in private entertainments and public concerts, and published for a middle-class audience.
text	By Goethe. (*See* pages 229–30.)

Robert Schumann

Robert Schumann was born in the town of Zwickau, near Leipzig, Germany, in 1810, and died in an insane asylum near Bonn in 1856.

His father had begun a publishing business by the direct method of writing many books himself. After his father's death, his mother wanted Schumann to become a lawyer, and he dutifully went to Leipzig University and later to Heidelberg. Not much law was learned, however. He devoted himself instead to the study of music and literature, to intense friendships, to philosophical discussions, and to prolonged drinking bouts; in other words, to acquiring a liberal education.

Eventually he convinced his mother to allow him to give up the law and to concentrate on music. He was already an excellent pianist, fond of improvising. His teacher was a man named Wieck, whose most talented student was his daughter Clara. Schumann and Clara Wieck fell in love. Wieck was bitterly opposed to the marriage and kept Schumann from seeing or even writing to his daughter. One of Wieck's fears was that Schumann would be unable to make enough money to support his daughter, since Schumann's potential career as a concert pianist was destroyed when he injured a finger by trying to strengthen it with a mechanical device. He did, however, have other means of support. He received a certain amount of money from the family publishing business, and, true to his father's spirit, embarked on a publishing endeavour of his own. This was the *Neue Zeitschrift für Musik, New Journal for Music,* which he edited and for which he wrote many of the articles.

That a journal devoted to music could succeed indicates that there was a large middle-class public devoted to music: not just a few bankers and doctors but many less wealthy professionals like pharmacists and teachers, as well as government workers and people with management positions in business and industry. This middle class had leisure time to enjoy concerts and to develop amateur music-making skills; it was hungry for music and information about music.

Leipzig was a particularly good city to start such a journal in. It had a rich musical tradition; it was Bach's city. The school Bach taught at and the churches he performed for continued their musical activities. There were teachers like Wieck, and, after 1843, a full-fledged music conservatory. In addition, the city supported a professional orchestra and was the home of a major music publishing house. All this in a community of fewer than 50,000 inhabitants.

Wieck's attempt to separate Schumann from Clara had the predictable result of making their love stronger. Finally Schumann took Wieck to court in an attempt to force him to free Clara for marriage (Schumann had apparently learned at least a few things about the law during his time at the universities.) He won the case, but only after Wieck had delayed things so long that Clara was practically 21 and thus free to marry anyway. They were married on the day before her twenty-first birthday.

Fairy tales always end with the prince and princess getting married, which saves the story-teller from having to deal with the grimy details of reality. In

Composers Clara and Robert Schumann were an example of a successful, two-career marriage.

fact Robert and Clara Schumann had a thoroughly successful two-career marriage. She gave concerts throughout Europe, often playing his music. He composed and sometimes conducted, although he was not very successful as a conductor. Publishers were, however, quick to buy and print his works. Clara's performances were always popular. In a sense, they made an ideal team. Their marriage was successful in other ways as well, producing seven surviving children in 15 years.

There were problems, of course. It is difficult to imagine how Clara managed to maintain a career as a concert pianist (with all that means in terms of practicing for hours every day, learning and memorizing new pieces, as well as arranging the practical details of concerts and tours) in and around the almost constant stream of pregnancies. It is not surprising that they greeted a miscarriage with relief rather than sorrow. Her career put strains on Robert as well. He hated travel, public appearances, and social occasions, all part of the concert pianist's life; but he hated being separated from her even more. Life, in short, may not have been like a fairy tale, but it was certainly productive—children, concerts, and compositions all poured forth in their years together.

The greatest difficulty they faced was Schumann's mental illness. He suffered from recurrent bouts of severe depression. This is a condition not well understood now and certainly not well understood then. In the most severe of these attacks he attempted in 1854 to drown himself in the Rhine. He was rescued, but asked to be put in an asylum. It was as though he were seeking out the fictional situation John Dowland—another composer subject to depression—had described in his song "In Darkness Let Me Dwell" (*see* Chapter 15). Like Dowland's narrator, whose own music becomes "hellish, jarring sounds, to banish friendly sleep," Schumann was plagued by imagined music which would not let him sleep. In asking to have himself committed to the insane asylum, Schumann was asking to be walled off from the world, buried alive like Dowland's narrator, who cries "Oh, let me living die, till death do come."

Dichterliebe

The Schumanns married in September of 1840, a year known as Schumann's "year of song." In that single year he wrote over a hundred songs, thus enriching song literature as much as any composer before or since, with the single exception of Franz Schubert.

Dichterliebe, A Poet's Love is a song cycle written between May 24 and June 1 of that year. It is a sequence of 16 songs all written to poems by Heinrich Heine (1797–1856). Heine, whom Schumann had met in his student days, was the greatest German poet of the generation after Goethe. He published the poems in a book he called *Buch der Lieder, Book of Songs.* Within that book, they form part of a section called "Lyrical Intermezzo," making it clear that Heine himself saw musical qualities in them.

The individual songs are not titled, simply named by their first lines, the first of which is "Im Wunderschönen Monat Mai," "In the Lovely Month of May." This is a conventional beginning, like that to many folk ballads: All in the merry month of May . . . What follows is not very folk-like. Its main concern is not to tell a story, but to describe a state of mind.

Im wunderschönen Monat Mai	In the lovely month of May,
Als alle Knospen sprangen,	when all the buds opened,
Da ist in meinem Herzen	love unfolded
Die Liebe aufgegangen.	in my heart.
Im wunderschönen Monat Mai,	In the lovely month of May,
Als alle Vögel sangen,	when all the birds sang,
Da hab ich ihr gestanden	I confessed to her
Mein Sehnen und Verlangen.	my longing and desire.

The music begins with a piano introduction. Throughout the cycle the piano will play an important role, not just accompanying but partnering the voice. Its very first notes are dissonant; the dissonance relaxes, the melody climbs, and then falls back.

Opening measures, piano accompaniment

The voice follows the folk-like character of the first line:

Opening two phrases of vocal line

These could be Classical-period phrases. What follows could not. The melody climbs, then climbs again and leaves off there, hanging, suspended, incomplete.

The second verse begins with the same words and music: "In the lovely month of May . . ." It is the last two lines of the lyric—"I confessed to her my longing and desire"—which explain what the song is all about. The melody's phrases which reach and fall, which question but remain unanswered, are qualities that mirror the narrator's statements. At the end the piano returns with its introductory music, ending on a dominant-seventh chord:

Closing measures, piano part

This is a chord which feels as though it *must* resolve. The absence of resolution leads us on to the next song. This kind of connecting is what makes a genuine song-cycle and not just a song-collection. More importantly, the absence of a resolution tells us that the narrator's confession of longing and desire will receive no welcoming response. This is the greatest of Romantic themes: longing and desire which rest unrequited and unreturned.

The second song of the cycle introduces another great Romantic theme: the "pathetic fallacy" (*see* color plate 8). This is a literary term which refers to a belief that nature's feelings correspond to the individual's. We all indulge in the pathetic fallacy to some extent, getting, for example, a certain glum satisfaction from a rainy day which matches our mood. The Romantic poet takes the idea to extremes:

Aus meinen Tränen spriessen	From my tears
Viel blühende Blumen hervor,	many blossoms spring,
Und meine Seufzer werden	and my sighs become
Ein Nachtigallenchor.	a choir of nightingales.
Und wenn du mich lieb hast, Kindchen	And if you will love me, child,
Schenk ich dir die Blumen all,	I will give you all the flowers,
Und vor deinem Fenster soll klingen	and at your window
Das Lied der Nachtigall.	the nightingales shall sing.

The song is organized into an AABA pattern. The voice leaves each phrase hanging—the vocal phrases end on V chords; the piano must complete the phrases and resolve the harmonies back to I. It does this with a pattern:

which is derived from the nightingale's song.

Schumann's melody is simple and delicate, as though shy of moving from its note. If there is word-painting for the word "tears" it occurs in the descending notes the left hand plays in the accompaniment.

"From my tears spring many . . ."

The narrator addresses his beloved as a child in this song, and the shyness, delicacy, and simplicity of the music help to convey this.

In the third song, Heine talks about the intensity and the all-encompassing sweep of love. The narrator lists powerful images of things he once loved; images, incidentally, with strong religious connotations. They have all been replaced by his love for a woman.

Die Rose, die Lilie, die Taube, die Sonne,	The rose, the lily, the dove, the sun—
Die liebt ich einst alle in Liebeswonne.	all these I once loved with passionate joy.
Ich lieb sie nicht mehr, ich liebe alleine	I love them no longer; I love only her
Die Kleine, die Feine, die Reine, die Eine;	who is so small, so gentle, so pure, so unique;
Sie selber, aller Liebe Wonne,	she herself, the joy of all passion
Ist Rose und Lilie und Taube und Sonne.	is rose, and lily, and dove, and sun.

First two measures of "The rose, the lily . . ."

Nothing in the words prepares us for the passionate rush of music Schumann gives us. There is no time for word-painting. Instead Schumann uses the quick rhythmic patterns in voice and piano to create a mood of euphoria, a sudden onset of joy. Love in this song is like the sudden "rush" of alcohol or drugs, flooding the brain, destroying sense, limiting the narrator's awareness to the happiness of the present moment.

The fourth song takes the narrator through a variety of emotions.

Wenn ich in deine Augen seh,	When I look into your eyes
So schwindet all mein Leid und Weh;	all my pain and sorrow vanish;
Doch wenn ich küsse deinen Mund,	and when I kiss your lips
So werd ich ganz und gar gesund.	I have all my health again.
Wenn ich mich lehn an deine Brust,	When I lay my head on your breast,
Komm's über mich wie Himmelslust;	heavenly bliss comes over me;
Doch wenn du sprichst: ich liebe	but when you say: "I love you!"
dich!	Then I must weep bitterly.
So muss ich weinen bitterlich.	

Why does he have to weep bitterly? She has just told him that she loves him—his longing and desire are returned—this should be his moment of greatest happiness. Somehow he can trust her eyes, her lips, her breast, but her words fill him with suspicion and despair. It is as though he is content only as long as he is creating their love himself, using her as a mirror for his emotions.

Schumann leads up to the song's central moment with a kind of dialogue between voice and piano. First one states a melody, the other imitating; then they reverse roles; then they speak together. The music builds towards her climactic statement, but at the word "sprichst," "say," it falls off with a diminished-seventh chord, telling us of the tension, doubt, and mistrust her statement will arouse.

"But when you say: 'I love you!'"

The seventh song is an illustration of Shakespeare's phrase "The lady doth protest too much, methinks," except here it is the man who is protesting too much. "Ich grolle nicht," he keeps saying, "I bear no grudge." He then proceeds to demonstrate the bitterest of grudges.

Ich grolle nicht, und wenn das Herz auch bricht,	I bear no grudge, though my heart is breaking,
Ewig verlornes Lieb! Ich grolle nicht,	O love for ever lost! I bear no grudge.
Wie du auch strahlst in Diamantenpracht,	Though you glitter with splendid diamonds
Es fällt kein Strahl in deines Herzens nacht.	no ray illuminates the darkness of your heart.
Das weiss ich längst. Ich sah dich ja im Traume,	This I have long known. For I saw you in a dream,
Und sah die Nacht in deines Herzens Raume,	and saw the night that reigns in your heart.
Und sah die Schlang, die dir am Herzen frisst,	and saw the serpent that feeds on your heart:
Ich sah, mein Lieb, wie sehr du elend bist.	I saw, my love, how wretched you are.

This is the first instance where we see Schumann making major changes in the structure of the poem as he turns it into a lyric. He repeats certain phrases to emphasize them and to expand the musical structure out of a simple strophic (repeated-verse) form into a through-composed form which builds to a powerful climax.

The throbbing repeated chords in the accompaniment are a familiar motif in Romantic music. It's hard to say exactly what they represent: the pulsing of the heart, or perhaps the throbbing of the soul, but they speak directly and unmistakably about the intensity of the passion underneath the singer's words. To see just how important these chords are, replace them with the Classical period's favorite accompanying device, the Alberti bass:

First three measures of Schumann's accompaniment

Not Schumann's accompaniment: same chords using Alberti bass pattern

The Alberti bass, revolving around a middle tone, speaks of balance and rationality. The repeated, throbbing chords of the Romantic accompaniment substitute passionate intensity for calm rationality. Above these chords the melody reaches higher and higher before finally falling back into the two last, ironic statements: "Ich grolle nicht, ich grolle nicht," "I bear no grudge, I bear no grudge."

Schumann's song cycle continues through a total of 16 poems. The young girl married someone else, we are told, but we really never do learn much about her or her situation. The narrator sometimes compares her to the Virgin Mary, sometimes sees her as a mercenary wretch; mostly he talks about himself. The song cycle is the history of his own feelings. We learn nothing about the circumstances of his life and everything about his emotional states.

Everyone assumes that Schumann wrote these songs under the impulse of his love for Clara. Yet it is obvious that the situation described in the song cycle is radically different from his own. It is as though Schumann's powerful feelings at this time in his life demanded expression, and Heine's poems provided the outlet. Schumann was able to pour his feelings into vessels—songs—shaped by Heine's poetry. The strongest point of connection between Schumann's life and Heine's poetry is that the composer was in the grip of powerful emotions he needed to express and the poetry is about powerful emotional states.

There is another point of connection. It was Schumann who titled the song cycle *Dichterliebe, A Poet's Love.* In identifying the narrator as a poet, he may be talking about something which he does have in common with the narrator of the poems. In the very first poem the narrator opens his heart, bares his soul to the girl. Ultimately his offering of love is rejected because she values diamonds over poetry. In this regard the narrator's situation has something in common with the situation of every Romantic artist, including Schumann. Schumann's music is very much the outpouring of his heart, the baring of his soul. The audience is not a single person whom he loves, but a general public. This is what separates the Romantic composer from the composers of other periods. They had patrons and audiences whom they knew well. The Romantic composer's audiences are the people who pay for admission to a concert or who walk into a music store to buy a collection of songs—the middle-class public, who do probably prefer things like diamonds to things like songs.

In his journalism, Schumann created his own literary drama around this situation. He invented a band of like-minded souls, dedicated to art (the

Davidsbund), named for the Biblical King David, who battled the Philistines. The *Davidsbund* included characters modeled on Schumann's friends as well as two characters, "Florestan" and "Eusebius," who represent contrasting aspects of his own personality. The Philistines, of course, were the ignorant public, more dedicated to diamonds than art. So although Schumann might not have been able to identify with the narrator as lover, he may have found it easy to identify with the narrator as artist.

SUMMARY: *Schumann's song cycle* Dichterliebe, A Poet's Love, *Songs 1, 2, 3, 4, and 7 (1840)*

melody	The cycle presents an extraordinary variety of melodies; the ideas which Schumann invented in a few days could have served the average composer for years. Although the melodies differ, they have in common a sense of natural, unforced flow, always fitting comfortably with their words, never seeming over-dramatic.
harmony	Schumann creates a general context of major tonalities and consonant harmonies. Within this, he introduces dissonance for powerful expressive effects. Harmonic movement is characterized by a general ebb and flow of tension and relaxation. Schumann calculates harmonic relationships between songs so that the end of one song leads naturally into the beginning of the next.
rhythm	Rhythms are generally free and variable, allowing the performers to respond flexibly to the moods expressed. Tempos vary widely, from very quick to stretched-out and slow. Several times Schumann uses rhythmic patterns derived from dance, but variations in tempo (*ritards* and *accelerandos*) add a lyrical, expressive quality removed from the dance mode.
form	A series of songs, each one of which presents a "snapshot" of a state of mind. The individual songs are short and succinct, often with piano introductions and/or postludes. Their melodies are distinct and well-matched to the individual poems; there is, however, a sense of flow from song to song within the cycle.
timbre	Voice and piano.
texture	Like Schubert, Schumann makes the piano an active partner in the song. More than Schubert, he gives the piano melodies of its own which relate contrapuntally with the voice part.
function	Designed for public performance in small concert halls and private performance in living rooms. Economically, the latter function was the most important, since the composer's primary income from the works was through the sale of published music.
text	Series of sixteen poems from the section "Lyrical Intermezzo" in Heinrich Heine's *Buch der Lieder—Book of Songs.*

Chopin and Brahms

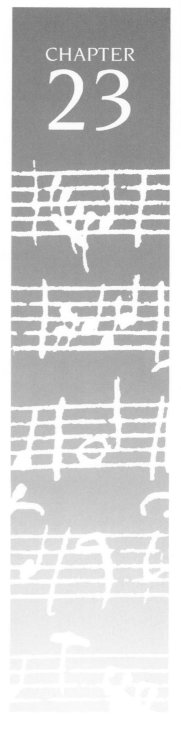

Chopin

Frédéric Chopin was born in 1810, far from Europe's musical capitals, in Zelazowa Wola, near Warsaw, Poland. He died, of tuberculosis, in Paris in 1849.

He was a gifted performer and improviser on the piano while still a child. As was often the case with musically gifted children, he was taken up by the local aristocracy; then, in his teens, he received formal musical training at the Warsaw Conservatory. To make a mark in the wider world he had to perform in the major cultural centers. First came Vienna, in 1829 and again in 1830, where Chopin performed a piece of his own composition, well-calculated to display his skill both as pianist and composer. This was a set of variations for piano and orchestra, based on a theme by Mozart—the duet "Là ci darem la mano," from *Don Giovanni* (discussed in Chapter 19).

At times the variations are fairly direct, with the theme still recognizable:

Original theme from Mozart's opera, transposed into Chopin's key

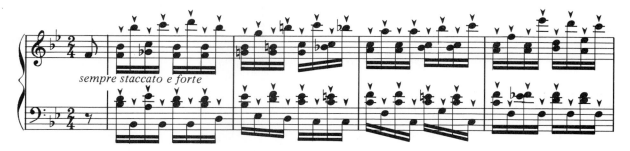

Opening measures of Chopin's fourth variation

At other times the variations are as free as a jazz musician's improvisation on a popular song:

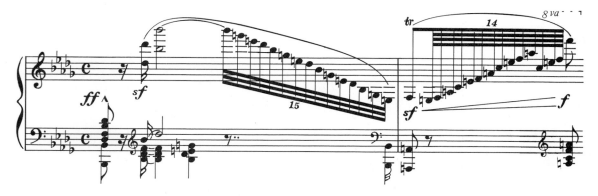

From the fifth variation

Schumann, almost exactly Chopin's age, wrote one of his first pieces of music criticism about this work. It is not the typical review, since it is written in the form of a conversation among several of Schumann's invented characters. One of them, Eusebius, lays the music on the piano rack with the comment "Hats off, gentlemen—a genius!" Later, he compares the finale to a sunset in the Alps, just the sort of imagery which Chopin most disliked. Nevertheless, the review was a major boost for Chopin's reputation.

The Paris *Salon*

Chopin did not stay in Vienna, but made his way to Paris, by tradition the second home of Poland's aristocratic and cultural elite. (Educated Poles and Russians at this time habitually spoke French rather than their native tongues.)

By the 1830s, Napoleon had risen and fallen, the monarchy had been restored and then toppled again. The "citizen-king" Louis Philippe was on the throne, and the French government did its best to protect the rights of the money-makers. French society was rigidly stratified and obsessed with status, with monied and aristocratic elites existing side by side. In this society "social climbing" was the great game, and its playing field was the *salon.*

A *salon* is simply the room in a house designed for receiving visitors. In nineteenth-century France "receiving visitors" had become elevated into an elaborate custom. Snobbism was involved—the status of your *salon* was governed by the social standing of your guests. Culture had a role to play in this: the best guarantee of desirable guests was the presence of brilliant talkers and talented performers. The polite fiction was that all were guests, artists and elites mixing on an equal footing. In fact, the artist was paid for his or her presence, although often indirectly. A painter might hope for a commission for a portrait, for example; a musician might expect sponsorship for a concert.

In this context, the artist was permitted a standard of behavior which would not have been tolerated in other guests. In effect, the artist could be a Bohemian and still be welcome. Chopin was not really a Bohemian—he dressed too well for that—but he and his friends did defy the conventional rules of polite society. His most important relationship was with the novelist George Sand (*see* Chapter 8). She was married but had left her aristocratic husband. She had had a number of well-publicized affairs—well-publicized largely because she wrote fictional accounts of them in her own novels. In fact, she included a fictional treatment of her relationship with Chopin in a novel called *Lucrezia Floriani,* written while the relationship was still going on (he is the model for the character "Prince Karol," who is made to seem incredibly intense and emotional and hopelessly idealistic about real human relationships). In addition, she smoked cigarettes and wore trousers, scandalous behavior for a nineteenth-century woman. A relationship with someone like this would have destroyed the chances of the average social climber; it merely made a musician like Chopin more interesting. He was interesting enough without George Sand: elegant and witty, foreign and frail of health, handsome but haunted-looking, brilliant and soulful in his music. The *salons* were perfect for him. He hated to perform in public concerts—in his entire career he gave only about 30. At the *salon,* a small number of cultured and educated guests could hear his music in comfortable, relaxed, and intimate surroundings. Of course he was not paid to perform, but the *salon* class of society provided him with pupils, and his piano lessons were very expensive. In addition, he published his works. Again, the *salon* experience was valuable. The market for published music was the middle class. An important sign of middle class status was a piano in the parlor and the ability of

In this picture of a salon performance by Chopin, the composer is performing for Prince Radziwill in about 1830.

some family member to play on it. The piano pieces which Chopin played in the *salons* were equally well suited for the parlors. Thus the *salon* hostess used Chopin, and Chopin used her, and both were reasonably content with the situation.

Nocturne in E♭ Major

In 1838 George Sand wrote to the painter Eugène Delacroix:

> To help you make up your mind to come this evening I must tell you that Chopin will play to a small group of us, quite informally; and it is at such times that he is really sublime. Come at midnight . . .*

Delacroix: *Chopin* (1857) *(Louvre, Paris)*

There is no way of knowing now what Chopin played that evening, but considering the hour, one of his nocturnes ("night-pieces") would have been appropriate. Perhaps the most famous of these is his Opus 9, No. 2 in E♭ Major.

The piece opens with a characteristically Romantic gesture—a melody which reaches and falls:

Chopin's E♭ Nocturne (measure 1)

*Translation by Arthur Hedley: *Selected Correspondence of Fryderyk Chopin,* Heinemann, 1962.

The second phrase begins with the same motion, but the harmonies change underneath, allowing the melody to continue with a second, higher reach before it falls.

Measure 2

The fall continues through the third phrase. The fourth phrase reaches and falls once again, this time over a wider interval and in a changed pattern—instead of reaching up to the downbeat, the reach starts *on* the downbeat, adding rhythmic energy.

Measure 4

These initial four phrases constitute a theme, which is next stated again, this time with decorations and variations in the right hand. These include the use of **chromaticism**—using not just the scale's steps, but also the half steps in between. For example, Chopin writes:

Measure 6

Take out all of the chromatic notes, and you would have the much simpler pattern:

Measure 6 without chromatic notes

Next, Chopin introduces a contrasting theme:

Measures 8–9

In a Classical sonata, this theme would modulate to a new key, and for a moment that is what seems to be happening. But as soon as we hear a brief cadence on the V key (B♭), the music quickly modulates back to the I key (E♭), for the opening theme in a new variation.

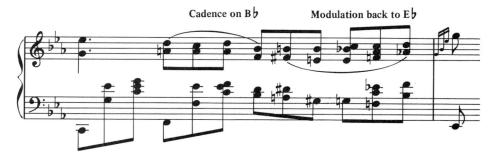

Measures 12–13

Each of the new variations is a little more free than the one before. What began as a simple and singable phrase has now become much more complex and ornate. The left hand remains fairly constant, giving us a repeated pattern of bass note and two chords, bass note and two chords. Against this consistency the right hand seems to develop a separate, almost independent rhythmic life.

The contrasting theme returns, varied slightly, and then the opening theme returns in another variation. Finally there is a closing theme. This begins mildly enough:

Measure 25

What is unusual is the chord underneath, an Ab minor chord not naturally found in the key of Eb. It is not dissonant, just unexpected, lending the music a suddenly different atmosphere. The theme's first appearances are very quiet, but the last time he uses it Chopin seems to discover in it a kind of folk-dance energy which bursts out of the dream texture *con forza,* with force. (*See* top of page 249.) This episode ends on a V chord which is held during a mini-cadenza, and which finally relaxes back into two measures of the tonic E♭ chord to end the piece.

The question is: what does all this have to do with the idea of a "nocturne," a "night-piece"? Part of the answer lies with the relationship between melody and accompaniment. The separation between the two is clear from the music's texture, organized around deep bass tones, bunched middle-register chords, and single note melody above. The separation is heightened by the dissonance

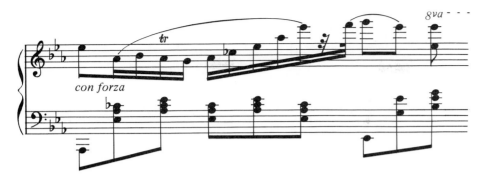

Measure 30

created through Chopin's use of chromaticism—the chromatic, non-chord tones in the melody create dissonance against the left-hand chords. But most important is the rhythmic separation. As we noted above, the accompaniment keeps a fairly steady "three" pattern going underneath in the left hand. The right-hand melody stretches out above this in long-held notes. We could easily miscompose this so that the time-scales of the two hands matched "better":

Not Chopin's version of the opening measures

This would transform the piece into a little waltz, not Chopin's intent at all. What he creates is an underlying beat which is consistent, even, regular, like—if I'm not being too fanciful here—the pulse of life, while above it the melody floats free, like the mind separating itself from the cares of daily existence and drifting off into fantasy.

As we listen to the music our minds naturally follow the dream-like melody. The variations Chopin creates help to give the illusion of spontaneity, as though the performer were improvising them in our presence. The more ornate they become, the more fantasy-like they seem. A Classical structure like sonata form, with its clear organization of themes and keys, would destroy the mood. Instead Chopin simply strings his ideas together in an episodic fashion. Only at the very end do left and right hands match their rhythms and harmonies perfectly together.

Measures 34–35

SUMMARY: *Chopin's* Nocturne in E♭ Major, *Op. 9, No. 2 (1831)*

melody	Long phrases, characterized by "reaching, then falling" motion. Each succeeding melodic statement includes more ornamentation, giving the effect of improvisation.
harmony	Much more dissonance than would be typical of a Classical piece. This is produced in several ways. One, the use of chromaticism in the right-hand melody involves non-chord tones which are dissonant against the left-hand chords. Two, the LH chords themselves often include added tones which increase their dissonance. For instance, instead of building a chord simply on the first, third, and fifth notes of the scale, Chopin might add the tones of the seventh, ninth, and eleventh steps. Three, the LH harmonies sometimes change slightly "out-of-step" with the RH melody, creating dissonance between the two parts.
rhythm	A steady "three" pattern in the left hand, over which the right-hand melody is free and variable in its pace and patterns.
form	Episodic. Two principal themes are used. The themes are given a new "improvisatory" variation with each repeat: A A′ B A″ B′ A‴ C.
timbre	Solo piano. Designed to exploit the particular timbres of the instrument. Chopin uses deep, ringing bass tones, compact mid-range chords, and clear treble melodies.
texture	The left hand maintains the bass line and chords, while the right hand plays single-note melodies above it. The clarity of this texture is the most Classical aspect of Chopin's style.
function	*Salon* performance and publication for use in middle-class parlors.

Brahms

Johannes Brahms was born in Hamburg in 1833 and died in Vienna in 1897. His family was poor. Before her marriage, his mother had been a seamstress and a maidservant. She was 41 when she married Brahms' father, then just 24. He was a musician—not a court musician and composer like Mozart's father, but an average, working, bass-viol player in dance bands—who only later made his way up to work in orchestras. When Brahms showed talent in his youth he was given lessons, and was lucky enough to find excellent teachers who taught him for free. But the family's poverty forced him to put his talent to work, and when barely a teenager he began to play piano in the bars and brothels of Hamburg's dockside district.

A little over 100 years later, the Beatles, at the beginning of their careers, would come from Liverpool to Hamburg to work in this same district. They survived the experience more or less intact, but Brahms—much younger than they when he started—felt himself permanently scarred. He confided in a friend that it had left him with an inability to associate love with sex. Sex for him meant prostitutes; love could only exist in the absence of a physical relationship.

He began to write music during this time, much of it popular music which he published anonymously. (Later in life he was to destroy all his early manuscripts.) He also began more ambitious compositions, and was hired as an accompanist by a touring violinist. The tour was not a huge success, but while on it Brahms met and became friends with another more important violinist, Joseph Joachim. Through Joachim he met Franz Liszt, the greatest virtuoso pianist of the day (perhaps of all time), and, most importantly, Robert and Clara Schumann.

Laurens: *Brahms* (1853)

Schumann had aided Chopin's career through his journalism when both were only 20. Now Brahms was 20, and Schumann was an established figure of 43. The day of their meeting he wrote in his diary: "October 1. Visit from Brahms (a genius.)" He listened to Brahms play and then called Clara in to hear the young man's compositions.

> Sitting at the piano [Schumann wrote] he began to disclose wonderful regions to us . . . he is a player of genius who can make of the piano an orchestra of lamenting and loudly jubilant voices. There were sonatas, . . . songs the poetry of which would be understood even without words, although a profound vocal melody runs through them all; single piano pieces, . . . again sonatas for violin and piano, string quartets, every work so different from the others that it seems to stream from its own individual source. And then it was as though, rushing like a torrent, they were all united by him into a single waterfall the cascades of which were overarched by a peaceful rainbow, while butterflies played about its borders and the voices of nightingales obliged.*

This is a little more poetic than our contemporary taste in music criticism allows; nevertheless, it was a great help to Brahms' career. It was also a great help to him personally. Every artist hopes for this kind of direct and complete understanding of what he is trying to say. Brahms was doubly lucky—not only did he find kindred souls to appreciate what he was doing, but they were also two of the musical world's greatest figures.

Schumann was to live only a few years after this meeting, most of that time in an insane asylum. Brahms returned the favor of friendship, visiting him there

*Translated by Paul Rosenfeld, in *On Music and Musicians,* McGraw-Hill, 1964.

often, serving as his contact with the outside world, bringing Clara there in Schumann's final days. After Schumann's death, the friendship with Clara stayed strong. It was a perfect sort of relationship for Brahms—almost a kind of courtly love, where a young knight devotes himself to a lady high above him. On another level it was simply an ordinary warm friendship: Clara exchanged recipes with Brahms' mother and wrote letters of advice to his sister.

On yet another level, the friendships with Clara Schumann, with the violinist Joachim, and later with the conductor Hans von Bülow had practical consequences for Brahms' career. Schumann had helped Brahms with some early publications, and publication of music was becoming an increasingly large part of the composer's profession. Brahms did other things: gave concerts, directed choirs, taught a few pupils, even for a time had a court appointment at a small German court (playing the piano, teaching the princess, and directing the choir for three months of the year.) More and more, though, he was able to direct his energies solely into composition, as the market for published music continued to expand. With performers like Clara Schumann, Joseph Joachim, and Hans von Bülow to première his works and make them known, he no longer needed to be a traveling virtuoso. There was one post which he really coveted, that of conductor of the Philharmonic orchestra in his hometown of Hamburg. That he was not given it was the great disappointment of his career. He moved to Vienna, and described himself, half-jokingly, as a "vagabond"—a wanderer. This is, of course, a stock Romantic image. In practice, his wandering was of a fairly pleasant sort. He liked to visit Italy in the spring, and he always spent the summer in some country village. The autumn was the time for concert tours, and the winter found him in his small apartment in Vienna, where he fixed his own breakfast, worked in the morning, and lunched at his favorite restaurant (The Red Hedgehog), after which he strolled, worked some more, and dined back at The Red Hedgehog, where his friends could always find him. In conversation he was often rude and sarcastic. In his relationships with his family and friends he was unfailingly generous and loving. When his friend and publisher, Simrock, invested and lost 20,000 marks of Brahms' money, Brahms wrote to him: "Do not make a useless fuss over the famous bankruptcy . . . I think of money only while I am talking of it."

Liebeslieder Waltzes

In the early 1600s, to be a gentleman or a lady meant to have musical skills. Composers attached to courts wrote music for aristocratic amateurs to sing and play. Monteverdi's "Si ch'io vorrei morire" was one such work (*see* Chapter 15). By the mid-1800s composers were writing music for a larger, more middle-class public, which, however, continued the tradition of devoting leisure time to music. One of the most popular mediums for amateur music-making was for two people, four hands, at one piano. Arrangers took works as complicated as Beethoven symphonies and transcribed them for this format. Before the invention of the phonograph, such transcriptions were the only way to bring music home from the concert hall into the living room.

Brahms and other Romantic composers also wrote directly for the medium. His series of waltzes for piano, four hands (Opus 39), was one of his most popular publications. He followed it in 1869 with a series of waltzes for piano, four hands plus a quartet of voices: soprano, alto, tenor, and bass. These are the *Liebeslieder, Lovesong* Waltzes, Opus 52.

Waltzing was the dance craze of the nineteenth century. It was at first thought to be immoral and dangerously sexual, since people paired off into couples to whirl around the room arm in arm. Brahms must have known the form well from his days as a popular pianist. In these *Liebeslieder* waltzes, then, he is taking music which was connected to a popular dance and using it in a medium suitable for a mixed company of amateur musicians to perform in a middle-class home.

The first song (there are 18 in all) begins with the men singing; the women respond; and then men and women sing together.

Brahms at about the time he wrote the *Liebeslieder* waltzes (c. 1866).

MEN:
Rede, Mädchen, allzu liebes,
das mir in die Brust, die kühle,
hat geschleudert mit dem Blicke
diese wilden Glutgefüle!
Willst du nicht dein Herz erweichen,

willst du, eine Überfromme,
rasten ohne traute Wonne,
oder willst du, dass ich komme?

WOMEN:
Rasten ohne traute Wonne,
nicht so bitter will ich büssen.
Komme nur, du schwarzes Auge,

MEN AND WOMEN TOGETHER:
(Women sing:)
komme, wenn die Sterne grüssen.
(Men sing:)
Willst du dass ich komme?

Speak, maiden, all too beloved
who in my cool heart
have stirred with a glance
these wild, passionate feelings!
Don't you want your own heart awakened?

Do you want to be overly devout,
to stay away from loving joy,
or do you want me with you?

Stay away from loving joy?
No such bitter penance for me.
Come near, you with dark eyes,

Come when the stars will greet us.

Do you want me with you?

There is a pleading quality to the men's first statement. Musically, it can be found in the dissonances which are struck and then relaxed.

Opening measures of song

The dissonances are made by tones out of the scale—they can be recognized by their accidentals—which are then relaxed back up into scale-tones. The use of these nonscale tones, chromaticism, tends to make the listener unsure of the tonal center. At the end of this section, the tonal center does shift, going briefly into G# minor. This harmonic uncertainty matches the men's uncertainty about how the women will respond.

"Don't you want your own heart awakened?" the men continue, and here the melody becomes more dance-like. The dance rhythm:

is treated contrapuntally, heard first in the tenor, then in the bass. The two voices then join for a typically Romantic melodic phrase, long and flowing, full of ups and downs:

The nature of the women's response is apparent immediately. They don't pause to think it over, they don't even wait for the men to finish, but enter over the men's last measure. Their music echoes the dance-like rhythm and melody of the men's "Don't you want your heart awakened?" line. For their next phrase, "Come near, you with dark eyes," the women start to repeat the melody of the men's long phrase. Then, in the middle of the phrase, the men pick up the melody, still asking "Do you want me with you?" as the women join them to answer "Come when the stars will greet us."

The song's expressions of longing and desire are typically Romantic; untypical is the fact that the longing is quickly answered. Like Monteverdi, Brahms brings his lovers together. Unlike Monteverdi, his lovers are not entirely sensual in their attitudes. They will kiss in the moonlight, listen to nightingales, and feel their souls tremble like a branch touched by a bird in flight. Not that everything is happy; the *Liebeslieder* waltzes present a variety of moods including fear of involvement, anger at gossip, despair from rejection, tenderness, joy, exuberance, and intimacy. Brahms gives us an extraordinary display of the waltz rhythm's versatility. But still the pulse of that rhythm underneath guarantees a certain buoyant feeling. Despair in a waltz can never be so desperate as despair in the flexible rhythms of songs like those of Schumann's *Dichterliebe*.

Brahms' song has many levels. One is the waltz itself, with its exuberant sense of physical movement. A second is that given by the medium (piano, four hands plus vocal quartet) which contributes a sense of relaxed intimacy—the cozy good feeling the Viennese call "Gemütlichkeit." Brahms sets up these two qualities as the "givens" of the song. At times he goes with them, but at times he works against them. For example, the particular instances we noted earlier—the strong dissonances, the rhythmic counterpoint, and the long flowing phrases—all go against the grain of the simple popular waltz. They are qualities you won't find in works like Johann Strauss's "Blue Danube." But it is just this working against the grain which sparks the songs into life, and gives them depth of interest.

SUMMARY: *First song from Brahms'* Liebeslieder *Waltzes, Opus 52 (1869)*

melody	The first section ("Speak, maiden . . .") is characterized by a melody which uses dissonance to reinforce its "pleading" effect. The second section ("Don't you want your own heart awakened?") is characterized by two melodies—the first a simple dance-like tune, the second an extended Romantic phrase. The third section (women's entrance) uses the same melodic materials as the second section.
harmony	Harmonic uncertainty conveyed by the use of dissonant tones out of the E-major scale (chromaticism) and by brief modulations to other keys. By the end of the piece, all is resolved into consonant major harmonies.
rhythm	The basic rhythm is a waltz rhythm: three beats per measure, where the first beat is a strong downbeat, the second beat relaxes from that, and the third beat leads into the new downbeat of the next measure. Brahms sometimes treats this rhythm straightforwardly, sometimes reinforces it with syncopation, sometimes works against it with flowing melodies and polyphonic effects.
form	A B B′. The men sing two sections alone; the women enter with music which echoes the men's second section.
timbre	Piano, four hands, plus vocal quartet. (Sometimes performed with more than one singer on each part.)
texture	Primarily homophonic, but with a wealth of polyphony as well. Brahms uses imitation and counterpoint between the singers' parts, between the pianists' parts, and between singers and pianists. It is a general characteristic of Brahms's music that he blends his parts so well together that the listener's first impression is that the texture is entirely homophonic. The more one listens the more polyphony appears.
function	Originally designed for amateur music-making. Now more often heard in concert, recital, and recording; also used by George Balanchine as music for ballet.
text	The poems are by (or translated by) Georg Friedrich Daumer (1800–1875), from his book of translations called *Polydora, a World-Poetry Songbook.*

Fourth Symphony

The most famous of Brahms' compositions is a simple lullaby which he wrote for a friend's child:

The slow rocking motion of the lullaby is characteristic of many of his melodies. The opening of his Fourth Symphony (composed in 1885) is no lullaby, but it does give evidence of this slow rocking characteristic.

Opening phrases of symphony

This melody is a "first theme"; that is, the first thematic statement of a sonata form. Sonata form was of course the favorite formal pattern of the Classical period composers. Brahms' fondness for such traditional forms is one of the reasons why he is thought of as the most Classical of the Romantics. The theme itself, however, is thoroughly Romantic in character. Where a Classical theme tends to break down into two- or four-measure units marked by cadences, Brahms' theme spins on for 18 bars. Even the end of those 18 bars is not marked by a clear cadence, but is obscured: as the theme comes to its close in the oboe and first violin parts, the second violin overlaps it to begin the second, varied statement of the melody.

End of first statement of theme

Beginning of second, varied statement

The melody itself is Romantic in that it reaches and falls, inhales and exhales like a series of sighs, each one of which flows into the next.

The Romantic fondness for "flow" shows up in the harmonies as well. Whereas Classical sonata form would begin with a series of basic V-I and IV-V-I statements, Brahms gives us a much more complex series of harmonies. In a simplified form, just listing the Roman numerals for the steps of the scale on which the chords are based, these harmonies are: I-IV-V-I (all over an E-pedal tone), then VI-III-VII-IV-#VII-IV-♭II-II-VI- #III-IV-#III-IV-II-I-V-I.

After a variation on the opening statement, characterized by fast running notes underneath the melody, there is a brief transition theme, marked by a downward-moving scale, which then rises on a broken chord:

Transition theme

This leads into the second theme section.

As Beethoven did in his Fifth Symphony, Brahms announces this section with a fanfare:

"Fanfare" introducing second theme section

The main melody of the second theme section is a rich, reaching, long-phrased theme, introduced in the 'cello:

Main melody of second theme section

The fanfare theme comes back, and then we hear a closing theme based on a downward-moving scale. The section seems about to end when we hear a tense, unstable, even mysterious-sounding chord over which the strings play arpeggios and under which the timpani rolls. This ushers in a return of the fanfare theme. What had first seemed only a melody used as an announcement now begins to assume larger importance. Brahms separates its two rhythmic components. One is a simple trumpet call, the other a more complicated playing of three beats where the underlying pulse gives two:

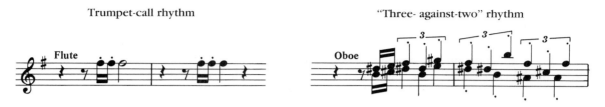

Trumpet-call rhythm   "Three- against-two" rhythm

Rhythmic components of "fanfare" theme

Brahms uses these two elements in counterpoint against each other, gradually building in intensity before suddenly relaxing the tension and leading into the development section.

The development starts with the first, "sighing" theme. This is played almost as it was in the beginning. Just at the end its phrases are rushed together, and Brahms begins to take the theme into different harmonies, playing contrapuntally back and forth across the orchestra. Next he brings back the "fanfare" theme. As a short, compact melody, it resembles a Classical period sonata-form theme more closely than one of Brahms' longer, more lyrical melodies. Its structure makes it well-suited for the kind of fragmentation that a traditional development section requires. Most importantly for the work as a whole, however, it stands up to those other, lyrical themes. With its trumpet-like notes, its three-against-two rhythm, its quick marching energy, it is the active partner which provides dramatic contrast to the lyrical melodies' more passive state. The lyrical melodies *feel;* this one *does.*

The recapitulation begins with the first theme in a stretched-out mode:

(instead of)

From there on it follows the traditional recapitulation pattern—after the first-theme group is played, the second-theme group arrives without modulating, instead staying in the home key. Again the "fanfare" melody takes over, with its energetic counterpoint and its complex rhythms. But where in the exposition this energy had been allowed to ebb away before the start of the development, it now continues to flow and even increases, leading to a coda section. This is marked by a final return of the first theme. But now it is as though that first "sighing" theme had been stirred up, awakened by the "fanfare" theme. Instead of languid, flowing phrases, it is transformed into active, accented, rhythmic ones:

which continue to build right to the climactic closing measures of the movement.

One of the hallmarks of Brahms' style is the sense of "blending." His timbres and textures include a variety of instrumental voices, but he blends them into a full, rich sound. In terms of melody, he develops various ideas, but makes them flow seamlessly together. This consistency of texture and flow of melody are part of what makes him a Romantic composer. A closer look at the music reveals a carefully-designed structure underneath, and shows that the texture is not just a smooth blend—there is a good deal of polyphonic writing, including both imitation and counterpoint, under the surface. The use of sonata form does not make Brahms an imitation-Classical composer, nor does the use of polyphonic techniques make him an imitation-Baroque one. Rather he uses the older techniques to serve his own Romantic style. Sonata form helps give an underlying structure; polyphonic techniques add to the intensity of the moment.

SUMMARY: *Brahms'* **Symphony No. 4 in E Minor,** *Op. 98, first movement (1885)*

melody	Strong, distinctive melodies. First theme in particular marked by characteristic falling and rising phrases, stretched out over 18 bars, making it unusually long.
harmony	Generally consonant, with less chromaticism than is found in other composers working at the same time. But still a powerful sense of the ebb and flow of consonance and dissonance, tension and release, qualities which make Brahms' music "breathe."
rhythm	Characteristically Romantic in its variability. At times languid and flowing, at times stirring and forceful. Rhythmic complexity given by frequent use of "three" against "two."
form	Sonata form: exposition-development-recapitulation plus coda.
timbre	Designed for a large orchestra, but one without the "extra" timbres (like harp, triangle, bass clarinet) popular with Wagner, Strauss, and Mahler.
texture	Predominantly homophonic in effect, but with a great deal of polyphonic writing under the surface.
function	Designed for large concert-hall performance. This is the kind of work for which our modern orchestras and the halls they play in were built.

Romantic Opera

Wagner

One of the reasons Robert and Clara Schumann greeted Brahms' music with such enthusiasm was because he represented to them a continuation of their own tradition. That tradition was being challenged by the New German School, whose principal exponents were Franz Liszt and Richard Wagner. Liszt (1811–1886) was one of the Romantic period's most fabulous figures. He was the nineteenth century equivalent of a present-day rock star, complete with long hair, women fainting in the audience, a tendency to break pianos in performance, and a somewhat scandalous love life (his principal relationships were with a princess and a countess, neither of whom he married). The word "Lisztomania" was coined to describe his immense popularity with audiences. He was, in addition, a kind and generous man and a gifted composer as well as performer. Nevertheless, the Schumanns were somewhat suspicious of him. His compositions were so extravagant and theatrical in their effects. Was there sub-

Inspiration flows to Liszt both from nature and from Beethoven's bust in this 1840 painting by Joseph Danhauser. His admirers are, from left, Alexandre Dumas, Victor Hugo, George Sand (wearing pants), Paganini, Rossini, and Liszt's mistress, the Countess Marie d'Agoult.

stance underneath the show, or was it all sound and fury, signifying nothing? Was Liszt a sincere artist, or a manipulating magician?

Richard Wagner

The same questions were to be asked about Richard Wagner, an equally flamboyant figure. Wagner was born in Leipzig in 1813 and died in Venice, Italy, in 1883. His parentage is unsure; his father may have been Friedrich Wagner, a clerk at the police department, or the artist Ludwig Geyer, whom his mother married shortly after her husband's death in the year of Wagner's birth. Wagner enrolled in Leipzig University in 1830, only a year after Schumann had left that school to go to Heidelberg. Like Schumann, Wagner neglected his academic studies in favor of music and the Bohemian pleasures of talk and drink. Soon, though, through his brother, a singer, he found work as a chorus-master in an opera house. From this he rose to various positions as an opera conductor, at the same time beginning the composition of his own operas. The great opera house of the age was the Paris Opéra, and it was to Paris that Wagner went in order to make his reputation as a composer. His years there, like those of many young musicians trying to make their ways in great cities, were years of poverty and struggle. The difficulties are especially great for a composer of operas. To organize a concert of piano works is relatively cheap and easy. But to produce an opera requires huge expense and the labor of hundreds of people over long stretches of time. It was in Dresden, in 1842, that one of his operas first received a successful performance. The performance led to his appointment as a conductor there, to the performance of other of his operas, and to work on new ones.

His career was by no means a settled or smooth one yet. His works were unconventional and received mixed reviews from both critics and audiences, veering from enthusiasm to antagonism. But the major disruption in his career was the result of politics. It was a time of revolution and counter revolution. In France, 1848 brought the toppling of the citizen-king Louis-Philippe. In Germany, revolutionaries attempted to unify the different princely governments into a republic. Marx and Engels published *The Communist Manifesto.* In 1849 there was an insurrection in Dresden, and Wagner was identified with the revolutionaries. A warrant was put out for his arrest, and he was forced to flee to Switzerland.

The fact that the public had not responded overwhelmingly to his works did not incline Wagner to modify his style to fit popular taste. Instead he strove to modify public taste to fit his style. In exile he devoted himself to theoretical writings designed to justify his approach. His aim was a "total-art-work" (*Gesamtkunstwerk)* where all of the various resources of poetry, music, and theatrical presentation would be totally united in style. Though in exile and in financial difficulties, Wagner began an incredibly ambitious project reflecting this ideal. It was an opera-cycle; that is, a series of four grand operas called *Der Ring des Nibelungen, The Ring of the Nibelungen.* Wagner had suffered a number of recent defeats: a Paris production of his *Tannhäuser* had lasted for only three performances (after 164 rehearsals); a Vienna production of his *Tristan und Isolde* received 57 rehearsals but never made it to performance. The "Ring" cycle must have seemed an impossible dream.

Rescue came from an unlikely source: King Ludwig II of Bavaria, later known as "Mad" King Ludwig. He was only 19 when he met Wagner, but already in control of incredible wealth. He became an enthusiastic proponent of Wagner's works, paid off 18,000 gulden of debt for him (Wagner lived extravagantly), and granted him an income of first 1200, then 4,000, then 8,000 gulden per year. In addition, he subsidized brilliant performances of Wagner's operas in Munich. There is irony in this situation. A composer exiled for his radical politics was being patronized by a king. A composer who advertised his music as "the art of the future" was being supported in the most ancient of fashions. There was a difference, however. Wagner was not employed by his patron the way past musicians like Machaut or Haydn had been. Ludwig served Wagner more than Wagner served Ludwig.

The performances in Munich were conducted by Hans von Bülow, who was Brahms' friend, and who had, as a pianist, premièred Tchaikovsky's first piano concerto (*see* Chapter 9). Von Bülow was married to Liszt's illegitimate daughter, Cosima. She and Wagner fell in love, resulting in three children while she was still married to Von Bülow. They finally married in 1870. In '1876, Wagner's dreams were realized with the opening of his own opera house in the town of Bayreuth, in King Ludwig's Bavaria. The project had King Ludwig's sup-

Wagner's opera house, the Festival Playhouse, opened in 1876 in Bayreuth, Germany.

port, but also contributions from hundreds of individual supporters and from Wagner Societies—fan clubs organized around Wagner's operas and ideas— around the world.

The theater was designed for the specific stage effects Wagner wanted and included a huge orchestra pit extending beneath the stage—large enough to accommodate an orchestra of well over one hundred musicians. Here the ideal of the "total-art-work" could be realized. Wagner could exercise personal control over sets, costumes, stage effects and direction, as well as over words and music. The "total-art-work" was designed to give more than an evening's entertainment; more, even, than powerful emotional effects. Wagner intended his operas to have a spiritual dimension. He wanted to transform the theater of popular entertainment into a theater of communal spiritual revelation, like that of the drama of the ancient Greeks. His followers spoke of making a pilgrimage to Bayreuth as though it were a shrine, as though not just musical but also spiritual experience awaited them there.

Lohengrin

Wagner completed his opera *Lohengrin* in 1848, while he was still conductor at Dresden. Because of his political troubles, it was not performed there and instead received its first production under Liszt's direction, at Weimar, in 1850. Exiled in Switzerland, Wagner was unable to attend.

In typical Romantic fashion, the opera is set in the world of Medieval knights. It begins not with a conventional audience-settling overture, but with an orchestral prélude which is an essay on the theme of the Holy Grail (the legendary chalice from which Christ drank at the Last Supper). Wagner provided a literary description of the picture he tries to paint in his prélude: "Out of the clear blue ether of the sky there seems to condense a wonderful yet at first hardly perceptible vision; and out of this there gradually emerges, ever more and more clearly, an angel host bearing in its midst the sacred Grail . . . " This kind of scene-painting is essential to his style. Purely abstract music— music as pleasing sounds or patterns—hardly exists for him. He only cares about music when it can stand for something, when it can *represent* objects, emotions, dramas, and ideas. To accomplish this representation, Wagner uses the technique of the **"leitmotif,"** or "leading motive." This is a melody associated with a particular object, emotion, or idea. The *leitmotif* of the Holy Grail begins like this:

First four measures of Grail *leitmotif*

Whenever the orchestra plays it later in the opera, the listener is to recall the image of the Grail.

The opera itself begins with a long—200 measures—section of exposition, in which two of the characters stand and explain the situation for us. By contrast, the action-packed first 200 measures of Mozart's *Don Giovanni* show us Leporello fantasizing about his (unlikely) future as a gentleman-lover; Don Giovanni physically forcing his attentions on the struggling Donna Anna; her father, the Commendatore, coming to her rescue and duelling with Don Giovanni; Don Giovanni reluctantly killing the old man; and, finally, Leporello asking Don Giovanni (from a safe hiding-place) "Who's dead, the old man, or you?" At first glance, the Mozart approach might seem the more dramatic. But Wagner has his own methods. Where Mozart sees a scene or an aria as a musical unit, Wagner sees the whole first act as a musical unit. Only slowly and gradually, over its hour-long length, does he build to a climax. When it arrives it is a stirring one, and one which makes all of the preceding music seem to fall into place.

It is easy to see how this method gave rise to detractors. Wagner's operas need an audience with the patience and trust to await the putting-together of the entire picture. The picture itself has more meaning once the *leitmotifs* are learned and understood. The situation is somewhat analagous to that of a person who tunes in for one episode of a soap opera. It may seem nonsensical if the viewer isn't aware of the allusions to past and future events and takes the episode as a separate thing, not part of a long development.

By the end of the first act of *Lohengrin,* we have met Elsa (the maiden falsely accused of murdering her brother), the evil sorceress Ortrud, her husband Friedrich, and the knight Lohengrin. Lohengrin appears in answer to Elsa's prayer. He arrives in a boat drawn by a swan, and we hear a "Swan" motive:

"Swan" motive

He defeats Friedrich in single combat, saving Elsa's life. They fall in love and agree to marry. He makes one stipulation—she must never ask his name, where or from whom he came:

"Fatal question" motive

The second act belongs principally to Ortrud. Her evil is represented in the act's prélude:

Ortrud's "harm" or "trouble" motive

Ortrud fakes repentance and insinuates herself close to Elsa so that she can poison Elsa's mind against Lohengrin. Nevertheless, the couple does get married, and the third act begins with the wedding march bringing the newlyweds back from the church. It is the most joyful moment in the opera and also the most famous one. The orchestral prélude describes the wedding festivities. It is characterized by an exuberant and energetic theme:

Theme from Prélude to Act III

Wagner orchestrates this by giving the melody to the lower strings, bassoons, horns, trombones, and tubas. Above, the chords are sustained in an excited *tremolo* by the violins, flutes, oboes, and clarinets. It is a characteristic Wagner moment. The combination of instruments creates an unusual and striking sound. Yet the texture itself is clear and simple: *tremolo* chords in one group, unison melody in another.

The Wedding March music itself opens the third act (which was, incidentally, the act which Wagner composed first).

This theme has had a continuing popularity partly because it has a simple, strong tune, characterized by consonant harmonies, regular phrases, and a consistent rhythmic pattern, and it is repeated several times, serving to place it firmly in the listener's memory. This is *not* characteristic of Wagner's style in general. Although he was capable of writing such music, he preferred more complex melodies, with tense harmonies, irregular phrases, flexible rhythms. These are the techniques which become apparent later in the act.

It's safe to assume that few of the couples who use the Wedding March from Lohengrin in their own weddings are aware of the subsequent events of

Lohengrin and Elsa in the bedroom scene, Act III, of *Lohengrin,* at the Metropolitan Opera.

Elsa's and Loehngrin's wedding night. Ortrud has succeeded in planting doubt and suspicion in Elsa's mind. Lohengrin asks that she have perfect faith and confidence in him, but her responses become increasingly anguished. Her melodies outline diminished-seventh chords, which also fill the orchestra's accompaniment. In addition, we can hear in her singing echoes of Ortrud's "harm" theme, which also uses melodies based on diminished-seventh chords.

ELSA:

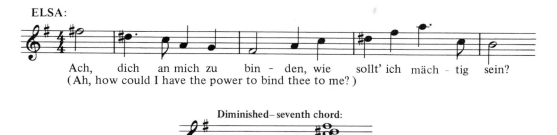

Ach,   dich   an mich zu   bin - den, wie   sollt' ich mäch - tig   sein?
(Ah, how could I have the power to bind thee to me?)

Her doubts and fears are increasing, and she seems to be reaching a point of hysteria, when she pauses suddenly, in the grip of an illusion. The orchestra plays the "swan" motive, as she seems to see the swan come to take Lohengrin away. Lohengrin attempts to quiet her, but she comes closer and closer to the fatal question. Finally we hear the "fatal question" motive in the orchestra and in Lohengrin's final appeal to Elsa not to ask it. But ask it she does.

Wie_____   dei - ne   Art?_____
(What is thy lineage?)

Before he can answer, Friedrich suddenly rushes in with sword drawn. Elsa cries out and hands Lohengrin his scabbard from which he draws his own sword to strike Friedrich dead. The sudden events are like a thunderstorm after oppressive humidity: they clear the air and release the built-up tension. Elsa collapses on Lohengrin's breast. But the fatal question cannot be withdrawn, and Lohengrin says, "All our happiness now is lost!" He places her on the couch, sternly orders Friedrich's henchmen to remove Friedrich's body, rings a bell for maidservants to prepare Elsa for their meeting with the King, at which he will reveal his identity. Dawn slowly glimmers, ending their unhappy wedding night.

In the opera's final scene, Lohengrin reveals that he is one of a group of knights who guard the Holy Grail. (Naturally, as he says this, the orchestra plays the "Grail" theme from the opening Prélude.) The swan returns to pull his boat away. Evil Ortrud exults since she knows that the swan is really Elsa's brother, transformed by her sorcery. But Lohengrin prays, and the swan is re-transformed back into a man, and it is into this man's arms that Elsa collapses, lifeless, as Lohengrin departs. In its plot, the opera is like a fairy tale. Evil Sorceress, Damsel in Distress, Knight to the Rescue, Fatal Question, Man turned into Swan. It is the music, with its constant ebb and flow, its heightened tension, its dramatic climaxes, which teaches us that the real drama is going on inside. The characters interest Wagner—and us—less for their actions than for the inner crises of their lives. The key figure here is Elsa. Beautiful, pure, and good, she is unable to have the perfect faith which Lohengrin demands. In this respect she represents us: the men and women of the modern world. We too are beset by doubts and fears, finding it difficult to make the leap of perfect faith.

SUMMARY: *Wagner's* Lohengrin *(1848)*

melody	Melody as "tune" shows up in the Wedding March, but is not a strong characteristic of Wagner's work. He prefers melody which represents, either by association *(leitmotif)* or by depiction (for example, Elsa's melodies based on diminished-seventh chords.)
harmony	Wagner uses stable and consonant harmonies to present images of peace and calm (for example, the "Holy Grail" motive.) To increase tension he uses dissonant harmonies, especially diminished-seventh chords. He uses frequent modulations both to create a constant sense of flow and the sense of instability necessary to the drama.
rhythm	Often free and flexible, following the emotions of the moment. Wagner creates rhythmic tension by moving his melodies off the beat of the music's pulse.
form	In his later operas, Wagner attempted what he called "endless melody," an extreme example of the Romantic love of "flow." While he had not fully developed this idea at the time he wrote *Lohengrin,* he had gone beyond the traditional operatic alternations between aria and recitative. In the wedding-night scene, for example, the form includes repeated melodic phrases, but these are not set off into separate aria sections. The result is something halfway between aria and recitative. In other words, instead of thinking in terms of musical numbers connected by recitatives, Wagner conceives of dramatic units, sometimes an hour or more in length, falling away from and building up to climaxes. The use of recurrent *leitmotifs* helps to create structural connections.
texture	In comparison with a composer like Brahms, Wagner's textures are relatively clear and simple. He is fond of strong unison melodies; he likes to organize his orchestra into two opposing but complementary groups. An unusual aspect of his texture involves *leitmotifs* introduced by the orchestra as counterpoint to the singers' melodies.
timbre	Wagner demands extraordinary power and range from his singers. The four principals do the lion's share of the singing, although

there are also several smaller parts, and a large chorus. The orchestra is larger than previous opera orchestras and features unusual timbres and striking effects—using, for example, the tuba and the bass clarinet.

function   Wagner wanted his works to function like the dramas of the ancient Greeks, where the community was united by the dramatic experience and found important spiritual and philosophical truths revealed there. Many did find a spiritual home in his works, and their immense popularity in the late nineteenth and early twentieth centuries owed a great deal to this extra-musical dimension.

text   (Excerpt from wedding-night scene, Act III)

ELSA
Ach, dich an mich zu binden
wie sollt' ich mächtig sein?
Voll Zauber ist dein Wesen,
durch Wunder kamst du her;
wie sollt' ich da genesen?
Wo fänd' ich dein' Gewähr? –
Hörtest du nichts? Vernahmest du
   kein Kommen?

LOHENGRIN
Elsa!

ELSA
Ach nein! Doch dort—der Schwan—
   der Schwan!
Dort kommt er auf der Wasserflut
   geschwommen—
du rufest ihm—er zieht herbei den
   Kahn!

LOHENGRIN
Elsa, halt ein! Beruh'ge deinen Wahn!

ELSA
Nichts kann mir Ruhe geben,
dem Wahn mich nichts entreisst,
als—gelt' es auch mein Leben!—
zu wissen, wer du seist!

LOHENGRIN
Elsa, was willst du wagen?

ELSA
Unselig holder Mann,
hör, was ich dich muss fragen!
Den Namen sag mir an!

LOHENGRIN
Halt' ein!

ELSA
Ah! How could I have the power
   to bind thee to me?
Thou art of magic nature,
through a wonder thou camest here;
how could I then recover,
where find protection?—
Hearest thou naught? Didst thou not
   hear someone come?

LOHENGRIN
Elsa!

ELSA
Ah no! But there—the swan—the
   swan!
There it comes swimming across the
   waters—
thou callest it—it draws the boat
   hither!

LOHENGRIN
Elsa, forbear! Rid thyself of this delu-
   sion!

ELSA
Nothing can give me peace
or tear me from this madness
but—even though it cost my life!—
to learn who thou art!

LOHENGRIN
Elsa, what wilt thou risk?

ELSA
Wretched, beloved man,
hear, what I have to ask thee!
Thy name thou shalt tell me!

LOHENGRIN
Forbear!

ELSA
Woher die Fahrt?

LOHENGRIN
Weh dir!

ELSA
Wie deine Art?

LOHENGRIN
Weh uns, was tatest du!

(Frederick and the four conspirators rush in with drawn swords.)

ELSA
Rette dich! Dein Schwert, dein
    Schwert!

(She hands Lohengrin his weapon from behind the couch. As Frederick lifts his arm to strike, Lohengrin fells him to the ground with one blow. The nobles, shocked, drop their swords and fall on their knees before Lohengrin.)

LOHENGRIN
Weh! Nun ist all under Glück dahin!

ELSA
Allewiger, erbarm dich mein!

LOHENGRIN
Tragt den Erschlagnen vor des Königs
    Gericht!

(The nobles lift Frederick's body and go out with it. Lohengrin rings a bell; four ladies enter.)

LOHENGRIN
Sie vor den König zu geleiten,
schmückt Elsa, meine süsse Frau!
Dort will ich Antwort ihr bereiten,
dass sie des Gatten Art erschau'.

ELSA
Whence didst thou come?

LOHENGRIN
Woe to thee!

ELSA
What is thy lineage?

LOHENGRIN
Woe to us, what hast thou done!

ELSA
Save thyself! Thy sword, thy sword!

LOHENGRIN
Woe! All our happiness is now lost!

ELSA
Almighty God, have pity on me!

LOHENGRIN
Bear the slain man to the King's judg-
    ment!

LOHENGRIN
Attire Elsa, my sweet wife,
to be led before the King!
There I will give her my answer
that she may learn her husband's
lineage.

(He withdraws, and the ladies lead Elsa away. Day has gradually come on, and the candles in the chamber have been extinguished. A curtain conceals the stage, as horns sound a summons from the courtyard beyond.)

Verdi

Giuseppe Verdi was born in 1813 (the same year as Richard Wagner) in a tiny town in Northern Italy, where his parents ran a small shop. He died in 1901, on a farm he had bought near his birthplace. His parents were poor and uneducated, and his own early education was minimal. He took lessons from the local church organist, advancing so quickly that he was able to take over that job when he was just ten. To help further Verdi's education, his father turned to a man named Barezzi, the wholesale grocer from whom he obtained his stock.

Barezzi was an amateur musician, much impressed with young Verdi's talent and intelligence. He took him into his own home, where Verdi learned the wholesale business while also continuing his musical studies. Eventually Barezzi arranged for him to go to Milan. There he was turned down in his application for admittance to the Music Conservatory. This action has been explained many ways (for one thing, he was a foreigner; Italy was so divided that it took a passport to go from one small state to the next), but it remains an outstanding example of academic short-sightedness.

With the conservatory closed to him, he studied privately with a minor opera composer, concentrating on exercises in harmony and counterpoint. His work as performer, conductor, and composer began to receive notice, and his first opera was performed with moderate success. Then tragedy struck. He had married the daughter of his benefactor Barezzi (who, unlike Clara Wieck's father at almost the same moment, was not afraid of taking a struggling musician into his family). They had two children. In 1838 Verdi's daughter died, followed by his son in 1839 and his wife in 1840. In the midst of these events he was asked to write a comedy. Not surprisingly, it was a failure.

He thought that his career as an opera composer was finished, but an impressario friend pressed a new libretto on him titled *Nabucco,* a re-telling of the Biblical story of Nebuchadnezzar. Although the story was Biblical, it had contemporary relevance. Italy had been conquered by Napoleon, and when, after Napoleon's retreat from Moscow, the Austrians had driven the French out of the country, they stayed on as occupiers themselves. The music-loving Viennese were not so charming as military rulers. There was strict censorship and no expressions of national patriotism were allowed, but censorship could not keep audiences from identifying with the ancient Jews in their captivity in Babylon, and from cheering wildly at the chorus in which they prayed for freedom. The opera was a huge success, and Verdi was famous overnight.

His subsequent career was filled with huge successes, but marked by a number of failures as well. This was in part the result of the commercial system of the day, which provided almost no copyright protection for the composer. By comparison, a composer who writes a successful Broadway musical could live for years off the royalty fees. Every time a high school, college, amateur or professional group wishes to perform the work, a royalty fee must be paid (for college productions, these average around $1200.) In the 1840s and 50s such arrangements were only just being introduced. Most of the composer's profit was tied to the work's first production. To increase his profits, he had to have many first productions. In one 11-year span, Verdi composed 16 operas. Considering that he was involved with rehearsing, staging, and conducting as well as composing, this becomes an astonishing feat. Naturally some of these productions were failures, but most have remained in the repertory from then until now.

La Traviata

Verdi wrote three of his greatest operas within a three-year span. *Rigoletto* was produced in 1851, *Il Trovatore, (The Troubador)* and *La Traviata, (The Fallen Woman)* both in 1853.

Violetta and Alfredo in *La Traviata,* 1984, in the San Diego Opera production.

Like Wagner's *Lohengrin,* Verdi's *La Traviata* is the story of two lovers. There the similarity ends. Wagner's lovers are a Medieval Princess and a Knight of the Holy Grail. Verdi's lovers are a pleasant young gentleman and a high-class Parisian prostitute. Whereas Wagner took his idea from an old legend, Verdi took his from a contemporary novel, *La Dame aux Camélias, The Lady of Camellias,* by Alexandre Dumas. The heroine of the novel—named Violetta in the opera—is known as the lady of camellias because she always wears them. The white flowers symbolize her own pale and fragile beauty; she suffers from tuberculosis.

Parisian society in the nineteenth century included what it called the "world," respectable upper-class society, and the "half-world" or *"demi-monde,"* which was disreputable upper-class society. The same men populated both worlds, but the women were kept separate: wives and mothers in one group, courtesans and mistresses in the other. Violetta was not a streetwalker. Her lovers were rich men and aristocrats, the society she moved in was filled with fine things and high fashion. In the novel, she explains quite openly that she requires at least 100,000 francs a year to maintain her lifestyle—not a bad living for a girl from a humble background. (A workingman in Paris might then have earned 1000 francs per year.) The price she paid for this rich life included exclusion from respectable society and total cynicism about love.

Although the existence of the *demi-monde* was generally known, Dumas' novel still had considerable shock value. He had turned it into a play, but Francesco Piave, Verdi's librettist, transformed the work further, compressing the action and creating the opportunity for brilliant theatrical and operatic effects.

After a brief orchestral prélude, we are plunged directly into the action. It is a party in Violetta's rich apartments. Alfredo is brought along by a friend and introduced to Violetta for the first time. In a sense their relationship has already begun; his fascination with her dates from his first sight of her, over a year before. She is of course sophisticated and teasing, but she can't help being attracted by his naïve and straightforward expressions of affection. As the company sits down to dinner, she asks him to propose a toast. Alfredo responds with a drinking song. It is in the style of a popular tune, a simple melody, a simple structure, a simple accompaniment patterned around an "oom-pah-pah" beat. Its meaning is given in the last two lines of Alfredo's first verse:

Li - bia - mo, a - mo - re, a - mor____ fra-i

ca - li - ci più cal - di__ ba - ci - a - vrà.

"Let's drink to love, to love in the wine that warms our kisses"

The guests echo Alfredo in chorus, and Violetta responds with her own verse. The two of them engage in a subtle flirtation. The atmosphere of the music continues gay, almost boisterous, but there is an underlying seriousness to their argument. Violetta says "Life is just pleasure." Alfredo responds "But if one still waits for love . . ." Violetta: "I know nothing of that—don't tell me . . ." Alfredo: "But there lies my fate."

Dance music starts in the other room, and the guests start towards it, when Violetta suddenly feels faint. Alfredo stays back with her, and tells her how much he loves her. She laughs off his passionate expressions, but they affect her. Later, when the guests have departed, she sings alone to herself. This is the first real moment of *recitative* in the act. All of the conversation we have heard has been carried along by the energy of the party and its music. Now the social energy fades away and the rhythmic energy with it; instead, the music follows her thoughts, responding to her brief phrases. "How strange," she says, "how strange!" perceiving unfamiliar feelings within her. The memory of Alfredo's words of love lingers. She starts to wonder what love would be like . . . real love, as opposed to the sensual pleasures her life is based on.

"Ah, fors' è lui," her aria begins, "Perhaps it is he," the one whose existence she has fantasized, the man she could love. Her melody is one of Verdi's finest inventions. It begins with a contrast. The first three notes are descending and disconnected, as though she is hesitant and uncertain. The very first note is a D♭, dissonant against the F-minor chord underneath. It relaxes on the second beat of the measure, creating a kind of rhythmic dissonance. Then, after this preparation, the melody turns *legato,* falls into rhythm and harmony, and soars with a great octave leap.

"Ah, perhaps it is he, the one whom my soul . . . "

To see the effectiveness of the hesitant, dissonant preparation, try moving the initial D♭ to a more conventional position, and see how the phrase becomes smoother—and blander.

The rhythm, a "three" pattern, is a continuation, like a memory, of the beat heard in the "party" section of the act. Here it is made to follow the singer's *rubato.* The harmonies are in F minor, but they shift to F major, as Violetta, the cynical sophisticate whose existence is based on her ability to treat love as a marketable commodity, suddenly finds herself becoming idealistic. The music expands (*con espansione,* Verdi marks it), as she says that "love is the pulse of the universe, mysterious and high, the cross and delight of the heart." Her melody and her words are echoes of Alfredo's wooing earlier. Again, a D♭ in the melody over an F in the bass, on the word "misterioso," helps to build tension which relaxes into a lyrical expansion.

mi - ste - ri - o - so,   mi - ste - ri - o - so, al te - ro,   cro - ce,

"Mysterious, high, cross . . . "

But this is a fantasy, she tells herself, and shakes herself awake: "Folly," she calls it, "a silly delirium." She must be realistic, giving herself to love would lead to being a poor woman, abandoned in Paris's desert. Better to forget fantasies of love and plunge herself into the whirlpool of sensual pleasures.

As she sings of this, her voice takes off on a wild cadenza, like an extended ornamentation Chopin would write for the piano, here to be managed by the human voice:

vor   -   -   ti - ci

"Whirlpool"

Next she begins her *"cabaletta"* (a short, rhythmic, ornamented aria): "Sempre libera," "Forever free." The basic melody contains a strong dance rhythm:

Sem-pre li - be - ra___ deg - g'i - o fol - leg - gia - re di gio - ja in gio - ja,

"Forever free, I go madly from joy to joy"

As the aria progresses, more and more ornamentation is added to the basic tune. Her *cabaletta* is interrupted by Alfredo, singing his love song in the street below her window. Violetta returns with ever wilder ornamentation, singing of madness and pleasure. The musical excitement mirrors her own, but Verdi deliberately, I believe, takes it too far. Perhaps all the swirling notes would have been believable in the midst of the party scene. But here, after the yearning lyricism of "Ah, fors' è lui," the excitement seems forced and artificial, almost hysterical. Violetta survives on her tough exterior. If love breaks through it she will become vulnerable, defenseless. She is right to be afraid of love, and her mad singing is her attempt to ward it off.

Of course she succumbs, as the succeeding two acts reveal. Alfredo and Violetta find idyllic happiness together in the country. She sells her Paris possessions secretly to help support them. But Alfredo's father comes to visit, telling her that the affair is spoiling his family's reputation, ruining Alfredo's younger sister's marriage prospects. He asks for her to renounce Alfredo in such a way that he will not pursue her. She does and returns to her life as a courtesan. Alfredo, convinced that she has spurned him to return to an old lover, the Baron, grows bitter with hatred. Again they meet at a party. There is gambling. Alfredo wins from the Baron ("lucky at cards, unlucky in love"), takes the money, and throws it in Violetta's face. It is a fitting gesture, since he believes that she prefers her life as a prostitute, but a shocking one—the ultimate insult, even if it were true—and the Baron challenges Alfredo to a duel.

The final act is in Violetta's bedroom. She is dying. A crowd celebrates Carnival in the street below. Alfredo, who has left town after wounding the Baron in the duel, returns with his father. All is explained and forgiven, but it is too late for Violetta, and after the last exhilarating flush of their reconciliation, she dies.

The opera's first production was a disaster. It was defeated by the problem of realism. The soprano playing Violetta was awkward, and the audience laughed all through her death scene. The fact that the opera's characters were taken not from Medieval legend, or ancient myth, or even the Spanish nobility, but from contemporary society gave the audience an expectation of realism which the production could not meet.

The *demi-monde* was real; tuberculosis was real; the well-intentioned hypocrisy of Alfredo's father was very real. In fact, Dumas' novel is based in part on his own experiences, and is full of concrete information about "the life," as contempoary Parisian prostitutes refer to their profession. Realism is not, however, the major concern of the opera. Its subject is a more general and thoroughly Romantic one—the power of love.

SUMMARY: *Verdi's* La Traviata *(1853)*

melody	Verdi is famous for his ability to write beautiful and memorable tunes, and this opera has several such. Although the melodies are lyrical, they are often based on strong dance rhythms, and sometimes include *coloratura* effects. Song-melodies are far more important to the opera than is *recitative*.
harmony	Generally consonant, with secure tonal centers. Dissonance and movements from major to minor important for expressive effects.
rhythm	Many dance rhythms; different types of "three" patterns are especially important.

form	Alternations between orchestral interludes, recitatives, arias, ensembles, and choruses.
timbre	Violetta is a soprano, Alfredo a tenor, his father a baritone. Strings dominate the orchestral texture. While the orchestra is used for expressive effects, it does not call attention to itself the way Wagner's does in *Lohengrin,* but plays a more supportive role.
texture	Thoroughly homophonic.
function	Opera in Verdi's Italy was a popular art form, more popular than musical comedy in the United States today. (Approximately 500 new operas premièred in Italy between 1842 and 1851.) Verdi's music was designed for this large public, although it played with equal success in the great international opera houses.
text	"Libiamo ne' lieto calici," "Ah, fors' è lui," and "Sempre libera."

"Libiamo ne' lieto calici" (drinking song)

ALFREDO
Libiamo ne' lieti calici,
Che la bellezza infiora;
E la fuggevol ora
S'inebrìì a voluttà.
Libiam ne' dolci fremiti
Che suscita l'amore,
Poichè quell'occhio al core
Onnipotente va.
Libiamo, amore, amor fra i calici
Più caldi baci avrà.

TUTTI
Ah! Libiam, amor fra' calici
Più caldi baci avrà

VIOLETTA
(s'alza)
Tra voi saprò dividere
Il tempo mio giocondo;
Tutto è follia nel mondo
Ciò che non è piacer.
Godiam, fugace e rapido
E il gaudio dell'amore;
E un fior che nasce e muore,
Nè più si può goder.
Godiam!
C'invita un fervido
Accento lusinghier.

ALFREDO
Let's drink from the happy cup
In which beauty flowers;
Let the fleeting moment
Become drunk with pleasure.
Let's drink to the sweet shivers
Stirred by love,
To those eyes which
Overwhelm the heart.
Let's drink to love, to love in the wine
That warms our kisses.

ALL
Let's drink to love, to love in the wine
That warms our kisses.

VIOLETTA
(rising)
Among you I could share
My time of happiness.
All in this world is folly
That doesn't lead on to pleasure.
Enjoy, for fleeting and swift
Is the bliss of love;
Like a flower, it blooms and dies
No longer to be savored.
Enjoy!
It still invites,
Fervently, enticingly.

TUTTI
Ah! Godiamo!
La tazza e il cantico
La notte abbella e il riso,
In questo paradiso
Ne scopra il nuovo dì.

VIOLETTA
(ad Alfredo)
La vita è nel tripudio.

ALFREDO
(a Violetta)
Quando non s'ami ancora . . .

VIOLETTA
(ad Alfredo)
Nol dite a chi l'ignora.

ALFREDO
(a Violetta)
E il moi destin così.

TUTTI
Ah! si godiamo . . .
La trazza e il cantico
La notte abbella e il riso;
Godiamo, in questo paradiso
Ne scopra il nuovo di.

ALL
Ah! Enjoy!
The cup of wine and the song
Make lovely the night and the laughter.
In a paradise like this
Discover a new day.

VIOLETTA
(to Alfredo)
Life is just pleasure.

ALFREDO
(to Violetta)
But if one still waits for love . . .

VIOLETTA
(to Alfredo)
I know nothing of that—don't tell me . . .

ALFREDO
(to Violetta)
But there lies my fate.

ALL
Ah! Let's enjoy . . .
The cup of wine and the song
Make lovely the night and the laughter.
Enjoy; in a paradise like this,
Discover a new day.

"Ah, fors' è lui" (Violetta) and "Sempre libera" (Violetta, joined by Alfredo)

VIOLETTA
(sola)
E strano! è strano!
In core scolpiti ho quegli accenti!
Saria per me sventura un serio amore?

Che risolvi, o turbata anima mia?

Null'uomo ancora t'accendeva.
Oh, gioia
Ch'io non conobbi,
Esser amata amando!
E sdegnarla poss'io
Per l'aride follie del viver mio?

Ah, fors'è lui che l'anima

Solinga ne' tumulti
Godea sovente pingere

VIOLETTA
(alone)
How strange! how strange!
His words are carved into my heart!
Would a real love be a tragedy for
   me?
What is your thought, o my troubled
   soul?
No man before has enflamed thee.
Oh, joy,
Joy which I've never known,
To love and be loved!
Would I scorn this
For the arid follies of the life I lead?

Ah, perhaps it is he, the one whom
   my soul,
Alone in the crowd,
Often loved to paint

De' suoi colori occulti.
Lui, che modesto e vigile
All'egre soglie ascese,
E nuova febbre accese
Destandomi all'amor!
A quell'amor ch'è palpito
Dell'universo intero,
Misterioso altero,
Croce e delizia al cor.

Follie! Delirio vano è questo!
Povera donna, sola, abbandonata
In questo popoloso deserto
Che appellano Parigi,
Che spero or più? Che far degg'io?
Gioire!
Di voluttà ne' vortici perir!

Gioir!

Sempre libera degg'io
Folleggiare di gioia in gioia,
Vo' che scorra il viver mio
Pei sentieri del piacer.
Nasca il giorno, o il giorno muoia,
Sempre lieta ne' ritrovi,

A diletti sempre nuovi
Dee volare il mio pensier.

ALFREDO:
(sotto al balcone)
Amor è palpito . . .

VIOLETTA:
Oh!

ALFREDO:
. . . dell'universo intero . . .

VIOLETTA:
Oh! Amore!

ALFREDO:
Misterioso altero
Croce e delizia al cor

VIOLETTA:
Follie!
Gioir!
Sempre libera degg'io . . . *etc.*

In the colors of fantasy.
He, modest yet vigilant,
Who guarded over my sick-bed,
And turned the fever of illness
Into the fever of love!
Such love is the pulse
Of the universe,
Mysterious and high,
The cross and delight of the heart.

What folly! A silly delirium!
A poor woman, alone, abandoned
In this populous desert
They call Paris,
What can I hope? What can I do?
To enjoy!
Plunge into the whirlpool of pleasure
    and drown there!
To enjoy!

Forever free, I go madly
From joy to joy.
Running headlong
Down the path of pleasure
As each day dawns, as each day dies,
Always living gaily in the world's gay
    places,
My thoughts always flying
To newer delights.

ALFREDO
(outside the window)
Love is the pulse . . .

VIOLETTA
Oh!

ALFREDO
. . . of the universe . . .

VIOLETTA
Oh! Love!

ALFREDO
Mysterious and high,
The cross and delight of the heart.

VIOLETTA
Folly!
Joy!
Forever free, I go madly . . . *etc.*

Strauss and Mahler

CHAPTER 25

Strauss

Franz Schubert was born just before the beginning of the nineteenth century; Schumann, Chopin, Verdi, and Wagner all were born around the end of that century's first decade. Of these, Verdi and Wagner continued active careers into the second half of the century. Brahms (born in 1833) and Tchaikovsky (born in 1840) represent the middle generation of the Romantic period. Two composers of the following generation were Gustav Mahler (1860–1911) and Richard Strauss (1864–1949). Although their careers extended into the twentieth century, both are considered Late Romantic composers.

Strauss was born in Munich, into a family situation which was ideal for a budding composer. His father, the first horn player at the Court Orchestra in Munich, was a skilled musician with an excellent reputation and many close contacts with the leading conductors of the day. His mother had money; she came from a prosperous brewery family, and as a result the Strausses were independently wealthy. Richard Strauss began piano lessons at age four, and started composing at age six. He attended a university for one year, but quit to concentrate on his music. Hans von Bülow (the conductor and pianist who had championed Brahms, Tchaikovsky, and Wagner) conducted his "Serenade for Winds" in Berlin when Strauss was just 19. Strauss then became von Bülow's assistant, beginning what was to become an illustrious career as a conductor.

This career by its very nature indicates a shift which had been going on all through the nineteenth century: the increased interest in larger forms. Most of the composers we have looked at were skilled performers; their primary skills involved keyboard instruments. Strauss was a skilled pianist, but his primary instrument was the orchestra. When orchestras were small, as they had been during previous periods, the separate role of the conductor was not needed. Bach could lead his groups from the organ, Mozart could lead his from the harpsichord. The first-chair violinist (still today referred to as the concertmaster) could lead an orchestra of the Classical period through the performance of a symphony. Such an orchestra would include about 40 players: two each of flutes, oboes, clarinets, bassoons, French horns and trumpets; timpani; and the rest strings. The *minimum* required to perform Richard Strauss's *Don Juan* includes five flutes (one doubling on piccolo), two oboes, English horn, two clarinets, two bassoons, contra-bassoon, four French horns, three trumpets, three trombones, tuba, timpani, triangle, cymbals, glockenspiel, harp, and about 60 strings—a total of around 90. Gustav Mahler offered a simple explanation for the growth of the orchestra: in addition to composers' desire for a wide variety of sounds, he said that "if we want thousands to hear us in the over-large auditoriums of our concert halls and opera houses we simply have to make a lot of noise." But probably more significant than the size and complexity of the orchestra was the expressive nature of Romantic rhythm. Even a large ensemble can play without a leader as long as the rhythm is strict—as is the case with, for example, a marching band. What the Romantic period hungered for was the direct and personal expression of emotion like that found in a Schumann song or a Chopin nocturne. This kind of expression is communicated in nuances of rhythm and volume, by *not* moving along in strict time like a marching band. Nor was the period content to have this expression limited to living rooms; it wanted it in the large concert halls and opera houses Mahler was talking about. In this situation the conductor is not merely necessary; in fact he becomes the key figure, the interpreter, the man (and until recently they were all men) who gives this giant orchestra all the nuances of volume and rhythm available to a solo performer at the keyboard.

Don Juan

Strauss completed his *Don Juan* in 1889. It is a one-movement work for orchestra, not called an overture or a symphony, but a "tone poem." It was written according to his theory of what was needed for the "music of the future": "New ideas," he said, "must search for new forms—this basic principle . . . in which the poetic idea was really the formative element, became henceforward the guiding principle for my own symphonic work." In other words, the music would not follow some abstract pattern of repetition and variation, but would instead have its form dictated by poetic ideas. Strauss, like Wagner, was fascinated by representation. He wanted music which would represent not just emotional or psychological states but also scenes, events, stories. Music which expresses such things with tones alone he called "tone poems." The more general term for such music is "program music." The concept is not original with Strauss. Vivaldi's flute concerto "Il Cardellino" (*see* Chapter 17) is representational, as is Haydn's "Military" Symphony (*see* Chapter 10). And of course the "scene-painting" heard in the accompaniments of many songs and operas is a type of musical representation. But Strauss in his tone poems takes the idea of representation a step further: not only will the music create the scenes a poem would describe, but the poetic ideas will control the very forms the music takes.

Richard Strauss in 1888, at about the time he was writing *Don Juan.*

The title page of *Don Juan* gives credit to Nicolaus Lenau, who wrote a poem of that name between 1842 and 1844, shortly before being committed to an insane asylum. Strauss quotes a portion of the poem as a frontispiece to the score. This might make it seem that Strauss is providing us with a handy guide to the music, but unfortunately the portion of the poem he quotes is a sort of general philosophical musing on the Don Juan character, and is not much help at guiding us through the intricacies and eccentricities of the music.

The work begins with a tremendous orchestral flourish, following a line which rises over three octaves:

"Flourish" theme

This "flourish" theme is introduced *fortissimo;* it is characterized by sudden, radical shifts in harmony and rhythm, moving rapidly from C major to E major, with three or four rhythmic ideas introduced in the first three measures—it is a whirlwind of a phrase.

Don Juan's theme comes next, slightly more conventional than the opening "flourish" theme, since its harmonies and rhythms are more consistent, but still marked by an exaggerated upward-thrusting motion:

"Don Juan" theme

A Classical-period composer might have written the first measure and a half of this melody, but a Classical composer would surely have felt the need for balance and stability, and might have completed the phrase something like this:

Fictional "Classical" version of "Don Juan" theme

The deficiency in this solution is that it expresses none of the raw energy and charged emotion Strauss wants to associate with his hero. If Don Juan is not balanced or rational in his behavior, why should his music be so? Seen in these terms, Strauss's music becomes a kind of critique of the Classical-period style and view of the world: Don Juan is not rational or balanced; humankind is not rational or balanced; the world is not rational or balanced; therefore music should not be rational or balanced.

After the "Don Juan" theme is reiterated in several varied forms, the first section closes with the "flourish" motive which opened the work. There follows an amazing sequence of contrasting ideas. First a dotted rhythm (a long-short-long pattern) dominates (horns):

Dotted-rhythm idea

Then, interrupting, a delicate little melody comes forth:

"Minuet"-like theme

In its question-answer format, this sounds like a snatch of a Classical-period minuet. It in turn is interrupted by another idea, two bars of lush melody:

"Lush" melody

Then the delicate "minuet" theme comes back for two bars. Again it is interrupted, this time by the opening "flourish" idea. Now the plot seems to thicken. The high woodwinds and strings create a twittering, almost giggling effect, while the lower winds present a slowly climbing motive. These two elements continue a kind of dialogue which suddenly breaks off. Into the silence steps the opening "flourish" idea, now heard in a tense, chromatic version in the low strings. It rises up to meet the oboe and clarinets, whose melody slowly falls. The music seems to hover for a second or two, and then the harp enters, and the glockenspiel, and a solo violin, and the texture relaxes into a dreamy, non-rhythmic state. Out of this appears the "lush" melody which had been given a brief two-measure appearance earlier. The clarinet states it, the strings follow, and it becomes more and more passionate in its intensity, seemingly headed for a tremendous climax when it is stopped cold by a series of full *fortissimo* minor chords, repeated in triplet patterns, while the timpani play in slow, syncopated beats beneath. Out of this dark sound the "Don Juan" theme rises in all its old exuberance.

There are two ways of looking at this first portion of the tone poem. We could see it as a kind of "new wine in old bottles"—new melodic material set into the traditional structure of sonata form. From this point of view, the "flourish" is an introductory theme; the "Don Juan" theme is the first theme. The succeeding episodes are all transition material. The "lush" melody is the second theme (and it is in the V key, B major.) The return of the "Don Juan" theme signals that the exposition has ended and the development section has begun.

Such an analysis is all right as far as it goes. The problem with it is that it ignores the most striking features of the music; that is, the incredible succession of disparate ideas. To explain how they fit we have to go beyond sonata form, and look for Strauss's "poetic ideas." Since the quoted portion of Lenau's poem is too general to serve as a guide, we have to invent our own. At any rate, I offer mine.

Both the "flourish" theme which raises the curtain and the "Don Juan" theme itself illustrate the hero's character—wild, undisciplined, irrational—with bounding energy and constant upward-thrusting movement to correspond to his aggressive *machismo*. The action begins. The dotted rhythm puts Don Juan on horseback (for me, at least.) At the delicate "minuet" theme I imagine him riding up to some palace where he hears a snatch of civilized entertainment within. Perhaps a girl from the party has wandered out onto the lawn. The two measures of "lush" melody are Don Juan's first approach to her. The politeness of the minuet returns, followed by the more vigorous "flourish" theme from Don Juan. Their dialogue commences. She twitters and giggles with the upper winds and strings, he continues to press her with the climbing motive in the lower range. She realizes that he is not teasing but serious. As the tense version of the "flourish" theme puts increased pressure on her, the descending line in the oboes and clarinets indicates her weakening resistance. For a long moment the music hovers as they tremble deliciously on the brink, and then their passionate love-making begins. The lush melody becomes a full-blown love theme, and the inter-weaving of voices indicates that Don Juan's seduction is progressing towards ecstatic completion when, with the series of triplet chords, the lovers are interrupted. For a moment it seems that tragedy will strike—perhaps a father or brother has discovered them and will seek revenge—but the exuberant return of the "Don Juan" theme signals that he has made good his escape and galloped off to his next adventure.

Written down like this, my interpretation seems a bit like an old silent movie. Nevertheless, I am convinced that Strauss had some such program in mind as he was writing the music. It isn't necessary to run a silent movie in your mind as you listen to the music, any more than it is necessary to think about exposition, development, and recapitulation every time you listen to a work in sonata form. My excuse for offering my silent movie is that a program, a story like this, explains the remarkable aspects of the tone poem more successfully than the traditional categories of first theme, second theme, and so on.

One defect in my explanation is that its story elements seem more like an episode from Mozart's *Don Giovanni* (which Strauss of course knew very well since it was the nineteenth century's favorite Mozart opera) than one from Lenau's poem. Lenau's Don Juan is a strange and tormented figure who yearns for death as much as he burns with lust, and who finds a religious element ("the warm pulse of God") in sensual desire. One episode finds him smuggling young girls into a monastery in order to tempt the monks (they are tempted); in another, he goes to a graveyard to let the "shudders of death" reawaken his sexual desire. Many writers feel that Strauss's plot has closer affinities to Mozart's opera than to Lenau's poem. Some have even named themes after Mozart's characters Donna Anna and Donna Elvira. It may be that the 25-year-old Strauss was offering a kind of challenge to Mozart, testing his own powers as a composer against the Classical period's great genius.

SUMMARY: *Richard Strauss's tone poem* Don Juan *(1889)*

melody	A wide variety of melodic types, each with strong individual characterization. Strauss does not gradually develop new melodic ideas, but "cuts" rapidly from one to another, as a movie-maker would cut from image to image, scene to scene.
harmony	The work is generally consonant, but the harmonies are not always stable. Many of the themes use chromaticism, which can blur the sense of a tonal center; others use sudden and unexpected harmonic shifts and momentary modulations. A glance at any given page of the score will reveal dozens of accidentals, perhaps the best indicator that a stable sense of "home key" is often lacking.
rhythm	*Allegro molto con brio* ("quick and very spirited") is Strauss's general instruction about tempo, but there are many tempo changes during the piece, and a tremendous variety of rhythmic patterns.
form	In abstract terms, an eccentric sonata form, with an extended development section. In representational terms, a series of episodes portraying the character and adventures of the hero.

texture	Predominantly homophonic. At any given moment, the texture is usually dominated by a single, clear, melodic idea. However, there is considerable use of counterpoint on a smaller scale (with Strauss using counter-melodies to support his principal themes) and occasional use of counterpoint on a larger scale (as when Strauss creates a sense of a "love-duet"). An important aspect of the texture is the way the melodies seem to move around the orchestra, travelling quickly from section to section, instrument to instrument.
timbre	Large orchestra, with many virtuoso passages. Strauss's tone poems are, in general, "showpieces" for orchestra, demonstrating the skill of the ensemble as well as the abilities of many of its individual members.
function	Intended for large-scale, public, orchestral performance.
text	The work is purely orchestral, but Strauss gives title-page credit to the poem "Don Juan," by Nicolaus Lenau, quoting brief selections from the poem as frontispiece to the score. In its musical description of Don Juan's personality and adventures, the tone poem may also refer to other versions of the Don Juan legend, including that developed by Mozart and Da Ponte in their *Don Giovanni.*

Salome

After *Don Juan,* Strauss went on to create a number of brilliant tone poems and operas while maintaining his status as one of the foremost orchestral and opera conductors of the day. Perhaps the most famous and well-loved of these operas is the period-piece comedy, *Der Rosenkavalier.* But the work which established his reputation as an opera composer was his *Salome,* the story of King Herod, his step-daughter Salome, and John the Baptist. The libretto was based on a play by Oscar Wilde (itself loosely based on an incident mentioned in the Bible). Herod desires his step-daughter; she desires Herod's prisoner, John the Baptist. When John refuses her, she turns to Herod, and, tempting him with the Dance of the Seven Veils, demands John's head as her reward. It is brought to her on a platter; she sings of her triumph and kisses John's dead lips. Herod, disgusted, orders the soldiers to kill her, and they crush her under their shields.

The work was a tremendous *succès de scandale,* banned in London and New York. It is not hard to see why it was shocking; nevertheless, the themes it is concerned with are traditional Romantic ones: the mingling of innocence and corruption, love and death, sex and violence, the exotic, and the irrational. These same themes can be found in Schubert's songs at the very beginning of the period. In Strauss's opera they are taken to extremes, almost caricatured, exaggerated in both content and treatment, and turned from small-scale private statement to a large public one.

Schubert, of course, had his life cut tragically short. There is a sense in which Strauss's life was tragically long. When the Nazis came to power in the early 1930s they persecuted artists for racial, political, and stylistic reasons. Many of the great figures of German culture went into exile, either forced or self-imposed. Strauss stayed, and was flattered enough by Nazi attention to accept an official appointment. The irony is that the Nazis campaigned against what they called "decadence," and it was *Salome,* a supremely "decadent" work, which first brought Strauss to prominence as an opera composer.

Mahler

Strauss's family owned breweries; Mahler's father had a distillery. Beyond this, there was little similarity in the two composers' backgrounds. Mahler was born in a little town called Kalischt, in Bohemia (now part of Czechoslovakia). The distillery was a purely local concern—probably not much more than what we would call a "still." Their house, Mahler recalled, did not even have glass in the windows. They stayed in that small town because they were Jews, and Jews were not allowed freedom of travel. When those laws were relaxed, the Mahlers moved to Iglau, a larger town. There Mahler had relatives who owned a piano. His father recognized his musical talent, and arranged lessons for him. At age ten, he gave a recital at the municipal theater. Five years later, his father sent him to Vienna to study at the music conservatory there. He concentrated first in piano, then in composition. There followed years of struggling work as a conductor, travelling to small provincial cities for limited seasons with inadequate opera companies. In one town, Mahler found excuses to have *Lohengrin* and *Don Giovanni* removed from the repertoire, simply because he couldn't bear to see his favorite works performed so incompetently.

Gradually his reputation for excellence grew, and he conducted better orchestras, in more prestigious houses, and in greater cities. Brahms, who was not a great concert-goer, heard him conduct *Don Giovanni* in Budapest, and admired the interpretation. In January of 1893 Mahler wrote to a friend, complaining that he had to give 13 performances involving five different operas within a span of 16 days. But still he found time to compose. He was offered the opportunity to complete an opera which the composer Carl Maria von Weber had left unfinished at his death. The work proved successful, and helped establish Mahler's credentials as a composer. In spite of this success, and his continued successes as an opera conductor, opera was not his chosen field of composition. His interests lay instead with symphony and song. For Mahler, these two categories were not so distinct as they are for us. His symphonies often included songs, and his songs were often symphonic in scale.

Gustav Mahler in 1892, around the time he was orchestrating *Songs of a Wayfarer.*

Songs of a Wayfarer

His *Lieder eines fahrenden Gesellen, Songs of a Wayfarer,* were written between 1883 and 1885, in a version designed for low voice and piano. He worked on orchestrating their accompaniment between 1891 and 1893, and they were first performed in 1896.

Four songs make up the cycle. The poems were written by Mahler himself. Their subject is reminiscent of Schubert's *Winterreise, A Winter's Journey,* and Schumann's *Dichterliebe, A Poet's Love.* The narrator suffers the pangs of unrequited love; he looks to nature for comfort, but finds only despair; he leaves to wander in lonely exile.

Behind the cycle lay genuine experience; Mahler had an unhappy love affair with a singer at the opera house where he was conducting, although he did not have to suffer through his sweetheart's wedding day, as his fictional narrator does. Still, it seems fair to relate the "I" of the songs to a fictionalized version of Mahler himself.

The first song begins with wedding music. Mahler uses his orchestra to create the image of a little wedding band. Two clarinets play the melody, a triangle and a harp accompany them. The melody has the characteristically "circular" quality of many Eastern European folk tunes. That is, the tune circles around a specific tone, in this case an A:

Opening melody, song no. 1

Also folk-like are rhythm and harmony. Although the piece is generally in "two," the second and fourth measures switch to a "three" pattern, a kind of rhythmic complexity heard frequently in folk dances. The harmonies are all based on a D-minor chord. The baritone voice enters with a version of the same theme, differing from the orchestra's version in *not* switching from "two" to "three," in having muted strings for accompaniment, and in being slower, softer, and more lyrical in treatment. The D-minor chord remains, droned in the lower strings even when the melody moves higher.

Mahler next does an audacious thing. He lets his "wedding band" interrupt the singer and strings, stepping on their last slow, soft note with a loud, cheerful blare. This dialogue repeats a little higher, as the singer explains that it will be a happy wedding day. But then he breaks out of the wedding song and into a Romantic phrase rich with reach and fall:

"Is a sad day for me"

Again the wedding band interrupts, this time even louder, augmented with flutes and oboes as well as timpani. The dialogue continues between the lonely, bitter singer and the happy wedding band. The words describe the situation, but it is the music which brings it to life. In a way, Mahler is telling us that he doesn't need the sets and costumes of opera, he can create the scene with his music. When we hear the wedding band play, it is as though we were with the narrator in his little room, hearing the music of celebration drift in through the window.

The mood changes and the musical texture with it. The narrator calls a halt to his inward-looking sadness and self-pity. Instead he looks out at nature, talking to the flowers he sees and the bird he hears, remarking on the beauty of the world. The orchestra perks up with him, in 6/8 time, E♭ major, imitating bird songs and nature sounds.

It doesn't work. Suddenly we are back to the wedding music, the narrator mourning his own sorrow, the wedding band, having picked up the collaboration of the strings, chiming in with its relentless cheerfulness, only slowly fading off into the distance. I say "cheerfulness" because the wedding-band music has such a springy rhythm, and because its dramatic function in the song is to contrast with the narrator's grief. But it is fair to say that one of the things the song teaches us is that the same wedding music contains within it both joy and sorrow.

SUMMARY: *Song No. 1 from Mahler's* Lieder eines fahrenden Gesellen, Songs of a Wayfarer *(1893)*

melody	Three principal melodic ideas are used: a circular, folk-dance melody is placed in contrast to a yearning Romantic phrase; contrasted to both of these is a slight, bouncy tune used in the "nature" section.
harmony	The first section begins with the "primitive"-sounding harmonies of the folk dance, all based on a D-minor chord which drones underneath. As the singer's expression becomes more personal, the harmonies begin to move, and the song modulates to G minor. The middle section moves from E♭ major to F major, the final section once again moving from D minor to G minor.
rhythm	The sense of "folk" rhythm is given by the shift back and forth between "two" and "three" in the opening phrase. For the singer's more personal expressions, the rhythm simplifies into a "two" pattern, but becomes more free and flexible. The middle, "nature" section is a bouncier 6/8 pattern.
form	ABA: first section a dialogue between singer and wedding band; second section a dialogue between singer and nature; third section a return to singer and wedding band.
timbre	Mahler begins with two distinct assortments: the "wedding band" and the singer plus string accompaniment. In the middle section he uses orchestral "scene-painting" techniques to imitate nature sounds.

texture	Predominantly homophonic. In the middle section, the imitations of nature range throughout the orchestra, almost as though "scattered" in the same way nature scatters her sounds in life.
function	Although first written in piano-vocal format, it appears that Mahler always intended these songs to be performed in orchestral concert, as they were heard first and are heard today.
text	

Wenn mein Schatz Hochzeit macht,
   fröliche Hochzeit macht,
Hab' ich meinen traurigen Tag!
Geh' ich in mein Kämmerlein, dunkles
   Kämmerlein!
Weine! Wein'! um meinen Schatz, um
   meinen lieben Schatz!

Blümlein blau! Verdorre nicht!
Vöglein süss! Du singst auf grüner
   Heide!
Ach! Wie ist die Welt so schön!
   Ziküth!

Singet nicht, erblühet nicht, Lenz ist ja
   vorbei!
Alles Singen ist nun aus!
Des Abends, wenn ich schlafen geh',
Denk ich an mein Leid', an mein
   Leide!

My sweetheart's wedding day, happy
   wedding day,
Is a sad day for me.
Then I go to my little room, dark little
   room,
and weep, weep for my dear love.

Little blue flower, do not fade;
sweet little bird, you
   sing in the green meadow—
Oh, how lovely the world is!
   Tirrah!

Do not sing, do not bloom,
   Spring is now over
and all singing must end.
In the evening, when I go to
   rest,
I think of my grief.

Mahler recovered eventually from his unhappy love affair and married Alma Schindler, the daughter of a well-known Viennese artist. She was a talented musician herself and had done some composing. In a typically Victorian interpretation of the wifely role, Mahler refused to allow her to continue her composing. He himself continued both to compose and to conduct, eventually becoming director of both Vienna's opera and its Philharmonic orchestra. Later he undertook similar responsibilities in New York. Considering the commitment and the pressures of such performing work, the amount of composing he accomplished is amazing. He wrote symphonies on a vaster scale than any composer before him. His Eighth Symphony is referred to as the "Symphony of a Thousand," since that is approximately how many performers took part in its première (although it can be performed with smaller numbers, as long as they include a large orchestra, chorus, boys' chorus, and eight solo singers.)

At one point in their marriage, Alma deserted Mahler briefly for an affair with the architect Walter Gropius. Mahler sought the advice of the famous psychotherapist, Sigmund Freud. After a long consultation during which the two great men walked around the streets of Leiden, Holland, Mahler reconciled with his wife. The composer realized that he had been asking Alma to live up to a Romanticized image. Later he helped her to publish some of her music. A fond

A silhouette by Hans Bohler of Mahler conducting.

father, he was deeply affected by the death of his young daughter. A long-term heart condition caused his own early death at age fifty-one.

Summary: Romantic Themes and Style Characteristics

The Romantic period, as we have seen, loved stories. Audiences were not content with abstract music; it had to be representational, it had to be *about* something. One result of this need was a tendency to re-make the music of the past. It was the Romantic period which invented the title "Moonlight" to tack on to Beethoven's famous sonata. Beethoven was not trying to describe moonlight when he wrote the piece, but the Romantics wanted to make the work their own, so they gave it a kind of retroactive representationalism.

It is the fact that the Romantics were so concerned about representation that makes it possible to discuss their favorite themes. Even in the few works we have looked at, certain ideas recur. One of these is the corruption of innocence (*see* color plate 9). The child is taken by the Erlkönig, Gretchen is corrupted by Faust, Elsa's innocence is spoiled by the witch Ortrud. Another theme is unrequited love, as suffered by the narrator of Schumann's *Dichterliebe* and by Mahler's narrator in his *Songs of a Wayfarer*. A third theme is the close relationship between love and death. The father's love cannot protect the child in "Erlkönig;" Gretchen is doomed, as are Verdi's Violetta and Wagner's Elsa. Even Don Juan meets his death at the end of Strauss's tone poem. We see these characters in love, and their love is given poignancy by its proximity to death. A fourth theme is that of the irrational. The child in "Erlkönig" cannot explain his fears, nor can Gretchen explain her desires. In *Dichterliebe* the narrator's emotions veer wildly from extreme to extreme. The taste for the supernatural, as found in both "Erlkönig" and *Lohengrin,* is evidence of another kind of fondness for the irrational. A fifth theme is that of the exotic. The Romantic period loved to place its dramas in distant times or places. *Lohengrin* is set in Medieval Germany, *Faust* (from which Schubert's "Gretchen" is drawn) from a slightly later period, Strauss's *Salome* in Biblical times. Verdi's *La Traviata,* a notable exception here, is set in contemporary Paris. A sixth theme is that of the wanderer or outcast. The narrators of Schubert's *Winterreise* and Mahler's *Songs of a Wayfarer* are both condemned to wander; Violetta's occupation puts her outside society, as does the occupation of the poet in *Dichterliebe.*

These themes reflect a vague quality we can call the mood or spirit of the times (in German, the *Zeitgeist*). Beethoven could still be an optimist, still believe wholeheartedly in humanity's capacity to solve its problems and live together in peace and harmony. The Romantics, having lived through revolution and counterrevolution and the social upheaval connected with industrialization, were more pessimistic and disillusioned. Humanity for them is neither perfect nor perfectable. Innocence is spoiled, love is flawed by bitterness or death, paradise is lost. The only hints of paradise left are found in nature—nature when it is unspoiled by civilization. Nature is of course the other great Romantic theme. There, in unspoiled nature, is the only place the Romantic hero can find communion for the soul (*see* color plate 10).

Even when the composers are more purely abstract, some sense of these themes persists. In Chopin's "Nocturne" and in Brahms' Fourth Symphony the music conveys a sense of yearning or longing, most clearly present in the characteristic Romantic melodic gesture of the reach and fall. The sense of love unrequited, innocence spoiled, paradise lost imbues abstract as well as representational works.

The popularity of these ideas is not just a question of shifting fashions. The audience for music expanded enormously during the nineteenth century, becoming large and middle-class, not exclusive and aristocratic. Of course this change in audiences had the obvious and immediate effect of requiring larger concert halls and bigger orchestras to fill them. But, more importantly, the audience was not refined or even thoroughly well-educated. It needed pegs to hang its culture on. Calling Beethoven's sonata "The Moonlight" made the work easier to listen to. From the composer's point of view, there was the problem of talking to such a mass audience. If I am the composer and you are the audience, I have to ask myself "How can we communicate? What common language do we share?" One answer is that we share certain very basic human concerns: concerns about love and death, for example. Even if I don't know you as an individual, I can be fairly certain that a story about the tragic love affair between a sensitive young man and a beautiful but doomed young prostitute will excite your interest. Such Romantic plots are still popular. "Erlkönig" is the story of a child possessed by an evil spirit; *The Exorcist* and at least half a dozen other movies have been made on that theme in the past decade or so. The theme of the wanderer or outcast has been a staple of popular culture for generations; think of television's "The Fugitive" or even "The Lone Ranger."

Because the Romantic style is so bound up with the search for significance, it becomes almost impossible to separate style from content. One way of looking at the Romantic style *without* trying to separate it from its content is through the general categories "Apollonian" and "Dionysian." Apollo here is the Greek sun-god, and the qualities associated with him are those we saw in the Classical period: clarity, discipline, order, a concern for universal truths, a faith in the rational mind. Against this, Dionysus is the god of wine. "Wine" is significant because it represents a way of escaping from rational, controlled consciousness, which is just what Romantic music wants to do. It wants to sweep you away, it wants you to lose yourself in its flow. So against the Apollonian quality of clarity, the Romantic period proposes suggestiveness: instead of the clear textures of Classical music, we have the scene-painting atmospherics of Schubert's accompaniments, or the dense orchestral texture of a Brahms symphony. Instead of discipline the Romantic period offers freedom: rather than the neatly balanced phrases of Classical music, it offers freely-flowing melodies. Where Classical rhythm is regular, Romantic rhythm ebbs and flows, as in the *rubato* of a Chopin piano piece, the *ritards* and *accelerandos* of a Schumann song, or the many unexpected tempo changes of a Strauss tone poem. Instead of order the Romantic period gives us spontaneity, or at least the illusion of spontaneity. Where Classical music is governed by clearly set-out forms, with divisions neatly marked, the Romantic period prefers the appearance that the piece is being improvised. It is fond of titles like "Impromptu" or "Fantasia" or "Nocturne": improvisations, fantasies, dream-pieces. Sonata form and other formal structures still persist, but they have to be searched for. The listener's impression is not that rules are being obeyed, but that they are being defied, the work governed only by the artist's need for self-expression.

In talking about "suggestiveness" I used examples relating to musical texture; in talking about "freedom" I used examples relating to melody and rhythm; and in talking about "spontaneity" I used examples relating to musical form. Perhaps more important than these—certainly much more difficult to express—is the question of harmony. Romantic harmonies are more dissonant than Classical ones, and, especially late in the period, the sense of tonal center is much less stable. These changes, I suggest, are related to the last two Dionysian categories: the concern for the individual and the loss of faith in the rational mind. For the Romantics, what is important takes place in the individual's heart or soul, beneath the level of conscious awareness. I mentioned the encounter between Freud and Mahler because of this significance. Freud is famous as the discoverer of the importance of the subconscious as the well-spring of human action. But in a sense he was only applying in a more scientific way the ideas which had been current from the beginning of the Romantic movement. In Schubert's "Gretchen" we can already see a composer recognizing and communicating the fact that hidden, ill-understood, irrational motivations are of more central importance than anything the character thinks or says. The tension and instability of the harmonies act to capture the tension between Gretchen's conscious beliefs and her subconscious desires, between the simplicities of her rational behavior as she spins, and the complexities of her irrational compulsions as she dreams.

Revolutionary Styles: Impressionism, Expressionism, and Primitivism

Debussy

Debussy Compared with Wagner

The Romantics aimed high. They wanted their music to have wave-like power, to lift with exultation or plunge into despair. As author Peter S. Hansen has suggested, the contrast between this Romantic style and the emerging Modern style can be seen in a comparison between melodies by Wagner and by the French composer Claude Debussy. When Wagner's Elsa tells her knight Lohengrin that she loves him, her melody reaches to a long, very high note, then falls over several drawn-out measures:

"Take all, all that I am"

When Debussy sets a declaration of love in his opera *Pelléas et Mélisande,* he avoids the grand Romantic gesture as completely as possible:

MÉLISANDE:

Je t'aime aus - si

"I love you too"

Debussy's Life

Debussy was born in 1862, in an apartment above his parents crockery shop. The city of his birth was St. Germain-en-Laye, a suburb of Paris, the city which he loved and in which he died in 1918. It may seem odd to begin a discussion of the Modern period with a composer who was born right between Mahler (1860) and Strauss (1864), but while these two composers were carrying on the Romantic tradition Debussy was rebelling against it.

His father was involved in a more political rebellion—the attempted communist revolution which led to the formation of the Paris Commune in 1871. When the Commune was defeated, Manuel Debussy was sentenced to four

Two strong influences on early 20th-century music: Claude Debussy (left) and Igor Stravinsky.

years in prison (the sentence was later suspended). An aunt first fostered young Debussy's musical ability and obtained piano lessons for him. His father evidently saw the possibility that Debussy might become a money-making child prodigy, and enrolled him in the Paris Conservatory when he was just 11.

Debussy did have the makings of a child prodigy; he performed a Chopin piano concerto when only 12. A career as a pianist did not interest him, however, and he soon switched his major field to composition. The conservatory training was structured around a series of prizes; a student had to win a prize at one level before moving on to the next. Debussy was not a model student—he found the conservatory instruction boringly tradition-bound—but he did succeed in winning the ultimate prize, the "Prix de Rome," in 1884.

This entitled him to three years of state-supported study in Rome, during which time he was supposed to soak up the atmosphere of classical civilization, mingle with other members of his generation's cultural elite, and create works which would be performed under official sponsorship back in Paris, thus guaranteeing a successful start to an officially-sanctioned career. Debussy didn't like Rome, didn't make friends, didn't complete the required number of compositions, didn't even endure the three years, and neglected to organize the exposition of his own compositions which was due to him.

Prélude à l'après-midi d'un faune

Instead of the approved path, he opted for the Bohemian life, living cheaply in a Paris garret with a working-class mistress, earning no steady income, studying the new poetry and evolving his own new style of music. The major work which he produced in this period was the *Prélude à l'après-midi d'un faune, Prélude to the Afternoon of a Faun* (completed in 1894.) This is an orchestral work based on a poem by Stéphane Mallarmé, the most important of the Symbolist poets who were creating a modern style in poetry. The "Faun" of the title is a mythological creature, half man, half goat, like the Greek god Pan. In the poem, the Faun awakes in a haze of love, unsure whether he has loved the nymphs he remembers or simply dreamed of loving them. Debussy captures this dreamy uncertainty in his music, basing his composition on a melody which recalls the Faun's traditional instrument, the "panpipes," especially in its first two measures, where we can imagine the Faun running his breath down across the pipes and back up again.

The Faun is a simple, sensuous creature; he isn't troubled or anxious about his experience, he merely wonders whether it was dream or reality. The melody, while quite chromatic (as can be seen from the accidentals) is suitably calm as well, moving up and down without a fixed sense of purpose or direction. A little later in the piece, the violins have a statement which seems to build towards a climax, but the climax never arrives. The clarinet takes over the idea, making it softer and slower, and returning it to the "panpipes" theme:

Like the "Je t'aime aussi" phrase from *Pelléas et Mélisande,* this work is a kind of criticism of the Romantic concept of "love." Love here is not deep, moving, and significant: it is only the confused memory of what was probably just a sensual dream. The Faun himself has no special significance, except that Debussy wants to teach us to be Fauns in our relationship to music. That is: as we listen, we should become simple and sensuous, not too concerned with meaning or significance, but lost in the moment-by-moment experience of the sounds of winds, strings, and harps.

The performance of the *Prélude à l'après-midi d'un faune,* and, more importantly, the production of *Pelléas et Mélisande* in 1902, made Debussy an established figure. Although his works were controversial, he was generally recognized as a major French composer, and in 1903 was awarded the ultimate badge of success, membership in the Legion of Honor.

He had married in 1899, but left his wife for Madame Emma Bardac, the wife of a wealthy banker. They had a daughter, Chouchou, in 1905, but were not able to marry until 1908. Although never free from worries about money, he was now, with this marriage and the success of his works, able to enjoy a more elegant style of life than had been available to him before. A photograph from 1916 shows him with his daughter, picnicking in a forest, wearing a suit and a boater hat. But a wife and child and a home on the fashionable Avenue Bois de Boulogne did not guarantee happiness. He had become estranged from many of his friends because of their support for his first wife; he was forced to undertake work, including conducting his own compositions, which was unpleasant to him; and in 1907 he developed cancer. From then until his death he suffered from the disease, often having to take drugs to counteract the pain. Even in the photograph shown on page 294, the effects of pain seem evident in his expression.

In spite of these obstacles, he continued to compose a wide range of works, including songs, choral works, music for dance, works for orchestra and for chamber groups, and works for the piano. Among the latter are his 24 préludes, in two books, written between 1909 and 1913. Like Bach's *Well-tempered Clavier* and like Chopin's 24 préludes, these were Debussy's attempt to define a new keyboard style. Probably the most famous among them is the tenth from the first book, *La Cathédrale Engloutie, The Engulfed Cathedral*.

Impressionism and *The Engulfed Cathedral*

According to Debussy's instructions at the head of the score, the work is to be "utterly calm (in a gently resonant mist)." It begins with a widely spaced chord, whose top and bottom notes are five and one-half octaves apart. The spaces within the chord are open as well—there are no thirds, only intervals of the fourth and fifth. As this chord rings, a series of more compact but still open-spaced chords climbs up within it:

These chords move in parallel motion, an effect not popular since the Middle Ages. The result is that all the chords seem equal; there is no sense of a chord *progression* to or away from a tonal center. Instead, the chords seem to float. As the music goes back and forth between widely-spaced, ringing chords, and climbing, middle-register chords, we lose a sense of the progress of time, and acquire instead a feeling of space: the ringing chords define the outer limits, the climbing chords fill the inner areas.

Out of this gentle mist a melody appears. Its characteristic gesture is up a step, then up a fourth.

It appears in a variety of settings, including some which become sharply focussed, but each time it seems to draw back into the mist, and it is to the opening mist that the piece returns in its closing measures.

Only after these closing measures does Debussy state the prélude's name, as a kind of afterword, in small letters, ". . . la cathédrale engloutie." Perhaps he does not want us to take the title too literally, perhaps he does not want us to "interpret" the piece in terms of the title. In fact the music does not describe an engulfed cathedral—a listener could hardly make a sketch based on what was heard—but the phrase "engulfed cathedral" does describe something about the music, as clear outlines appear out of, and disappear back into, a mist of sound.

What is modern about the music is not the clear outlines, but the mist; not the cathedral, but what engulfs it. At one moment, for example, Debussy introduces a series of dominant-seventh chords. In traditional harmonic practice, these are the chords which lead directly to the tonal center. Here Debussy introduces them in parallel, completely defusing their traditional function. Instead of progressing, they float; instead of functioning as a means to an end, they become an end in themselves. If we no longer can hear these chords as supports for other chords, we are forced to listen to them as themselves, forced to concentrate on their textures and timbres, forced to notice them purely as sounds.

Debussy takes this process even further in the next few measures with chords like this:

These are placed so deep in the piano that it becomes hard to distinguish the individual tones. It is the *sound,* not the tone, which has become crucial. Two different substitutions may help demonstrate this. One calls for the same notes in a different register; one calls for different notes in the same register:

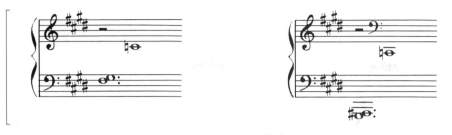

Right notes, wrong register   Right register, wrong notes

If, of the two versions, the second seems preferable, it is because timbre has be-come more important than tone. Debussy is composing with sounds in the same way that Monet painted with light. This is why the word "Impressionism" is an appropriate one for both their styles. It is not, as is commonly thought, that Monet and Debussy were trying to give the viewer a quick "impression" of a cathedral, a kind of sketch. It is rather that both artists are principally con-cerned with sensory impressions: the effects of light and sound are their subject matters. Monet is not concerned with the stones and structure of the cathedral, but with the way light reflects off it and through the atmosphere to the eye. Similarly, Debussy's principal concern is with the way certain sounds strike the ear. (*See* color plate 11, Monet's *Rouen Cathedral at Dawn.*)

Not that the prélude is empty of Romantic emotional content. In the clearly focussed sections Debussy gives a hint of a regretful look back at the lost cathedral. But especially in the passages where he frees chords from their tradi-tional functions, making us hear them not for what they mean but just for how they sound, he is taking a revolutionary step whose consequences would be felt throughout the century.

Maurice Ravel

A large part of this Impressionist influence came not directly from Debussy but through his younger contemporary, Maurice Ravel (1875–1937). A gifted melo-dist, Ravel in general departs less radically from tradition than does Debussy, but his orchestration techniques benefit from an Impressionist concentration on pure timbre. The brilliant orchestral colors he created in works like his orchestration of the Russian composer Modest Mussorgsky's *Pictures at an Exhibition* had a powerful influence on the young American composers Aaron Copland and George Gershwin, as we shall see in Chapters 28 and 31.

SUMMARY: *Debussy's* The Engulfed Cathedral *(1910)*

melody	Melodic outlines appear and disappear. A characteristic pattern is up a step, then up a fourth.
harmony	Many "open"-sounding chords, without the third (thus not defined as major or minor); harmonies treated in parallel (thus without a

	sense of chord progression); pedal-tones; "static" harmonies where the underlying harmony stays the same over a long period.
rhythm	Time signature is ambiguous: Debussy writes "6/4 = 3/2," probably (there is disagreement on the subject) to indicate that the beat can shift back and forth from two groups of three to three groups of two.
form	Principal unifying element is the melodic idea of movement up a step, then up a fourth. Debussy alternates between focus and fog; each new "focussed section" presents the melodic material in a new way.
timbre	This is the area which acquires heightened prominence in Debussy's music. He likes to combine the very high and low registers of the piano; to find ways to allow series of chords to blend together; to contrast a blurry texture with a sharply defined one; to create dense chords which look dissonant but in context become pure sounds without harmonic tension.
texture	One of Debussy's favorite effects is that of the pedal-tone, or, as in the opening measures, whole chords which are sustained while other chords play within them. The variety of pedal-tones and pedal-like effects was one of the new approaches to the piano which his préludes helped to define.
function	Debussy's préludes were intended for publication (which is how they provided a source of income for him). Amateur, student, and professional pianists have been performing them ever since.

Schoenberg

In developing a style opposed to the Romantic tradition, Debussy had an advantage in being French. He was able to use his national identity to distance himself from a tradition which was dominated by composers from Germany and Austria. This was the tradition Arnold Schoenberg grew up in. He was born in Vienna in 1874 and spent most of his life there and in Berlin. He emigrated to the United States in 1933, driven out of Europe by the Nazis, and died in Los Angeles in 1951. His parents were not well-off; his father ran a shoe shop. There was no piano in their home. Schoenberg began violin lessons when he was eight, and these lessons were all he ever received in the way of formal training. He played in amateur chamber groups with friends who could not afford tickets to concerts—making the music themselves was their only access to it. The leader of one of these groups was Alexander Zemlinsky, a well-schooled musician who was able to assist Schoenberg in what was really a course of self-study. Zemlinsky's sister became Schoenberg's first wife.

Being self-taught is not a bad thing for a potential revolutionary. Schoenberg studied traditional music with meticulous care, and he approached it free from the academic prejudices of his day. His own music was grounded in the

German Romantic tradition, but it benefitted from his wide-ranging knowledge of traditional musical styles, especially from the ages when polyphony reigned.

Both Richard Strauss and Gustav Mahler recognized Schoenberg's abilities and gave him assistance, but his work did not receive popular support and never attracted a wide audience. In his early years he made his living by conducting for choral societies and by orchestrating operettas. (Opera composers do their own orchestrations; writers of operetta and musical comedy have traditionally relied on outside help for theirs.) Later he devoted himself increasingly to teaching, a vocation to which he brought the same seriousness and sense of moral purpose which he brought to his composing.

"Seriousness" and "moral purpose" are related to Schoenberg's failure to attract a wide audience. It is not that audiences necessarily dislike these qualities. It is just that Schoenberg had a particular kind of truth he wanted to express, and the Viennese audiences were not particularly interested in hearing it. They preferred the operettas he was arranging: romantic, nostalgic tales, idyllic fantasies with happy endings. As an example, one famous operetta, Franz Lehar's *The Merry Widow,* is about a nobleman trying to arrange a marriage between a young man and a wealthy widow, in order to get his (fictional) country of Pontevedro out of debt. Schoenberg's subject matter was less sugar-coated. In fact, Schoenberg was not concerned with the coating at all, but with the core, and it was, in his view, an acid one.

Expressionism and *Erwartung*

Schoenberg's *Erwartung, Expectation,* might be said to concern a widow, but she is hardly merry. The work is an opera in one act, four scenes, for solo soprano and full orchestra. The soprano sings the role of a woman searching for her lover. It is night. Moonlight floods the field at the edge of a dark forest. The woman enters. The orchestra plays in quick, fragmented motives, scattered through the winds, harp, celesta (a small piano-like instrument in which steel bars are struck instead of strings), and strings. "Is it here?" the woman asks. "I can't see the way . . ." She remarks on the silvery shine of the tree trunks, and is reminded of their garden. "The night is so warm," she continues. "I am afraid." She moves back and forth between past and present, noticing the crickets with their love song, then talking to her lover as though he were with her: "It is so sweet beside you." She berates the moon for fading, then sees horror in it. "Does it look within itself?" she asks. In the second scene she continues to shift back and forth between her present in the tangled forest and her past in the garden, but now she is afflicted by other imaginings: the forest seems to be alive, grappling at her; she thinks she stumbles on a body, then realizes it is only a tree trunk; later, in the final scene, she will find her lover's body, but the intensely subjective words never let us know if we are seeing real experience or her nightmare.

Her melodic line, just as the text, is broken up into short, disconnected phrases. The effect of "disconnection" is communicated by more than mere

Munch: *The Cry* (1895). The Expressionist painter Munch creates an image of a woman's inner pain echoing through a landscape. Schoenberg creates the same image in *Erwartung*. *(Oslo Municipal Collection, Munch Museum)*

gaps between the phrases; there is also a formal lack of connection. Here, for example, are the first five phrases of the second scene:

Five consecutive phrases from the vocal part of *Erwartung*

These show the essential quality which makes the music difficult for the listener. We are accustomed to patterns in music. We expect something like what Haydn gives us in the first four phrases of his F-Major Piano Sonata, where each phrase is a logical-sounding response to the previous one:

Opening phrases from Haydn's F-Major Piano Sonata

Schoenberg avoids patterns in his rhythms as much as in his melodies. As the conductor and author Robert Craft points out, the tempo changes 111 times in 427 measures of music; in addition there are 65 other tempo modifications indicated (faster, slower, and so on).

Perhaps in part because Schoenberg's training was as a violinist, not as a pianist, his harmonies result not so much from chords as from the overlapping of individual musical lines. The resultant harmonies are dissonant, sometimes extraordinarily so. Here, for example, are all the notes heard on the second half of the first beat of measure 40:

Although this sort of extreme dissonance is what Schoenberg's music is famous for, it is not really as important as the absence of resolution. On the following beat of the measure, this particular harmony does not relax into consonance but becomes even more dissonant.

These harmonies are not as dissonant as I may have made them seem, because they are not heard as block chords. The constant interplay of voices gives the music a thin, even delicate and transparent texture. But as dissonance succeeds dissonance, we are never allowed the sense of repose which a tonal center could provide. Schoenberg deliberately disrupts the normal patterns of melodic, rhythmic, and harmonic connection. He does this not arbitrarily but in pursuit of the reality he thinks it is essential to capture. This is the reality of the "core": the sub-conscious, the Freudian strife-torn inner self where thoughts and words lose their neatness and logic and become confused and disconnected; where wounds have not healed; where psychic pain resides.

Erwartung is full of Romantic themes: the individual, alone, in an irrational state, relating to nature which reflects her mood back to her, a victim of unrequited love, regretting a lost paradise ("our garden"). But these themes are developed to such a heightened extreme that the result overturns Romantic practice. The usual translation of the title is *Expectation,* but what the music is about is the *defeat* of our expectations. Romanticism taken to these extremes turns on itself and becomes revolutionary, giving rise to a new style. The new style was developing in painting as well as in music, and it would come to be known by the term "Expressionism." Schoenberg was involved with these developments not just as a musician but also as a talented amateur painter. One of the Expressionist painters, Franz Marc, wrote in 1911 that "Schoenberg, like our society [of painters], seems convinced of the continuous dissolution of the laws of European art and harmony."

SUMMARY: *Schoenberg's* Erwartung, *scenes one and two (1909)*

melody	Extremely chromatic. Characterized by "jagged" lines, with wide intervals over a wide range, making it very difficult to sing. An absence of conventional repetitions of melodic phrases leads to a sense of "disconnection."
harmony	Extraordinarily dissonant, with an almost complete absence of tonal center.
rhythm	Extremely variable. No strong pulse or beat and constant shifts of time signatures and tempo indications.
form	An opera for one singer in four scenes. The form is Wagnerian in

	that there is no separation of *aria* and *recitative,* but a continuing development in the singer's melody.
timbre	Full, large orchestra, including harp, celesta, and percussion effects (gong, rattle, cymbals, triangle). The various instruments often play in isolation or in small combinations, making the orchestral sound much thinner than it was for Wagner, Strauss, or Mahler.
texture	The writing in general is extremely linear. At any given moment, each instrument's part is likely to look like a melodic line. Although the orchestra is a large one, it is presented in a fragmentary form: we might hear the woodwinds against the first violin, then the celesta against the 'cello, both played over the vocal line. The vocal part dominates, but the instrumental parts create a fragmented polyphonic texture around it.
function	*Erwartung* was designed for theatrical performance, but did not receive a performance of any sort until 1924, 15 years after it was composed. It has been performed consistently though never frequently since then.
text	Written by Marie Pappenheim (at the time a young medical student in Vienna).

SCENE I—Moonlight floods the fields at the edge of a dark wood. A woman enters.

THE WOMAN:

Hier hinein? . . . Man sieht den Weg nicht . . .	Is it here? I can't see the way.
Wie silbern die Stämme schimmern . . . wie Birken! oh—unsern Garten.	How silvery shine the tree trunks . . . like birches. Oh—our garden . . .
Die Blumen für ihn sind sicher verwelkt.	the flowers are probably faded . . .
Die Nacht ist so warm. Ich fürchte mich . . .	the night is so warm. I am afraid . . .
was für schwere Luft heraus schlägt . . .	what heavy air comes out from there . . .
Wie ein Sturm, der steht . . .	like a storm, suspended . . .
So grauenvoll ruhig und leer . . .	so horribly calm and empty . . .
Aber hier ists wenigstens hell . . .	but here it is at least light . . .
der Mond war früher so hell . . .	earlier the moon was so bright . . .
Oh noch immer die Grille . . .	oh, the crickets . . .
mit ihrem Liebeslied . . .	with their love song . . .
Nicht sprechen . . . es ist so süss bei dir . . .	don't speak . . . it is so sweet beside you.
der Mond ist in der Dämmerung . . .	The moon is fading . . .
feig bist du, willst ihn nicht suchen? . . .	cowardly moon, won't you search?
So grauenvoll ruhig und leer . . .	so die here . . .

Wie drohend die Stille ist . . .	how threatening the quiet is . . .
der Mond ist voll Entsetzen . . .	the moon is full of horror . . .
sieht der hinein? . . .	does it look within itself?
Ich allein . . . in den dumpfen Schatten.	I, alone in the muted shadows.
Ich will singen, dann hört er mich . . .	I will sing, then he will hear me.

SCENE II—Deep darkness. She gropes her way forward.

Ist das noch der Weg? . . .	Is this still the path?
Hier ist es eben. Was? lass los! . . .	Here it is level . . . what? Let go!
Eingeklemmt? . . . Nein es ist was gekrochen . . .	Hemmed in . . . No, it is something crawling . . .
Und hier auch . . . Wer rührt mich an? . . .	and here also . . . who's touching me?
Fort—Nur weiter . . . um Gotteswillen . . .	Away—further away. For God's sake . . .
So, der Weg ist breit . . .	the path is broad . . .
Es war so still hinter den Mauern des Gartens . . .	it was so quiet behind the garden wall.
Keine Sensen mehr . . . kein Rufen und Gehn . . .	No more mowing . . . no more calling and going . . .
Und die Stadt in hellem Nebel . . .	and the city in bright fog . . .
so sehnsüchtig schaute ich hinüber . . .	so yearningly I looked across . . .
Und der Himmel so unermesslich tief über dem Weg	and the heavens so immeasurably deep over the path
den du immer zu mir gehst . . .	on which you always walk to me . . .
noch durchsichtiger und ferner . . .	more transparent and distant . . .
die Abendfarben . . .	the evening colors . . .
Aber du bist nicht gekommen . . .	but you have not come . . .
Wer weint da? . . . Ist hier jemand?	who is crying there? Is someone here?
Ist hier jemand? Nichts . . .	Is someone here? Nothing . . .
aber das war doch . . .	but there was something . . .
Jetzt rauscht es oben . . .	now it is rustling overhead . . .
es schlägt von Ast zu Ast . . .	it strikes from branch to branch.
Es kommt auf mich zu . . . Nicht her! . . .	It approaches me . . . not here!
lass mich . . . Herrgott hilf mir . . .	Leave me . . . Lord God, help me . . .
Es war nichts . . . nur schnell, nur schnell . . .	it was nothing . . . only quick . . .
Oh, oh, was ist das? . . . Ein Körper . . .	oh, oh, what is that? A body . . .
Nein, nur ein Stamm.	no, only a tree trunk.

The Twelve-Tone System

A great part of Schoenberg's subsequent fame and influence arose through his work at creating *new* laws to replace the old ones he had worked to dissolve. He codified his revolution by developing a system, called the "twelve-tone" or "serial" method of composition. The method almost guarantees the absence of a

George Gershwin: *Arnold Schoenberg* (1937) (*See* page 359.)

tonal center by requiring that each of the twelve half-steps be treated with equal importance. To show how the method works, we can first list the twelve half-steps of the chromatic scale as follows:

Then we can make a melody, or "tone row," from this list, using all of the notes and repeating none:

When actually writing the composition, we would be allowed to use these tones in different registers, high or low, and in combinations, but we would not be allowed to repeat any tone until all twelve have been used. We would, however, be permitted variations on the original tone row: the row in retrograde (played backward), inversion (upside down), or retrograde-inversion. Using just the original row, we can create a miniature twelve-tone composition:

As a method, the twelve-tone system is disciplined and limiting. At the same time, it is in one sense liberating: it frees the composer from the four centuries of tradition in which music was organized around a tonal center. The method was used with greatest effectiveness by Schoenberg's two most famous pupils, Alban Berg and Anton Webern. It would become important again in music after World War II.

Igor Stravinsky

A Schoenberg concert on March 31st, 1913, led to a near riot in the concert hall. A ballet performance with music by Igor Stravinsky on May 28th of the same year created an even greater and more famous tumult.

Stravinsky was born in 1882 in what is now Lomonosov, Russia, and died in New York City in 1971. His father was a musician, a bass at the Imperial Opera in St. Petersburg (now Leningrad), but Stravinsky was sent to study law. Like

Schumann, he never completed his degree, becoming instead increasingly involved with music.

Nationalism

His early (1903–1906) teacher was Nikolay Rimsky-Korsakov, who was a leader of the Russian "nationalist" group of composers. The political history of the nineteenth century is largely the story of the establishment of national identities. The concept of a nation is a familiar one to us, but it was relatively unknown in earlier centuries, when loyalties were focussed on communities, churches, or monarchies. In the latter part of the nineteenth century, composers like Rimsky-Korsakov, Alexander Borodin, and Modest Mussorgsky in Russia, Edvard Grieg in Norway, and Antonin Dvořák and Bedřich Smetana in Bohemia (Czechoslovakia) wrote concert music which was strongly colored by the folk idioms of their native cultures, although the music still retained the dominant characteristics of the Romantic style. The inclusion of folk idioms identified the music with its nation and helped to define the nation's identity for its people.

Stravinsky's early music was strongly characterized by folk idioms, but his purposes in using them were fundamentally different from those of the "nationalist" composers like his teacher. One of Stravinsky's early works was played in a concert in St. Petersburg where it was heard by Serge Diaghilev, the impressario of the *Ballets Russes.* Diaghilev hired Stravinsky to compose and arrange music for his ballet company. This was not a purely local concern. The *Ballets Russes* toured throughout Europe, and its seasons in London and Paris were viewed as major cultural events in those capitals. This was, in short, a tremendous opportunity for a young composer. Right at the start of his career, large audiences including Europe's cultural elite would experience his music in splendid performances combined with innovative choreography and visual presentation. Of course a great opportunity like this is also a great opportunity to fail, but Stravinsky met the challenge with a series of brilliant works including *The Firebird, Petrushka, The Rite of Spring,* and *Les Noces.*

Primitivism and The Rite of Spring

The most famous of these is *The Rite of Spring, Le Sacre du printemps,* composed between 1911 and 1913, and performed with riotous results in May of 1913. Part of the audience tried to shout the music down, another part tried to shout the shouters down, and fights broke out. The famous Russian dancer Nijinsky, who had choreographed the ballet, stood in the wings shouting out counts to dancers who couldn't hear the music over the crowd.

The best way to see why the audience found the music outrageous is to look at the last, climactic, section of the ballet, the "Sacrificial Dance." In this section, the maiden who has been chosen as the victim to be sacrificed to spring must dance herself to death. The music opens with a prolonged series of driving, heavy, dissonant chords. Stravinsky uses a technique called "bi-tonality"

"The Sacrifice" from Stravinsky's *The Rite of Spring* with Maurice Bejart's Ballet of the Twentieth Century.

(for instance, mixing a D chord with an E♭ chord) at the beginning of the movement:

The chords are presented in a wildly eccentric rhythm. Here is the first-violin part during the opening measures:

A performer might count to himself or herself while playing it: "one TWO three, one TWO, one TWO three, one TWO three, one TWO THREE FOUR . . ." Meanwhile, basses and timpani play on downbeats against this pattern. It *is* a pattern, although its complexities are such that the listener never quite catches up with it and is constantly being caught by surprise. Nevertheless, the complexity never obscures the driving, propulsive beat.

Dissonant harmonies and eccentric rhythms were not enough to cause a riot. What was offensive to the audience was the sheer violence of the music and the violence which was being done to musical tradition. The symphony orchestra which had evolved to play the rich melodies and harmonies of Haydn, Mozart, Beethoven, Schubert, Brahms, and Mahler, was being treated as a gigantic primitive drum. Here we have to distinguish between *sounding* primitive and *being* primitive. Stravinsky's score gives the illusion of crude, unbridled energy, but is in fact worked out with extraordinary finesse. The smallest details of rhythm and inflection are carefully notated, as they must be to create the sense of conflict between different timbres, different rhythms, and different motives. Stravinsky builds towards a climax by creating a sense of ever-increasing chaos; to accomplish this requires, paradoxically, a tremendous degree of organization.

Still, "primitive" is a key word. Once again a comparison with painting is appropriate. Painters attempting to liberate themselves from their cultural traditions sought out radically different cultural traditions. Picasso, for example, brought elements of African art into his *Demoiselles d'Avignon* (1906–1907). The "Demoiselles" of the title are the women of a brothel on Avignon Street in

Picasso: *Les Demoiselles d'Avignon* (1907) The faces of the figures on the right are derived from the features of African masks. *(Museum of Modern Art)*

Barcelona. The work is a direct contradiction of one of painting's principal functions in the Western world: to make attractive images of pretty women. Picasso assults that tradition with blatant poses, masks for faces, and an overall sense of confrontation with the viewer. He uses African art to help liberate himself from tradition's bonds.

"Primitivism" had the same liberating function for Stravinsky. *The Rite of Spring* is subtitled "Scenes of Pagan Russia." This "Pagan Russia" is an imaginary country, having little to do with the modern nation. The world Stravinsky pictures is harsh, violent, and filled with brutal energy, although it can still create moments of singular beauty. Stravinsky and his collaborators in the ballet company were challenging the audience. They were asking, in effect, which offered the truer picture of the world—the elegant images of Classical ballet, or the crude energies of *The Rite of Spring?* Is the world a polite and civilized place, or is it closer to the imaginary pagan Russia? Events were to prove Stravinsky's vision the truer one, although it was not nearly harsh or violent enough to match the horrors of World War I. His "Pagan Russia" sacrifices a maiden to the Spring; civilized Europe was about to sacrifice millions of young men to the ideals of nationhood. But there is a sense in which *The Rite of Spring* really is a rite of spring: the rioting audience was acting out a ritual of renewal in which old traditions were sacrificed and new ones created.

SUMMARY: *Stravinsky's* The Rite of Spring, *final movement,*
           "Sacrifical Dance" (1913)

melody	The composition is centered around rhythmic patterns rather than melodies, but there are certain melodic ideas (for example, a six-note, descending chromatic phrase) which gather force through repetition.
harmony	Stravinsky creates strong dissonances, sometimes by using "bitonal" chords; like Debussy, he creates a context in which they neither demand nor receive resolution. His principal method for creating that context is by treating each chord as a particle of rhythmic energy.
rhythm	Characterized by powerful, driving, eccentric patterns of beats. The time signatures shift constantly: 3/16, 2/16, 3/16, 2/8, 2/16, and so on, changing with almost every change of measure. In addition, Stravinsky creates contrasting rhythmic patterns which play against each other.
form	The work as a whole is divided into sections corresponding to the "scenes" of the subtitle. This final section is marked by a gradual increase in chaotic energy, with orchestral texture becoming denser and rhythmic energy more frenetic.
texture	The texture is basically homophonic, as Stravinsky lines the instruments up together to create huge chords. A polyphonic element enters with the introduction of conflicting rhythmic patterns.

timbre
: Full orchestra, used to create a full sound. Stravinsky stretches the orchestra to create unusual effects, for example, writing for instruments at the extremes of their ranges. In a famous section near the beginning of the work, he creates a chord by giving different notes to each of six bass viols.

function
: Music for ballet. After its first tumultuous reception, the work achieved general acceptance. The music has outlived its dance, and is now heard most often in concert performance.

Stravinsky's subsequent career took him through many changes of style. He wrote music which was dry and satirical *(The Soldier's Story);* "neo-classical" music which reused certain traditional forms *(The Rake's Progress);* music which was serious and religious *(Symphony of Psalms);* even music written according to Schoenberg's twelve-tone system. After the Russian revolution in 1917 he lived in Switzerland and then in France, later moving to the United States. He was always a working musician, performing, conducting, and composing commissions, including such oddities as a circus polka for baby elephants (a commission from Barnum and Bailey). But his early ballet compositions for the *Ballets Russes,* for all their early shock, became his most popular works.

Summary of the Three Early Modern Styles

Debussy's Impressionism, Schoenberg's Expressionism, and Stravinsky's Primitivism are immensely different in sound. What they have in common is that they all deny fundamental aspects of the Western musical tradition. Their melodies do not follow traditional shapes and are not based on conventional scales. Their harmonies do not offer a series of chord progressions to and from a tonal center. Their rhythms do not march along in regular measured patterns.

Of these changes, the most important is that involving the tonal center. The invention of the tonal center in music was equivalent to the invention of perspective in painting. Centuries of art-making were based on these two discoveries, but in the early years of the twentieth century, composers and painters repudiated these essential aspects of their traditions. The familiar space of Masaccio's *Tribute Money* is absent from Picasso's, Munch's, and Monet's works, just as the familar sense of tonality is gone from Stravinsky's, Schoenberg's, and, to a lesser degree, Debussy's music.

Another quality which unites these composers is that they were conscious of their roles as musical revolutionaries. They knew that their works were attempting fundamental changes in the musical tradition. To some degree, this revolutionary process becomes the subject of the works; the works can be seen as comments on the process. For example, *The Afternoon of a Faun* teaches the listener to accept a Faun-like, sensual approach to musical sounds. In *The Engulfed Cathedral,* the cathedral, a symbol of old art, is lost in the mist of the new Impressionist style. Schoenberg's *Expectation* is about music which defeats the listener's expectations. Stravinsky's *The Rite of Spring* is about the Spring-like birth of a new style.

Music about music is part of a larger trend known as "art for art's sake." According to the Russian theorist Plekhanov, art for art's sake arises when artists and those closely involved with art feel disaffected from the middle-class public which supports them. We do not have to look hard at either the composers' works or their situations to see this process at work in the early modern period. The composers have an increasingly difficult struggle for recognition. They are less and less willing to compromise their ideals to meet the public's tastes. Their works show an increasing emotional distance from the audience, at times amounting to an almost agressive antagonism. This is an attitude best summed up in a phrase which modernist poets and painters liked to use: *"épater les bourgeois,"* "astonish, dumbfound, flabbergast the middle-class."

Music of the Times

Weill

As musicians came to feel out of harmony with their society, their concerns became, increasingly, purely musical ones. Problems of form seemed more important than problems of content. In other words, they were interested in making innovations in melody, harmony, rhythm, form, texture, and timbre more than they were concerned with using contemporary stories, issues, or images—more than they were concerned with subject matter in general. *Music* seemed subject matter enough.

At least, this is the attitude which dominated the musical scene in Berlin when Kurt Weill arrived there as a student in 1920. Weill was born in Dessau, Germany, in 1900, and died in New York City, another refugee from Nazism, in 1950. His father was the cantor (a trained singer who leads the musical portion of worship in a Jewish synagogue) and the musical director of the synagogue in the city. Dessau, in the years before World War I, was still a court city, with a resident Duke. The Jewish and aristocratic communities co-existed comfortably, and young Weill gave concerts at the court, worked as an accompanist at the court theater, and gave piano lessons to the Duke's daughter. Weill was just young enough to miss active service in the war, and when it was over he made his way to the capital city of Berlin. He attended a music school for just half a year, later studying privately with the composer Busoni. He made a somewhat precarious living by teaching, composing, conducting, and doing music criticism for a radio station, in addition to accepting financial help from relatives.

His compositions during the early 1920s fit into the dominant Schoenberg-influenced mold, with a symphony, an oratorio, a string quartet, and a violin concerto as well as several one-act operas. His work was achieving increased respect in the German musical world, as evidenced by a contract from a leading publisher, Universal Edition.

Although this career was proceeding satisfactorily, it did not live up to an ideal which Weill and others were formulating. They wanted *Zeitoper*—opera for the times. These were exceptional times. Berlin had become a pleasure-seeking city, and the pleasures were not all innocent ones. It was filled with dance-halls, taverns, and cabarets, and with prostitutes of both sexes. Decadence was fashionable, as seen in a taste for cross-dressing (women as men, men as women.) This was the Berlin of the Weimar Republic, the government which had replaced the Kaiser's reign at the end of the war, but which was ill-equipped to deal with the economic problems which followed in the war's wake. Chief among these was inflation. In one year, the German mark sank first to 48,000 marks to the dollar, then to four hundred million marks to the dollar, then to four trillion marks to the dollar. Barter replaced cash; Weill told a student that his charge for lessons would be one-half pound of butter. The war was behind the inflation; the war, or the memory of war, was behind the hedonism as well.

It has often been said that Schoenberg's nightmare Expressionism and Stravinsky's violent Primitivism were forecasts of the horrors of World War I. In fact, no artistic expression could have forecast those horrors. They were on a scale beyond art, beyond even imagining, and I will not try to describe them here, but only say that the ideals which people were told they were fighting for did not survive the realities of trench warfare. A residue was the deepest kind of cynicism. If these were the times, what could a *Zeitoper,* an "opera of the times," be like?

Weill found his answer in working with the poet-playwright Bertolt Brecht, a collaboration which began in 1927 and in 1928 produced their most famous work, the *Threepenny Opera, Die Dreigroschenoper.* The work was based directly on John Gay's work from exactly two centuries earlier, *The Beggar's Opera* of 1728 (*see* Chapter 16).

Threepenny Opera

In creating the libretto, Brecht moved the story up to the early years of the twentieth century, but kept the same low-life characters: Macheath becoming "Mackie Messer" or Mack the Knife. He also kept the same basic outline of

Lotte Lenya and Kurt Weill at the time of *The Threepenny Opera*. Lenya (Weill's wife) played Jenny.

events and the general format of a "ballad" opera, a play interspersed with songs. The work is of course in German, but we will look at it in its English translation by Marc Blitzstein, since that version is the one most often used for performance in the United States.

Bertolt Brecht was later to become famous for his politics. He was a Communist and chose to make his home in Communist East Germany after World War II. However, it is not Communism which the opera teaches so much as nihilism; that is, the belief that "all traditional values and beliefs are unfounded and that all existence is consequently senseless and useless." This attitude finds direct expression in Peachum's "Useless Song." If first you don't succeed, the lyric begins familiarly, then try and try again. But

Useless, it's so useless, our kind of life's too tough.
Take it from me, it's useless, trying ain't enough.

These are words which could provoke music of pity and despair. Instead, Weill supplies a melody which is cheerful, danceable, and somehow positive in its outlook:

Use-less, it's so   use-less,   our kind of life's too tough.   Take it from me, it's   use-less

Here, in the tension between the lyrics and the music, lies the opera's great theatrical energy. We, the middle-class public who buy theater tickets, see people who reject middle-class values like the value of trying again if at first you don't succeed. Surely, we think, the person who rejected such values must be depressed and despairing. Instead, he comes to us expressing happiness and finding joy in alienation. Brecht and Weill are teaching one of the great and surprising lessons of modern art: that alienation can be fun.

Peachum and his wife teach us their philosophy of love in the "Instead of Song." The orchestra, its instrumentation taken from contemporary dance bands rather than traditional opera, introduces the song with a dry, minor-key melody, like the drum beat of a march:

Peachum enters over this accompaniment, his vocal line often in conflict with it. Like his character in *The Beggar's Opera,* he is dismayed that Polly has fallen in love with Macheath. Not that he disapproves of Macheath particularly; rather, what he disapproves of is love. With a cold and brutal melody he sings his cold and brutal philosophy: love is a waste of time.

In - stead of,   in - stead of   stay-ing home in bed at night be - hav - ing,
(Anstatt dass,   Anstatt dass   Sie zu bleiben und in ihrem Bett)

Peachum's section ends with a series of open, repeated chords, the first of which arrives unexpectedly, crashing down on his last word. Over this harsh texture (the repeated chords continue, though softer), Mrs. Peachum's half of the verse begins. She speaks sarcastically of lovers' Romanticism: gazing at the moon, singing love songs, thinking like Ruth in the Bible that "anywhere you go, I will go with you." Her melody, however, is anything but sarcastic. It reaches and falls with true Romantic yearning, struggling against the mechanical beat of the accompaniment like a flower breaking through the pavement. But her conclusion at the end of the second verse is as cynical as ever:

Call   that   old - fash - ioned   love   tick - le   last   year's   news.
(Wenn   die   Liebe aus ist und   im   Dreck   du verreckst?)

Musically, Weill has returned to basics: strophic songs, phrases in balanced patterns, measured rhythms, melodies based on major and minor scales, harmonies with a clear sense of tonal center. His sources for his style are not, however, old-fashioned high-art music, but the popular music from the streets, bars, dancehalls and cabarets of Berlin (*see* color plate 12). How his music is different from both the popular music and the old high-art music is in the tensions it creates—between melody and accompaniment, between words and music. It is this tension which communicates the irony, the distance, and the cynicism with which all emotions are viewed. The play's great attack is on hypocrisy. "You don't really believe in love, honor, or duty, either," it says to us. "The characters you are watching are better than you because at least they aren't hypocrites; they don't pretend to believe in these things. They're capitalists, just like you. They believe that anything, including love, honor, and duty, can be bought or sold." Weill's Berlin was ready for such cynicism and preferred it to more sugar-coated sentiments. And yet, and this is one source of the work's enduring popularity, even after we accept the distance, irony, tension, and cynicism, we can still feel the emotions as real ones.

SUMMARY: *Weill's "Instead of Song" from* The Threepenny Opera *(1928)*

melody	Three distinct types: a march-like accompanying figure in the orchestra; short, brutal phrases in Peachum's half of the verse; and yearning, Romantic phrases in Mrs. Peachum's half.
harmony	Often dissonant in clashes between melody and accompaniment, but with a clear, even obvious, sense of tonal center.
rhythm	Weill matches different rhythmic types to the melody types discussed above. Throughout the work, rhythms are simple and basic, often borrowed from popular dances. What is more complex is their combinations.
form	Strophic song, ABAB: Peachum's half (A), Mrs. Peachum's half (B); repeat.
timbre	The orchestra includes no strings, and uses dance-hall instrumentation, including saxophones, trumpets, trombones, and banjo. An onstage hurdy-gurdy is used elsewhere in the work. The vocal timbre called for is that of the actor, not the trained singer.
texture	Weill presents two or three musical lines with clarity and simplicity. He keeps the textures thin, making the tension between melody and accompaniment readily apparent.
function	*Threepenny Opera* was a commercial venture, produced by a Berlin theater-owner. It was a financial success as well as an artistic one, and it ran for years, until the Nazis came to power.

text   Note: Marc Blitzstein's English words are a performing adaptation rather than an exact translation of Brecht's text.

PEACHUM:

Anstatt dass,	Instead of,
Anstatt dass	instead of
Sie zu Hause bleiben und in ihrem Bett	staying home in bed at night behaving,
Brauchen sie Spass	they want love,
Brauchen sie Spass	they want love
Grad als ob man ihnen eine Extrawurst gebraten hätt.	chasing up the alley with a sentimental craving.

FRAU PEACHUM:

Das ist der Mond über Soho	They got those "Moon Over Dock Street."
Das ist der verdammte "Fühlst-du-mein-Herz-Schlagen"-Text	They got the "You Feel My Heart Beating" blues.
Das ist das "Wenn du wohin gehst, geh auch ich wohin, Johnny!"	They got that "Anywhere You Go, I Will Go With You."
Wenn die Liebe anhebt und der Mond noch wächst.	For that old fashioned love tickle still makes news.

PEACHUM:

Anstatt dass,	Instead of,
Anstatt dass	instead of
Sie was täten, was 'nen Sinn hat und 'nen Zweck	going about their business and behaving,
Machen sie Spass,	they make love,
Machen sie Spass	they make love
Und verrecken dann natürlich glatt im Dreck.	till the man is through and she is sorry that she gave in.

FRAU PEACHUM:

Wo ist dann ihr Mond über Soho?	Now where's your "Moon Over Dock Street?"
Wo bleibt dann ihr verdammter "Fuhlst-du-mein-Herz-Schlagen"-Text	What happened to the "You Feel My Heart Beating" blues?
Wo ist dann das "Wenn du wohin gehst, geh ich auch wohin, Johnny!"	Where is that "Anywhere You Go, I Will Go With You?"
Wenn die Liebe aus ist und im Dreck du verreckst?	Call that old fashioned love tickle last year's news.

Weill and Brecht collaborated on other works, the finest of which may be their opera *The Rise and Fall of the City of Mahagonny.* It is more obviously anticapitalist and also more obviously nihilist than even *The Threepenny Opera,* closing with a marching hymn whose refrain is "Cannot help a dead man." Forced into exile by the Nazis, Weill came to the United States, where he continued to work in musical theater. His collaboration with Brecht demanded that he write bitter, ironic songs in a mockery of popular styles. One of the things he learned from the experience was that he had a wonderful aptitude for composing melodies in the popular styles. In his work for the Broadway stage much of the irony and bitterness drops away, but the gift of song remains.

Bartók

Béla Bartók was born in the Torantál district of Hungary (now part of Romania) in 1881. He died in New York City, yet another refugee from Nazism, in 1945. His father died when he was just seven years old, and his mother, a schoolteacher, gave him his first piano lessons. When he was eighteen he enrolled in the Academy of Music in Budapest, aiming towards a career as a concert pianist. He began to develop two other interests as well: music composition and the study of folk music.

Béla Bartók

These two interests were closely related. A feeling of national pride coupled with the sense that a truly Hungarian voice had never really been heard helped inspire his efforts to compose. Other composers, notably Liszt, who was of Hungarian descent, had used what they thought were Hungarian folk themes. In fact these turned out to be Gypsy melodies, and their treatment was heavily romanticized. Bartók's approach to folk music was scholarly and scientific. He and his collaborator and fellow-composer Zoltán Kodály visited the peasant villages and farms with an Edison phonograph. They captured the authentic folk music on wax cylinders, which permitted them to study the songs, work out accurate notations, and begin the massive task of categorizing and cataloguing. There was an urgency to this work since Bartók knew that the old oral folk culture was in its last days and could not long survive the changes the modern era was bringing to peasant villages.

Although he used precise methods to capture and categorize the folk music he heard, he wanted also to communicate its beauties to a wider audience. To this end, he selected certain favorite examples and rewrote them in more conventional concert-music formats; thus creating works for chorus, for example, or for solo piano. Typical of these efforts are the *Seven Romanian Folk Dances* for piano, written in 1915.

"Pe Loc" from Seven Romanian Folk Dances

The third dance of the group is called "Pe Loc," a dance on one spot. The left hand begins with an *ostinato*—a constantly repeating accompanying figure— which will continue unchanged for twelve measures, changing only slightly through the rest of the work:

Left-hand *ostinato* figure

High above this, the right hand plays the melody in a thin, reedy texture, with a tune that hardly moves, circling around a small pattern of five notes:

Right-hand melody

There are two strong elements of tension. One is harmonic—the E# in the melody clashes against the *ostinato* pattern underneath. The other is rhythmic—each of the accented "turns" gives a rhythmic spark, and these are often set off in syncopation against the straightforward rhythm of the accompaniment.

A slightly contrasting melody is introduced, and then the initial melody and contrasting melody return, making an ABAB pattern. The subtle change which Bartók introduces into this pattern is a harmonic one. The left hand *ostinato* slowly shifts, becoming momentarily more consonant, then pauses, slows, and sinks back down to the original harmony, this time an octave lower, while the melody stays above, high and thin.

When Liszt treated a folk tune he used it as a trampoline for his own astonishing pianistic feats. With Bartók, the texture is so clear, the form so simple and direct, that we are hardly aware of the composer's presence. Nevertheless, Bartók is present in his exact calculations of the piano's timbres and in the subtle harmonic and rhythmic changes which communicate an elegiac sadness. This feeling may belong to the folk dance, or it may represent Bartók's feeling about the folk dance. In either case, he has captured it successfully, and given us something more than the sounds on the Edison wax cylinder.

SUMMARY: *"Pe Loc" from Bartók's* **Seven Romanian Folk Dances (1915)**

melody	Based on a six-note scale: B, C#, D, E#, F#, G#. The tune moves around these notes in a step-wise motion, with turns and grace notes added for rhythmic emphasis.
harmony	The left-hand *ostinato* pattern is based on B, from which it departs and returns. The melody often moves into dissonance against this pattern.
rhythm	A steady two-beat pattern in the left hand, against which right-hand accents are syncopated.
form	ABAB
texture	A single-line melody, widely separated from an *ostinato* bass.

timbre	Piano, concentrated in the mid- and upper-ranges.
function	Intended primarily for amateur and student pianists as a means of translating folk music into a more accessible form. He later (1917) wrote a version for small orchestra.

Rise of Nazism

Bartók continued to mix three interests in his career: concert piano performance, scholarly study of folk music, and composing. In addition, he taught and did research at the Academy of Music in Budapest, and he married twice, both times to students. He was a man who could have been made content by only a reasonable amount of peace and tranquillity—collecting folk songs in tiny villages, working at the Academy, performing his own works on concert stages. The times, however, would not let him be tranquil. Better than most, he understood what the growth of Nazism meant. His own Hungary was becoming increasingly under Nazi influence. He wrote of his shame at being part of a Hungarian Christian middle class all too ready to flow with the Nazi tide. He refused even to set foot in Fascist Italy. As Hungary's most famous composer, he wrote a will specifying that "neither square nor street nor public building" be named after him as long as streets and squares in Hungary were still named for the two dictators, Hitler and Mussolini.

It was in 1937 that he wrote his *Sonata for Two Pianos and Percussion*. On one level this perfectly fits the definition of music whose concern is music. The work was commissioned by the Basel, Switzerland, section of the ISCM, the International Society for Contemporary Music. This was (and is) an organization of musicians and people closely involved with music and devoted to the cause of contemporary high-art composition.

The mere fact that such an organization should be necessary reveals something about the state of contemporary music then. Its issues and concerns were not those of the wider public. The separation between artist and audience had grown larger. The mass audience was listening to popular music. The educated, music-loving, middle-class audience was increasingly devoted to the music of the past and was not looking for modern masters. Only small numbers were committed to the new music; it was they who supported the ISCM.

The artists and audiences for the new music were interested in exploring music's possibilities and potentials, and this is also one of Bartók's goals in his sonata. The work is scored for an unusual ensemble: two pianos, timpani, xylophone, drums with and without snares, bass drum, triangle, cymbals and tam-tam (gong). Two pianists and two percussionists are required for performance. By making the pianos part of a percussion ensemble, Bartók asks us to imagine the instrument in a new way. The percussion instruments reinforce the piano's percussive qualities and allow Bartók to explore this aspect of the instrument's capabilities.

The work begins with a timpani roll, over which the first piano enters:

Piano I, measure 2

This is a chromatic theme; it uses all of the half steps between D# and A. Low and dark in timbre, it communicates a sense of foreboding which is realized with the sudden dissonant clash in the sixth measure. Here the second piano has a phrase which shows Bartók using the piano to create pure timbre and rhythm. The chromaticism of the first phrase may remind us of Schoenberg, but the coloristic effect of this flourish reminds us of Debussy and Stravinsky.

Piano II, measure 6

The work builds to an episode of rhythmic complexity, where the timpani play what looks like a quarter-note rhythm, and the pianos play what looks like a quarter-note rhythm a little off from the timpani, the two combining to make a new, eccentric eighth-note pattern (I have underlined the accented counts):

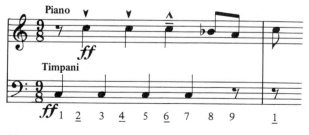

Measure 33

The next theme to be introduced is a gentler one ("a little more tranquil," Bartók instructs), but it still continues this rhythmic complexity, while the grace notes create an exotic timbre:

Measures 87–88

The last motive to be introduced has a genuine folk-dance energy. This is a place where we can see Bartók's folk-music researches crossing over to influence his composition.

Piano II, measures 105–108

All these themes are filled with rhythmic energy and harmonic tension, qualities which Bartók heightens by creating layers of counterpoint among his instruments, and by placing the themes in contrast and conflict with one another. Along the way he explores new timbres and combinations of timbres, creating a synthesis between the chromaticism of Schoenberg's Expressionism and the rhythmic exuberance of Stravinsky's Primitivism.

He may be doing something more. The first theme, heavy with fear, and the second theme, barbaric in its force: might these communicate some of his anguish at the inexorable growth of Nazism? Might the more fragile third theme and the folk-like fourth theme say something about the tradition which Bartók would have fight against it? It may be that Bartók puts these ideas together for purely musical reasons—he likes the way they combine and contrast. Certainly Bartók was not writing a Strauss-like tone poem. Nevertheless, it seems possible that real events were bleeding over into musical ones, and just as Weill had written an opera for the times, Bartók was writing a sonata for the times.

SUMMARY: Bartók's Sonata for Two Pianos and Percussion, *first movement, (1937)*

melody	Four main themes. First theme highly chromatic; second uses repeated notes for rhythmic excitement; third based on a non-traditional, folk-like scale; the fourth creates a strong folk-dance rhythm.
harmony	Much parallelism (a legacy from Debussy and Stravinsky), as well as much dissonance.
rhythm	Active and eccentric rhythmic patterns. Most of the work is in the time signature of 9/8, allowing Bartók to place accents where they will create a variety of patterns.

form	After the four themes are stated, they are developed, but no traditional recapitulation occurs.
texture	At times the texture is heavily chordal, but it usually includes contrasting lines being played at once. Frequent use of imitative counterpoint.
timbre	Two pianos plus percussion instruments, creating an overall sound which brings out the piano's percussive capabilities.
function	Commissioned by the ISCM for concert performance. Bartók and his second wife toured with the work soon after its first performance.

Bartók went into exile in 1940 and spent the last five years of his life in the United States. He was ill a good deal of the time and beset with worries about the progress of the war, about his son in the Navy, about family and friends still in Hungary, and about Hungary itself. Still he managed to continue his folk music work, his composing, and even some performing. In 1943, two years before his death, he completed his *Concerto for Orchestra,* which became one of the small number of twentieth-century works to enter into the standard orchestral repertory.

Britten

Benjamin Britten was born in Lowestoft, Suffolk, England, in 1913, and died in Aldeburgh, Suffolk, England, in 1976. His father was a dentist, his mother an amateur musician. He started piano lessons at five and began composing in the same year.

Benjamin Britten

He began the serious study of composition with the English composer Frank Bridge when he was 14. After prep school, he attended the Royal College of Music in London. This turned out to be a disappointment; in his three years at the college, only one of his works was given a performance.

When he told some acquaintances that his ambition was to be a professional composer, they asked "Yes, and what else?" as though it were impossible to imagine a full-time English composer. Nevertheless, Britten succeeded in his ambition almost immediately. From 1935 to 1939 he composed for a film company which specialized in producing documentaries. Through this work he met the poet W. H. Auden, the leading artistic and intellectual figure of the generation which came of age in the England of the 1930s. Auden's positions were left-wing: anti-fascist, anti-war, and generally anti-establishment. He and Britten collaborated on a number of works for the theater and concert stage. From this time on, Britten's compositions were to be heavily involved with literature, and he was to show unusually fine judgment in his choice of texts.

In 1939, shortly before war broke out in Europe, Britten came to the United States. In doing this, he was following Auden, who eventually became a U.S. citizen. Although he was a pacifist, Britten could not remain away from England, and he returned there in 1942. He asked for and received conscientious objector status, and fulfilled his service requirement by taking part in government-sponsored concerts.

Serenade for Tenor, Horn, and Strings

It was a dark time for England. The Allied forces had suffered significant defeats in the early part of the war. Ultimate victory seemed distant and uncertain. This was the moment during which Britten composed his *Serenade for Tenor, Horn, and Strings.* The tenor part was written for Britten's lifelong companion, Peter Pears; the French horn part for the gifted virtuoso Dennis Brain, who died just a few years later after crashing his sports car.

The work includes settings of six poems and a "prologue" and "epilogue" for solo horn. Britten titles the third of these "Elegy," a song of sorrow over a death. It is a setting of "The Sick Rose," a poem written by the English Romantic poet William Blake in 1794.

> O Rose, thou art sick;
> The invisible worm
> That flies in the night,
> In the howling storm,
> Has found out thy bed of crimson joy;
> And his dark, secret love
> Does thy life destroy.

William Blake was an artist as well as a poet. This is his own engraving of "The Sick Rose."

The poem is about what its title says, but about other things as well—things which could be applied to human experience, like love's capacity to corrupt innocence.

Britten's setting begins with a long introduction. Violins, violas, and 'cellos provide a soft pattern of open chords, just off the beat. The basses play fragmented, separated arpeggios underneath. The horn has the melody. Its characteristic motive is a motion of a half step, up or down. The motion occurs throughout a huge range of octaves and volumes, illustrating an astonishing flexibility in the intrument. The last half-step motion begins pianissimo at the very top of the horn's range, crescendoes to fortissimo and tapers away to triple pianissimo, introducing the voice.

The strings now settle down into long sustained chords in the 'cellos. The tenor begins with the characteristic half-step motion:

and continues with a free-flowing melody which builds to a climax, supported by the strings, on the word "found." From there it declines, ending with a reversal of the initial half-step motion:

life_____   des - troy_____

The horn and strings return with the music from the introduction. At the very end the horn plays the same half-step motion which began and ended the tenor's melody:

The little "o"'s and "+"'s indicate the horn player is to achieve the half-step down by stopping up the bell of the horn with his or her hand (+), then move back up by opening the bell again (o). It is a small but telling effect, typical of Britten's fine ear for the instrumental possibilities. Twentieth-century composers are in general much more wary of scene-painting than nineteenth-century composers were. There is a hint of scene-painting here, though—the horn insinuates itself among the strings like the worm among the petals of the rose.

The next song in the *Serenade* Britten titles "Dirge," a funeral song. It originated as a folk song called the "Lyke-Wake Dirge," where its function was to be sung by women mourners around the casket of a dead person, giving the spirit instructions on how to proceed, listing way stations to the afterlife, in hopes that the spirit would find its way there efficiently and not return to haunt the living.

> This ae nighte, this ae nighte,
> Every nighte and alle,
> Fire and fleet and candle-lighte,
> And Christe receive thy saule.
>
> When thou from hence away art past,
> Every nighte and alle,
> To Whinnymuir thou com'st at last;
> And Christe receive thy saule.
>
> If ever thou gav'st hos'n and shoen,
> Every nighte and alle,
> Sit thee down and put them on;
> And Christe receive thy saule.

If hos'n and shoen thou ne'er gav'st nane,
Every nighte and alle,
The whinnes sall prick thee to the bare bane;
And Christe receive thy saule.

From Whinnymuir when thou may'st pass,
Every nighte and alle,
To Brig o'Dread thou com'st at last;
And Christe receive thy saule.

If ever thou gav'st meat or drink,
Every nighte and alle,
The fire sall never make thee shrink;
And Christe receive thy saule.

If meat or drink thou ne'er gav'st nane,
Every nighte and alle,
The fire will burn thee to the bare bane;
And Christe receive thy saule.

This ae nighte, this ae nighte,
Every nighte and alle,
Fire and fleet and candle-lighte;
And Christe receive thy saule.

Britten uses the fifteenth-century folk lyrics with a melody which is ancient in character. The words describe the path the soul ("saule") must take this very night: through Whinnymuir, through Brig o'Dread, through Purgatory, until Christ receives the soul. If in life it has been charitable, these steps will not be too dreadful. If, though, it has not given away shoes, stockings, meat, or drink, it is in for a number of unpleasant moments.

The melody starts very high, and works its way down in stages, ending up an octave lower than at the start.

This is the folk-song idea, simple, strong, and strophic. The accompaniment Britten creates is a fugue for strings and horn. The 'cellos and basses enter over the last phrase of the singer's first verse. The melody, the fugue subject, is quick and rhythmic, with moments of speed and moments of stillness, in deliberate contrast to the sustained vocal line.

Four measures later—the tenor is in the middle of the second verse—the violas enter with the subject while the 'cellos and basses play counterpoint. The third voice to enter is the second violin, and the fourth voice to enter is the first violin. The key relationships from voice entrance to voice entrance are not those of a traditional fugue, but the pattern of subject and counterpoint is clear and recognizable.

After all of the strings have entered, they play an extended episode, preparing for the entrance of the French horn. Except that the listener is deliberately *not* prepared. To this point, the entrances have generally been eccentric and have arrived in the middle of lines and phrases. The horn enters with the fugue subject, taking the orchestra into a new key (E minor, against the tenor's G minor), arriving right on the downbeat of the sixth verse. It is one of the most highly-charged moments in twentieth-century music, not because the techniques it uses are radically new (having the singer in a different key from the orchestra is an example of the technique of bi-tonality which Stravinsky used in *The Rite of Spring*) but because of the combination of preparation and surprise. Britten prepares us for the moment using the most traditional of structures, the fugue, and yet the moment when it arrives is dramatic and surprising, even after repeated hearings. Afterwards the horn withdraws again, the strings gradually soften, only the bass viol is left, then it drops out, leaving the song to conclude in the hands of the singer.

Not all of the songs in the *Serenade* are as dark in effect as these two are. Nevertheless, it is a serenade, a song to greet the evening. Edward Sackville-West, to whom the *Serenade* was dedicated, said that "The subject is Night . . . the lengthening shadow, the distant bugle at sunset, the Baroque panoply of the starry sky, the heavy angels of sleep; but also the cloak of evil."

In other words, this too is music of its time. European culture had produced men like Mozart, Beethoven, Schubert, Goethe, Heine. It could with justice claim to be a civilization. Now it had produced Hilter and the Nazis and given them the power to murder millions. The civilization was destroying itself. Whoever won the war, there was no turning away from this knowledge: that "civilized" humanity was capable of crimes against humanity, evil on a scale never before imaginable. This at least is my interpretation of the work's title: the evening Britten writes about is the evening of our civilization.

SUMMARY: *Two songs from Britten's* Serenade **for Tenor, Horn, and Strings** *(1943)*

melody	In "Elegy," the horn melody is based on a half-step motive. The tenor melody starts and ends with half-step motion, but in between follows the contours of the poetry. In "Dirge," the vocal melody is folk-like, following a descending pattern. The fugue subject on which the accompaniment is based is quick and rhythmic.
harmony	In "Elegy" there is an underlying sense of tonal center based on E. However, Britten departs from it freely, moving to unrelated

chords, creating considerable dissonance between melody and accompaniment, switching between major and minor. In "Dirge," the folk-like melody has a consistent strong sense of tonal center, but the accompanying fugue keeps changing tonal centers, climaxing with the horn entrance, where the voice is centered on G and the accompaniment on E.

rhythm   In "Elegy," accents are often placed off the beat, not to create a syncopated beat but to blur the sense of pulse. In "Dirge," the tenor's song has a relatively straightforward six-measure rhythmic pattern. The accompanying fugue has a livelier, more eccentric rhythm, and its patterns do not line up with those of the folk melody.

form   The "Elegy" 's form is ABA: introduction (horn and strings), song (tenor and strings), postlude (horn and strings, almost identical to the introduction.) The "Dirge" 's form is strophic in its melody, with a fugue structure in the accompaniment.

texture   In "Elegy," the most important element in the texture is the tense relationship between the horn melody and the accompanying string chords. In "Dirge," the accompanying figure has a polyphonic texture; more important are the opposed characters of melody and accompaniment.

timbre   The work as a whole explores the full range of possibilities which the modern French horn allows when in the hands of an extraordinary performer. Britten limits his range of colors—no percussion, no chorus, no other winds besides the horn—but uses what he has with great sensitivity and dramatic effect.

function   Intended primarily for concert performance.

text   "Elegy" is written to William Blake's "The Sick Rose;" "Dirge" is written to an anonymous fifteenth-century poem called the "Lyke-Wake Dirge."

After World War II, Britten became increasingly well-known as a composer of operas, the most famous of which is *Peter Grimes,* whose hero is a fisherman ostracized by his community for his cruelty to young apprentices. Perhaps because Britten, as a homosexual and a conscientious objector, knew what it was like to be an outsider, he was able in his operas to treat outsiders like Peter Grimes with sympathy and compassion. He became England's most famous composer, a successful and established figure, but one who never compromised his beliefs. In an officially-commissioned *War Requiem* the pacifist Britten used the harsh words of the poet Wilfred Owen, killed in World War I: "What passing bells for those who die as cattle?"

In America: Ives and Copland

Charles Ives

During the early part of the twentieth century, the United States was something of a cultural backwater. A typical composer from the period was Horatio William Parker, who taught at Yale and wrote in a style derived from Romantic models. His song "Love in May," as an example, uses such Romantic devices as a "trembling" motive in the piano accompaniment, but it lacks any trace of Romantic emotional force.

One of Parker's pupils at Yale was Charles Ives. Ives was born in Danbury, Connecticut, in 1874 (the same year as Schoenberg) and died in West Redding, Connecticut, in 1954. His father was a bandmaster who had led a band for the Union Army during the Civil War. He taught Ives the rules of music and also taught him to question those rules and to experiment. Ives showed talent as a pianist, and his father suggested a concert career for him, but Ives was too shy and diffident a personality for that kind of life. He wasn't too shy, however, to play the organ in church, or to play baseball for his prep-school team, which once beat the Yale freshman team, causing the school reporter to write that

"Ives is a little wild, but he plays coolly and is very quick at catching men napping at bases."

After graduating from Yale (with a D+ average) he went into the insurance business, eventually forming a partnership and creating his own very successful company. Meanwhile, he was spending all his available free time writing music. His studies under Parker had not put him in touch with the revolutionary developments in Europe. Nor did he seem eager to make those contacts himself. He was a true independent. "Listening to concert music seemed to confuse me in my own work," he once stated, ". . . to throw me off from what I had in mind." Nevertheless, though out of touch, he was somehow still in tune with new developments, and in the radical nature of his experiments he matched his European counterparts and even went beyond them.

A composition called "The Unanswered Question," from 1908 (the year before Schoenberg's *Erwartung*) shows him creating an unusual musical texture which contrasts tonality with atonality. He begins with big, hymn-like chords:

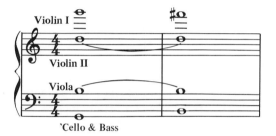

against which he has the trumpet play an atonal melody:*

Not only are the tones dissonant, but the rhythms are also in conflict, with the chords moving on every four beats, while the melodic motion plays in patterns of three.

This fondness for a musical texture in which the different layers are largely independent of each other shows even more clearly in the "Fourth of July" movement from his *A Symphony: Holidays*. What he is creating here is a kind of musical *collage*. He takes fragments of music and sounds from the real world: a band playing "Columbia, the Gem of the Ocean;" a bugle call; "The Battle Hymn of the Republic;" a military drumbeat; and a skyrocket and pastes them together, not trying to make them all blend smoothly, but letting them jangle against each other like experiences jumbled in a child's memory. This is in fact how Ives described the work: "It's a boy's '4th' . . . His festivities start in the

*An atonal melody is a melody without a tonal center.

Braque: *Le Violin* (1913–14)
(Private Collection)

quiet of the midnight before and grow raucous with the sun . . . The day ends with the skyrocket over the Churchsteeple just after the annual explosion sets the Town-Hall on fire."

The *collage* technique was to become an essential aspect of modernism. Painters like Picasso, Braque, Ernst and Schwitters started putting "found" objects, scraps of material, and bits of newsprint into their paintings. In literature, James Joyce put together scraps of conversation, momentary images, and random thoughts into his "stream-of-consciousness" writing. These artists all shared with Ives an affection for the vernacular: the images, words, and music of everyday life.

Ives' desire to experiment was something else he had in common with the advanced composers, painters, and writers of the time. The difference was that the European composers, painters, and writers found audiences for their works. Ives did not. It is true that the Europeans all received a good measure of public rejection, but the public indifference which greeted Ives was harder to take. After suffering a heart attack in 1918 (when he was 41) he wrote very little. Near the end of his life, he did have the satisfaction of witnessing a revival of interest in his work.

Copland

Ives studiously avoided influence from the developments in Europe. But it was clear to the next generation of Americans that European influence was essential if the United States was not to remain a cultural backwater. Their mecca was Paris, the center of advanced art-making. Paris had traditionally been the place Americans went to study painting. Now it became the place to be for novelists, for example Ernest Hemingway; for poets, such as E. E. Cummings; or for composers, for example Aaron Copland.

Copland was born in 1900, in Brooklyn, New York. He went to public schools, worked in his father's store on weekends, and took piano lessons from his sister. When he was 20 and knew that he wanted to be a composer, he scraped together enough money to go to Paris, where he studied with Nadia Boulanger, who was to become a kind of *guru* for American composers over the next 40 years.

Stravinsky had given European composers an interest in Primitivism. A side-effect of this interest was a fascination with American jazz. Copland's works from the 1920s show the influence of this taste, combining jazz idioms with the sophisticated orchestral techniques which were a heritage from Impressionism. Later, in the early 1930s, he shifted to a more personal and abstract style. But in the later 1930s, his style shifted again.

He was back in the United States at this time, and the change in his style was influenced in part by the severe economic depression the country was going through. The Depression had caused a deeply-felt desire for change in American political life. Artists and intellectuals like Copland became committed to the forces for change, and this committment influenced their styles in a direction away from high-art complexity and towards a more populist simplicity.

A performance of *Applachian Spring* by Martha Graham's dance company.

The most famous example of Copland's work in this new style is his *Appalachian Spring,* commissioned by Martha Graham's modern dance company for a 1944 performance. Towards the end of the work's first movement, he quotes a hymn taken from the worship services of the Shakers, a religious community who believed in a severe sort of simplicity, dedicating their lives to work and to worship, serving God and the poor:

First verse of Shaker hymn, "The Gift to Be Simple"

This becomes for Copland a statement of an artistic as well as a political ideal. He had learned from European music, but now he was ready to create works in a distinctly *American* style. He was certainly not going to carry simplicity to the extremes that the Shakers did, but he recognized that the complexities, difficulties, and dissonances of the European style were taking music away from the common listener. For Copland, simplicity meant democracy—music for the common man, an ideal which he made explicit in his 1942 composition *Fanfare for the Common Man*.

Works like these represented a successful solution to the problem of finding a way to combine European sophistication with an identifiably American voice. But other developments pressed in a new direction. Where Copland's generation had gone to Europe to study, Nazism was forcing a generation of Europeans to America. Among the principal figures we have studied, Schoenberg, Stravinsky, Weill, and Bartók, all came to the United States, as did many more influential composers and teachers. The result was a new melding of European and American cultures, making the United States for the first time a center for the musical *avant-garde*.

The Post-War Avant-garde

In the period between the start of World War I and the end of World War II, the pressures and urgency of events forced many composers away from purely musical issues. A similar process took place in other art forms. When the forces of General Franco terror-bombed a village in Spain, Picasso turned away from his previous style to create an impassioned testament about the destroyed town of Guernica. But in the relatively peaceful and increasingly prosperous years after World War II, music led the other arts in turning inward, in becoming involved with its own processes. The idea of "experimental" composition, of the *avant-garde,* took hold as it never had before.

The word *avant-garde* derives from French military terminology, where it refers to the vanguard, the troops who precede the main body of the army. It has traditionally been associated with any group of artists whose work is more "advanced" than their contemporaries'. In the post-war period, however, its meaning became more specific, and the *avant-garde* came to be seen as a kind

Composer Milton Babbitt
at the synthesizer.

of scouting-party. In a military situation, the scouting party doesn't have to win any battles. It simply has to explore and learn and report back. This metaphor became a rationale for "experimental" music. To be successful meant to break new ground, try out new techniques, explore uncharted territory. If audiences were not moved, or excited, or even interested, it didn't really matter. One composer, the American Milton Babbitt (b. 1916), went so far as to write an article entitled "Who Cares If You Listen?" For Babbitt, composition was comparable to scientific or mathematical research. The public at large has no way of judging the validity of an advanced mathematician's (or musician's) work. The discoveries may look meaningless now but may still benefit some future public enormously—even if they only prove some theory false, some line of research unprofitable.

Music may not be quite so comparable to mathematics or the military as these analogies seem to suggest. After all, those two fields are ones in which there are hard, objective measures of success or failure. The ultimate proof of the worth of any piece of music is still a subjective one: the responses of generations of listeners. Nevertheless, the rationale itself was successful in that it was productive; the post-war generation of composers was inspired by the experimental, *avant-garde,* ideal.

Total Control

Milton Babbitt's own experiments led him in the direction of "total control." This was an expansion of the twelve-tone technique developed by Schoenberg. In that technique of composition, the twelve tones are fixed in a certain series, and the order of that series governs the entire composition. Composers like Babbitt extended the idea of the governing series to other aspects of musical sound: the durations of notes, for example, the degree of loudness at which they are played, and the instrumental timbres through which they are produced. In this kind of composition, numerical sequences lie behind every aspect of musical production.

The importance of numbers led some composers in this style to use computers as aids in writing their works. They also began to use synthesizers and tape machines as aids to performance. (Photographs from the time show composers sitting in rooms filled with machinery. Later, under the impetus of commercial rock 'n' roll's interest in electronic music, much smaller and more practical devices were invented.) Problems of rhythm made electronic aids particularly useful. Simply put, when the durations of tones are tightly controlled by a numerical sequence, not by a rhythmic pulse, they become extremely difficult to play. Earlier, discussing Schoenberg's twelve-tone technique, I wrote a tiny twelve-tone composition (*see* page 306). The numerical sequence for the tone-row I used was: 1, 12, 11, 6, 7, 2, 3, 9, 5, 8, 10, 4. Suppose I create a series of durations:

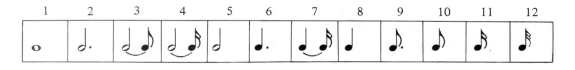

then arrange them in the same numerical sequence I used for my tone-row, and assign this sequence of durations to my piece:

Even this very primitive use of the method makes a composition which is extremely difficult to count. The difficulties multiply if each of several instruments has a complex pattern and the patterns must be coordinated. If, however, the patterns can be programmed into a computer and the sounds generated by a synthesizer (*see* Chapter 4), the difficulties disappear. Except, of course, for the listener who has become used to hearing human emotions, pulses, breaths behind the notes. Such a listener, that is, the average listener, has typically found considerable difficulty in communicating with music whose note-choices are based on numerical sequences.

John Cage

Another American, John Cage (b. 1912), championed another sort of experiment. Cage had studied with Arnold Schoenberg in California in the 1930s and with the American composer Henry Cowell, who was a friend of Charles Ives. But Cage's work departs radically from even their advanced styles. His compositions rely heavily on chance. (A term for his style is "aleatoric music," meaning simply "chance music.") One of his favorite techniques is to draw notes at the points where there are imperfections on the blank sheet of music paper; another is to make decisions by using the "I-Ching"—a Chinese device in which numbered sticks are shaken from a box. His *Imaginary Landscape No. 4* puts 12 performers in command of radios, which they tune to certain frequencies for certain lengths of time. His *Concert for Piano and Orchestra* allows performers freedom to play their parts in different ways, different sequences, or not to play at all. His *4'33"* instructs a performer to sit at a keyboard—but not to play. The music is the ambient noise of the room during the four minutes and 33 seconds of the title.

Cage's works, often theatrical and funny, express a certain philosophy: chance governs his music as chance governs life and the universe. Babbitt's works depend on a certain definition of beauty: it is abstract, to be found in formal but hidden patterns. Their tendencies seem opposite, yet in an important way they are similar. Both ask the composer to relinquish making certain decisions. Why do I hear a particular sound at a particular instant? If I am listening to a Babbitt piece, I must assume that certain pre-decided sequences of pitches, durations, volumes, and timbres have coincided to create the moment. If I am listening to a Cage piece, I assume that the moment has been created by a throw of the dice or the accidental combination of performers' whims.

Of course, to some extent these things are true of all music. Beethoven didn't worry over every note. He let certain conventional patterns of rhythm, harmony, and form govern many of his choices. Once a time signature is decided on in the Classical style, the composer stays with it fairly faithfully. There are rules for chord progressions which Beethoven usually followed. And he based many of his works on sonata form. Similarly, a concert of his music is subject to chance sounds and performers' whims. Beethoven gives the performer a great deal of freedom to interpret, and he even allows for improvisation in some of his concerto cadenzas. Nevertheless, experimenters like Cage and Babbitt seem far more distant from their works than Beethoven does from his. Cage and Babbitt are visible as the makers of the systems which control the music, but they are absent in the moment-to-moment choices where the composers in more traditional styles can be found. To some degree, this is an inescapable consequence of being *avant-garde*. Where past composers strove to say new things in the traditional musical language, the *avant-garde* composer strives to create a whole new language.

Luciano Berio

Luciano Berio was born in Oneglia, Imperia, Italy, in 1925. Where Copland's generation of Americans had gone to Europe to study, Berio, a European, came to study in America, where, as it happens, one of his principal teachers was the Italian Luigi Dallipiccola. He also learned from John Cage and from the French composer Pierre Boulez, who like Babbitt was involved with systems of "total control."

Since *avant-garde* music has not as a rule attracted large audiences, one of the questions to be asked about it is "Who pays?" In the case of Berio's *Circles,*

Luciano Berio

the work was commissioned by a foundation. This represents a new kind of patronage. The patron no longer hires a musician to work for him, as Esterhazy hired Haydn, and no longer commissions specific works, as Beethoven's aristocratic friends had; nor does the government subsidize music the way England under King George subsidized Handel's operas. Instead the patron decides to benefit music in a more general way and enlists the government as a kind of silent partner. The system works like this: the patron donates money to the foundation he or she creates. Since the foundation is a not-for-profit organization, donations to it are tax-exempt. Forty million dollars of capital gains might earn the government ten million dollars in taxes. If the 40 million is donated and tax-exempt, other taxpayers make up the missing ten million, creating a form of government subsidy.

In this case the patron is Paul Fromm, who founded the Fromm Foundation, which, operating under expert advice, commissioned Luciano Berio's *Circles,* a song cycle for female voice, harp, and two percussion players on a variety of instruments. Although it is true to say that the work was written for the Fromm Foundation, it is equally true to say that it was written for Cathy Berberian, who was Berio's wife from 1950 to 1966, who premièred the work, and who was one of the few singers with the technical abilities required to learn and perform it.

Circles

Berio composed the song cycle to poems by the American poet E. E. Cummings. The first poem in the cycle is the fifth from a group Cummings called "Impressions."*

<blockquote>

stinging
gold swarms
upon the spires
silver

    chants the litanies the
great bells are ringing with rose
the lewd fat bells
           and a tall

wind
is dragging
the
sea

with

dream

-S

</blockquote>

Cummings liked to experiment with the look of words on the page. He wanted to break the reader's normal habits of seeing words, in order to make

*E. E. Cummings, poem No. 5, "Impressions" (New York: Harcourt Brace Jovanovich, 1954), p. 43

them stand out individually and gain their meanings from how they sound and how they look as much as from how they function in a sentence.

The poem as a whole revolves around the mixture and confusion of the senses. What you see (gold), you feel (stinging); what you hear (chants), you see (silver); or what you hear (bells) you see or smell (rose). This is not a complete analysis of the poem, but it is enough to indicate that Berio has given himself a challenging work to turn into music.

He begins with the soprano voice alone. Her melody line is not a twelve-tone row, but it is highly chromatic, going through nine of the twelve tones before a note repeats. Its movement—up, down, hovering, seeming to come closer as it crescendoes or move away as it becomes softer, is like the movement of a hummingbird, or, perhaps, to match the images of "stinging" and "swarming," like a bee.

(Voice)

But the melody's most obvious characteristic is its disorienting departure from the vocal patterns of everyday speech. This departure, present right from the beginning, becomes most obvious at the sudden accent on the "ging" of "stinging." With effects like these, Berio is providing a musical equivalent to the disorienting effects of odd typography in the poem. The disorienting effect is furthered by the avoidance of repeated melodic or rhythmic patterns. Berio here is following the Schoenberg we saw in *Erwartung*. The resemblance carries over into actual melodic structure. Here is a harp figure from *Circles* compared to a violin figure from *Erwartung*:

From *Circles*   From *Erwartung*

There is, though, a major difference. Schoenberg's language is expressive; it uses dissonant music to capture a tormented state of mind. In Berio's song, the dissonant language is disassociated from a state of mind. The soprano isn't telling us how she feels, she is simply trying to create a series of vocal images. When Berio creates a dissonant chord like this one for the harp:

its effect is that of pure timbre (as in Debussy) rather than that of a stressful emotion (as in Schoenberg.)

At the very end of this first song, the percussion instruments enter, coming in over the soprano's hissed "S" sound. The score instructs her to conduct the two percussionists at this point and then to join them playing the *claves* (Cuban rhythm sticks). The word "dreams" becomes, in the poem, "dream - S." Then in Berio's setting it becomes its "S" sound, then becomes the purely percussive noise of the sand block and maracas. Through this process a word—and a thoroughly Romantic word at that—is gradually deprived of its meaning and transformed into pure sound.

SUMMARY: *The first song from Luciano Berio's song cycle* Circles *(1960)*

melody   Extremely variable in terms of melodic and rhythmic patterns. Frequent use of grace notes.

harmony   No sense of tonal center. Harmonies occur when lines coincide, but we are far more conscious of the separate lines than of their coincidence. When chords appear they are used as percussive timbres.

rhythm   No strong sense of beat; no time signature is given until the entrance of the percussion instruments near the end of the song.

form   The song cycle as a whole has a circular form: first poem, second poem, third poem, second poem, first poem. The music is not repeated along with the words, however.

texture   Predominantly linear and polyphonic.

timbre   Soprano voice, harp, and two groups of percussion instruments. The voice and harp are both used more percussively than in traditional styles. Each of the groups of percussion instruments is set up in a circle, and organized into three sections: wood, skin, and metal. The two groups play opposite each other to create antiphonal or "stereophonic" effects.

function   Composed on a commission from the Fromm Foundation, and designed for concert performance. Certain effects (for example, the soprano moves to different positions during the performance of the piece) are visual and cannot be captured in recording.

text   Poem by E. E. Cummings.

Steve Reich

The present-day high-art music scene includes composers working in every conceivable combination of the various twentieth-century styles which have been discussed here. One style among these many seems significantly different and apart. It is usually called "Minimalism," and its foremost exponent is Steve Reich.

Reich was born in New York in 1936. His education took him to Mills College in California, where he studied with Luciano Berio, and to Ghana, where he studied African drumming. The method of composing which became identified with his style was revealed to him in a semi-accidental way. He set two tape recorders to playing the same tape loop simultaneously. Because of minute differences in speed the tapes got gradually out of phase with one another, creating complexities which then simplified as the tapes came back into phase.

This discovery led Reich to compose works for tape recorders, but he became dissatisfied with tape as a medium. At a time when most high-art composers support themselves by teaching in universities, Reich wanted to resurrect the old idea of composer-as-working-musician, to participate in the process of rehearsing and performing his own music. To accomplish this, he needed to invent a way of capturing the gradual transformations he desired while using live musicians. *Music for Mallet Instruments, Voices and Organ* illustrates his methods.

There are two rhythmic streams. On top, women's voices and organ repeat a basic pattern (a vibraphone enters this stream later):

Underneath, a second rhythmic stream is provided by glockenspiels and marimbas. Here Reich uses the process he has become famous for—rhythms going out of phase and then coming back into phase. His technique is to fashion a pattern, and then gradually to build up a second pattern one and one-half beats out of phase.

These two patterns are in the marimbas; another two patterns build up out of phase in the glockenspiels. When they are all going at once, the patterns become denser, more hectic. Reich calls this gradual increase in density "rhythmic construction." As the density builds up it triggers a change in the upper stream, which begins to "augment"—that is, its rhythmic pattern stretches out, for example moving from

Steve Reich and musicians performing *Music for Mallet Instruments, Voices and Organ*.

So rhythmic construction triggers rhythmic augmentation. Once the maximum rhythmic augmentation has occurred (the notes can't be stretched any farther than a human voice can hold them out), the rhythms in the glockenspiel–marimba stream begin to simplify, going back towards unison, and this return to rhythmic unison triggers rhythmic diminution (reversal of the augmentation) in the voice-organ stream. The whole process—construction triggering augmentation, return to unison triggering diminution—occurs four times through the course of the entire work.

Reich's music represents a radical departure from the past. It has been called "Minimalist" music, named after the Minimalist movement in sculpture. The word seems appropriate because there are such few changes in melody, harmony, form, texture, and timbre. Change is concentrated in the rhythmic patterns, and even there the changes are not rapid, but are the products of gradual transformation. The problem with the term "Minimalist" is that the sculptures it is associated with tend to be drab and bleak in appearance. Closer in spirit might be the color-field paintings of artists like Jules Olitski (*see* color plate 13). Reich, like those painters, creates works which are pleasing, even pretty—a quality long missing in music's *avant-garde*.

SUMMARY: *Steve Reich's* **Music for Mallet Instruments, Voices and Organ** *(1973)*

melody   Three different melodic lines: voice-organ, glockenspiel, and marimba. All are built on traditional scales or modes. The voice-organ line is the one most easily recognized.

harmony	Generally consonant, sometimes revolving between two chords, sometimes content to maintain the feel of a single chord over long stretches.
rhythm	Defined through two processes. In one, the rhythm becomes more complex as out-of-phase elements are introduced (construction), then returns to a simpler unison. In the other process, the pattern is stretched out (augmentation) and then brought back to its original shape (diminution).
form	"Construction" triggers augmentation; return to unison triggers diminution; the process is repeated four times, with different thematic material used each time.
texture	Two basic streams: one is dominated by organ and voice, with vibraphone entering later; the other by marimbas and glockenspiels. The separateness of the two streams is defined as much by their differing rhythms as by their timbres.
timbre	Based on percussion instruments; all the instruments used, including the voice, function as percussion instruments. The exact orchestration is: Two women's voices, organ, vibraphone without its vibrato effect, two glockenspiels, four marimbas.
function	Designed for both concert and recorded performance. Reich is one of the few *avant-garde* composers who has been able to attract large audiences to concerts, to sell significant numbers of recordings, and to attract commercial (as opposed to foundation-grant) commissions.

Twenty years ago, it would have been easy to name twentieth-century music's most influential revolutionary: Arnold Schoenberg. Today, Schoenberg's influence seems not so certain. Berio's *Circles* uses a Schoenberg-influenced language, but it rebels against the idea of music as emotional expression. Steve Reich goes much further. His *Music for Mallet Instruments, Voices and Organ* is not heavy with emotional expression; nor is it invested with the kind of spiritual meaning contained in the African drumming he studied. And, going still further, it completely ignores the Schoenbergian musical language: the dissonances, the angular twelve-tone melodies, the fragmented phrases. In its separation of sound from meaning and its desire for music which will flow in a steady state, Reich's music has closer affinities with Debussy than with Schoenberg, and it may in fact appear to some future historian that Debussy's revolution was the more fundamental one. Reich returns us to the status of the Faun: we become simple, sensuous beings, who enjoy watching the music move, but do not need to be moved by it ourselves. Reich himself has likened the experience of listening to his music to that of standing at the ocean's edge, and watching, feeling, and listening as the waves gradually sink your feet into the sand.

Blues and Jazz

Introduction to the Popular-Art Tradition

Modern composers in the high-art tradition were *self-consciously* modern. That is, they knew that they had broken with tradition, and they worked deliberately to maintain and increase the distance between their own music and that of the style which had preceded it, Romanticism. The history of modern high-art music can be understood as a series of revolutions against the Romantic style, revolutions which searched for ways to present modern truths in a modern manner.

Audiences, however, were not quite so ready for revolution as composers were. The new truths being expressed were often not very pleasant ones, and the new manner was not always easy to listen to. A good part of the audience didn't want to hear about the horrors of war, or capitalism, or modern life in general, and was not prepared for eccentric rhythms, harsh dissonances, atonal melodies or nonrepeating forms. This audience in general preferred the old, comfortable forms and the old, comfortable ideas which fit the old forms. The best way to obtain them was simply to play the old music over and over. This had not been common practice since the days of Gregorian chant, but it became a twentieth-century habit. Opera companies and symphony orchestras became museums for eighteenth- and nineteenth-century music. Record companies and "classical" music stations devoted themselves to playing music of the past.

"New" old music was still being written; that is, new music in the old styles, or at least in watered-down versions of the old styles. The Viennese operettas which Schoenberg had to orchestrate to make a living exemplify the trend. It was almost as though Romanticism had been driven underground, out of the concert halls and into popular entertainment. Some of this music was high in quality, but much of it was second- or third- or even tenth-rate, aping the superficial effects of the Romantic style but capturing nothing of its essence. You can hear music like this piped into drugstores, or buy it in late-night TV offers where a pianist plays popular tunes in a lush, "Romantic" style, with a lush, "Romantic" orchestra playing in the background.

If this sort of "underground" Romanticism were all that twentieth-century popular music had to offer, it would not be worth our attention. But the world of popular music was completely transformed by the influence of another cultural tradition, that of black music. The events are too recent and the results too close for us to get a good perspective on them, but some future historian may well see this change—the introduction of the black musical tradition into Western culture—as the most far-reaching development in twentieth-century music's history.

Black Music and Its Influence

Slavery

It is a sad fact that much great music has human misery in its origin. Poor peasants paid taxes so that aristocrats could patronize Mozart and Beethoven. The black cultural tradition entered Western music because of slavery. Wherever slaves were forced to work in the New World, there was some tendency for their African culture to mix with the dominant European culture. In the French- and Spanish-speaking areas, this tendency was less marked; apparently, those slaveholders were more willing to allow Africans to maintain their own culture. In the English-speaking, Protestant areas (principally the southern United States), slaveholders were not so tolerant. Stamping out African cultural traditions, it was thought, would help destroy social organization, and thus the capacity to revolt. Perhaps more importantly, indoctrinating the slaves with Protestant religious beliefs helped salve their owners' consciences: they could tell themselves that they weren't holding slaves for profit, but to save them from damnation. Whatever the rationale, it seems clear that black slaves were compelled to convert to Protestant religious worship. While many of their music-making activities were prohibited, hymn-singing was encouraged. This was the point of contact between the two cultures.

Blues and jazz artists found a large and responsive black audience in the 1920s through widely distributed "race record" labels.

Bessie Smith

The easiest way to see how the mixture works is to look at an example of a blues song. Our example is "Lost Your Head Blues," written and sung by Bessie Smith. Smith was born in Chatanooga, Tennessee, in 1894, and died in an automobile accident in Clarksdale, Mississippi, in 1937. In her teens, she joined a touring black minstrel show led by Ma Rainey, the most famous blues singer of the previous generation. An executive from Columbia Records heard Smith singing in a small club in Selma, Alabama, and brought her to New York to record. She made a long series of successful records with some of the best jazz musicians of the day as back-up artists. Her audience was almost entirely black; "race" records directed at this audience were practically a separate industry in the 1920s. That her music struck a responsive chord in the audience is evidenced by the fact that she sold over two million records in her first year of recording. Her later career supplies an all-too-familiar scenario: declining popularity, alcohol addiction, violent death. The world of popular music would see many such stories in the decades that followed. But in 1926 her fame was at its height.

Bessie Smith (1920's)

Blues Form in "Lost Your Head Blues"

There is no one way to write a blues song, but "Lost Your Head Blues" follows one of the most familiar blues patterns.

I was with you, baby, when you didn't have a dime.
I was with you, baby, when you didn't have a dime.
Now since you got plenty money, you have throwed your good gal down.

Once ain't for always, two ain't but twice *(2 times)*
When you get a good gal, you better treat her nice.

When you were lonesome, I tried to treat you kind. *(2)*
But since you've got money, it done changed your mind.

I'm gonna leave, baby, ain't gonna say good-bye. *(2)*
But I'll write you and tell you the reason why.

Days are lonesome, nights are long. *(2)*
I'm a good old gal, but I've just been treated wrong.

It is a "twelve-bar blues"; that is, one verse takes twelve measures. The twelve bars are broken down into three phrases. The first phrase is sung over a I chord (in this case a chord based on E♭). The second phrase uses the same words and melody as the first phrase (or, if not exactly the same, varied only slightly) with new harmonies underneath, a shift up to the IV chord, then back down to the I chord (in this case up to A♭, back down to E♭). The third and final phrase "answers" the first two phrases with new words and melody. The harmonies underneath go further away, to the V chord, before returning to the I chord for the last time (in this case up to B♭ before returning to E♭). In the most familiar variation on this form, the harmonies in the third phrase go through the IV chord on the way from the V to the I. If there is another verse, a

V chord is commonly added at the end to lead back to the beginning. Each of the singer's phrases takes approximately two measures, leaving the other two measures for an improvised response, here provided by the trumpet player Joe Smith. Improvisation here means that Joe Smith invents his trumpet part on the spot, basing his melody on a scale which will fit with the chord underneath.

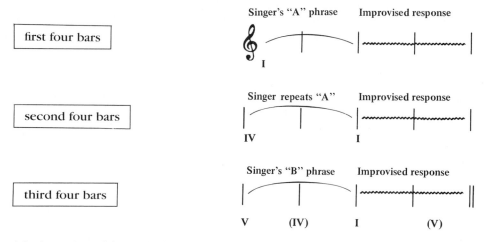

A basic version of the twelve-bar blues form

This is the basic pattern which the performers hold fairly close to until the last verse. Here Bessie Smith introduces a variation. The technical term is rhythmic augmentation (a technique also used by Steve Reich, *see* Chapter 29). She stretches out her phrase "Days are lonesome, nights are long" to cover the entire four bars. All through the song the singer has been tough and critical towards the man who left her. Here she expresses other feelings, feelings of loneliness and despair. The change to the stretched-out melody signals the switch to a different level of expression and communicates the feeling of time lengthening through lonely days and nights.

On the word "long" in the first phrase she sings:

Or at least that's what the written music would look like. A more accurate representation might be something like this:

The Mixing of Western and African Musical Traditions

In other words, Smith sings notes which conventional Western notation cannot capture because they bend around both pitches and beats. If we could understand everything about the history which produced this phrase we would know a great deal about how African music mixed with the Western tradition. Unfortunately, much of the history is hidden from us, and it is complicated by the fact that it includes not just two, but three strands. In addition to the African and European traditions, there are the new inventions and discoveries made by the black people in America who put those two traditions together.

The African tradition is visible in a number of aspects of the song. African musicians search for complex rhythms, often layering different patterns to create a kind of rhythmic polyphony. In "Lost Your Head Blues," the basic beat is in the piano's left hand; the pianist's right hand, the trumpet's lines, and the singer's lines all play both on and slightly against this basic beat.

African music frequently uses a five-tone (pentatonic) scale, and most of Smith's melody can be found in the following five-note pattern:*

Another African tradition is that of the "cutting" song which, like "Lost Your Head Blues," offers improvised criticisms of the person it speaks about. In general, African music relies to a great extent on improvisation from basic patterns, as this song does, especially in the trumpet part.

The way the trumpet responds to the voice represents another African carry-over: the "call and response" pattern is essential to African musical structure.

The principal Western contribution is in the harmonies. These are at their root the simple chords of the Protestant hymn, with their clear and direct sense of tonal center, departure, and return. They carry with them some of Western music's rhythm and phrase structure, since if the chord changes are going to be powerful they must also be regular, creating a strong harmonic rhythm.

Western music also contributes its instruments, in this case piano and trumpet. The musicians invent new approaches to these instruments, and find ways to bend their tones and create rhythmic attacks. The Western tradition asks the player to concentrate on producing a tone; the African tradition asks the player to focus attention on the tone's location in time, and therefore on the points of attack and release. The bending of tones is possible even on the piano, which can create an illusion of a bent tone. The pianist, Fletcher Henderson, plays patterns like this, "crushing" the F against the G♭ which makes the G♭ seem to bend:

---

*The G♭ in this scale creates a tension against the G♮ which is part of the underlying harmony of E♭ major. This tension is an important part of the characteristic blues sound.

Another Western influence is the focus on the individual's feelings. If the "criticizing" verses are from an African tradition, the emotional last verse of the song owes more to a Western one.

After all is said and done, the whole is simply greater than the sum of its African and Western parts. And in fact the blues song doesn't sound like either African chant or Protestant hymn. Its rhythm is certainly not Western, but the kind of beat it gives doesn't sound like African music either. The harmonies are certainly not African, nor do they sound much like Protestant hymns. The melody may combine Western and African elements, but its particular emotional flavor is something not found in either tradition. In short, the two traditions may have supplied the raw materials, but the black musicians who created the mixture added a great deal which was purely their own.

SUMMARY: *Bessie Smith's "Lost Your Head Blues" (1926)*

melody	Based on a five-tone scale. Much bending of pitches. Characteristic motive is a fall of a minor third, from G♭ to E♭.
harmony	Based on a tonal center, with departures and returns. Basic pattern of chord progression: I-IV-I-V-I.
rhythm	An underlying four-beat measure, with the pulse found principally in the pianist's left hand. Other lines play both on and against this beat.
form	Twelve-bar blues form.
texture	Piano supplies bass line and middle-range harmonies; voice and trumpet play melodies above, sometimes overlapping in polyphony, more often in "call and response" pattern.
timbre	Piano, trumpet, and voice. All three, but especially the trumpet, create timbres not traditionally heard on those instruments.
function	Designed specifically for commercial recording, although similar performances would have been heard in nightclubs and bars.

Louis Armstrong and New Orleans-Style Jazz

The most famous song from Kurt Weill's *Threepenny Opera* is "Mack the Knife." The reason it is so famous is that the jazz trumpet player Louis Armstrong recorded a version of it—a version which has since been copied by dozens of other artists. But the song had particular meaning for Armstrong. The world of whores, pimps, beggars, and thieves was the world he grew up in. He was born in 1900 in a poor, black quarter of New Orleans, and died, a wealthy man, in New York City in 1971. At seven, he sang on streetcorners for small change. Later he hauled coal in a cart for 75 cents a day, and still later he pimped for a prostitute. She stabbed him in the shoulder, which, fortunately, discouraged him from continuing that career. When he was 13 he was arrested for shooting a gun into the air to celebrate New Year's Eve and was sentenced to spend a year and a half in a "Colored Waifs' Home," where he began to play the cornet. He was helped by his idol, the jazz cornetist Joe "King" Oliver, who brought him to Chicago in 1922. In 1925 he began to make records under his own name for a company called Okeh Records.

Improvisation: "Potato Head Blues"

"Potato Head Blues"—despite its title, it is not in blues form—was recorded in May of 1927. The work starts with a New Orleans-style ensemble. A tuba plays the bass line (tubas came through better than stringed basses on the primitive recording equipment of the time), and the piano and banjo fill in the harmonies in a steady, block-like "four" pattern. The trumpet, clarinet, and trombone play simultaneously above this rhythm section. They create the rhythmic polyphony of an African drum ensemble, while also staying within the bounds of the Western harmonies given by the chord progressions, and all the while improvising their melodies. The trumpet plays short, strong, rhythmic melodies in patterns like this one:

while the clarinet plays filigree-like patterns above and around it in a "swinging" rhythm:

and the trombone keeps a slow, legato line going, mostly in half and whole notes.

After this group improvisation, Armstrong takes a short, melodic solo, leading into Johnny Dodds' solo on clarinet. This is followed by a brief banjo interlude which does nothing to prepare us for what is to come: Armstrong's "stop-time" chorus. The rhythm section is reduced to the barest outline, hitting only a downbeat every eight beats. The 32 bars belong to Armstrong alone. He gives us an encyclopedia of improvisational ideas: a variety of melodic patterns, an assortment of timbres, but most of all a huge range of rhythmic ideas. Notes held long, notes held short, accented notes, unaccented notes, notes just barely anticipating the beat, notes which seem to delay it. And yet the beat is always

Louis Armstrong

there. No one is playing it—the rhythm section only hits one quick note every two bars, Armstrong plays against the beat as much as on it—but it is still there, perhaps even more there than it was with the rhythm section pounding away. This is, I think, a central principle of the black musical tradition: that the implied beat is stronger than the played one. A jazz or blues or rock group with four or five players can create a stronger sense of beat, a stronger rhythmic "feel," than can a military band of 200. The military band can hit the beat with brute force, but once the listener has heard and learned the pattern, it loses its mental force. When Louis Armstrong plays slightly away from the beat, he creates a tension between his note and the implied beat we hear in our minds. After 32 bars this tension accumulates, needing the release it receives in the final group improvisation which brings the piece back to the New Orleans-style ensemble for its joyful conclusion.

"Potato Head Blues" works on two levels. One level is that of the New Orleans ensemble, which achieves a kind of "take-off" through combined improvisations. But for the ensemble to stay together, the individual improvisations have to stay within well-defined limits; the players have to be role-players. In his solo on the "stop-time" chorus, Armstrong is introducing another level: the complete freedom of the solo improvisation. Except, of course, that the freedom isn't complete. The rhythms and harmonies of the form are still there, and they help to create the excitement and drama. We feel the freedom of the improvisation more because we sense it in relationship to the form which it is based on. The form is like a tightrope, and Armstrong does cartwheels on it.

SUMMARY: *Louis Armstrong's "Potato Head Blues" (1927)*

melody	The piece has no easily-recognizable tune; it gives instead a series of melodic improvisations over a set of chord changes.
harmony	Strong sense of tonal center in a major key. The improvised melodies must all conform to these changes. That is, if the chord underneath is an F chord, the clarinet player cannot play notes from an E scale.
rhythm	The rhythm section creates a steady "four" pulse, but the soloists play more complex patterns above this. The pulse ceases in the "stop-time" section, and the rhythm comes to reside in the tension between Armstrong's notes and our mental sense of the beat.
form	Group improvisation; individual solos; group improvisation.
texture	Polyphonic in the group improvisations; homophonic in the individual solos.
timbre	Rhythm section of tuba, piano, bass, and drums; trombone, clarinet, and trumpet play leads.
function	Designed for the three-minute span of commercial recordings; similiar but longer performances would have been heard in the Chicago clubs where these musicians played.

CHAPTER 31

American Popular Song

Bessie Smith's and Louis Armstrong's recordings are among the purest statements of 1920s blues and jazz. Their works were popular in the black community and among white listeners who were seriously interested in jazz. The general public was hearing jazz too, but in a more diluted form, as the jazz idiom filtered through the commercial music system and made its influence felt in popular dance music, in musical comedy, and in popular song.

In retrospect, the years 1920 to 1950 seem to be a golden age of American popular song. Composers like George Gershwin, Cole Porter, Irving Berlin, Jerome Kern, and Richard Rodgers created a body of song literature which ranks with some of the great past periods in the high-art tradition. At the time, however, the critical and academic establishments ignored this work—it was just the commercial music of the day. There is nothing intrinsically wrong with commercial success, of course; we have seen a number of great composers who were commercial successes. But in the modern period, "commercial" developed the connotation of having no artistic integrity or individual identity. It was possible, and it still is, to achieve success by creating warmed-over, watered-down versions of other peoples' successes. There were writers, for example, who pulled themes out of Tchaikovsky concertos and made songs from them.* What Gershwin and others did was different. They staked out their own territory. What they wrote was not modernist in the sense of being experimental or *avant-garde,* but it was modern: not cheapened Romanticism, but something new and of its time.

George Gershwin

George Gershwin was born in Brooklyn, New York, in 1898 and died of a brain tumor in Hollywood in 1937. Like Aaron Copland, who was born in Brooklyn two years after Gershwin, his parents were Jewish immigrants. His father had left Russia to avoid conscription in the Czar's army, a mandatory 25-year term. In 1910, the family bought a piano, intended for Ira, the oldest son. George immediately monopolized it (as he later became famous for doing at parties) and began a musical education which took advantage of the excellent teachers and

Collaborators on both films and Broadway musicals, Ira Gershwin wrote the lyrics while his brother George composed the music.

*For example, a song called "Tonight We Love" was made from the Tchaikovsky concerto discussed in Chapter 9.

rich concert life of New York City. Another kind of education was available as well. In those days of safe streets, the Gershwin brothers could walk the city all night long, soaking in the atmosphere, speech, sounds and music coming from bars, clubs, and playhouses.

Gershwin left high school at 15 to become a piano "plugger" in Tin Pan Alley, as the music publishing district was called. Until the record player and radio became dominant in the 1930s, sheet music was the way most music was sold. The "plugger" sat at a piano in the music store and played sheet music selections so that customers could hear what they were buying. From this lowly job he graduated to writing songs for publication, then to having songs included in musical revues, then, in the 1920s, to composing scores for Broadway musicals, and in the 1930s to writing scores for Hollywood film musicals.

At the same time he continued to develop his abilities to write concert music. In 1924 he wrote his *Rhapsody in Blue,* which mixed jazz and Romantic-concerto idioms; in 1928 the orchestral work *An American in Paris,* which demonstrated his increasing command over modern techniques of orchestration; and in 1935, his opera *Porgy and Bess.* Gershwin himself believed that his musical comedy songs were ephemeral, to be forgotten after momentary popularity, and that only his concert music stood a chance of surviving.

"A Foggy Day"

In fact Gershwin's concert works have survived. But so have his songs, which have never lost their currency since the day they were written. One example is "A Foggy Day," written in 1937, the year of his death, for the film *A Damsel in Distress.* His lyricist here, as in his Broadway musicals, was his brother Ira, and his star, also as in many of his Broadway musicals, was Fred Astaire. Miraculously, no one in Hollywood forced them to alter their styles, and the songs they wrote for film have the same qualities as the ones they wrote for theater.

"A Foggy Day" begins with a verse, a section of the song which is designed to effect a transition from spoken dialogue in the film to the song proper—it corresponds to the recitative sections of opera, and is more conversation-like than the main part of the song, the refrain which follows.

(verse)
I was a stranger in the city,
Out of town were the people I knew.
I had that feeling of self-pity,
What to do? What to do? What to do?
The outlook was decidedly blue.
But as I walked through the foggy streets alone,
It turned out to be the luckiest day I've known.

(refrain)
A Foggy Day in London town
Had me low and had me down.
I viewed the morning with alarm,
The British museum had lost its charm.

How long, I wondered, could this thing last?
But the age of miracles hadn't passed,
For suddenly, I saw you there,
And through foggy London town the sun was shining everywhere.

The narrator is a stranger, wandering through a town, a victim of the pathetic fallacy—the foggy weather corresponds to his mood—depressed and filled with self-pity. These are all recognizable as Romantic themes. In fact, they can all be seen in a Romantic song-cycle like Schubert's *Die Winterriese, The Winter's Journey,* written to poems by Müller. Again the narrator is a stranger ("A stranger I came, a stranger I depart"), a wanderer ("I bruised myself on every stone in my hurry to leave the town"), afflicted with the pathetic fallacy ("My heart sees its own likeness painted on the sky; it is nothing but winter, cold, savage winter"), depressed ("My heart seems dead"), and filled with self-pity ("So I go on my way with dragging step, passing solitary and unregretted through bright, joyful life.")

The difference is that the Gershwins are setting up these Romantic themes only to knock them down. Ira Gershwin uses vernacular language and a matter-of-fact tone to help deflate the sentiments. His narrator is a stranger only because his friends are out of town. He doesn't bother with metaphor to tell us "I had that feeling of self-pity" and renders his depression with slang: "The outlook was decidedly blue;" the fog "had me low, had me down." Where Müller strives for the mythic, Gershwin sticks with the mundane.

The published sheet-music version of the song opens with a piano introduction which "scene-paints" by mimicking the sound of Big Ben, perhaps even the sound of Big Ben echoing through the fog, for the chords, based on fourths, are reminiscent of those which Debussy used in the opening measures of *The Engulfed Cathedral.*

The verse itself is recitative-like since it lets the rhythm and melody follow the patterns of speech. In its last two measures, it relaxes into a beat, leading us into the refrain.

The refrain shows its debt to the black music tradition immediately, using both a syncopated rhythmic pattern, which creates tension between note and beat, and melodic intervals borrowed from the blues. (Gershwin's relationship with the jazz tradition was a reciprocal one. He made use of jazz and blues idioms, and his songs became popular with jazz musicians, who use them as "standards," that is, favorite tunes to improvise on.)

Syncopation is evident as the rhythmic pattern puts notes on normally-stressed beats (beats one and three) only once every two measures; the other accents are displaced to beats two and four.

The melody stresses the blues interval of the minor third, in this case C to E♭ and F to A♭, on its way up. On its way down, it relaxes into the regular intervals given by the major scale; the E♭ and A♭ become E natural and A natural.

Rhythmic accents away from the beat have the effect of strengthening the feel of the beat. A key aspect of Romantic music is that its rhythm ebbs and flows, following the emotion of the moment. Gershwin gives at least a hint of this in the recitative-like verse. But in the refrain it is the beat, not the emotion, which dominates the rhythm, and the effect is to make the individual's feelings seem not so all-important. Similarly, when Gershwin first uses the notes from the blues, and then wipes them away, his music is saying that the "blue" emotions are similarly temporary. In other words, George Gershwin's music, like Ira Gershwin's language, serves to deflate the song's supposedly Romantic content.

To see what the music would sound like without its jazz elements, we could try the first few measures with the interval of the minor third smoothed out, the syncopation removed, and some Romantic "throbbing" chords added to the accompaniment:

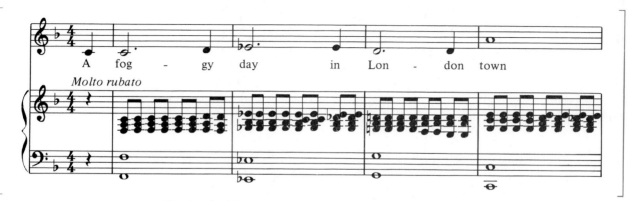

Not Gershwin's setting

These changes effectively ruin the song, but, amazingly, something of its flavor still remains. This "something" is locked into the basic structure of the melody, and cannot be lost even with all those changes in the setting. If we reduce the melody's phrases to their principal notes, we get a pattern which looks like this:

This is an angular melody which breaks into very short phrases. The short phrases help to give the song its offhand, casual air; the angularity of the tune contributes to its almost jaunty bouyancy.

In discussing the Romantic themes which the song sets up only to knock down, I left out the principal Romantic theme of unrequited love, the state of passionate yearning. It is clear that the Gershwins have no patience for this sort of thing. How long, they wonder, could this "down" feeling last? No more than three eight-bar phrases. By the arrival of the fourth phrase, Big Ben is striking clearly.

In fact the depressed feeling never has a chance. The buoyancy of the tune and the wit of the words will not allow it. Where Romantic songs let their narrators

George Gershwin before his portrait of Arnold Schoenberg.

tinge past accounts with present sorrows, the Gershwins use present laughter to contradict past depression and make it seem as insubstantial as the fog.

Gershwin uses none of the "difficult" techniques employed by high-art contemporaries like his friend Arnold Schoenberg (they were neighbors in Hollywood, played tennis together, and admired each other's work). Unlike Schoenberg, Gershwin writes tonal music; he uses rhythmic, melodic, and harmonic patterns that repeat. But this does not make him a leftover Romantic. His music is as much of its time as Bartók's or Stravinsky's. It is his path to modernity which differs from theirs. He uses the jazz and blues traditions to help create a new musical language—a language through which his own voice speaks as clearly as Big Ben ringing through the sunshine at the end of that foggy day.

SUMMARY: *George Gershwin's "A Foggy Day" (1937)*

melody	In the verse, flowing and step-wise. In the refrain the melody is angular, with intervals of a minor third characterizing its upward motion, and intervals from the major scale characterizing its descents.
harmony	Consonant. Brief movements away from and back to tonal center of F. At the climax of the melodic line, there is a stronger shift to B♭ before the final return.
rhythm	Accents placed off the beat consistently, until the final six bars, when the melody imitates Big Ben ringing clearly.
form	Verse and refrain; refrain's form can be summarized as ABAC.
texture	Homophonic.
timbre	In the film context, voice and orchestra; published for voice and piano (the version I have been using); played and sung in many other combinations when used by jazz musicians.
function	Originally intended for use in a film musical; also sold as sheet music; frequently used by jazz artists.

Bop and Cool Jazz

From Big Bands to Bop

The jazz tradition itself continued to evolve from the styles that were popular in the 1920s. In the 1930s and 1940s the Big Band sound came to dominate popular music: as dance music, as music bought on records and listened to on the radio, even, occasionally, as music heard in concerts. The big bands maintained a rhythm section like that of the small group (now generally piano, drums, string bass rather than tuba, and sometimes guitar), but increased the number of horns, with three- or four-man sections of trumpets, trombones, and saxophones replacing the individual trumpet, trombone, and clarinet players of the groups like those which Armstrong recorded with. The big bands, led by men like Count Basie, Benny Goodman and Duke Ellington, required a more regimented approach to music than the small groups had. Their musicians developed tremendous ensemble skills, whole sections playing complex rhythmic patterns together in harmony.

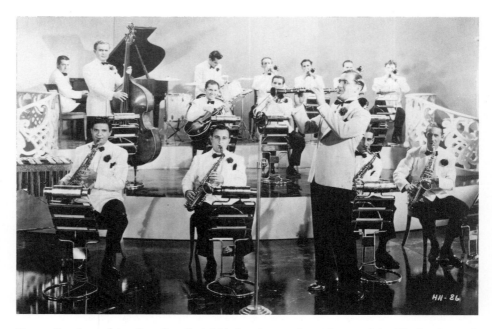

Benny Goodman (standing, front) and his band were the epitome of the Big Band sound of the 1940s.

For many black musicians the popularity of the sound offered an unprecedented chance for success with the mass public. Musicians who performed only for knowledgeable black audiences might keep their styles purer, but the musicians themselves would end up considerably poorer. Nevertheless, there was a reaction against the commercialized style, and many talented musicians in the 1940s resorted to playing at "after-hours" clubs—places like Minton's Playhouse in Harlem, where long, late-night jam sessions allowed soloists the freedom to experiment and invent. The style they developed in those sessions became known as "bebop," usually shortened to "bop."

"Experiment" and "invent:" these words are reminiscent of high-art music's *avant-garde,* and indeed bop was jazz's *avant-garde.* The musicians at Minton's Playhouse were playing for themselves and for people closely involved with their music; they were disaffected from the larger audience which populated the commercial music-making scene. As the jazz historian Frank Tirro remarked, "Jazzmen were already on an island; bopsters built a raft and moved offshore."

Charlie Parker

The greatest bop musician and innovator was Charles (Charlie) Parker, Jr., nicknamed "Bird." He was born in Kansas City, Kansas, in 1920 and died in New York City in 1955, the victim of a heart attack brought on by an almost lifelong addiction to drugs and alcohol. His mother bought him his first saxophone when he was eleven, and she gave him his first lessons on it. In the late 1930s and early 1940s he worked with several big bands; as his playing became better known in the late 1940s he was able to lead small groups in jazz clubs, where he could command salaries as high as $1200 per week (equivalent to about $5000 per week in 1985 dollars)—a sign that his music, though advanced, had not left the jazz audience completely behind.

He was, from all accounts, a difficult person, capable of inspiring great affection and equally capable of antagonizing those who loved him. Young musicians idolized him, and he was dismayed that they would do things like take heroin in an attempt to emulate him. Hearing his playing, it is easy to see why he attracted such adulation, and why young players might believe in a magic potion to make such playing possible. It is not just that he played fast, and he played very fast, but that he *thought* fast. In the wake of the great fame which followed his death, record companies began to issue "outtakes"—rejected takes from recording sessions. In these tapes, Parker can be heard starting up the same tune several times, each time embarking on a solo of incredible speed and complexity, each solo totally different from the previous one.

"Parker's Mood"

"Parker's Mood" is a 1948 recording made with Parker on alto saxophone, John Lewis (who also takes a short solo) on piano, Curley Russell on bass, and Max Roach on drums. It starts with a somewhat dramatic six-bar introduction, and then goes into a blues form. The basic pattern is the same twelve-bar blues form that Bessie Smith used in "Lost Your Head Blues," with the difference that the bop style likes to add extra chords to keep the harmonic pulse moving and changing. For example, instead of going directly from the I chord to the V chord, bop players might go from I to III to VI to II to V. Perhaps more importantly, the rhythm section's whole approach has changed since the 1920s. The bass plays the beat in a "walking" pattern: creating lines in a generally step-wise motion.

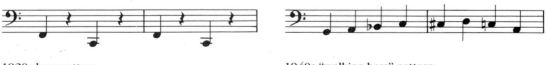

1920s bass pattern   1940s "walking bass" pattern

The piano plays chords sometimes on, sometimes off the beat, while never letting a consistent pattern build up. The drummer stays away from the bass drum, preferring the higher timbres of the cymbals and snares, again sometimes accenting on, sometimes away from the beat. The background texture as a whole is thin and clear—it gives support but also leaves space for the solo improviser. Although Louis Armstrong didn't like the bop style, there is a sense in which he was responsible for it. Solos like his stop-time chorus on "Potato Head Blues"

Charlie Parker (left) and Miles Davis (1945)

were simply too powerful for the old-style rhythm section; the desires of players to equal the kind of individual expression he achieved in that piece created some of the pressure that led to the development of the newer kind of rhythm section represented here.

Parker's solo has several qualities in common with Armstrong's. Like Armstrong's, it is a little encyclopedia of timbres and rhythms. Sometimes his tone is edgy and almost strident, at other times soft and feathery. His rhythm plays with the beat in an almost dizzying way. For example, in the fifth and sixth measures of his solo, he creates a little pattern:

which he then brings in four times, each time finding a different rhythmic spot for it: on the second beat, on the fourth beat, a little after the first beat, and on the third beat.

He plays teasing melodic games as well. He likes to use a blues "cliché," like this one at the start of the second 12 bars:

A traditional blues player would repeat a pattern like this several times:

Not Parker's solo

Parker plays it once, builds up our expectations for a repeat, then follows with a swirling, unexpected run:

But for all the sophisticated playing with rhythms, melodies, and timbres, this really is Parker's mood. Dramatic, bitter, sad, lonely, joyful, strident, pretty, wry, funny, gentle—not any one mood, but a contradictory, mercurial assortment, reflecting, no doubt, the man. (*See* color plate 14.)

SUMMARY: *Charlie Parker's "Parker's Mood" (1948)*

melody	The brief introduction and postlude are set melodies; the rest of the work is improvised. Parker repeats ideas only to vary them. His melodic style is characterized by fast, curving runs, with considerable chromaticism.
harmony	The underlying harmonic pattern is that of the twelve-bar blues, but bop musicians vary that with the addition of extra chords to maintain a strong sense of harmonic movement between the chord changes of the traditional blues form. The chords themselves are often characterized by added tones. Instead of the simple A, C, E for an A-minor chord, the pianist will keep adding thirds: A, C, E, G, B, D. These harmonies are reflected in Parker's solo as well.
rhythm	A steady four-beat pulse, where each of the beats is treated relatively evenly, producing a sense of even horizontal motion.
form	Introduction; two twelve-bar chorus improvisations on alto saxophone; one twelve-bar chorus on piano; one twelve-bar chorus on alto; postlude which repeats the introduction.
texture	Homophonic. The rhythm instruments' function is to support the improvised melodic line.

Miles Davis

| timbre | Alto saxophone, piano, bass, and drums. |
| function | Designed for recording, but similar to performances which would be given in jazz clubs. |

Miles Davis and the "Cool" Style

By the early 1950s, jazz had entered its "cool" period. This was as much an attitude as a style. To be cool, you had to slouch, wear sunglasses, never smile. There was a serious meaning behind this; the attitude said to the audience: we are not here to entertain you; if you are interested in the music, you will have to make the effort to understand it.

Miles Davis was born in Alton, Illinois, in 1926 and studied briefly at the Julliard School of Music in New York before working with Charlie Parker in the late 1940s and taking part in the development of the cool style in the early 1950s. In 1959 he put together a group of the best jazz musicians of the day for a record called "Kind of Blue." (A cool title—not *completely* blue, just *kind of* blue.) Paul Chambers plays bass, James Cobb plays drums. The pianist is Bill Evans, the tenor saxophone is played by John Coltrane, alto sax by Julian "Cannonball" Adderly, and the trumpet by Davis. The cool attitude is also evident in the title of one of the numbers from the album: "So What."

"So What"

The tune itself of "So What" is unusual. Instead of being based in a major or minor key, it is based on an ancient mode, the Dorian mode, which we first encountered in Gregorian chant. The four eight-bar phrases which make up the tune are almost identical; the principal difference is that the third eight-bar phrase is one-half step higher than the first, second, and fourth phrases. Miles Davis is credited with its composition, but pianist Bill Evans may have had a hand in it as well. On the album's liner notes, Evans reports that the musicians had not seen the music before the recording session and that the first complete version was also the final take.

The other unusual aspect of the tune is that it is played by the bass. After a free, floating introduction, the bass settles into the beat, introducing the melody:

(This is how the melody looks in notation, but jazz players "swing" their eighth notes in a long-short, long-short pattern, creating an effect which looks like this:)

The piano responds with two chords—a pattern which no doubt inspired the work's title:

These chords bear the characteristic Bill Evans stamp. They are built on fourths, and they are thus related to the opening chords from Debussy's *The Engulfed Cathedral.* The relationship is not accidental. Evans made deliberate use of Impressionist techniques in his playing. The jazz authority Martin Williams quotes Miles Davis as remarking that "when Bill Evans plays a chord it's not just a collection of notes but a sound"—which is a good summary of what musical Impressionism is all about.

After the tune has been stated, the solo improvisations begin. The soloists are given a new kind of freedom by this sort of work. Instead of having to worry about making their solos fit with chord changes which occur every two beats or so, they know that anything in a Dorian mode starting on D will fit over the first, second, and fourth eight-bar phrases, and that anything in a Dorian mode starting on E♭ will fit over the third eight-bar phrase.

Miles Davis takes the first solo and uses this freedom to create what is in effect a structured composition. The principal idea is heard right at the beginning. After an initial downward statement which functions as his lead-in, he states a motive which has a kind of circular motion to it—starting on D, going up, and then returning to it.

He gradually builds up to a second, related motive, which starts higher and moves downward in a stretched-out rhythm:

Variations on these two ideas form the substance of the solo. The use of silences, the vibrato-less tone, and the melodic motion which turns back on itself, all contribute to a sense of contemplation and introspection—attitudes befitting the cool style.

The next soloist is the tenor saxophone player John Coltrane. His solo is in tremendous contrast to Davis's; there is nothing cool and contemplative about

John Coltrane in Amsterdam (1962)

it. Where Davis's principal idea was based on a circular motive, Coltrane's opens up and out:

His solo gradually builds in intensity, with swirling lines which focus at times on certain repeated notes. There is a hypnotic kind of power to Coltrane's solo—a quality he would develop further in his work during the 1960s. What comes across most strongly here, through the raw timbre and high volume as well as the swirling patterns of notes, is sheer exuberant, extroverted energy.

Cannonball Adderly's alto saxophone solo which follows continues the rapid stream of notes, but rhythmically it is easier and more relaxed. He, like Davis, and like the tune itself, uses a "swinging" rhythm, the long-short, long-short pattern. Coltrane's rhythms seem more intense, in part because he gives up the relaxed swing feel in favor of even streams of notes.

The last major solo is by Bill Evans, who takes one chorus, with horns punctuating on the "So What" chords. He returns in mood to Davis's solos, perhaps even more exploratory in feel, putting denser and denser chords against the modal harmonies. Then a brief bass solo leads back into the tune, until it fades off to end.

"So What" is as distant from Romanticism as any *avant-garde* work from the high-art tradition (*see* color plate 14). The whole idea of the "cool" is completely contradictory to nineteenth-century attitudes; it is a perfect expression of a particular mid- twentieth-century point of view. There is one Romantic aspect to the work, however—its stress on the spontaneous. Romantic composers liked to create the illusion that the performance captured the impulses of the moment. A jazz performance really *does* capture the impulse of the moment; that's what improvisation is. Even here, though, Miles Davis contrives to give such thematic structure to his solo that it seems both spontaneous and rational—a rare accomplishment.

SUMMARY: *Miles Davis's "So What" (1959)*

melody	The tune's principal melody is played in the bass, and is formed from the Dorian mode. The melodies of the solos are improvised; they are also formed from the Dorian mode, but take different characters reflecting the different approaches of the different soloists.
harmony	The basic harmonies of the tune are built up in fourths taken from the Dorian scale.
rhythm	The tune uses a relaxed, four-beat swing. Of the soloists, Coltrane moves farthest from this rhythmic feel.
form	Introduction; tune; solos; tune; fade.
texture	Homophonic. The focus is always on the soloist's melody, with the rhythm section in support.
timbre	Trumpet, alto saxophone, tenor saxophone, piano, bass, and drums.
function	Designed for the recording studio, where this particular version was created. The tune itself has become a standard for jazz groups and is heard frequently in live performances.

Miles Davis continues to perform today, although his style has gone through several transformations since the days of "Kind of Blue," including involvement with heavily electronic jazz-rock.

Bill Evans, who was born in Plainfield, New Jersey, in 1929, died in 1980, after influencing a generation of pianists with his jazz-Impressionist harmonies.

John Coltrane was born in 1926 in Hamlet, North Carolina, and died in New York City in 1967. He played in rhythm and blues groups in his youth—an influence which may show in his use of even, as opposed to "swung," eighth notes. After working with Davis he went on to lead his own group, one of the most influential of the 1960s. His saxophone playing became more and more free in style and less and less structured in form. Eventually he developed a style of almost pure intensity, with sheets of sound obscuring rhythmic, melodic, or harmonic patterns. At the same time, he was capable of immensely lyrical playing. Soloing on the song "My One and Only Love," on an album made with the singer Johnny Hartman, he plays the melody without improvising, using only slight changes and subtle inflections, but still somehow communicating his typical intensity.

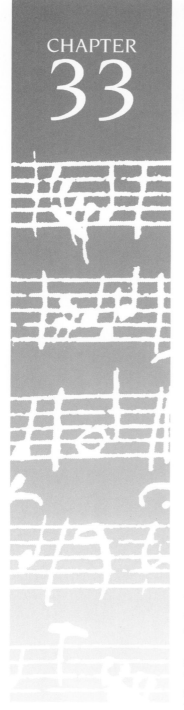

Rock 'n' Roll

The Birth of Rock 'n' Roll

The bop and cool jazz styles were both commercially successful, at least to the point of providing a fair number of musicians with the opportunity to perform and record under conditions which enabled them to remain full-time musicians. (Most high-art *avant-garde* composers earned their living as teachers; their composing activities were often supported by grants). But the number of working jazz musicians was smaller than it had been in the Big Band era, when jazz had reached the mass market. One simple difference was that the bop and cool styles were intended for listening, while the Big Band sound was designed for dancing. Jazz fans liked to listen; the mass audience wanted to dance.

The black members of that audience had never lost their fondness for blues, and as jazz evolved in new directions, many of them looked to the blues tradition for a new popular music. This was **"rhythm and blues,"** an updated blues style with a strong beat, group vocals, and grown-up, city-life subject matter. When, in 1951, Alan Freed, a disk jockey in Cleveland, noticed white teenagers listening to rhythm and blues records, he began featuring the style on his radio programs. The response was tremendous. The phenomenon Freed had noticed became a trend, then a huge trend. Rhythm and blues groups began to tailor their music to fit the tastes of the new, wider audience, and other groups began to tailor their styles to fit the audience's desire for rhythm and blues. Rock 'n' roll was born.

Chuck Berry's "Rock and Roll Music"

Rock 'n' roll has always had a fondness for self-reference. Usually when a style starts talking about itself, it is a sign of decadence—it has run out of things to say about the world. But in the case of songs like Chuck Berry's "Rock and Roll Music" it is more a matter of education: the song explains what rock 'n' roll is all about.

Berry was born in 1926, in San Jose, California, but grew up in St. Louis, Missouri, and still lives near St. Louis. He was influenced by rhythm and blues and also by the urban blues style of musicians like Muddy Waters. More unusually, he heard and was influenced by country music. This was a background ideally suited to writing rock 'n' roll music and to composing "Rock and Roll Music."

Just let me hear some of that rock and
  roll music,
Any old way you choose it,
It's got a backbeat, you can't lose it,
Any old time you use it.
It's got to be rock and roll music,
If you want to dance with me.

I've got no kick against modern jazz,
Unless they try to play it too darn fast,
And change the beauty of the melody,
Until they sound just like a symphony.

That's why I go for that rock and roll
  music, etc.

I took my loved one over 'cross the
  tracks,
So she can hear my man wail a sax;
I must admit they have a rockin' band,
Man, they were goin' like a hurrican!

That's why I go for that rock and roll
  music, etc.

'Way down South they gave a jubilee,
The jokey folks they had a jamboree.
They're drinkin' home-brew from a
  water cup,
The folks dancin' got all shook up.

Chuck Berry

And started playing that rock and roll
   music, etc.

Don't care to hear them play a tango.
I'm in no mood to hear a mambo.
It's 'way too early for a congo,
So keep a rockin' that piano.

So I can hear some of that rock and
   roll music, etc.

The melody's rhythmic pulse is defined by the series of eighth notes which start the song.

This even eighth-note beat provides a hard-driving rhythm which is derived from a style of piano playing popular in the 1930s and 1940s called "boogie-woogie."

Typical boogie-woogie bass line

To get a sense of how this differs from a jazz style, try "swinging" the eighth notes:

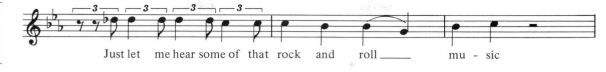

Just let me hear some of that rock and roll ___ mu - sic

Not a rock rhythm

This thoroughly destroys the rock feeling, creating instead the effect of a lounge-singer who has listened to too many old Frank Sinatra records.

Underneath the even eighth-note beat is a basic pulse which Berry talks about in the song's third line: "It's got a back beat you can't lose it." This is the essence of rock 'n' roll: the back beat you can't lose. Generations of beginning drummers have discovered it with joy. Just hit beats two and four good and hard, and you're playing rock 'n' roll: one TWO three FOUR, one and TWO and a three and FOUR and so on. It may be simple, but it is probably the most potent device yet invented for evoking a physical response from a listener. This is what Berry is talking about when he compares rock 'n' roll to jazz and various Latin dance rhythms like the mambo and the tango. The rock 'n' roll rhythm is the one you have to use "if you want to dance with me."

Elvis Presley (1956)

The rhythm is also the quality which keeps getting rock 'n' roll in trouble with the authorities; the slow backbeat pulse can, given the right context, remind the listener of sexual movement. Sexual love is one of the things people write songs about, and they wrote them as much in the 1590s as in the 1950s. What made the 1950s' songs seem different and dangerous is the backbeat, which amplified the physical, sexual aspect of the lyrics. Elvis Presley made the quality visible in his performances, which is why when he first appeared on the Ed Sullivan television show he was photographed only from the waist up. But Presley was just trying to make visible what was already obvious to his audience.

In the second verse, Berry creates a kind of real-life situation. The narrator takes his love across the tracks to hear a "rockin' " band. Who is the narrator and where is the band? Berry has said that "everything I wrote about wasn't about me, but about the people listening to my songs." In the context of that remark, the "I" who takes his love across the tracks sounds like a white teenager, and " 'cross the tracks" sounds like a journey to the "wrong" side of the tracks—into the black ghetto. Berry is creating a kind of guided tour to the sources of rock 'n' roll. In the third verse he goes down South to a Georgia jamboree. This of course refers to the importance of country music in forming rock 'n' roll style. That influence is more evident in other Berry songs like "Maybellene," and in the work of Presley, Bill Haley, Buddy Holly, and the Everly Brothers. It may surface a bit in this song in the verse sections. The refrain sections, though, spell out rock 'n' roll's major debt to the black music tradition—they are in blues form.

The fact that Bessie Smith's "Lost My Head Blues" and Charlie Parker's "Parker's Mood" and Chuck Berry's "Rock and Roll Music" are all examples of twelve-bar blues should indicate just how elastic that form can be, and what a huge range of expression it can contain. In this instance, the song is not even "blue" in the conventional sense of feeling down or moody or depressed. It is instead full of physical energy and teenage exuberance.

SUMMARY: *Chuck Berry's "Rock and Roll Music" (1957)*

melody	Characterized by fast repeated notes, more concerned with creating rhythmic life than melodic contours.
harmony	Based on the I, IV; and V chords traditionally used in the blues form.
rhythm	Even eighth notes characterize the melodic line; stress on "backbeat" forms the basic pulse.
form	Refrain, verse, refrain, verse, refrain, verse, refrain. The refrains are cast in the twelve-bar blues form.
texture	Homophonic.
timbre	Voice, supported by electric guitars, bass, and drums.
function	Designed principally for recorded performance on 45 rpm records (thus limited to a three-minute format). Also used in live performances in clubs and at dances, later in concerts.

The Beatles

England in the mid-1950s was just coming out of the dark period of economic hardship which it had suffered in the wake of World War II. John Lennon (1940–1980), Paul McCartney (1942–), George Harrison (1943–), and Ringo Starr (1940–) were from working-class Liverpool backgrounds, which traditionally would have meant that there was little room for them in the class-conscious English cultural world. But 1950s England saw a renaissance of artistic expression from provincial and working-class men and women, especially in literature and drama. The range of possibilities open to these particular four young men may have been limited, but it was vast in comparison to what had been open to their parents' or grandparents' generations. In addition, their generation was the first in a long while that was not subject to the military draft. The new sense of growing prosperity and freedom allowed them to do previously unthinkable things, like enrolling in art school and playing rock 'n' roll.

Rock 'n' roll had a raw energy and exuberance which seemed tailor-made for the attitudes the four musicians wanted to express. It was still a kind of outlaw art, perpetually under attack from the Establishment (a status which the music has tried to maintain), a working-class music which was defiant rather than servile, rebellious rather than conformist. These are qualities which probably seemed more strange and wonderful in the context of the English tradition than the American. This may help to explain how it happened that an essentially American art form was so thoroughly taken over by English groups. An expert in cultural history would probably have predicted that any English rock 'n' roll

The Beatles

would be a pale imitation of the American original. In fact, it was the American groups who were just going through the motions in the late 1950s. Rock 'n' roll represented a new kind of freedom and identity for the English groups. Using rock 'n' roll to express their own ideas, they helped revitalize the style. (Two other trends which helped in the revitalization of rock music were the new folk songs being written by musicians like Bob Dylan and the gospel-based soul music of artists like Stevie Wonder—*see* Chapter 6.)

In 1957, John Lennon formed a group called the Quarry Men. Paul McCartney joined them later that year and George Harrison the next. (Ringo Starr would not join the group until 1962.) They changed their name to the Silver Beetles and later, in 1960, to the Beatles. They played lunch-hour performances at a Liverpool basement club called The Cavern for twenty-five shillings per man (about nine dollars in 1985 currency). They were offered work in Hamburg, West Germany, and went there in 1960 and again in 1962. It was the same Hamburg district Johannes Brahms had worked in as a young man: the dockside area of bars, clubs, strip shows, and brothels. They played four hours every night, six hours on weekend nights. The living and playing conditions were poor, as was the pay, but the performing experience was a kind of trial by fire: the group that could survive it would be prepared for the rigors of a performing career.

Between the two Hamburg visits they had acquired a manager, Brian Epstein. After seeing the group rejected by several major recording companies,

The Beatles at Shea Stadium, New York, 1964

Epstein finally secured a contract with E.M.I. They recorded their first single in September of 1962, their first album in February of 1963. The speed of their rise from that point on was incredible. Within a year they were the world's top rock group. Between 1963 and 1966 (when they stopped touring) the total attendance at their concerts was approximately 2,676,000. Between February 1963 and January 1972 they sold approximately 545 million records. As John Lennon noted—not as some thought, proudly, but with some dismay—they had become more popular than Jesus.

This amazing kind of success begs for explanations. And many were offered: some crediting their publicity machine, some their sense of humour, some the squeaky-clean image Epstein had given them, some their moplike haircuts. But the most obvious explanation still makes the most sense: they had enormous talent coupled with energy and desire, and they offered these gifts to a world which was ready for them.

Their early work was squarely within the rock 'n' roll tradition—they recorded a version of Berry's "Rock and Roll Music," for example. But right from the beginning they were making original contributions in songs like "If I Fell" and "I Saw Her Standing There." By 1967 they were no longer touring, partly because of the unhappiness of the touring life ("a room and a car and a car and a room and a room and a car," in Lennon's phrase), partly because the screaming audiences didn't allow much music to be heard. They concentrated instead on work in the recording studio and in June of 1967 brought out *Sgt. Pepper's Lonely Hearts Club Band.* It was the most thoroughly worked-out, coherent album-as-total-artwork yet produced, with visual as well as musical and lyrical aspects taken seriously.

This occurred partly under the influence of Pop Art, a high-art movement which took for its subject matter the images of mass culture, the most famous example probably being Andy Warhol's painting of a Campbell's soup can. Mass culture images, Warhol seemed to say, were now more real than the things they represented. Where a traditional artist might paint soup, he painted the image a contemporary person holds: the name, the label, the can. Similarly, his portrait of Marilyn Monroe is not of her person but of her media image (*see* color plate 15). The Pop Art attitude towards mass culture, ironic but affectionate, shows up on the album cover, where popular culture images are arranged in a photographic collage. The odd thing here is that the Beatles were part of the mass culture they were commenting on, and knew it; their own images and their waxwork-museum images are both included in the scene they create.

The process continues in the music, where old music-hall styles are quoted with irony and affection. Here, though, there is an additional function. If styles are viewed ironically and are used to create collage-type effects, all styles become equal, and the artists can choose among them freely. On the cover, Fred Astaire and Marilyn Monroe mix with Dylan Thomas and Edgar Allan Poe. In the music, not just popular art but high-art traditions are open to them, and they take advantage of that opening.

"She's Leaving Home"

The sixth song on the first side is "She's Leaving Home," written principally by McCartney. Lennon collaborated, helping with the chorus, and the two of them do all of the singing (using tape to double their voices) while session musicians perform the accompaniment on harp and strings.

The song is a ballad in the old-fashioned sense—a story song. Like the old English folk song "False Sir John," it begins by locating the time, not folk time ("the merry month of May") but modern time, "Wednesday morning at five o'clock." A girl, the "she" of the title, sneaks out of her room, leaves a slightly unsatisfactory note, and steps outside "to be free." The refrain consists of two musical lines: one, the narration, saying "She's leaving home after living alone for so many years," the other responding with the words the parents will use— all of them particularly tired clichés—"We sacrificed most of our lives," "We gave her everything money could buy." The second verse captures the parents, first poignantly, the mother standing with the note, alone at the top of the stairs, then exposing their selfishness—"How could she do this to me." The third verse takes us forward to Friday morning. She is far away, exercising her freedom by meeting "a man from the motor trade." This is her own phrase, her slightly pretentious way of regarding a mechanic or car salesman. She is fantasizing about her freedom.

After an introduction led by the harp, the accompaniment moves along with a steady pulse, a "tick-tock-tock" steadiness (the work is in 3/4 time), of just the sort you would expect from classically-trained musicians playing a score. The melodic phrases are more free, rhythmically—we can hear McCartney anticipating or delaying the beat—but not enough to make the piece seem rhythmic, just enough to make the narrator seem casual and offhand. This quality is reinforced by the vocal style, which has the easiness allowed by microphoned singing, as opposed to the more strenuous effects of the voice trained for operatic production. The melody itself shows a return to Romantic habits, with a long reach and fall:

But what is un-Romantic is that each phrase comes back up after its fall, in each case to the same note, a C#. This constant little lift to the same spot removes any tendency the narrator's melody might have to be "expressive," to say how he feels about the events being described. It creates instead a sense of reporting, of objectivity.

The refrain sails away from this matter-of-factness, as the narration flies up into a falsetto range, with long, stretched-out notes which seem to symbolize her sense of freedom and escape, while underneath the parents utter their clichés in a boring chant:

She   (We gave her   most of our ____ lives)   is   leav-ing   (Sac - ri - ficed

The narrator's line changes the last time through, right after the reference to "the motor trade." "She is having fun," it says, "something inside that was always denied for so many years." The final "she's leaving home" returns to the same C# repeated so often before, leaving room for the parents' closing "bye-bye"—a final and fairly contented-sounding "bye-bye." Perhaps they aren't all that disappointed to see her go. But if the parents are hypocrites, the girl is self-deluding. She is right to leave, but her chances of finding real freedom seem poor.

This is not a song which has much to do with rock 'n' roll, although there is a hint of it in the refrain, where the narrator enters on the beat, and the parents' entrance then feels a little like a stressed back beat. It is, instead, a rare moment in the history of twentieth-century music, where artists from the popular tradition step over and use high-art materials to create a song not confined to either category.

SUMMARY: *Paul McCartney's and John Lennon's "She's Leaving Home" (1967)*

melody	Characteristic motion includes a Romantic-sounding reach and fall, followed by a lift to mid-range C#, which takes away the Romantic tendency for emotional heaviness.
harmony	The chords change slowly, and at times keep the same basic harmony for eight or ten measures. During the verse, the melody floats above a long-held V chord, developing a sense of uncertainty.
rhythm	The basic pulse is in three. The accompaniment interprets the beat strictly; the voice treats it freely.
form	Verse-refrain.
texture	Homophonic in the verse. In the refrain, the two voice parts create polyphony, although the accompaniment remains chordal.
timbre	Two voices, sometimes using tape to create the effect of four, plus harp and strings.
function	Designed purely as recorded performance, although it has been performed "live" by groups other than the Beatles.

The later history of the Beatles is both sad and fascinating. In terms of audiences reached and affected, and in terms of money earned, they were, without a doubt, history's most successful musicians. Such success is only possible in the day of mass communications, and these same mass communications tend to destroy the artist's chances of leading a normal life, isolating the artist, and removing him or her from the roots and sources of his or her art. *Sgt. Pepper's Lonely Hearts Club Band* sings about lonely hearts, not just in "She's Leaving Home," but all through the album. Themes like these became common in the Beatles' later work.

When the group broke up, partly from a sense of being burned out, partly from the pressures of dealing with the huge sums of money they had accumulated, the creative tension between Lennon and McCartney deteriorated into bitter feuding. The songs they wrote while they were members of the Beatles had all been credited to "Lennon and McCartney" even if just one of them was responsible. There was truth to this fiction; both deserve credit for their songs, whether written individually or in collaboration. The challenge each presented to the other, the sense of competition, the freedom to criticize which was allowed to no one else—all these contributed to the high standard of their work together, and that high standard declines in their work apart. McCartney lives with his family on a farm in Scotland and continues to compose and to perform. Lennon continued to compose and perform, mostly in the recording studio, until he was murdered outside his apartment building in New York City in December 1980.

Summary of Twentieth-Century Styles and Trends

A hundred years from now, some of the twentieth-century examples I have included will be regarded as historical masterpieces, some will be regarded only as historical curiosities, and some will be entirely forgotten. There is no way of knowing which category which work will fall into.

The general trend we can note about our century is more sociological than musical. Starting in the early 1800s, the audience for professionally-produced music (as opposed to folk music) began to expand. In the twentieth century, this expansion accelerated.

Some see technology as the cause of that expansion, but it is fairer to see technology as the response. More and more people had money and leisure; the twentieth century was ingenious at finding ways to use the money to fill the leisure time with music.

This has not been an unmixed blessing. Folk music has largely disappeared as an organic part of community life. Techniques of mass reproduction require only a very few performers and composers at the top of the music industry pyramid, and the distance from that peak to the audience below is a great one.

The style which was associated with the expanding audience in its early days at the beginning of the nineteenth century was Romanticism. In theory, Romanticism was finished by the early years of the twentieth century. In practice, it still continues, especially in forms of popular entertainment like television, films, popular novels, and journalism. There the Romantic themes and styles still reign, forming a great undercurrent of popular taste. Romanticism in this form is often despised for being "mushy," "sentimental." Nevertheless it is always there, a kind of sticky trap for music to fall back into.

Much of the best of twentieth-century music set itself against this easy, popularized, debased Romanticism. There were different ways of doing this. The principal rebellion of the high-art tradition was against tonality (although all of the traditional habits of music-making came under challenge). The popular-art tradition preserved tonality, but rejected traditional rhythmic structures, replacing them with rhythms derived from black music. In both traditions, the development of a distinctly twentieth-century musical language seemed necessary before distinctly twentieth-century voices could speak.

One of the reasons the modern period is difficult to define is that we are in it, and we have trouble seeing the forest for the trees. Another reason is that there really are a lot of trees. The struggle to find the modern voice has taken many different forms with many different degrees of success. No one style has emerged to lead or dominate, nor does one seem likely to emerge in the few years remaining in the century. The period, in short, has been as confused and messy as modern life, and the only mistake is to expect it to be more rational or neater.

Text Credits

Page 96: Translation of Latin mass. Copyright © 1946, 1949 by the President and Fellows of Harvard College; © 1974, 1977 by Alice D. Humez and Willi Apel. Reprinted by permission.

Pages 224–25: "Erlkönig." *The Penguin Book of Lieder,* edited and translated by S. S. Prawer, Penguin Books, 1964, copyright © S. S. Prawer, 1964, pp. 33–35. Reproduced by permission of Penguin Books Ltd.

Pages 229–30: "Gretchen am Spinnrade." Edited and translated by S. S. Prawer, Penguin Books, 1964, copyright © S. S. Prawer, 1964, pp. 33–35. Reproduced by permission of Penguin Books Ltd.

Pages 236–40: *Dichterliebe.* Edited and translated by S. S. Prawer, Penguin Books, 1964, copyright © S. S. Prawer, 1964, pp. 81–82. Reproduced by permission of Penguin Books Ltd.

Page 251: Schumann diary entry from *On Music and Musicians.* By Robert Schumann, translated by Paul Rosenfeld, edited by Konrad Wolff; McGraw-Hill, 1964. Copyright © Pantheon Books, a Division of Random House, Inc.

Pages 269–70: *Lohengrin.* EMI Music Limited and Capital Records, Inc. Used by permission.

Pages 302, 304–305: *Erwartung.* Used by permission of Belmont Music Publishers.

Pages 315–318: *Threepenny Opera.* Used by permission of Warner Bros. Music.

Pages 319–20: "Pe Loc" from *Seven Romanian Folk Dances.* Copyright 1918 by Universal Edition; renewed 1945. Copyright and renewal assigned to Boosey & Hawkes, Inc. for the U.S.A. Reprinted by permission of Boosey & Hawkes, Inc.

Pages 325–27: *Serenade for Tenor, Horn, and Strings.* Copyright 1944 by Hawkes & Son (London Ltd., renewed 1981). Reprinted by permission of Boosey & Hawkes, Inc.

Page 331: *The Unanswered Question.* © Copyright 1953 by Southern Music Publishing Company. Copyright renewed 1984 by Peer International Corporation. Used by permission.

Pages 339–40: *Circles.* © Copyright 1961 by Universal Edition (London) Ltd., London. All rights reserved. Used by permission of European American Music Distributors Corporation, sole U.S. agent for Universal Edition. Used by permission.

Page 342: *Music for Mallet Instruments, Voices and Organ.* Copyright 1978 by Hendon Music Inc., a Boosey & Hawkes Company. Reprinted by permission.

Pages 347–50: "Lost Your Head Blues." © 1925 Frank Music Corp. © Renewed 1953 Frank Music Corp. International Copyright secured. All rights reserved. Used by permission.

Pages 356–59: "A Foggy Day." Words by Ira Gershwin. Music by George Gershwin. Copyright © 1937 by Gershwin Publishing Corporation. Copyright renewed, assigned to Chappell & Co., Inc. All rights reserved. Used by permission.

Pages 364–65: "Parker's Mood." © 1948 Atlantic Music Corp. © Renewed and assigned 1976 Atlantic Music Corp. Used by permission. All rights reserved.

Pages 366–67: "So What." Used by permission of Warner Bros. Music.

Pages 371–73: "Rock and Roll Music." Reprinted by permission of Isalee Music Pub. Co.

Pages 378–79: "She's Leaving Home." © 1967 Northern Songs, Limited. All rights for the U.S., Canada and Mexico controlled and administered by Blackwood Music Inc. under license from ATV Music (MACLEN). All rights reserved. International Copyright Secured. Used by permission.

Photograph Credits

Chapter 21: Page 209, Editions Recontre; 202, Photo by Nick Rossi; 217, Photo courtesy of Stephen Brown; 218, The Bettmann Archive, Inc.

Chapter 22: Pages 223, 234, The Bettmann Archive, Inc.

Chapter 23: Page 246 top, The Bettmann Archive, Inc.; 246 bottom, Cliché des Musées Nationaux; 251, Photographie Bulloz; 253, The Bettmann Archive, Inc.

Chapter 24: Pages 261, 263, The Bettmann Archive, Inc.; 266, Copyright © Beth Bergman 1987; 272, Courtesy of the San Diego Opera

Chapter 25: Pages 281, 286, 289, The Bettmann Archive, Inc.

Chapter 26: Page 294, The Bettmann Archive, Inc.; 306, The Gershwin Collection at the Library of Congress; 308, © Fred Fehl; 309, © ARS, NY/SPADEM 1988

Chapter 27: Page 315, The Bettmann Archive, Inc.; 319, Columbia Records; 324, The Bettmann Archive, Inc./BBC Hulton; 325, Reproduced from the collections of the Library of Congress

Chapter 28: Page 332, Giraudon/Art Resource, © ARS, NY/ADAGP 1988; 333, © Martha Swope

Chapter 29: Page 336, Electronic Music Center, Columbia University; 338, Radiotelevisione; 343, Courtesy of Lynn Garon Management

Chapter 30: Page 352, © Dennis Stock/Magnum Photos; 346, Reproduced from the collections of the Library of Congress; 347, Photo Trends

Chapter 31: Page 359, The Bettmann Archive, Inc.; 355, Photo Trends

Chapter 32: Page 364, © William Gottlieb; 366, © David Redfern; 368, UPI/Bettmann Newsphotos; 362, The Bettmann Archive, Inc.

Chapter 33: Page 372, Music Division, The New York Public Library at Lincoln Center, Astor, Lenox, and Tilden Foundations; 373, UPI/Bettmann Newsphotos; 375, © David Redfern; 376, © Jan Lukas/Photo Researchers

Color Plates: Color Plates 2, 3, 5, Scala/Art Resource; Color Plate 6, Hirmer Fotoarchiv München; Color Plate 9, Copyright © 1979 By The Metropolitan Museum of Art; Color Plate 10, © Walter Steinkopf, Berlin; Color Plate 14, © ARS, NY-Pollock/Krasner Foundation, 1988; Color Plate 15, ESM Documentations/Art Resource

Index

Note: The numbers in bold type indicate the page on which the term is defined.

A 7
B 8
C 9
D 0
E 1
F 2
G 3
H 4
I 5
J 6